PEOPLE AND PLACES
Essays in Honour of Mick Aston

Professor Michael Aston

PEOPLE AND PLACES

Essays in Honour of Mick Aston

Edited by
Michael Costen

OXBOW BOOKS

Published by
Oxbow Books, Oxford

ISBN 978-1-84217-251-3

A CIP record for this book is available from the British Library

This book is available direct from

Oxbow Books, Oxford
www.oxbowbooks.com

and

The David Brown Book Company
PO Box 511, Oakville, CT 06779, USA
(Phone: 860-945-9329; Fax: 860-945-9468)

Front cover: Wells and its cathedral (photo. Mick Aston)

Back cover: The cloister garth of the abbey of Notre-Dame at Arthous
(Dép. Landes, Dioc. Aire et Dax).

Printed and Bound in Great Britain by
CPI Antony Rowe Ltd, Chippenham

Contents

List of Contributors vi

Foreword (*Michael Costen*) vii

Acknowledgements viii

Mick Aston – An Appreciation (*Trevor Rowley*) ix

Mick Aston – Principal Publications 1970–2004 (*Prepared by Teresa Hall*) xi

1   Experiencing the Prehistoric Landscape of Somerset (*Jodie Lewis*) 1

2   Chasing the Tail of Hunter-Gatherers in South Western Landscapes (*Paula Gardiner*) 23

3   Keeping the Faith: The Physical Expression of Differing Church Customs in Early Medieval Britain (*Teresa Hall*) 53

4   Anonymous Thegns in the Landscape of Wessex 900–1066 (*Michael Costen*) 61

5   Stategy, Symbolism and the Downright Unusual: The Archaeology of Three Somerset Castles (*Stuart J. Prior*) 76

6   The Premonstratensian Canons in South-Western France: A Preliminary Survey (*James Bond*) 90

7   Angevin Lordship and Colonial Romanesque in Ireland (*Tadhg O'Keeffe*) 117

8   The Peripatetic Life of the Medieval Bishop: The Travels of Salisbury and Bath and Wells (*Naomi Payne*) 130

9   An Aristocratic Mausoleum at Grosbot Abbey (Poitou-Charente, France) (*Mark Horton and Katharine Robson Brown*) 137

10   Not All Archaeology is Rubbish: The Elusive Life Histories of Three Artefacts from Shapwick, Somerset (*Christopher Gerrard*) 166

11   'Of Naked Venuses and Drunken Bacchanals': Tong Castle, Shropshire, and its Landscapes (*Paul Stamper*) 181

12   Clear Fountains and Turbid: Archaeology's Crisis of Communication? (*Nick Corcos*) 195

13   Reconstructing Past Landscapes: What Do We See? (*Christopher Taylor*) 205

Index 209

List of Contributors

JAMES BOND, The Anchorage, Coast Road, Walton-in-Gordano, Clevedon, BS21 7AR

NICK CORCOS, Flat 4, Tresco Mansions, 30 Highbury Road, Weston-super-Mare, BS23 2DN

MICHAEL COSTEN, Department of Archaeology and Anthropology, University of Bristol, Bristol, BS8 1UU

PAULA GARDINER, Department of Archaeology and Anthropology, University of Bristol, BS8 1UU

CHRISTOPHER GERRARD, Department of Archaeology, University of Durham, South Road, Durham DH1 3LE

TERESA HALL, Farthings, Hill road, Sandford, Winscombe, BS25 5RH

MARK HORTON, Department of Archaeology and Anthropology, University of Bristol, BS8 1UU

JODIE LEWIS, Department of Applied Sciences, Geography and Archaeology, University of Worcester, Henwick Grove, Worcester, WR2 6AJ

TADGH O'KEEFFE, Department of Archaeology, Newman Building, University College Dublin, Belfield, Dublin 4, Ireland

NAOMI PAYNE, Somerset County Museum, Taunton Castle, Taunton, TA1 4AA

STUART PRIOR, Department of Archaeology and Anthropology, University of Bristol, Bristol BS8 1UU

KATHARINE ROBSON BROWN, Department of Archaeology and Anthropology, University of Bristol, Bristol, BS8 1UU

TREVOR ROWLEY, 3 White Forge, Appleton, Abingdon, Oxon

PAUL STAMPER, English Heritage, 1 Waterhouse Square, 138–142 Holborn, London EC1N 2ST

CHRISTOPHER TAYLOR, 11, High Street, Pampisford, Cambridge, CB2 4ES

Foreword

Michael Costen

This volume springs from a two day conference held in December 2004 at the Department of Archaeology and Anthropology, Bristol University, to celebrate the career of Mick Aston, Professor of Landscape Archaeology, on the occasion of his retirement. The speakers were drawn from among his colleagues, students and friends and they set out to pay tribute to Mick's energy, commitment, enthusiasm and pioneering spirit as a landscape archaeologist and as a teacher. The talks and the essays are of course, a reflection of the interests of the speakers, but they all touch on aspects of his work and interests.

All historical studies are ultimately attempts to understand the societies of the past and the people who animated them. To make the imaginative leap which carries us beyond our own assumptions about the past and into the lives of our ancestors is difficult enough. To convey our ideas and to be at once intelligible and true to that past is enormously difficult. We rearrange the parts of the jig-saw puzzle in many different ways as we try to understand the difficult and fragmentary evidence left us. Much of Mick's work has involved pioneering efforts to find new sources of information and to interpret them to build new ways of understanding the past. His labours have often involved many years of careful research, often in cold and wet fields and long hours of careful analysis, but the result has been seemingly effortless interpretations expressed with clarity and economy and always illustrated to illuminate. Mick has always been deeply concerned to persuade people to *look* and his devotion to illustration through maps, plans and drawings reflect his spatial and visual understanding of landscapes. After working with him, or being taught by him, it would be difficult to look at a house, a village, a field or wood without seeing something more than the immediate image.

This set of essays reflects the variety of Mick's enthusiasms, in landscape and monastic studies particularly and they range in time from the Mesolithic to the Victorian and from south-west England to south-west France and Ireland. The landscapes and the monastic enclosures are seen for what they are – places where people lived out their lives and upon which they were in some way dependent. They vividly illustrate the way in which people appropriated and shaped their surrounding to meet their needs, whether they were Mesolithic hunter-gathers in Somerset or noble families in twelfth and thirteenth century Aquitaine.

Mick is the first to acknowledge that he has been deeply indebted to earlier workers and to other contemporaries in his efforts to build models of the past which satisfy today. He also knows that others will find his efforts unsatisfactory and set out to rebuild the model to suit their own times, but in doing so they will stand on the shoulders of someone we are happy to acknowledge as an inspiration to us. We offer these essays as a token of our affection and esteem.

Acknowledgements

The two day conference where these papers were first given was held in the Department of Archaeology of the University of Bristol. Thanks are due to Mark Horton as Head of Department for hosting the event and to numerous unpaid helpers who kept a noisy and full house fed, watered and seated. Special thanks are due to Sue Grice who gave much time, effort and expertise to making the illustrations of the various authors meet the publishers specifications. The copyright of authors and organisations, other than contributors, are acknowledged with each illustration. Finally the editor thanks the contributors for their efforts at the conference and for their understanding during the editing process.

Mick Aston – An Appreciation

Trevor Rowley

The first time I met Mick Aston he was still a student at Birmingham University. He and his fellow post-graduate in the Geography Department, James Bond, came to visit the rescue excavations I was conducting on Metchley Roman forts. The site lay in the grounds of Queen Elizabeth Hospital, about half a mile from the famous Byzantine campanile of the university. Mick was very indignant about the lack of interest and involvement of the university in the excavations on its doorstep, and of its archaeologists, who at that time were almost entirely classicists. Mick and James helped to redress the situation by immediately and enthusiastically joining in with the rescue work.

Even then Mick demonstrated very unusual skills. He was a geographer who took delight in gathering historic information in a variety of forms and mapping it in his inimitable style. It seemed that everywhere he visited he had made drawings and kept notes, and thus by his early twenties had already compiled an impressive dossier of original material, particularly on historic towns and ecclesiastical sites. His plans were often annotated with his own range of cartoon characters. Nevertheless I did not become fully aware of his talents until he undertook a survey of the earthworks at Bordesley Abbey in Redditch New Town. These covered more than forty hectares in the Arrow Valley and included the disturbed earthworks of the conventual site, a set of large fishponds, outlying industrial earthworks and a surrounding perimeter bank. Mick not only produced a clear plan of the extensive earthworks, but on the basis of his survey he was able to postulate a convincing chronology of development. This demonstrated that the location of the original abbey buildings was in a bend of the River Arrow and was followed by a progressive extension of monastic activity, which involved the diversion of the river. This explains a straight section of the river, which otherwise follows a distinctly winding course. Mick was already deeply involved in the analysis of medieval water management, which was the topic of his thesis and later of a two-volume publication by British Archaeological Reports. His work on fishponds, moated sites and mills opened up a new area of previously little studied and recorded medieval earthworks. He was already showing a rare understanding of landscape and an ability to employ architectural and documentary evidence in addition to earthworks and topography.

Mick's unique skills as a fieldworker and draughtsman were put to excellent use in his first full-time job at the Oxford City and County Museum, based at Woodstock. He joined the Field Department under Don Benson, who was pioneering a new systematic way of recording the county's archaeology in the form of a Sites and Monuments Record. Mick took to this work with the enthusiasm he has shown in all the ventures he has tackled in his career. Despite the fact that Oxfordshire was already a well-worked county he was able to identify hundreds of new sites and record them for the new inventory. Mick's interest in the post-Roman landscape ideally complemented Don Benson's prehistoric speciality.

It was at this time that I shared a house in Wheatley with Mick and got to know and like him as a trusted companion as well as an excellent colleague. He already held strong views on a wide range of topics, but he always expressed them wittily and rarely with rancour. Apart from the joys of his company and unfailing sense of humour I have three particular memories from that period. Eating and sleeping were simply a means to the end of fieldwork as far as Mick was concerned, although his penchant for a glass or two of red wine developed at this time. Mick, as a vegetarian since the age of 15, used to have a never-ending vegetarian stew kept in a bright orange pan on the kitchen stove. Every couple of days he would top it up with some fresh produce. Mick always used to pronounce that the meal was 'bostin' or some similar Black Country expression; this Sorcerer's Apprentice like concoction had the other important advantage of being very cheap, a major consideration for Mick! My second enduring memory is of his precarious journey to work each morning. He used to wake up about half an hour before he was due to start work, roll downstairs straight into his 'half-timbered waggon' (a Morris Minor estate), and drive the ten miles or so to Woodstock in what I can only describe as a state of 'sleep driving'. My final memory was of his obsession with that quintessential 1960s musical 'Hair'. I don't know if this show prompted his later interest in naturism, but it almost certainly contributed.

During the Wheatley phase we decided that there was a need for a book which would help extra-mural students in particular to recognize and record earthworks and historic topographic features. David and Charles agreed to publish *Landscape Archaeology* under our joint names in 1974 and through it a much wider audience was introduced to Mick's ideas and skills. Although the book creaks a bit after thirty years, it still finds its way regularly on to Landscape History reading lists. Mick has a rare talent in his ability to analyse and interpret landscape – a talent that was later revealed in his excellent Batsford book *Interpreting the Landscape* (1985).

In the late 1960s and early 1970s the grand extra-mural tradition of archaeology teaching was still thriving, before the educational bureaucrats and accountants had arrived on the scene to vandalize it and destroy a century-old tradition of genuinely democratic adult education. Mick was a gifted teacher, immensely knowledgeable, enthusiastic and eager to share his skills and scholarship with others. He first taught for Birmingham University Extra-Mural Department and then for the Delegacy of Extra-Mural Studies at Oxford. It was clear that Mick was a natural communicator and he soon found his way on to the recently founded Radio Oxford with his own long-running archaeology series. He viewed the mass media as an extension of the extra-mural class and even at that stage it was clear that he had more than a touch of the David Bellamy about him.

His appointment as Somerset's first County Archaeologist was followed by a move to become a full-time extra-mural tutor, firstly at Oxford, then at Bristol. He resumed his media career on local television, and then in 1988 he began working with Tim Taylor, the producer of the long-running Channel 4 series *Time Team*. Mick had caught Tim's imagination by making the claim that if he were dropped blindfolded into any part of Britain he would be able to locate his position through examining local building styles and materials as well as settlement shape, type of field boundary and so on. It was the justifiable claim of a true landscape historian and was the beginning of this most popular archaeology programme.

An unusual aspect of Mick's career has been that he has never been tempted to take up the trowel himself and although he is fully conversant with the interpretation of excavated evidence, he sees excavation as just another tool of the landscape historian. It is this breadth of vision and his ability to explain it to a broad-based audience that has rightly earned Mick the title of 'The Ambassador of British Archaeology'.

Mick Aston – Principal Publications 1970–2004

Prepared by Teresa Hall

1970

Earthworks at the Bishop's Palace, Alvechurch, Worcestershire, *Transactions of the Worcestershire Archaeology Society* 3rd Series No. 3, 55–9.

(edited with P. D. C. Brown) Notes and news, *Oxoniensia* XXXV, 103–5.

1971

Wychwood: A Motor Trail Around the Historic Sites of the Area. Woodstock, Oxford City and County Museum.

1972

The earthworks of Bordesley Abbey, Redditch, Worcestershire, *Medieval Archaeology* 16, 133–136.

Cherwell: A Motor Trail Around the Villages of the Cherwell Valley, Oxfordshire. Woodstock, Oxford City and County Museum.

1973

Fieldwork. In R. T. Rowley and M. Davies (eds), *Archaeology and the M40 Motorway: An Interim Report*, 7–13. Oxford, Department for External Studies, Oxford University.

1974

Stonesfield Slate. Woodstock, Oxfordshire County Council, Department of Museum Services Publication 5.

(with T. Rowley) *Landscape Archaeology: An Introduction to Fieldwork Techniques on Post-Roman Landscapes.* Newton Abbot, David and Charles.

Archaeology in Somerset, *Somerset Farmer* 43, No 6, June, 24–6.

1975

A county planning department – Somerset. In T. Rowley and M. Breakell (eds), *Planning and the Historic Environment*, 50–2. Oxford, Department for External Studies, University of Oxford.

A stone axe from Taunton, *Proceedings of the Somerset Archaeological and Natural History Society* 119, 70–1.

1976

(with C. J. Bond) *The Landscape of Towns.* London, Dent. (Reprinted 1987 by Alan Sutton, Gloucester).

(with A. P. Munton) A survey of Bordesley Abbey and its water-control system. In P Rahtz and S Hirst (eds), *Bordesley Abbey 1969–73*, 24–37. British Archaeological Reports 23, Oxford.

Warstone Farm, Frankley, Worcestershire, *Transactions of the Worcestershire Archaeological Society*, 3rd Series 5, 75–8.

(with F. Condick and A. Ellison) A Somerset field monument and land use survey, *Proceedings of the Somerset Archaeological and Natural History Society* 120, 85–94.

(edited) Somerset Archaeology 1974–5, *Proceedings of the Somerset Archaeology and Natural History Society* 120, 69–80.

1977

(with R. Leech) *Historic Towns in Somerset.* Bristol, Committee for Rescue Archaeology in Avon, Gloucestershire and Somerset.

Deserted settlements in Mudford parish, Yeovil, Somerset, *Proceedings of the Somerset Archaeological and Natural History Society* 121, 41–53.

Archaeology. In D. Denton-Cox, *Consultative Report and Survey: Somerset Structure Plan*, 167–71. Taunton, Somerset County Council.

(edited) Somerset Archaeology 1976, *Proceedings of the Somerset Archaeological and Natural History Society* 121, 107–128.

1978

Gardens and earthworks at Hardington and Low Ham, Somerset, *Proceedings of the Somerset Archaeological and Natural History Society* 122, 11–28.

(edited with B. Murless), Somerset Archaeology 1977, *Proceedings of the Somerset Archaeological and Natural History Society* 122, 117–52.

1979

A Sheela Na Gig at Fiddington, *Proceedings of the Somerset Archaeological and Historical Society* 123, 111–113.

1981

(with L. Viner) Gloucestershire deserted villages, *Glevensis* 15, 22–9.

(Review) *Medieval England* by M. W. Beresford and J. K. S. St Joseph (1979). In *Bristol Archaeological Research Group* No. 2, 79–80.

1982

(edited with I. Burrow), *The Archaeology of Somerset: A Review to 1500 AD.* Taunton, Somerset County Council. (Reprinted in 1992).

(with I. Burrow) The Early Christian Centres 600–1000 AD. In M. Aston and I. Burrow, *The Archaeology of Somerset: A Review to 1500 AD*, 119–21. Taunton, Somerset County Council. (Reprinted in 1992).

The medieval pattern 1000–1500 AD. In M. Aston and I. Burrow, *The Archaeology of Somerset: A Review to 1500 AD*, 123–33. Taunton, Somerset County Council. (Reprinted in 1992).

Aspects of fishpond construction and maintenance in the sixteenth and seventeenth centuries, with particular reference to Worcestershire. In T. R. Slater and P. J. Jarvis (eds), *Field and Forest: an Historical Geography of Warwickshire and Worcestershire*, 257–80. Norwich, Geo Books.

Recording historic landscapes. In R. Simpson (ed.), *Conserving Historic Landscapes: Seminar Reports*, 9–14. Peak National Park Study Centre with the Historic Landscape Group.

(review) *The Somerset Landscape* by Michael Havinden (1981). In *Bristol and Avon Archaeology* No. 1, 60–61.

(review) *Rescue Archaeology in the Bristol Area*, edited by N. Thomas (1979). In *Bristol and Gloucester Archaeological Society Transactions* 99, 184–5.

1983

Anglo-Saxon towns in Somerset. In J. Haslam (ed.), *Anglo-Saxon Towns in Southern England*, 167–201. Chichester, Phillimore.

Deserted farmsteads on Exmoor and the Lay Subsidy of 1327 in West Somerset, *Proceedings of the Somerset Archaeology and Natural History Society* 127, 71–104.

The making of the English landscape – the next 25 years, *The Local Historian* 15, No 6 (May 1983), 323–332.

(review) *Models of Spatial Inequality: Settlement Patterns in Historical Archaeology* by R. Paynter (1982). In *Journal of Archaeological Science* 10, 547–8.

1984

(with R. J. E. Bush) Taunton's town defences: a history and itinerary. In P. J. Leach (ed.), *The Archaeology of Taunton: Excavation and Fieldwork c1920–1980*, 59–63. Bristol, Western Archaeological Trust.

(with R. J. E. Bush) The town: history and topography. In P. J. Leach (ed.), *The Archaeology of Taunton: Excavation and Fieldwork c 1920–1980*, 75–9. Bristol, Western Archaeological Trust.

(with L. Viner) The study of deserted villages in Gloucestershire. In A. Saville (ed.), *Archaeology in Gloucestershire*, 276–83. Cheltenham, Cheltenham Art Gallery and Museums and the Bristol and Gloucestershire Archaeology Society.

(review) *The Lost Villages of England* by Maurice Beresford (republished by Alan Sutton in 1983). In *The Local Historian* 16 No. 3, 172–3.

(review) *Village and Farmstead: A History of Rural Settlement in England*, by C. Taylor (1983). In *The Local Historian* 16 No. 3, 173–4.

(review) *Village and Farmstead: A History of Rural Settlement in England*, by C. Taylor (1983). In *Bristol and Avon Archaeology* No. 3, 66.

1985

Interpreting the Landscape: Landscape Archaeology in Local Studies. London, Batsford. (2nd edition 1992).

(with I. Burrow) Monks in the landscape: the place of religious communities in English medieval archaeology. In M. Thompson, M. T. Garcia and F. J. Kense (eds), *Status, Structure and Stratification: Current Archaeological Reconstructions*, 139–43. Proceedings of the Chacmool Conference, University of Calgary, Canada.

Somerset, *Medieval Village Research Group* 33rd Annual Report, 11–14.

(review) *Marshfield: An Archaeological Survey of a Southern Cotswold Parish* by V. Russett (1985). In *Bristol and Avon Archaeology* 4, 69–70.

(review) *Historic Landscape Study of the Manor of Englishcombe* edited by M. Stacey and R. Iles (1983). In *Avon Past* 11, 38.

1986

The Bath region from late Prehistory to the Middle Ages, *Bath History* Vol 1, 61–89.

(with D. Hill and C. Wickham) New horizons for the blind, *University of Bristol Newsletter* Vol 17 No. 4 (13 November 1986), 14.

(review) *Invitation to Archaeology* by P. Rahtz (1985). In *Young Archaeology* (February 1986), 12–13.

1987

(with R. Iles) *The Archaeology of Avon: A Review from the Neolithic to the Middle Ages.* Bristol, Avon County Council.

Medieval settlements in Avon. In M. Aston and R. Iles (eds), *The Archaeology of Avon: A Review from the Neolithic to the Middle Ages.* 94–106. Bristol, Avon County Council.

Rural settlement in Somerset: some preliminary thoughts. In D. Hooke (ed.), *Medieval Villages.* 80–100. Oxford, Oxford University Committee for Archaeology, Monograph No 5.

Post-Roman central places in Somerset. In E. Grant (ed.), *Central Places, Archaeology and History*, 49–77. University of Sheffield, Department of Archaeology and Prehistory.

(review) *Avon's Past From the Air* by R. Iles (1984). In *Avon Past* 12, 31.

(review) *Cranfield: Bedfordshire Parish Surveys: Historic Landscape and Archaeology 5* by S. Coleman (1986). In *Landscape History* 9, 87–8.

1988

(edited), *Aspects of the Medieval Landscape of Somerset: Contributions to the landscape history of the county.* Taunton, Somerset County Council.

Editor's preface. In M. Aston, *Aspects of the Medieval Landscape of Somerset: Contributions to the landscape history of the county*, 8–9. Taunton, Somerset County Council.

Settlement patterns and forms. In M. Aston, *Aspects of the Medieval Landscape of Somerset: Contributions to the landscape history of the county*, 67–81. Taunton, Somerset County Council.

Land use and field systems. In M. Aston, *Aspects of the Medieval Landscape of Somerset: Contributions to the landscape history of the county*, 83–98. Taunton, Somerset County Council.

(edited) *Medieval Fish, Fisheries and Fishponds in England.* Oxford, British Archaeological Reports, British Series 182.

Medieval fish, fisheries and fishponds – forethoughts. In M. Aston, *Medieval Fish, Fisheries and Fishponds in England*, 1–6. Oxford, British Archaeological Reports, British Series 182.

Aspects of fishpond construction and maintenance in the sixteenth and seventeenth centuries. In M. Aston, *Medieval Fish, Fisheries and Fishponds in England*, 187–202. Oxford, British Archaeological Reports, British Series 182.

(with E. Dennison) Fishponds in Somerset. In M. Aston, *Medieval Fish, Fisheries and Fishponds in England*, 391–408. Oxford, British Archaeological Reports, British Series 182.

(with C. J. Bond) Warwickshire fishponds. In M. Aston, *Medieval Fish, Fisheries and Fishponds in England*, 417–434. Oxford, British Archaeological Reports, British Series 182.

(with C. J. Bond) Worcestershire fishponds. In M. Aston, *Medieval Fish, Fisheries and Fishponds in England*, 435–455. Oxford, British Archaeological Reports, British Series 182.

(review) *The Medieval English Village* by B. K. Roberts (1987). In *Antiquity* 62 No. 234, 191–3.

1989

(edited with D. Austen and C. Dyer) *The Rural Settlements of Medieval England: Studies Dedicated to Maurice Beresford and John Hurst.* Oxford, Blackwell.

A regional study of deserted settlements in the West of England. In M. Aston, D. Austen and C. Dyer (eds) *The Rural Settlements of Medieval England: Studies Dedicated to Maurice Beresford and John Hurst*, 105–128. Oxford, Blackwell.

The development of medieval rural settlement in Somerset. In R. Higham (ed.), *Landscape and Townscape in the South West*, Exeter Studies in History Vol 22, 19–40. Exeter, Exeter University.

The Shapwick Project, *Medieval Settlement Research Group*, Annual Report 4, 33–4.

The Shapwick Project: A Topographical and Historical Study: 1988 Report. Bristol, University of Bristol.

1990

(edited) *The Shapwick Project. A Topographical and Historical Study. The Second Report.* Bristol, University of Bristol.

Fieldwork. In M. Aston (ed.), *The Shapwick Project. A Topographical and Historical Study. The Second Report*, 13–20. Bristol, University of Bristol.

Air survey. In M. Aston (ed.), *The Shapwick Project. A Topographical and Historical Study. The Second Report*, 71–73. Bristol, University of Bristol.

Somerset – The Shapwick Project, *Medieval Settlement Research Group* Annual Report 5, 30–1.

Shapwick Project, *Proceedings of the Somerset Archaeological and Natural History Society* 134, 211–13.

(with P. Stokes) Somerton Park, *Proceedings of the Somerset Archaeological and Natural History Society* 134, 215–17.

The monastic site at Hinton Charterhouse, *Avon Past* 15, (Autumn), 14–20.

1991

Being a landscape detective. In D. Jones (ed.), *Landscape Detective*, 2–4. London, Channel 4.

A dip into prehistory: from Burrington Combe to Dolebury in the Mendips. In D. Jones (ed.), *Landscape Detective*, 5–9. London, Channel 4.

Prehistoric farmers, medieval rabbits and tinners: Trowlesworthy Warren, Dartmoor. In D. Jones (ed.), *Landscape Detective*, 10–13. London, Channel 4.

Agriculture, continuity and settlement persistence: Bagley and Sweetworthy, Dunkery, Exmoor. In D. Jones (ed.), *Landscape Detective*, 14–17. London, Channel 4.

Somerset – the Shapwick Project, *Medieval Settlement Research Group Annual Report* 5, 30–31.

(with P. G. Hardy), The pre-Minoan landscape of Thera: a preliminary statement. In, Hardy, D. A. (ed.), *Thera and the Aegean World III*, Vol 2 of Earth Sciences, 348–361. London, The *Thera Foundation*.

1992

(edited with M. D. Costen) *The Shapwick Project. A Topographical and Historical Study. The Third Report*. Bristol, University of Bristol.

An analysis of the village plan. In M. Aston and M. D. Costen (eds), *The Shapwick Project. A Topographical and Historical Study. The Third Report*, 21–6. Bristol, University of Bristol.

Aerial survey work in 1990. In M. Aston and M. D. Costen (eds), *The Shapwick Project. A Topographical and Historical Study. The Third Report*, 37–8. Bristol, University of Bristol.

(with M. D. Costen) A holy well at Northbrook. In M. Aston and M. D. Costen (eds), *The Shapwick Project. A Topographical and Historical Study. The Third Report*, 39–40. Bristol, University of Bristol.

The Shapwick Project, Somerset: A study in need of remote sensing. In P. Spoerry (ed.), *Geoprospection in the Archaeological Landscape*, Oxbow Monograph 18, 141–54. Oxford, Oxbow.

1993

'The development of the Carthusian order in Europe and Britain: a preliminary survey', in Carver M. (ed.), *In Search of Cult: Archaeological Investigations in Honour of Philip Rahtz*, 139–151. Boydell and Brewer, Woodbridge.

Monasteries. London, Batsford.

(with R. Croft) *Somerset from the Air*. Taunton, Somerset County Council.

(edited with M. D. Costen) *The Shapwick Project. A Topographical and Historical Study. The Fourth Report*. Bristol, University of Bristol.

Mounds, barrows, watermills, windmills and limekilns. In M. Aston and M. D. Costen (eds), *The Shapwick Project. A Topographical and Historical Study. The Fourth Report*, 10–13. Bristol, University of Bristol.

Regressive map analysis of Shapwick Parish. In M. Aston and M. D. Costen (eds), *The Shapwick Project. A Topographical and Historical Study. The Fourth Report*, 14–23. Bristol, University of Bristol.

1994

Time Team: An Archaeological A–Z. London, Channel 4 Television.

(edited with C. Lewis) *The Medieval Landscape of Wessex*, Oxbow Monograph 46. Oxford, Oxbow Books.

Medieval settlement studies in Somerset. In M. A. Aston and C. Lewis (eds), *The Medieval Landscape of Wessex*, Oxbow Monograph 46, 219–237. Oxford, Oxbow.

(with C. Lewis) Introduction. In M. A. Aston and C. Lewis (eds), *The Medieval Landscape of Wessex*, Oxbow Monograph 46, 1–12. Oxford, Oxbow.

(edited with M. D. Costen) *The Shapwick Project. A Topographical and Historical Study. The Fifth Report*. Bristol, University of Bristol.

More regressive map analysis of Shapwick parish. In M. A. Aston and M. D. Costen (eds), *The Shapwick Project. A Topographical and Historical Study. The Fifth Report*, 19–26. Bristol, University of Bristol.

(with J. Penoyre) Analysis of the village plan. In M. A. Aston and M. D. Costen (eds), *The Shapwick Project. A Topographical and Historical Study. The Fifth Report*, 27–44. Bristol, University of Bristol.

(with J. Bond and C. Ingle) The site of the early church. In M. A. Aston and M. D. Costen (eds), *The Shapwick Project. A Topographical and Historical Study. The Fifth Report*, 57–62. Bristol, University of Bristol.

Four eighteenth-century watercolours of Shapwick. In M. A. Aston and M. D. Costen (eds), *The Shapwick Project. A Topographical and Historical Study. The Fifth Report*, 81–6. Bristol, University of Bristol.

1995

Monks and Monasteries in Twelfth Century Wessex. Bristol, University of Bristol.

(edited with C. M. Gerrard) *The Shapwick Project. A Topographical and Historical Study. The Sixth Report*. Bristol, University of Bristol.

1997

The Carthusian Project in the British Isles. In G. De Boe and F. Verhaeghe (eds), *Religion and Belief in Medieval Europe. Papers of the 'Medieval Europe Brugge 1997' Conference* 4, 34–41. Zellik, Belgium. Institute for Archaeological Heritage.

The Shapwick Project, Somerset, England. In G. De Boe and F. Verhaeghe (eds), *Rural Settlements in Medieval Europe. Papers of the 'Medieval Europe Brugge 1997' Conference* 6, 195–210. Zellik, Belgium. Institute for Archaeological Heritage.

(with C. M. Gerrard and T. Hall) Shapwick, *Medieval Settlement Research Group Annual Report* 12, 36–7.

(edited with C. M. Gerrard) *The Shapwick Project. A Topographical and Historical Study. The Seventh Report*. Bristol, University of Bristol.

1998

(with M. H. Martin and A. W. Jackson) The potential for heavy metal soil analysis on low status archaeological sites at Shapwick, Somerset. *Antiquity* 72, No. 278, December 1998, 838–847.

(with M. H. Martin and A. W. Jackson) The use of heavy metal soil analysis for archaeological surveying, *Chemosphere* 37, 465–477.

(with T. Taylor) *The Atlas of Archaeology*. London, Dorling Kindersley.

(edited with T. Hall and C. M. Gerrard) *The Shapwick Project. An Archaeological, Historical and Topographical Study. The Eighth Report*. Bristol, University of Bristol.

General introduction. In M. Aston, T. Hall and C. M. Gerrard (eds), *The Shapwick Project. An Archaeological, Historical and Topographical Study. The Eighth Report*, 6–8. Bristol, University of Bristol.

The Shapwick Project: Progress from 1994–96. In M. Aston, T. Hall and C. M. Gerrard (eds), *The Shapwick Project. An Archaeological, Historical and Topographical Study. The Eighth Report*, 11–14. Bristol, University of Bristol.

Fieldwalking: 1994 to Spring 1996. In M. Aston, T. Hall and C. M. Gerrard (eds), *The Shapwick Project. An Archaeological, Historical and Topographical Study. The Eighth Report*, 17–20. Bristol, University of Bristol.

(with M. H. Martin and A. W. Jackson) Soil analysis as part of a broader approach in the search for low status archaeological sites at Shapwick, Somerset. In M. Aston, T. Hall and C. M. Gerrard (eds), *The Shapwick Project. An Archaeological, Historical and Topographical Study. The Eighth Report*, 53–68. Bristol, University of Bristol.

(with M. D. Costen, T. Hall and M. Ecclestone) The medieval furlongs of Shapwick: attempts at mapping the 1515 survey. In M. Aston, T. Hall and C. M. Gerrard (eds), *The Shapwick Project. An Archaeological, Historical and Topographical Study. The Eighth Report*, 103–168. Bristol, University of Bristol.

The development of settlement at Shapwick: current ideas. In M. Aston, T. Hall and C. M. Gerrard (eds), *The Shapwick Project. An Archaeological, Historical and Topographical Study. The Eighth Report*, 235–243. Bristol, University of Bristol.

The new village: a story. In M. Aston, T. Hall and C. M. Gerrard (eds), *The Shapwick Project. An Archaeological, Historical and Topographical Study. The Eighth Report*, 247–249. Bristol, University of Bristol.

(with J. Bettey) The post-medieval rural landscape, c1540–1700: the drive for profit and the desire for status. In P. Everson and T. Williamson (eds), *The Archaeology of Landscape: Studies Presented to Christopher Taylor*, 117–138. Manchester, Manchester Univ. Press.

1999

(with C. M. Gerrard) "Unique, Traditional and Charming", The Shapwick Project, Somerset, *The Antiquaries Journal* 79, 1–58.

2000

Mick's Archaeology. Tempus, Stroud.

(reprinted 2000), *Monasteries in the Landscape*. Tempus, Stroud.

(with J. Bond) (reprinted 2000), *The Landscape of Towns*. Sutton, Stroud.

(with C. Lewis and P. Harding) *Time Team's Timechester: A Companion to Archaeology*. London, Macmillan.

Medieval rural settlement. In C. J. Webster (ed.), *Somerset Archaeology: Papers to Mark 150 Years of the Somerset Archaeology and Natural History Society*, 93–98. Somerset County Council, Taunton.

Monasteries in Somerset. In C. J. Webster (ed.), *Somerset Archaeology: Papers to Mark 150 Years of the Somerset Archaeology and Natural History Society*, 99–104. Somerset County Council, Taunton.

2001

(edited with G. Keevill, and T. Hall) *Monastic Archaeology*. Oxford, Oxbow.

The expansion of monastic orders in Europe from the eleventh century. In G. Keevill, M. Aston and T. Hall (eds), *Monastic Archaeology*, 9–36. Oxford, Oxbow.

(with V. Ambrus) *Recreating the Past*. Tempus, Stroud.

2002

Interpreting the Landscape from the Air. Tempus, Stroud.

(with T. Robinson) *Archaeology is Rubbish: A Beginner's Guide*. London, Macmillan.

(with G. Coppack) *Christ's Poor Men: The Carthusians in England*. Tempus, Stroud.

2003

Early Monasteries in Somerset – Models and Agendas. In M. Ecclestone, K. Gardner, N. Holbrook and A. Smith, *The Land of the Dobunni*, 49–55. Oxford, Parchment Ltd.

2004

(with T. Hall) Donyatt Park House, *Proceedings of the Somerset Archaeology and Natural History Society* 147, 206–208.

(with T. Hall) Shepton Mallet, Downside Farm, *Proceedings of the Somerset Archaeology and Natural History Society* 147, 214–215.

Various short notes have been published over the years in *Council for British Archaeology 8* and *9*, and the Channel 4 Time Team Magazine, *Trench One*.

Chapter 1

Experiencing the Prehistoric Landscape of Somerset

Jodie Lewis

Somerset is a large county and the landscape is one of contrast, with upland hills and plateaux, river valleys and gentle undulating land, wetlands and a sea coast. The prehistoric period is well-represented at many of these places, from Palaeolithic deposits in many of the Mendip caves; Mesolithic open-air sites in upland and lowland settings; Neolithic monuments from the hills of Exmoor to the river valleys of northern Somerset; Bronze Age barrows occurring in their hundreds on the high ground and a wealth of Iron Age sites widely distributed, from hillforts to specialised industrial and trading sites. The prehistoric repertoire extends, albeit interrupted, half a million years in the county, providing a unique insight into how certain places within this landscape were used, visited, reused and revisited. The traces of earlier activity at some sites were still visible when they were reused at a later time and it is from this we can begin to imagine the changing histories and myths that may have been created to make sense of this. Yet, certain locales may have become special places rich in meaning, not only because of remembered and invented histories, but because of the unique qualities of the landscape. These distinctions may have also become blurred, as landscape can act as a repository of memory, certain locales recalling specific or mythic events and people. If landscapes are socially constituted, human interaction ascribing them with meaning, then we can begin to look at landscape in a different way: the way in which it may have been experienced.

The Development of Landscape Approaches

Experiencing the prehistoric landscape of Somerset requires a different approach to simply describing it. The view taken here is that landscape is not a passive backdrop to human activity but an integral part of that activity, intimately tied up with life and with an effect on behaviour. The use of the term landscape is not unproblematic, however, as the proliferation of recent works suggest. The concept of landscape is not universal and is a relatively modern Western construct (Ingold 2000) so we must question the validity of applying it to the prehistoric past. To do this it is important to look at how landscape approaches have developed within archaeology.

Landscape archaeology originally grew out of dissatisfaction with individual site-based analyses and a desire for a multi-disciplinary approach in order to 'understand' how these sites fitted into the wider exploitation of the landscape. Archaeologists aligned themselves with scholars from other disciplines, most importantly geographers, anthropologists and environmentalists, and began to write a new kind of archaeology. The first *explicit* use of the term 'landscape archaeology' was in 1974 in the book "Landscape Archaeology", by Aston and Rowley:

> Indeed, if one is to fully understand the landscape, one needs a combination of all possible disciplines. Such an approach has been called 'total archaeology' but 'landscape history' or 'landscape archaeology' would possibly be more apt, for they incorporate all aspects of the natural and man-made landscape and their relations. (Aston and Rowley 1974, 24)

The quintessentially English fascination with landscapes can, however, be traced back much further than the 1970s. Britain has enjoyed a long tradition of the observation of archaeological sites and monuments, dating back to the antiquarians of the sixteenth and seventeenth centuries. Nevertheless, it was the advent of the twentieth century that really set the scene for the development of a landscape archaeology. The foundation of the Royal Commission on Ancient Historic Monuments in 1908 and the establishment of the Victoria County Histories saw the preparation of county-based inventories of ancient and historical monuments across England. The 1920s saw important contributions made by individuals such as O. G. S. Crawford who, whilst working for the Ordnance Survey, was one of the first to realise the importance of aerial photography in helping increase the number of archaeological sites. Crawford could also be said to be the first to appreciate the insights to be gained from distribution maps of archaeological phenomena (Goudie 1987, 14). Sir Cyril Fox was also instrumental in developing landscape approaches, combining geographical and environmental models with archaeology and Crawford's distribution approach. Fox developed these ideas within the "Archaeology of the Cambridge Region" (1923) and the approach reached its zenith in the "Personality of Britain" (1932). Throughout the twentieth century the numbers of archaeological sites increased due to diligent fieldwork and individuals such as Leslie Grinsell continued the tradition of county-based observation, compiling detailed inventories of prehistoric burial monuments. Distribution and location analysis, themes originally borrowed from Geography, became the dominant approach within the study of prehistory.

These kinds of approaches have been criticised for their emphasis on the description of sites rather than their analysis. They were seen as simply putting 'dots on the map', increasing the number of sites, rather than an understanding of them. It was not until the beginning of the 1970s that archaeologists sought to do something with these 'dots on the map' and began to look at the relationships between them: this was to become a hallmark of 'Landscape Archaeology'. However, archaeology did not have an adequate methodology to do this and had to borrow heavily, once again, from Geography. The links between archaeology and geography reach back to the nineteenth century when travellers and geographers such as Morritt at Troy, Forster in Arabia and Major Rawlinson near Baghdad combined their work with antiquarian research (Goudie 1987, 13). It was the 'New' Geography of the 1960s, borne out of dissatisfaction with the empiricist outlook and based around the new idea of geography as a spatial science, however, to which archaeology turned. Equipped with Thiessen polygons, site catchment analysis and gravity models, the New Geography provided the basis for a mathematically spatial archaeology (Tilley 1994, 10: for a contemporary example see Clarke 1977). In Britain, the revolutionary "New Archaeology" was based heavily on the "New Geography", and embraced the idea of archaeology as a science of the past. Tilley (1994, 10) notes that the links between the two disciplines were obvious, with Clarke's "Models in Archaeology" (1972) modelled on Chorley and Haggett's "Models in Geography" (1967), likewise

Watson's "Explanation in Archaeology" (1971) followed Harvey's "Explanation in Geography" (1969).

Landscape archaeology was only really able to develop after the genesis of these spatial approaches to the past, providing an empirical methodology that had previously been lacking. The emphasis was still, however, predominantly on networks of sites and "a history of things that had been done to the land" (Barrett 1999, 26), the landscape being seen as a passive backdrop to human activity. Although landscape archaeology was embraced with a passion, archaeologists initially showed themselves reluctant to engage with the debates surrounding the "landscape" that embroiled geographers. These have a direct relevance on the landscape archaeology practised today and must be explored.

The etymology of the word 'landscape' is usually traced to the Dutch word *lantscap*, (Old English: landscipe) borrowed from Dutch painters of the sixteenth century (Coones 1992, 23). What was originally a painter's technical term has come to have a multiplicity of meaning. Geography, and to a lesser extent history, are disciplines that have long grappled with concepts of landscape. Both have drawn heavily on landscape studies and both have divided the landscape into 'natural' and 'cultural'. The seminal work by the American Geographer Carl Sauer "The Morphology of Landscape" (1925) argued strongly for this distinction, the transformation from natural to cultural being brought about by the dynamism of human agency (Coones 1992, 24). In Britain, similar themes were being propounded by the historian W. G. Hoskins in the classic "The Making of the English Landscape" (1955). Here Hoskins traced the historical evolution of the English landscape and the various ways in which man has 'reclaimed the land'. So-called 'natural' landscapes such as Dartmoor were viewed as 'wastes' and 'desolate' (1955, 18). The common thread running through the works of Sauer and Hoskins is the absolute rejection of environmental determinism: human culture is viewed as dynamic, inducing change, whilst the idea that 'Man Made the Land' dominates (Baker and Harley 1973).

It was the separation of 'natural' and 'cultural' landscapes that led to the separation of geography into 'physical' and 'human'. Geographers, historians and archaeologists rejected the influence of the natural environment on society, looking instead to social and economic processes, stressing the resourcefulness of humans, with man as the conqueror of nature. Environmental determinism, popular with geographers of the nineteenth century and many archaeologists of the twentieth, was thus firmly rejected. Yet, it has been argued that the weakness of this approach was that 'man' was merely substituted for 'environment', cultural determinism for environmental determinism (Coones 1985, 8).

What, then, actually *is* landscape? Coones (1992, 23) argues that it is the element of physical place – province, territory, tract of land – that is common to all ideas of landscape, and for this reason it has been closely tied up with concepts of locale, region and environment. Others such as Cosgrove (1984, 13) argue that landscapes are experiential and subjective; they represent 'visual ideologies' that alter depending on the social, economic and historical context. These approaches, with their rejection of "the quantifiable world of spatial scientists" (Coones 1992, 32) and their replacement with "human values, symbols and aesthetic concerns" (Coones 1992, 32) influenced new archaeological approaches to studying landscapes, widely classified as "phenomenological" (e.g. Bender 1992, 1997, Tilley 1994, 1996, Darvill 1997). Interestingly, Hodder predicted such a move in 1987:

> It seems likely that a rediscovery of such authors (Collingwood, Vico), *along with a discovery of phenomenology*, will occur in archaeology as its attempt to integrate mental and material phenomena matures and catches up with developments in geography. (Hodder 1987, 140, my emphasis)

Phenomenology, derived from the work of Edward Husserl, investigates people's 'lived world of experience' and how this world is understood (Hodder 1987, 140; Cummings and Whittle 2004, 11). It depends primarily on a contrast between 'space' and 'place'. Place is the focus of emotional attachment and provides an individual with a sense of personal and cultural identity. Places have distinctive, subjective meanings, whereas space is "…a situational context for place" (Tilley 1994, 15). Spaces can be transformed into places by the actions of individuals or groups, space becoming place by the attachment to it of values by human beings. The landscape, when viewed in this way, is mentally constructed rather than physically definable, concerned with people's perceptions of their environment. The landscape becomes a mode of experiencing (Tilley 1994, 34).

The phenomenological approach to archaeological landscapes is best seen in works by Tilley (1994, 1997), Bender (1992, 1993, 1997), Darvill (1997) and Cummings and Whittle (2004). Traditional landscape approaches are explicitly or implicitly critiqued in these works for their emphasis on topography, technology and resources, rather than people's emotional engagement with the land (Bender 1992, 148). There is an argument that metaphysical and social aspects of landscapes have been neglected, and instead the natural environment is viewed as meaningfully constituted through associations and memories that humanise and enculture the landscape (Tilley 1994, 24). There is an attempt to move beyond site-specific approaches and look at the interaction of people, sites and monuments with their wider landscape. The visual relationship between sites and the natural landscape is considered to be of the utmost importance as this 'symbolic continuum' is the way in which people would have understood their world (Bender *et al.* 1997, 150). Particular prominence is also placed on the location of sites and monuments within the landscape and it is argued that their situation controls topographical perspectives and how the world is experienced (Tilley 1994, 204). The act of moving through the landscape is also emphasised, with pathways seen as the link between the natural environment and societal space (Tilley 1994, Barrett 1994). Many of these "experiential studies" have been applied to the prehistoric period, particularly the Neolithic and Bronze Age (though see Corcos 2001 and Altenberg 2003 for medieval studies). For this reason, the appropriation of the landscape through the building of monuments, and the effect this would have had on the creation of individual and group identities, is central to many works. Whilst phenomenological approaches are not without their problems – the importance of individual perception and the multiplicity of landscape interpretation therefore possible mean "…there comes a point when selection of a particular viewpoint has to be justified." (Cummings and Whittle 2004, 11) – they provide us with an alternative way of studying the past and make us think about the possible, innumerable experiences of the people and groups who inhabit it.

As already stated, the concept of place is intimately linked with experiential approaches and it has been argued that whilst *landscape* may not be universal, *place* might be (Cummings and Whittle 2004, 9). Places are apperceived physical environments, locales that become meaningful through human encounter. Places are not static and meanings can be manipulated through actual and remembered experiences. The fallible nature of memory has been stressed by many authors, reminding us that an understanding of place can be deliberately distorted and manipulated (for example see Mullin 2001). Places of significance are often named and these names may be linked to distinctive characteristics, either natural or humanly created. Cummings and Whittle (2004, 10) argue that places exist for different people at different levels and different spatial scales. Ultimately we may argue that landscape is, in fact, composed of places and that places influence the meaning of landscape.

Ideas about prehistoric Somerset that will be recounted here embrace concepts of a dynamic landscape, a network of places that people lived in, understood, manipulated and experienced. The landscape that will be described calls upon ideas of memory, identity, biography, myth and temporality (Cummings and Whittle 2004, 11). However, as Thomas has argued (Thomas in Hodder 2001, 181), we still need to "...identify and plot the traces of past activity..." so it is the archaeological evidence from places within this landscape that is the starting point for considering such meanings and experience.

The Physical Environment

> On Mendip... a phrase that implies more than a mere geographical location – a deep respect for those who live and work where nature demands a stubborn toughness and where success is hard won. (Coysh 1954, 1)

The examples that will be drawn on here range in date from the Mesolithic to the Bronze Age and come mainly from northern Somerset, a region dominated by the Mendip Hills (Figures 1.1 and 1.2). Mendip is largely composed of a ridge of carboniferous limestone, stretching for approximately 40 miles from Brean Down in the west to Frome in the east. The highest points are rounded uplands of Old Red Sandstone, attaining heights of 325m OD though much of the plateau undulates at around 280m. West Mendip, the plateau proper, has sides that fall steeply to the low-lying central and north Somerset Levels and to the west, the ridge becomes a series of hills before ending at the sea (Figure 1.3). The plateau has a landscape unity and archaeological homogeneity that suggests a certain "otherness" may have been perceived in prehistory, and indeed possibly also in the historic period.

Mendip has a reputation of "...remoteness and strange desolation" (Coysh 1954, 2), and the lack of nucleated settlement on the hills is noticeable. In the medieval period it was a Royal Forest and by the sixteenth century much of the western plateau fell into one of the mining liberties, administered by the four Lords Royal of Mendip (Atthill 1976, 146). This, together with its use as common pasture (the sheepwalks), meant Mendip was unenclosed land for much of the historic period. Neale (1976, 97) eloquently notes:

> Uncouth and 'faery' names, tracks and crosses, prehistoric barrows, mine workings and a few scattered springs and pools, supplemented by boundary stones: all add up to an open, bleak, undeveloped landscape. Its unchanging appearance is emphasised by the perpetuation of these simple descriptions...from the tenth right into the eighteenth century.

It is interesting that Neale (1976, 97) makes the point that the small size of landmarks, and their individual names, evidence the intimate local knowledge Medieval people had of this landscape. Similarly, people in later prehistory would also have had an "intimate knowledge" of their Mendip landscape, even if this landscape were radically different.

Landuse and land division before the medieval period is difficult to determine. The important Roman mining settlement at Charterhouse demonstrates rapid mining activity at this, and several other, locations on Mendip within a few years of AD43. Yet the plateau itself has very little evidence for non-industrial activity, with most villas and farms developing in the valleys north and south of Mendip (Fowler 1976, 71). In the Iron Age, at least twenty hillforts cluster to the east and the west of the hills yet other forms of settlement are mainly found in lower-lying areas off the plateau. There are, however, a few small areas of so-called "Celtic Fields" on the western plateau – above Cheddar Gorge, around Dolebury Warren hillfort and at Stock Hill, for example – although these may date to any period from the Late Bronze Age to the Roman period. They do, however, represent land division although seemingly restricted in size and extent. There exists no strong evidence for the large-scale physical division of the Mendip plateau before eighteenth century enclosure.

The paucity of environmental evidence makes it difficult to reconstruct the later prehistoric environment of Mendip. The idea that the British Isles became covered by a dense wood panoply after the end of the last glaciation has recently been challenged by environmental archaeologists and a model of different regional and local environments suggested, with open and closed woodland and natural clearings. Manipulation of this environment is apparent from the later Mesolithic, evidenced by episodes of burning. The Mendip uplands probably supported a mixed woodland of lime, oak, ash and elm, analogous with other limestone uplands of the south-west, such as the Cotswolds (Straker and Wilkinson 2005). Animal bones associated with Neolithic sites on Mendip include domesticated cow, pig and sheep as well as wild deer, boar, wolf and auroch. Evidence for cereal cultivation is extremely limited however and it appears that the environment was one of woodland and small clearances (Lewis 2005). The idea of pioneer Neolithic farmers, intensively clearing and exploiting their landscape has been rejected for much of Britain and a model of shifting pastoralism and small-scale clearance, for allotment-type cultivation, settlement and monument construction, is now thought more likely. The evidence for Mendip would seem to fit with

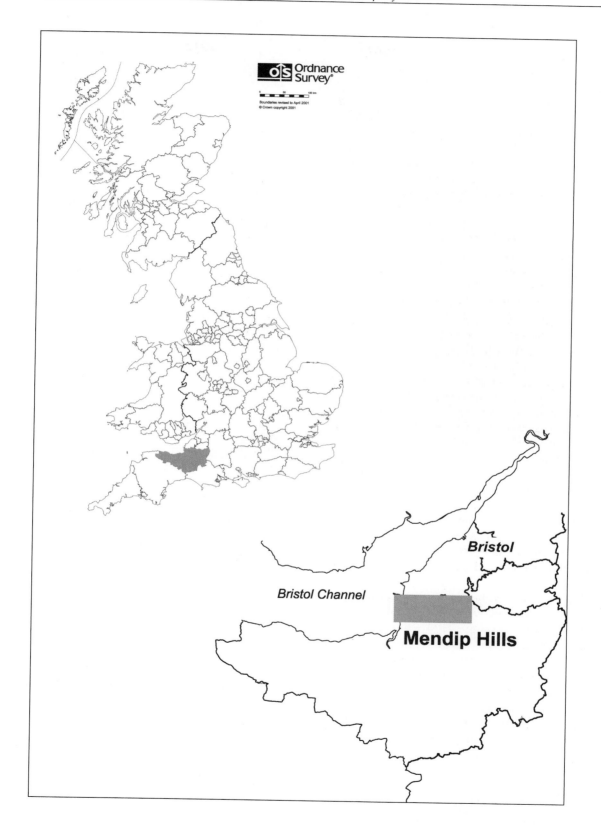

Fig. 1.1 Location of Somerset and the Mendip Hills.

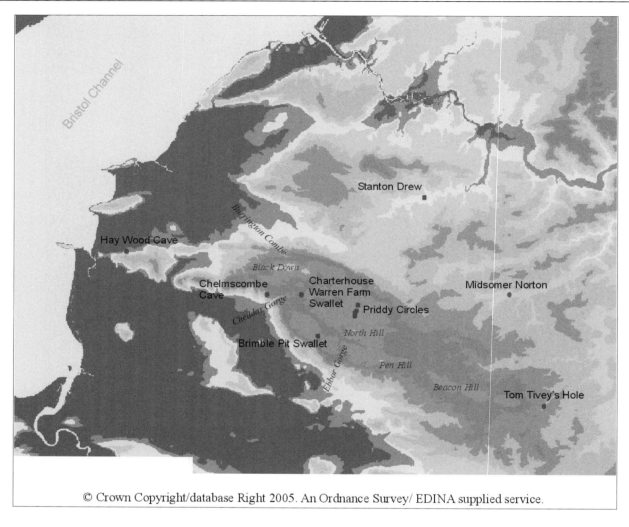

Fig. 1.2 Terrain map of northern Somerset, showing sites mentioned in the text.

this more comfortably and it is probable that, like other regions, extensive woodland clearance did not become a significant feature until the Middle or Late Bronze Age or possibly even later. Parts of the landscape may have been naturally open, however, such as the acidic Old Red Sandstone uplands, the significance of which will be considered later. The lowlands to the north and south of the hills would have been a very different environment. Peat formation probably began in the Somerset Levels in the late fifth millennium and the detailed environmental data from this region suggests a landscape of freshwater fen and reed swamp, with some alder carr (Straker and Wilkinson 2005). To the west, rising sea levels from the very late Mesolithic

meant that the coastline would have undergone dramatic change and the coastal fringe environment itself eventually becoming tidal mud flats.

Thus, by the early Neolithic, *c*.4000 calBC, it is possible to envisage Mendip as an upland environment of mixed woodland with small natural and artificial clearings, edged by wetlands on three sides. At certain times – seasonally, yearly – this wetness would increase, making Mendip appear island-like. These are its boundaries, sometimes permeable sometimes impassable, helping maintain the sense of "otherness" of Mendip, that may have been understood and even enhanced by the prehistoric inhabitants of the region.

Fig. 1.3 Looking west along the Mendip Plateau.

Neolithic Mendip

The Mendip Hills contain evidence for concentrated and varied Neolithic activities including monument construction, cave exploitation and the deposition of large artefacts scatters, presumably related to temporary and/or permanent settlement. Recent work by the author (Lewis 2005) suggests that there are at least 18 long barrows within the hills, with a further 8 lying in the valleys between Mendip and the (Bristol) River Avon to the north. There is also one possible bank barrow, 8 henges, 3 stone circles and 20 caves and swallets with Neolithic/Early Bronze Age deposits. Huge quantities of lithics have been recovered as surface scatters within the ploughsoil, with numbers of struck flints from Mendip probably well in excess of 100,000 pieces (Lewis 2001). A selection of these sites will now be considered in more detail.

The physical environment of Mendip is shaped by the characteristic features of karst limestone – rocky gorges, combes, dry valleys, caves and the closed depressions known locally as swallets. Neolithic exploitation of many of these features can be recognised or hypothesised. Travelling onto the plateau, the gorges and combes offer a ready-made, though not necessarily easy, approach to the plateau top (Figure 1.4). Besides their functionality as routeways we can imagine a more esoteric role. These are unique environments, enclosed by rock faces and rock strewn, wooded and dark, with caves hidden in their crevices. The caves evidence that wild animals were present in the gorges and thus the journey through may also have afforded danger. Cheddar Gorge is the largest gorge in Britain and has the highest inland cliffs (Figure 1.5). This is a dramatic journey, shut-off, confined to the immediate gorge environment. When the top is reached, the Mendip landscape stretches away, the contrast with the gorge and the lowlands immense. Other gorges such as Ebbor and Burrington Combe are similarly impressive (Figure 1.6).

At the head of Cheddar and Ebbor gorges, where fieldwalking has taken place, large multi-period lithic scatters have been found (Lewis 2001). These indicate concentrated activities taking place at these locales over several millennia, favoured places perhaps for hunting or for gatherings of people. If we envisage a mobile population, possibly seasonally visiting the hills, these may have been the places where people repeatedly stopped after journeying to the upland and prepared for the activities to come.

Fig. 1.4 The view across the top of Ebbor Gorge.

Fig. 1.5 Cheddar Gorge.

The gorges and combes contain caves and the use of caves is part of the distinctive Mendip archaeological signature. Caves are not particularly inviting environments – there is constant water percolation; they are slippery; they have sharp edges and uneven surfaces and are often difficult to access; they can be subject to roof collapse and flooding; they are often the lairs of wild animals and they are of course, dark. It is not difficult to imagine how caves could have been interwoven into myths about place and separateness, the locations where strange events occurred. Caves also evidence particular practices and with these we start to witness just how this otherness might have been played out. Whilst it is possible that some lend themselves to opportunistic exploitation, the inaccessibility of some, coupled with the nature of the deposits, suggests intentional ritual usage.

Mendip has a long tradition of cave burial, dating back to at least the early Mesolithic, as sites such as Aveline's Hole (Burrington Combe) and Gough's Cave (Cheddar Gorge) illustrate (Figure 1.7). During the Early Neolithic, a time when mortuary monuments start to be constructed, it is possible to see the use of some caves for burial. Yet the caves are not being used as an *alternative* for such monuments, as the practices represented are different. On East Mendip, excavations at Tom Tivey's Hole revealed a Neolithic layer containing sherds of a Windmill Hill style vessel, the

Fig. 1.6 Burrington Combe.

fragmentary remains of an adult female, a broken leaf shaped arrowhead, a few flints, a bone point broken in half and the tip of another, and a few sheep bones (Barrett 1966). At Chelmscombe Cave (a gorge adjacent to Cheddar Gorge), 2 round-bottomed bowls, which appear to be of Windmill Hill type, and rim sherds representing another 4 similar vessels were found, along with flint scrapers, two bone points and a fragment of a polished bone pin. The remains of four individuals, two of which were identified as adult and one a child, are most likely associated with this deposit (see Lewis 2005).

These two sites give us a glimpse of the varied nature of burial traditions practised in this region during the early Neolithic, with both single and small (kin?) group burial, associated with artefacts that may be interpreted as grave goods. This is in marked contrast to the larger number of individuals and the lack of grave goods from contemporary long barrows. It is thought that interment within a barrow was selective and not available to all of the population, though the inclusion of both sexes and all ages has been taken to mean that those afforded this rite were representative of the broader group. Cave burial does not seem to have been common and caves cannot be

seen as simple barrow skeuomorphs. It appears that this too was a proscribed activity, potentially linked to the significance of particular caves and particular people. Historically and ethnographically, caves are seen often as entrances to other worlds, liminal places where the living may encounter the ancestors, the gods or other forces. They may be explained as ancestral creations, the wild animals that inhabit them seen as guardians or incarnations of the gods themselves. These are richly symbolic arenas for ritual, places where myths may be created and remembered. Traces of earlier activities may have been visible, *in-situ* or disturbed by animals, merging history with the present.

It is worth considering another site, Haywood Cave, here. Haywood is to be found further west, near to the sea. At Haywood, the archaeological deposits had suffered 'gross disturbance', due to animal burrowing, but lithics representative of the Mesolithic and Neolithic were found, along with Iron Age and Roman pottery (Everton and Everton 1972). In addition, however, were the remains of 28 individuals of both sexes and all ages. One skull had a lump of ochre placed in the mouth. A further two skulls showed evidence of mutilation of the teeth, interpreted as

Fig. 1.7 Aveline's Hole Cave.

'ritual mutilation' (*ibid.*). These practices hint at hunter-gather rituals, the association of ochre with human burials having precedents in Palaeolithic Europe, and it can be argued that the red ochre is symbolic of blood and indeed life itself. Yet a sample of human bone (skull IV) was submitted for radiocarbon dating and returned a calibrated date range of 3790–3510 cal BC, firmly within the early Neolithic. This raises some interesting possibilities. Potentially, all of the skeletons may date from this period, making this a burial site where links with the past were possibly being made, through multiple cave inhumation (apropos Aveline's Hole), the use of ochre and teeth mutilation. Alternatively, it may be that we are seeing a cave used for burial in the Mesolithic *and* the Neolithic, the latter directly influenced by the former. Either possibility suggests the coalescence of past and present practises in a place beyond the normal world, somewhere that was suitable and safe for such actions.

Caves are a distinctive part of the Mendip landscape yet Mendip is distinctive in other ways. The altitude results in specific weather conditions – it is wetter, colder and windier than the surrounding lowlands (as anyone who has carried out fieldwork on Mendip in winter, or even summer, is all too aware). Mendip is often covered by cloud and mist yet sometimes it is also above it, the Levels themselves turning into a swirling sea (Figure 1.8). From the levels and out to sea, the Mendip ridge looms, impressive, dark and sometimes hidden by mist. The high plateau can allow excellent visibility and it is possible to see other land, not just the levels but also the hills far beyond – the Quantocks and Exmoor, the Blackdown Hills, the Wessex Chalk and over the sea, the Welsh mountains, areas with different archaeological repertoires and possibly very different myths (Figure 1.9).

Mendip is full of strange natural sounds – wind is channelled by the deep gorges and echoes within caves. The resurgence of the River Axe in Wookey Hole and the changing water levels result in the famous "Noises of Wookey Hole", first described by Clement of Alexandria in about AD220 (Barrington and Stanton 1976, 181). There is another extremely distinctive feature of the Mendip landscape: swallets, closed depressions concealing fissures or shafts in the limestone. Swallets are formed by dissolutional activity and, very rarely, by ground collapse into an underlying cave system (Barrington and Stanton 1977, 222–223). Many occur at the junction of the impermeable Old Red Sandstone and the free-draining limestone; water

Fig. 1.8 The Somerset Levels and Glastonbury Tor from Mendip.

Fig. 1.9 The view towards Exmoor and the Bristol Channel from Mendip.

enters cracks & fissures in the limestone that become enlarged and form swallets. They also form in valley floors, dry valleys and where clay caps the limestone (*ibid.*). In the latter case, water will find leakage points in the clay, eventually causing a depression in the limestone into which the clay slumps. Research has shown how many of these features would have opened for the first time in the Holocene (Stanton 1986) and many are still opening today, with accounts of tractors being literally swallowed by the earth not uncommon on Mendip. Swallets have been the focus of excavation for many years by cavers hoping to gain access to new cave systems, and occasionally, these have been carried out with enough care to reveal archaeological deposits within the shafts. The material that has been found indicates a fascination with these features in the Neolithic, some being used as the focus for highly structured deposits. The most outstanding example of this is Charterhouse Warren Farm Swallet, a 21m deep natural shaft that contained four distinct late Neolithic-early Bronze Age horizons (Levitan *et al.* 1988). At the base were juvenile human bones, animal bones and fine flint, stone, antler and bone items (including a flint

dagger and "sponge finger stones"). The other three horizons were formed of deliberate deposits of stone and clay and contained more human and animal bone and Grooved Ware and Beaker pottery. Similarly, at Brimble Pit Swallet, excavations revealed a range of deposits in a c.10m deep shaft including human bone, flint, the largest Grooved Ware pottery assemblage yet found in Somerset and a pristine greenstone axehead (Figure 1.10) (Lewis and Stanton, forthcoming).

Analyses of these and other swallet sites on Mendip by the author suggest that the deposits within them are deliberate emplacements (Lewis 2000). It appears that people were deliberately lowering themselves into the confined, deep, dark places and depositing human remains, pottery and fine flint and stone items. This may have been in response to the changing nature of this landscape, as the ground opened and the land was literally swallowed back into the earth. The deposits may have been attempts at appeasement to mythical beings be they gods, the ancestors, deities, who were changing the very landscape in which people lived. Like caves, these natural shafts may also have been liminal places, between worlds, where it was possible to communicate with other worlds or other beings. Swallets have very unusual properties: water percolation can lead to strange gurgling sounds; the wind whistles around and in them; they act as natural frost hollows and mist lingers in them. Large areas of the plateau can, at times, be covered by what appears to be holes of mist, sinking into the earth. As well as the deliberate placement of material within swallets, monuments may have exploited their special properties, which leads to the next site to be discussed, the Priddy Circles.

The Priddy Circles are four large "henge-type" circular enclosures which extend in a NNW – SSE line for 1.2kms (Figure 1.11). The Priddy Circles have external ditches and internal banks, in contrast to the usual outer bank, inner ditch layout of henges. This arrangement is, however, reminiscent of the initial phases of Stonehenge and the Llandegai A henge in North Wales, both of which date to the "Middle" Neolithic (c.3000 cal BC) (see Cleal *et al.* 1995, and Lynch and Musson 2001). This non-standard layout is also echoed by other aspects of their construction, revealed by the 1950s excavation within the most southerly monument: Circle 1 (Tratman 1967). This showed a complex sequence of bank construction, almost without parallel. The bank structure, rather than being simply formed of upcast material from the ditch, was made up of posts, stakes, wattle-work, drystone walls, turf walls and imported stone. Tratman's excavations suggests the following sequence (see Table 1.1 opposite):

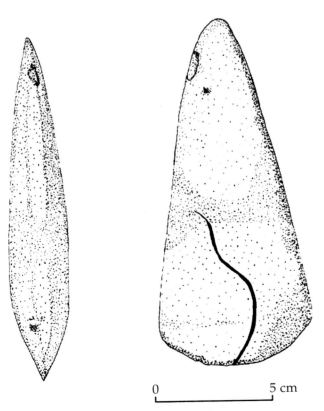

0   5 cm

Fig. 1.10 Greenstone axehead from Brimble Pit Swallet. Drawn by David Mullin.

Phase	Activity
Phase 0	Pre-monument activity? (Pits in entrance that either predate or are contemporary with monument construction.)
Phase 1	Marking out trench?
Phase 2	Digging of two concentric rings of postholes, in radial pairs. Stakeholes driven in alternatively between the postholes. ?Hurdles set behind the rows of postholes and stakeholes (possibly attached).
Phase 3	2 circuits of drystone or turf wall constructed behind the hurdles (niches show pre-existence of postholes).
Phase 4	Locally collected stones placed between walls.
Phase 5	Ditch dug outside bank, leaving berm. Ditch material placed between and over walls. Additional material (stones, soil) collected from North Hill and added to the bank structure?

Table 1.1 Simplified sequence of construction for Priddy Circle 1 (based on Tratman 1967).

Fig. 1.11 Aerial view of the Priddy Circles, taken by Jim Hancock. The southernmost circle is at the top of the photograph.

This unusual construction style is echoed at only one other Later Neolithic site – Blackshouse Burn in Lanarkshire – a large subcircular enclosure, enclosed by a low stony bank (Lelong and Pollard 1998). This does not necessitate a link between the builders of the two sites, but it does suggest that both were drawing upon a similar broad repertoire of techniques current, if not somewhat unusual, at this time. Ellis has suggested that the physical form of Priddy Circle 1 reflects a conscious use of symbols, the timbers and hurdles representative of an animal pen, the drystone walls a field boundary (Ellis 1992, 16). However, the different materials utilised at the site are also symbolic in their own right, the physical landscape of Mendip – earth, wood, stones, turf – captured and encapsulated within these monuments. We may also be witnessing the "capturing" of different traditions of monumentality, the outer ditch/inner bank arrangement reminiscent of earlier Neolithic enclosures; the drystone and turf walls suggestive of earlier Neolithic megalithic and non-megalithic long barrows; the two rings of timbers calling to mind later Neolithic timber circles and the circular enclosed space indicative of later, more "standard" Neolithic henges. The ceremonies and rituals carried out at the Priddy Circles may have been lent potency by this merging of time and traditions.

Greater strength may have been added to this potency by the location of the Priddy Circles: they are centrally placed on the Mendip plateau and the land on which they sit is riddled with hollows, long assumed to be mine workings. However, a close examination and survey of the hollows by Stanton (1986) has shown that in fact nearly *all* are natural swallets and not mine workings. Stanton was also able to demonstrate that most of the swallets are of considerable antiquity, being older than the Circles. This has astounding implications as it suggests that the Priddy Circles were constructed in an area with one of the highest concentrations of swallets on Mendip. It has already been demonstrated that swallets were significant features in the Neolithic landscape and it is argued here that the Circles were located where they are *precisely* because of the high density of swallets, the artificial monuments drawing on the associations of a natural 'ritual' landscape. Yet, this is more than an act of appropriation. The construction of huge enclosures literally on top of the swallets also contains them and changes the meaning of that landscape, making it both *physically* and *ideologically* altered.

The number and arrangement of the Priddy Circles is also of great interest. Although groupings of henges are known elsewhere (at Thornborough, Yorkshire, for example), nowhere else are there *four* in alignment. It may be that at the Priddy Circles we are witnessing the appropriation of a monumental idea and the expression of it in a way that is unique to Mendip. Such idiomatic expressions could have been used to reinforce the boundary between Mendip and the "outside" world, a bold statement of regional and/or group identity. In layout, Priddy Circles 1, 2 and 3 are spaced 60m apart, with Circles 3 and 4 360m apart. This large gap between Circles 3 and 4 has led some scholars to search for a putative "missing" circle to fill it, but there is no evidence to suggest that another circle once existed. It has been noted that the Roman road to Charterhouse passes through this gap and Ellis has argued that the Circles may have been divided by some feature at the time of their construction (Ellis 1992, 14). Rather than look for a monument to fill the gap, it is possible that it was occupied by an earlier track or pathway. Such a hypothesis is potentially supported by examining human activity that both pre and post dates the Circles. Work by the author has identified large flint scatters, extending in a broadly linear spread in the fields alongside the Roman road and current B3134 to the north-west of the Circles. Whilst these scatters are of mixed date it is interesting to note that they are dominated by Mesolithic and Early Neolithic material, evidence for human activity in the area near the Circles prior to their construction. Moving forwards into the early Bronze Age, it is possible to identify significant round barrow groups in the same area, running in a linear alignment from Circle 4. The south-east/north-west orientation of the Roman road and the barrow groups, together with the large lithic scatters, might indicate that they follow the course of a prehistoric (?Mesolithic, ?Neolithic) routeway, off which the Circles were set, and which passed through the gap between Circles 3 and 4. It is worth noting here that Richard Bradley (1998, 121) has suggested that larger henges may have been sited for accessibility from surrounding areas. He draws attention to the occurrence of these monuments and major rivers and other topographical features that lend themselves to communication routes. Yet, along with issues of accessibility, it is also important to consider the social role of pathways, for, as Tilley (1994, 30) argues, "paths are also fundamentally to do with establishing and maintaining social linkages and relations between individuals, groups and political units". This becomes particularly apposite if the path connects to a ceremonial monument, where activities involving the establishment, maintenance and manipulation of social relations come to the fore.

The Symbolism of Materials

In the preceding discussion the symbolism of raw materials was touched upon and this needs expansion, in relation to other sites and monuments. Recent works have highlighted how materials used in some monument construction had different sensory and visual properties that may have been fundamental to the experience of the monument. Studies by Jones (1997) and Lynch (1998), for example, have highlighted both the symbolic and aesthetic effects of the use of different coloured stone in Neolithic and Early Bronze Age monuments and striking examples of the deployment of particular materials can be seen by the use of quartz at monuments such as Newgrange passage grave and the Clava cairns. In Somerset such concepts may be useful to furthering our understanding of certain key sites, beginning with its most famous stone monument, Stanton Drew.

Stanton Drew

The complex of prehistoric monuments at Stanton Drew covers a large area - indeed, only the stone circle at Avebury has a greater diameter than the Great Circle at Stanton Drew (Figures 1.12 and 1.13). A magneto-meter survey by English Heritage in 1997, within the Great Circle, revealed pits interpreted as the remains of the largest timber circle arrangement in Britain and the ditch of a henge, predating the stone circles and other stone settings (David *et al.* 2004). Although no excavations have been carried out at the Stanton Drew complex it is possible to assign it broad chronological dates to the phases, based on comparisons with other sites (see Table 1.2).

This monument complex went through phases of timber and earth before its final manifestation as stone – from timber circles to henge to stone circles. It is an important and fascinating site but the aspect that will be explored in more detail here is the "lithicisation" phase, the final manifestation in stone.

The stones that make up the Stanton Drew megalithic complex are varied in their composition and their origins have been the subject of speculation since the time of John Aubrey (Lewis 2005). The most detailed analysis of the raw materials used in the stone monuments is that by Lloyd-Morgan, undertaken over 100 years ago (1887), and which is in need of some refinement. Visual examination, in conjunction with this account, does, however, allow some preliminary statements to be made. The geology of the Stanton

Fig. 1.12 The Great Circle at Stanton Drew.

Fig. 1.13 The North-East Circle at Stanton Drew.

Drew region (the upper basin of the River Chew) is predominantly formed of Mercia Mudstone, rarely exposed at the surface (Lloyd-Morgan 1887, 45). This stone is not used in the construction of the stone circles. By contrast, the stones used include sandstones, limestones and conglomerates. At least two types of sandstone are represented, a coarse-grained and a finer-grained stone, the former suggested to be probably Old Red Sandstone by Lloyd-Morgan (*ibid.*). There are also at least two types of conglomerate, a rough, coarsely-cemented example and a smoother conglomerate, with smaller inclusions. The limestone used at Stanton Drew has been identified as oolite. None of these stones are local to Stanton Drew and, whilst the *precise* location of the sources have not been identified (the *general* areas where such stones naturally occur are, however, known), it is possible to calculate that certain stones would have been transported distances of between 2.5 and 12 kilometres (see Table 1.3).

The stone that occurs most locally to the site is the Inferior Oolite limestone from the Dundry ridge, which is visible from Stanton Drew. This material (if not this source) has a long history of use within Neolithic monuments, being used for drystone walling within megalithic long barrows in Somerset and the Avebury district of Wiltshire. It was also used as a tempering agent in early Neolithic pottery. Yet, even though this is the most accessible stone source to the site, it is used in very small quantities. Contrast this with the common use of conglomerates, which would have had to have been imported between 5 and 8 kilometres from either the northern edge of Mendip (Harptree area) or Broadfield Down (a wide ridge of Carboniferous Limestone to the north of the higher Mendip ridge) or most likely both areas. The coarse (Old Red?) sandstone would have been imported from even further afield, the closest source being Black Down, the highest point of the Mendip Hills. It may be significant that Black Down can be seen from the south-west circle at Stanton Drew.

The geology of the Chew Valley does not provide stone suitable for megalithic construction, so any stone monument placed here would need to use imported stones. What is interesting is the choice of these stones. Elsewhere, the author has argued that this was not simply a matter of practicality, but intrinsically tied up with aesthetic, cultural, symbolic and ritual concerns (Lewis 2005). Each of these may have been of differing importance at different times or even in

Phase	Area	Activity
I (c. 2500 – 2000BC)	Great Circle	9 concentric rings of pits, each measuring c.1m in diameter and 1m apart. 5 central pits.
	NE Circle	4 pits in quadrilateral arrangement (or contemporary with Phase II).
	SW Circle	3 concentric rings of pits.
Ia (c. 2500 – 2000BC)	Great Circle	Henge, with inner ditch and suggested (but not seen on geophysics) outer bank, entrance to NE.
II (2000 – 1800BC)	Great Circle	Stone circle within the henge enclosure but outside the outer ring of timbers. 26 stones survive today.
	NE Circle	Stone circle, formed of 8 large stones.
	SW Circle	Stone circle, formed of 12 (?) stones.
	Avenues	2 stone avenues, leading from the Great Circle and the North-East Circles, extending for 45.7m and 30m respectively, towards the River Chew.
	Cove	3 large stones in horseshoe arrangement. Today, 2 large standing stones, c.3m apart, and 1 broken recumbent stone lying between them.
	Hauteville's Quoit	Standing stone, c.500m to the NNE of the Great Circle. Once over 4m high.
	Tyning's Stones	Pair of standing stones, c.700m to the W of the Great Circle.
	Tollhouse Stone	Standing stone, recorded by William Stukeley, no longer survives.

Table 1.2 Elements of Stanton Drew monument complex, with putative phasing.

Type of Stone	Estimated Number of Stones	Source	Minimum Distance from Stanton Drew (kms)
Conglomerates	54	Harptree area of Mendip	8kms south-west
		Leigh Down area of Broadfield Down	5–6kms west
Oolitic Limestone	7	Dundry Ridge	2.5kms north
Sandstones: Coarse (Old Red Sandstone?) Fine Grained	7	Black Down area of Mendip? ?	12kms south-west ?

Table 1.3 Distance of stone sources from Stanton Drew (after Lewis 2005).

different parts of the site. A striking characteristic of the stones however, is their very different physical and visual properties (Figure 1.14). The oolitic lime-stone is a soft, yellow, fossily, powdery rock. Certain sandstones are a distinctive pinky-grey colour, the quartz inclusions sparkling in light, the surfaces smoothed. Some of the conglomerates are fantastically knobbly, with 'shaggy' surfaces and large numbers of hollows, conspicuously red from iron impregnation, whilst others are a smoother, more muted grey. The conglomerates also contain quartz and William Stukeley poetically noted how the "...fluours and transparent crystallisations... shine eminently and reflects the sunbeams with great lustre." (Stukeley, quoted in Lloyd-Morgan 1887, 39). Quartz, or rocks with a high concentration of quartz, as already

Fig. 1.14 Photographic montage of four different stone types at Stanton Drew.

mentioned, often occurs as deliberate inclusions in Neolithic monuments suggesting that it had particular meaning. The deployment of these different stones may have been linked to these particular aesthetic and textural qualities.

The stones may also have referenced their place of origin, places with their own mythologies and histories. The raw materials may have been imbued with meaning prior to their incorporation in the monuments. For example, the huge blocks of conglomerate do not appear to have been quarried and historical records suggest that large blocks of this stone lay on the surface in the East Harptree area of Mendip. If these stones were visible in prehistory, the blocks of conglomerate may have been significant places, the stones explained in terms of actions of the gods or the ancestors. Indeed, Lloyd-Morgan stated:

> I have no doubt that superstition or religion supplied the motive force for the energy which displayed itself in the removal...of blocks of rock so huge; and I should suggest that the germ of this lay in the attribution of the occurrence of huge blocks of stone lying on the surface to superhuman or diabolic agency. (Lloyd-Morgan 1887, 49)

By incorporating the stone into the monuments at Stanton Drew, the narrative of such places becomes caught and entangled within the broader meaning of the site. The origins of materials, the memories of other places and other people, become part of the story of Stanton Drew, recalled and recounted during its use.

Linking Objects, Monuments and Landscape

The preceding discussion mentioned Old Red Sandstone, a type of stone found on the Mendip Hills. Old Red Sandstone forms the five rounded hills that rise from the flatter Mendip plateau: Black Down, North Hill, Pen Hill, Stock Hill and Beacon Hill (Figure 1.15). All of these hills have large and impressive round barrow cemeteries upon them, Pen Hill also having an earlier Neolithic long barrow and possible bank barrow near its summit. Mendip Old Red Sandstone was used extensively in the Neolithic and Bronze Ages, turned into artefacts such as quern stones and whetstones that were circulated widely. Items made from this material have been found at monuments in

Fig. 1.15 North Hill from the Mendip plateau. Note the Priddy Nine Barrows skylined.

neighbouring Wessex, for instance, at the Windmill Hill and Hambledon Hill causewayed enclosures (Smith 1965, Mercer and Healey forthcoming) and also on Mendip and in Northern Somerset. During excavations at the non-megalithic Priddy long barrow, a "pavement" of Old Red Sandstone was found, the nearest source being North Hill, c.2½ kilometres north-east of the site (Lewis 2002). At Gorsey Bigbury henge, small pieces of Old Red Sandstone were found within entrance postholes (ApSimon 1976) and at Priddy Circle 1, the stone was introduced as bank material (Tratman 1967). Whilst sources of Old Red Sandstone lie closer to the latter two sites than they do at Stanton Drew and the Priddy barrow, its inclusion at these monuments, as well as in numerous round barrows and cairns, indicates deliberate selection and deposition. Whilst there might be many explanations for this, it is possible that the incorporation of this material into monuments, both as unworked stone and as finished artefacts, might indicate that reference was being made not only to the peculiar (magical?) qualities of the material, but also to its place of origin.

But what of these hills, what might make them special? It is likely that the acid boggy soils formed on the Old Red Sandstone meant that they were never wooded (Findlay 1965). It is also perhaps significant that surface water and springs on the sparsely watered West Mendip plateau are largely confined to areas of impermeable rocks like Old Red Sandstone, the water vanishing at the junction with the permeable limestone. Thus, these are high places, wet places, bare and prominent places and from them it is possible to see off the plateau, to places that include the Welsh mountains, Exmoor, the Cotswolds, the Wessex chalk and even the Malvern Hills. The hills connected *places* across the landscape and might thus have connected *people*. Also, as Cummings and Whittle (2004) have recently pointed out, high places such as hills and mountains are often, ethnographically, associated with mythical beginnings and have a central role in cosmologies. They become sacred places. The deliberate incorporation of stone from these places within monuments can then be seen as an act of sacred incorporation. Viewed this way, the placing of monuments on these hills could be an even more powerful act of appropriation, of harnessing their meaning and associating individuals or communities with the legends of the place.

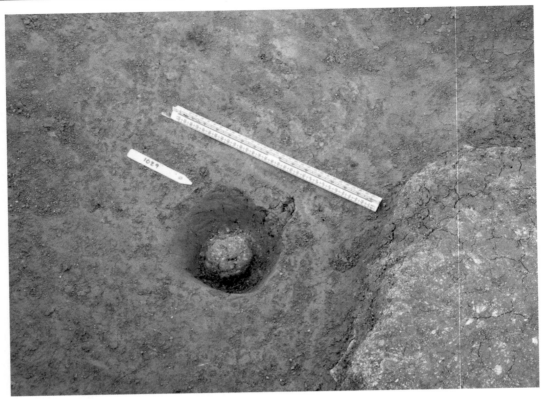

Fig. 1.16 Tufa ball in small pit at Langley's Lane, Midsomer Norton.

Looking Backwards

Most of the sites and monuments discussed in this paper have been of Neolithic and Bronze Age date but it is important to remember that properties of landscape were appreciated and manipulated before this time, though probably in very different ways. In this respect it is necessary to consider one final site, this time of Later Mesolithic date. Recently (2004), the author and Paul Davies started a research project at Langley's Lane, near the town of Midsomer Norton on East Mendip. The site under investigation is a low, naturally formed tufa mound in the valley of the Wellow Brook. Tufa is a striking white substance formed of calcium carbonate, precipitated from water. The mound seems to have been a focus for Later Mesolithic activities, with flint, charcoal and animal bone stratified throughout. However, of particular interest are features noted during excavations at the edge of the mound. These take the form of a series of small pits, dug against the edge of the tufa mound. Placed within them were small deposits of struck flint, fossils and different coloured stones. A single pit contained a small hand-formed ball of possibly "non-local" tufa and no other finds (Figure 1.16). What might

these activities mean? Whilst the project is in its very early stages and any conclusions must remain hypothetical, the deposits are difficult to explain on utilitarian grounds, and might best be seen as evidence for ritual activities. Tufa and tufa depositing springs have had a powerful symbolism attached to them throughout history, many of them becoming holy wells and springs in the medieval period. This is not to espouse continuity of sacred meaning but it does demonstrate human fascination with these unusual landscape features. At Langley's Lane substantial tufa deposition would at times render the landscape white, covering vegetation and soil, the mound growing through time. Davies and Robb (2002) have argued elsewhere that tufa deposits may have been viewed as magical, appearing from ordinary looking water. Perhaps the pits and the deposits within them were a way of demarcating the edge of the tufa, formalising the boundary, delimiting and defining a significant locale in the landscape. Further excavations will provide a fuller understanding of this unusual and important site but it appears that people were recognising and attaching symbolic meaning to parts of the Mendip landscape long before the start of the

Neolithic. The continued importance of this unusual material may be seen at the Bronze Age round barrow *Chewton Mendip 34* (numbering from Grinsell 1971), where a cremation deposit in a pit was covered by a small mound of soil and tufa (Williams 1949).

Conclusions

The prehistoric landscape of central Somerset that has been presented here was a landscape redolent with meaning, myth and history. It is a spectacular landscape, a landscape of contrast from the hills to the levels, from the hidden world of caves and swallets to the open hilltops. People living within and those visiting this landscape have long been aware of its particular qualities and attempted to understand, incorporate and even manipulate these meanings in different ways. The bleak, rather mysterious Medieval landscape that Neale describes (1976) is one example of this, with the traces of earlier activities an integral part of the Medieval inhabitant's "taskscape" (see Ingold 1993). Throughout the prehistoric periods discussed here, it is possible to see human fascination with natural features within the Mendip landscape, though we cannot assume that they would necessarily have been perceived as "natural", for dualistic concepts of nature and culture are not universal. Richard Bradley has discussed how the concept of nature may be a feature of Western philosophy but warns against dismissing it out of hand "…where it is still useful" (Bradley 2000, 34). Archaeological deposits at places such as caves and swallets are, however, material evidence of the significance of these locales and this may be linked to ideas of gods, ancestors or other beings, important places for situating allegoric histories and ritual enactment. A link may also be made between natural features that had demonstrable meaning and the placement of certain monuments, such as the locating of the Priddy Circles in an area with a high concentration of swallets. This is not meant to be a crude predictive model that works for all monuments in all regions, but a way of stressing localised, nuanced understandings of particular landscapes. Such meaning may also carry over into items extracted from places within the landscape, as has been suggested for artefacts of Old Red Sandstone: the biography of the object being intrinsically bound up with its origins. The selection and use of particular materials was not dictated by functionality alone, though it may be impossible to divorce the different elements that make up its significance. The aesthetic and symbolic properties of different stones seems to have been important at Stanton Drew, but these may have been enmeshed within broader meanings of people, places and histories.

In this discussion an attempt has been made to look at how the Mendip landscape may have been experienced at different times in prehistory. Such experiences would have been dependent upon a detailed knowledge of the region and we can speculate whether access, and thus experience, was available to all. Perhaps visits to certain places were arcane, restricted socially or temporally, and experienced by some through story and song rather than viscerally. Yet, it is possible to document the particular uses of particular places and this gives us a glimpse into how meaning may have been inscribed and the Mendip landscape conceptualised in the prehistoric past. That meanings are not static should remind us "horizons for experience are always open and changing." (Tilley 1994, 205).

Acknowledgements

Many thanks must go to Dr Michael Costen for inviting me to present the conference paper that this work is based upon. I would also like to thank David Mullin for the time and energy he put into reading and commenting upon this paper and for allowing me to reproduce his illustration of the axehead from Brimble Pit Swallet. Charlotte Phillips (External Research and University Liaison, Ordnance Survey) kindly sorted out copyright issues, for which I am most grateful. Last but by no means least, the support and encouragement of Mick Aston over the last 10 years is gratefully acknowledged!

References

Altenberg, K. (2003) *Experiencing Landscapes.* Lund Studies in Medieval Archaeology No. 31, Stockholm, Almqvist and Wiksell International.

ApSimon A. M. Musgrave J. H. Sheldon J. Tratman E. K. and van Wijngaarden-Bakker L. H. (1976) Gorsey Bigbury, Cheddar, Somerset: radiocarbon dating, human and animal bones, charcoals, archaeological reassessment. *Proceedings of the University of Bristol Spelaeological Society* 14(2), 155–183.

Aston, M. and Rowley, T. (1974) *Landscape Archaeology.* Newton Abbot, David & Charles.

Atthill, R. (ed.) (1976) *Mendip, a New Study.* Newton Abbot, David and Charles.

Baker, A. and Harley, J. (eds) (1973) *Man Made the Land: essays in English historical geography.* Newton Abbot, David and Charles.

Barrett, J. (1999) Chronologies of Landscape. In P. Ucko and R.Layton (eds), *The Archaeology and Anthropology of Landscape,* 21–30. London, Routledge.

Barrett, J. (1994) *Fragments from Antiquity: An Archaeology of Social Life in Britain, 2900–1200 BC.* Oxford, Basil Blackwell Ltd.

Barrett, J. H. (1966) Tom Tivey's Hole Rock Shelter, near Leighton, Somerset. *Proceedings of the University of Bristol Spelaeological Society* 11(1), 9–24.

Barrington, N. and Stanton, W. (1976) *Mendip: The Complete Caves.* Bath, Dawson & Goodall.

Bender, B. Hamilton, S. and Tilley, C. (1997) Leskernick: Stone Worlds; Alternative Narratives; Nested Landscapes. *Proceedings of the Prehistoric Society* 63, 147–178.

Bender, B. (ed.) (1993) *Landscape Politics and Perspectives*. Oxford. Berg Publishers.

Bender, B. (1992) Theorising Landscapes, and the Prehistoric Landscape of Stonehenge. *Man* 27, 735–755.

Bradley, R. (2000) *An Archaeology of Natural Places*. London, Routledge.

Bradley, R. (1998) *The Significance of Monuments*. London, Routledge.

Clarke, D. (ed.) (1977) *Spatial Archaeology*. London, Academic Press.

Cleal, R. Walker, K. and Montague, R. (1995) *Stonehenge in its Landscape*. English Heritage Archaeological Report Number 10.

Coones, P. (1992) The Unity of Landscape in Macinnes, L. and Wickham-Jones, C. *All Natural Things: Archaeology and the Green Debate*. Oxford, Oxbow Monograph 21, Oxbow Books, 22–40.

Coones, P. (1985) One Landscape or Many? A Geographical Perspective *Landscape History*, 7, 5–12.

Corcos, N. (2001) Churches as Pre-Historic Ritual Monuments: A Review and Phenomenological Perspective from Somerset. *assemblage 6* [Online]. Available from: http://www.shef.ac.uk/~assem/issue6/Cessford_text_web.htm. [Accessed: 15-05-2005].

Cosgrove, D. (1984) *Social Formation and Symbolic Landscape*. Totowa NJ, Barnes and Noble.

Coysh, A. Mason, E. and Waite,V. (1954) *The Mendips*. London, Robert Hale Ltd.

Cummings, V. and Whittle, A. (2004) *Places of Special Virtue Megaliths in the Neolithic Landscape of Wales*. Cardiff Studies in Archaeology. Oxford, Oxbow Books.

Darvill, T. (1997) Neolithic Landscapes: Identity and Definition. In P. Topping (ed.) *Neolithic Landscapes*. Neolithic Studies Group Seminar Papers 2, Oxbow Monograph 86, 1–14.

David, A. Cole, M. Horsley, T. Linford, N. Linford, P. and Martin, L. (2004) A rival to Stonehenge? Geophysical survey at Stanton Drew, England. *Antiquity*, 78 (300), 314–358.

Davies, P. and Robb, R. (2002) The Appropriation of the Material of Places in the Landscape: the case of tufa and springs. *Landscape Research*, Vol. 27, no. 2, 181–185.

Ellis, P. (1992) *Mendip Hills: An Archaeological Survey of the Area of Outstanding Natural Beauty*. Survey Funded by English Heritage & Somerset County Council.

Everton, A. and Everton, R. (1972) Hay Wood Cave Burials, Mendip, Somerset. *Proceedings of the University of Bristol Spelaeological Society*, 13(1), 5–29.

Findlay, D. C. (1965) *The Soils of the Mendip District of Somerset*. Harpenden: Memoir of the Soil Survey of Great Britain, Agricultural Research Council.

Fowler, P. (1976) Early Mendip. In R. Atthill (ed.) *Mendip A New Study*, Newton Abbot, David and Charles, 50–74.

Fox, C. (1923) *The Archaeology of the Cambridge Region*. Cambridge, Cambridge University Press.

Fox, C. (1932) The *Personality of Britain*. National Museum of Wales, Cardiff.

Goudie, A. (1987) Geography and Archaeology: The Growth of a Relationship. In J. Wagstaff (ed.) *Landscape and Culture*. Oxford, Basil Blackwell, 11–25.

Grinsell, L. (1971) Somerset Barrows, Part 2. *Proceedings of the Somerset Archaeology and Natural History Society*, 115, 44–137.

Hodder, I. (1987) Converging Traditions: The Search for Symbolic Meanings in Archaeology and Geography. In J. Wagstaff (ed.) *Landscape and Culture*. Oxford, Basil Blackwell, 134–145.

Hoskins, W. G. (1955) *The Making of the English Landscape*. London, Hodder and Stoughton.

Ingold, T. (2000) *The perception of the environment: essays on livelihood, dwelling and skill*. London, Routledge.

Ingold, T. (1993) The Temporality of Landscape. *World Archaeology* 25 (2), 152–174.

Jones, A. (1997) On the Earth Colours of Neolithic Death. *British Archaeology* 22, 6.

Lelong, O. and Pollard, T. (1998) The Excavation and Survey of Prehistoric Enclosures at Blackhouse Burn, Lanarkshire *Proceedings of the Society of Antiquaries of Scotland* 128, 13–53.

Levitan, B. Audsley, A. Hawkes, C. Moody, A. Moody, P. Smart, P. and Thomas, J. (1988) Charterhouse Warren Farm Swallet, Mendip, Somerset. *Proceedings of the University of Bristol Spelaeological Society* 18 (2), 171–239.

Lewis, J. (2005) Monuments, Ritual and Regionality: the Neolithic of Northern Somerset. *British Archaeological Reports*. Oxford, Archaeopress

Lewis, J. (2002) Reconsidering the Priddy Long Barrow, Mendip, Somerset. *Proceedings of the University of Bristol Spelaeological Society*, 22 (3) 269–288.

Lewis, J. (2001) *Monuments, Ritual and Regionality: the Neolithic of Northern Somerset*. Unpublished Ph.D. thesis, University of Bristol.

Lewis, J. (2000) Upwards at 45 degrees: the use of vertical caves during the Neolithic and Early Bronze Age on Mendip, Somerset. *Capra* 2. Available at http://www.shef.ac.uk/~capra/2/upwards.html

Lewis, J. and Stanton, W. (Forthcoming). Brimble Pit Swallet, Westbury, Mendip: a focus for Later Neolithic deposition.

Lloyd-Morgan (1887) The Stones of Stanton Drew: Their Source and Origin. *Proceedings of the Somerset Archaeological Society*, 33, 37–50.

Lynch, F. (1988) Colour in Prehistoric Architecture. In A. Gibson (ed.) *Prehistoric Ritual and Religion*. 62–67, Stroud, Alan Sutton.

Lynch, F. and Musson, C. (2001) A Prehistoric and Early Medieval Complex at Llandegai, near Bangor, North Wales. *Archaeologia Cambrensis*, 150, 17–142.

Mercer, R. and Healy, F. (Forthcoming). *Hambledon Hill, Dorset, England. Excavation and Survey of a Neolithic Monument Complex and its Surrounding Landscape*, English Heritage Archaeological Report. Swindon, English Heritage.

Mullin, D. (2001) Remembering, Forgetting and the Invention of Tradition: Burial and Natural Places in the English Early Bronze Age. *Antiquity* 75, 533–7.

Neale, F. (1976) Saxon and Medieval Landscapes. In R. Atthill (ed.) *Mendip A New Study*, 75–101, Newton Abbot, David and Charles.

Sauer, C. O. (1925) The Morphology of Landscape. University of California Publications in Geography 2, 19–54.

Smith, I.F. (1965) *Windmill Hill and Avebury: Excavations by Alexander Keiller, 1925–1939*. Oxford, Clarendon Press.

Stanton, W. (1986) Natural Sinkholes Affecting the Priddy Circles, Mendip. *Proceedings of the University of Bristol Spelaeological Society* 17(3), 355–358.

Straker, V. and Wilkinson, K. (2005) Neolithic and Early Bronze Age environments in South-West England. In *South West Archaeological Research Framework Draft Resource Assessment for the Neolithic and Early Bronze Ages*, held with Somerset County Council, Culture and Heritage Department, Taunton.

Tilley, C. (1994) *A Phenomenology of Landscape*. Oxford, Berg.

Tilley, C. (1996) The Powers of Rocks: topography and monument construction on Bodmin Moor. *World Archaeology* 28 (2), 161–176.

Thomas, J. (2001) Archaeologies of place and landscape. In I. Hodder (ed.) *Archaeological Theory Today*, 165–86. Cambridge, Polity Press.

Tratman, E. K. (1967) The Priddy Circles, Mendip, Somerset – Henge Monuments. *Proceedings of the University of Bristol Spelaeological Society* 11 (2), 97–125.

Williams, A. (1949) Bronze Age Barrows near Chewton Mendip. *Proceedings of the Somerset Archaeological and Natural History Society*, 93, 39–67.

Chapter 2

Chasing the Tail of Hunter-Gatherers in South Western Landscapes

Paula Gardiner

There are many of us at Bristol who have been influenced by the approaches taken by Mick Aston in the discipline of landscape studies. The effect that this has had on how we view sites in the landscape and how we contextualise landscapes has been considerable and many of us have continued this thinking into our own particular areas of research, not least my own which have been in the prehistoric period. My research into the Mesolithic-Neolithic transition has focused on landscapes in Somerset and more recently on Exmoor. While we may have significant evidence of Mesolithic flint knapping, or postholes from temporary structures and interpret sites as hunting camps or residential bases, we also need to understand the strategies for raw material procurement and subsistence as well as group territories. More importantly, we need to know why some sites were chosen within a particular environment. It is these principles that have formed the basis of my research in south west England and which is summarised in this paper.

Introduction

The Mesolithic-Neolithic transition has traditionally been seen as an economic phenomenon of colonising farmers who moved across Europe bringing polished stone and pottery, domesticated animals and cereals that made up a Neolithic "package". It was believed that they rapidly absorbed or transplanted the indigenous population. Sedentism and a growing population were linked with this colonisation as a result of intensive food production. This view has partly been due to Childe's label of a "Neolithic Revolution" (1936) and by Ammerman and Cavalli-Sforza's model of *demic diffusion*, the 'Wave of Advance' (1971; 1984). A widespread view of this economic model has led to the presumption that with farming came sedentism and this link between farming

and permanent settlement has been a difficult association to erase.

These views have been challenged more recently, however, and thirty years on from the 'Wave of Advance' the concept of indigenous populations having manipulated their environment and having some influence in the adoption of farming has carried weight. The idea that a colonising mechanism, like that of the *Bandkeramik (LBK)*, which brought a complete village based system to north western Europe at the beginning of the 7th millennium BP, is generally considered not applicable to Britain (Dennell, 1985, 136). However, it is very difficult in a British context to test Zvelebil and Rowley-Conwy's 'Availability' model for the transition to farming (1984; 1986; Zvelebil, 1995b). An agricultural 'wave of advance' may indeed have started in the Near East, but the mechanisms underpinning the adoption of agriculture changed as the phenomenon spread throughout Europe. Ammerman and Cavalli-Sforza's "ripples on a pool" became disordered and fragmented by the time they reached western Europe and there is no reason to suppose that the same model for explaining culture change should be applied to both sides of the North Sea Basin.

These arguments have become polarised into a debate between *diffusionists* and *indigenists*, but neither of these models fit precisely on the British evidence. Researchers in both the late Mesolithic and the early Neolithic often persist in trying to manipulate the data on to the European models, even though it is apparent that Britain has a different database to that in Europe. The *indigenists* have used palaeoenvironmental evidence to suggest social complexity in hunter-gatherer communities. This is seen as some form of woodland management or manipulation of the environment and some researchers argue for a "farming frontier" through which ideas could be filtered (Dennell 1985; Rowley-Conwy 1986; Zvelebil

1995a). The *diffusionists* often see change purely in terms of economy and take no account of monument building and the social changes that were also occurring at this time.

The late Mesolithic in Britain has much regional variation, both in the tool typology and in topographical location. Once Britain became an island our cultural development and transition to agriculture occurred quite differently to that in Europe and Thomas's implication that "there was more than one Neolithic" (1988) is a cautious reminder that we have a very different set of data to that in Europe. We must look critically at the evidence we do have and assess the regional differences that exist in this country, rather than expecting the kind of uniformity that has been found in some parts of western Europe (Waddington 2007).

It is difficult to evaluate accurately the late Mesolithic period in Britain, as we lack a comprehensive database. This hinders any serious test of the 'Availability' model. Many Mesolithic sites have been lost through submergence (Coles 1998), destroyed by modern ploughing, or deeply buried due to alluviation and colluviation processes. It is difficult to predict where these sites might be and although extensive fieldwork has been carried out in the Vale of Pickering, Yorkshire, it has failed to find a site of the calibre of Star Carr (Mellars and Dark 1998). However, the recent discovery of Mesolithic sites with house structures at Howick (Waddington 2003; 2007) and Bowman's Farm (Green 1996) has increased both our database and our understanding of Mesolithic activity in Britain, without borrowing from European analogies.

The excavation of three late Mesolithic sites in Somerset, with the addition of radiocarbon dates has allowed a crucial testing of the current debates surrounding the transition. The sites at Birdcombe (Wraxall), Totty Pot (Mendip) and Hawkcombe Head (Exmoor) are sites where hunter-gatherers were moving between coastal lowlands and uplands for their raw materials and hunting. Birdcombe and Hawkcombe Head have very distinct cut-off points at the end of the late Mesolithic with no continuity into later periods. This evidence will be restructured into a model that is more applicable for the British evidence and allows for more cultural and regional variation than that put forward by the 'Wave of Advance' or the 'Availability' models.

There is a range of evidence for the Mesolithic in Somerset, but it is mainly confined to isolated flint scatters, with the exception of the burial evidence on the Mendip Hills (Gardiner 2001). At Aveline's Hole, Burrington Combe, there is a multiple burial site with possible grave goods, where an estimated fifty to a hundred skeletons were found in 1797 (Tratman 1977; Jacobi 1982; Schulting and Wysocki 2002; Schulting 2005). The most complete Mesolithic skeleton is 'Cheddar Man' from Gough's (New) Cave, Cheddar (Davies 1904; Stringer 1986). Human remains from the Mesolithic have also been found at the Totty Pot swallet hole, Cheddar (Gardiner 2001, 110).

Recent excavation by the author (Gardiner 2000; 2001; 2006) was undertaken on late Mesolithic sites in Somerset, to increase the British database and to test the 'Availability' model in order to assess whether the three sites under excavation could be regarded as 'transition' sites (Zvelebil 1995b).

Birdcombe Case Study

Birdcombe lies at the foot of a south facing slope which forms part of the Failand Ridge and adjacent valley, five miles south of Bristol (ST475718) (Figures 2.1 and 2.2). The site is bordered by the wooded limestone hills of Tower House Woods in the north and a thin band of alluvium that forms the valley bottom. It lies upon Mercia Mudstone at 10m OD. It is well watered by many local springs in the vicinity (Green 1992), with two of them immediately adjacent to the site, the larger of which is named the Whirly Pool. The site was originally discovered in the 1950's by two amateur archaeologists, Mr C. M. Sykes and Mr S. Whittle, when they found hundreds of worked flint, including microliths in the plough soil (Sykes and Whittle 1960).

Subsequent excavation revealed a "chipping floor" which contained worked flint from the early and later Mesolithic periods (Sykes and Whittle 1960). Excavation by the author and students from the University of Bristol in 1997 was carried out to assess and interpret a lowland hunter-gatherer landscape and to re-examine Sykes and Whittle's "chipping floor". Trial trenches were laid in the vicinity of Sykes and Whittle's 1955 trench, approximately 25m from the Whirly Pool and smaller spring (Figure 2.3). A large amount of flint was recovered from Trench D which was extended to 4m × 3m and northwards 1 metre wide to the full length of the field (45m).

There was a distinct flint horizon in Trench D which was 30cm thick and which was sealed by 46cm of deposits. 1600 pieces of worked flint (1628.45g) were recovered from the trench of which 97 were retouched tools, together with 23 cores (469.54g) (Figure 2.4). The retouched tools included a non-geometric element from the earlier Mesolithic period (Figure 2.4, Nos. 1–12), but the collection was dominated by geometric microliths (Figure 2.4, Nos. 15–46) from the later Mesolithic period (Clarke 1932; 1934; Pitts and Jacobi

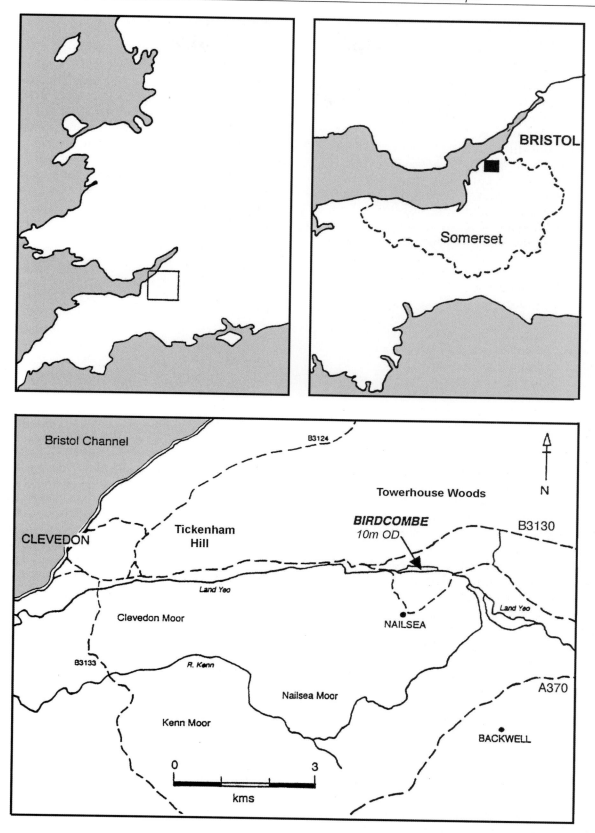

Fig. 2.1 Location map of Birdcombe, Wraxall, North Somerset (Gardiner 2001, 82).

Fig. 2.2 The Birdcombe Mesolithic site is marked 'X'.

1979, 164), together with a quartzite hammerstone, microburins and a fragment of a Horsham, hollow-based point (Figure 2.4, No.12) (Jacobi 1978).

Flint is not found within the natural geology of Somerset and the large quantity of debitage suggests that the raw material was brought to the site in small nodules for knapping. It was used economically and some of the raw material derives from river gravels (chert), but much of it is high quality flint that was probably taken directly from chalk of the Marlborough Downs, Wilts. (Gardiner 2001). Three fragments of charred hazelnut (*Corylus avellana*) were also recovered from Trench D.

Two radiocarbon dates were obtained from charcoal samples from Trench D. Sample 1 was associated with 3 microliths and a Mêche de foret; Sample 2 was associated with 3 scalene triangles (see Table 2.1).

The radiocarbon dates suggest that there was very late hunter-gatherer activity at Birdcombe into the early Neolithic period. Sample No. 2 overlaps with Neolithic monument dates from Broome Heath, Norfolk (4492–3979 cal BC), the Whitwell long cairn (4433–3981 cal BC) and the Hembury causewayed enclosure (4450–3700 cal BC) (Zvelebil and Rowley-Conwy 1986). Sample No.1 suggests that hunter-

gatherers were lingering into the Neolithic period and up to the time of the construction of the Sweet Track (3806 calendar years) (Hillam *et al.* 1990).

10m north of Trench D (D Extension) there was an area of concentrated burning. Little flint was found here (a core and 6 microliths). The charcoal was predominantly oak (*Quercus sp.*) with some hazel (*Corylus avellana*).

Interpretation

Birdcombe is not a 'transition' site as defined by Zvelebil (1995b), as there is no evidence from the flint collection of continuity into the early Neolithic, but the presence of four residual Bronze Age scrapers suggests the area may have been used by farming communities at a later date. The radiocarbon dates, together with the flint typology, suggests prolonged use of the site by hunter-gatherers, possibly into the Neolithic period. There are separate areas of activity for flint knapping and lighting fires. The absence of flint tools above the top of the main flint horizon suggests that the site went out of use fairly abruptly at the end of the Mesolithic. The deposit of approximately 1m of colluvium which sealed the Mesolithic layers, suggests clearance at a later date,

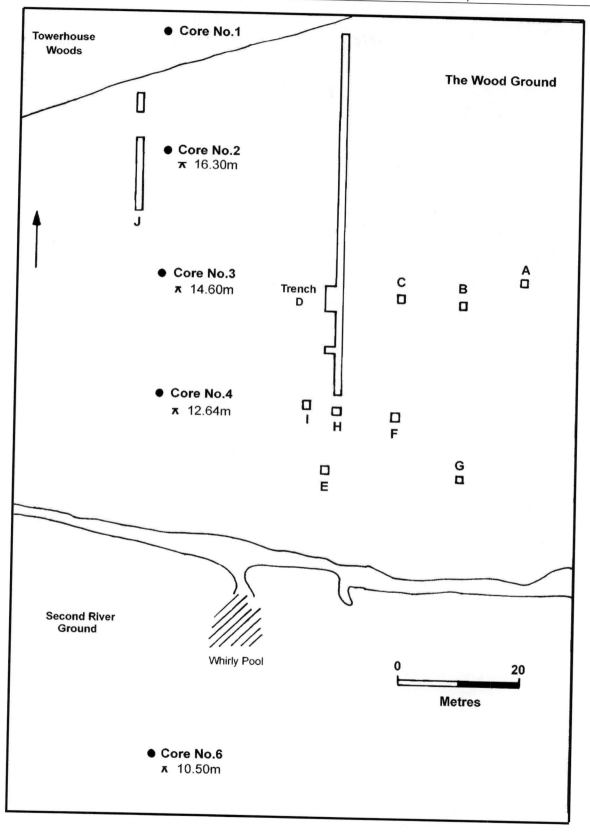

Fig. 2.3 Plan of trial trenches at Birdcombe (Gardiner 2001, 89).

Birdcombe, Somerset

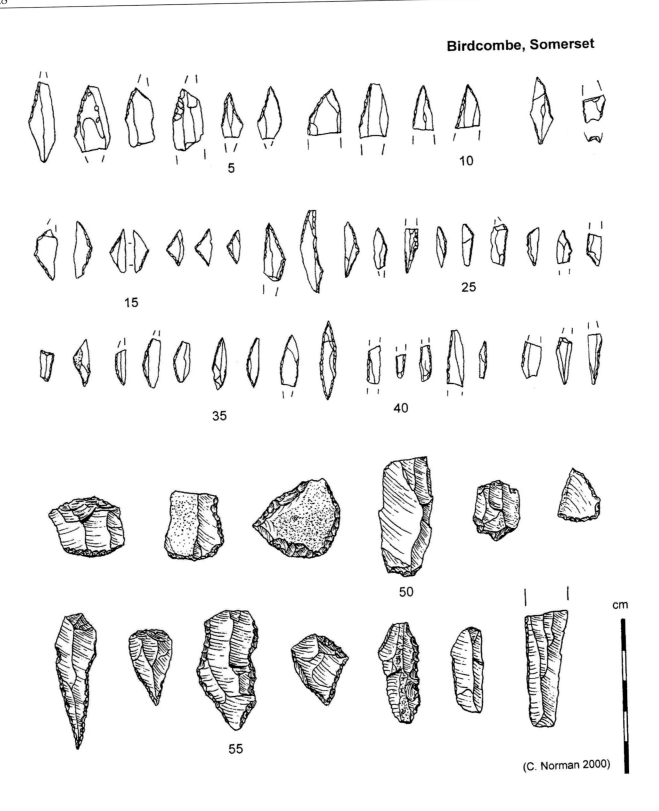

Fig. 2.4 Flint from the 1997 Birdcombe collection (Gardiner 2001, 98).

Sample No.	Material	Lab Code	Radiocarbon Years	Calibration 95%
1	Oak charcoal	Beta-147105	4700 ± 50	3637–3362 cal BC
2	Oak charcoal	Beta-147106	5420 ± 60	4358–4047 cal BC

(Stuiver and Reimer 1993; Stuiver *et al.* 1998)

Table 2.1 Radiocarbon dates from trench D, Birdcombe, Wraxall (Gardiner 2001).

which might have begun in the Neolithic. The location is sheltered and south facing and environmental evidence suggests that there was a steeper valley slope and deeper, wetter, valley bottom in the Mesolithic (Gardiner 2001). This would have provided an essential food resource with the assumption that edible, aquatic plants and wildfowl and fish were available, with nuts, berries and game coming from the higher slopes behind the site on the Failand Ridge. This is an ideal location for a winter stop-over.

The archaeological evidence does not suggest any reason why such a frequently visited site might be abandoned. It is a site where it is conducive to longer visits, especially if resources are to hand, but as will be seen below, the hunters from Birdcombe may have moved up to the higher ground of the Mendip Hills for summer hunting.

Totty Pot Case Study

The entrance to the Totty Pot swallet-hole lies on the level plateau of a limestone rock outcrop at 245m OD at the top of Cheddar Gorge (ST482535) (Figure 2.5). The location affords good all-round visibility, but also exposes it to the weather. It is probable that there was an open woodland environment, as aurochs horn and bone have been recovered from the swallet-hole and from the neighbouring Charterhouse Warren farm swallet (Burleigh and Clutton-Brock 1977).

The swallet-hole was discovered by a caver, Chris Hawkes, in the 1960's and subsequently excavated by the Wessex Caving Club with the objective of discovering a cave chamber. The present entrance to the cave is by a shaft which is 4m deep and 75cm wide (Figures 2.6 and 2.7). A corridor runs for 10m from the base of the shaft into small chambers. Archaeological finds were recovered during excavation of the chambers and also from the spoil heap. The finds include both human and animal bone. The human remains from the chambers comprised six individuals, including children, but some of them were subsequently destroyed by the Leicestershire Police (C. Hawkes pers. comm.). There is a radiocarbon date from a remaining humerus (BM-2973) 8180 ± 70 BP (7450–7050 cal BC) (Schulting 2005). The flint

recovered from the chambers in the 1960's includes 20 microliths from the late Mesolithic period (Figure 2.9, Nos.1–20) (C. Hawkes pers. comm.).

Other finds from this excavation include a small number of early Bronze Age pottery sherds, together with larger flint blades and flakes, also from the Bronze Age. None of the material is stratified and the excavation has not been published. There is a note in Barrington and Stanton (1970), Smith and Drew (1975) and Norman (1982).

In 1998 the author with students from Bristol University excavated around the mouth of the swallet-hole to try and establish whether there was any occupation evidence (Figure 2.8). This consisted of five trenches: Trenches 1 and 2 each side of the mouth of the swallet hole; Trench 3 was 5m east of Trench 2; Trenches 4 and 5 on the lower plateau were sterile. There was little stratigraphy in Trenches 1 and 2 as the bedrock was close to the surface. Trench 3 contained deeper soils of the Nordrach Series. There was evidence of the original spoil heap and this was also excavated (Gardiner 2001).

The 1998 flint collection consisted of 7 retouched tools, including 4 retouched pieces from the 1960's spoil heap and 18 pieces of debitage. The retouched tools are diagnostic of the late Mesolithic period and include 3 lanceolates (Figure 2.9, Nos. 21, 23, 24), a backed bladelet (Figure 2.9, No. 25) and a convex backed microlith (Figure 2.9, No. 26). Also recovered was a Beaker arrowhead (Gardiner, 2001).

There was a small concentration of charcoal in Trench 2, but not in any density to suggest a hearth and not in a suitable stratigraphic position that could be sampled for radiocarbon dating, although three fire-crackled flint fragments hint that there may have been a fire on the site.

Interpretation

There is no evidence of occupation or flint knapping around the mouth of the swallet-hole and it appears that the cave was deliberately used for burial. The difficult access, via the shaft, suggests that it is unlikely that the finds were washed in. The flint debitage is not in any quantity to suggest that flint knapping was carried out to any extent and the finished tools can be

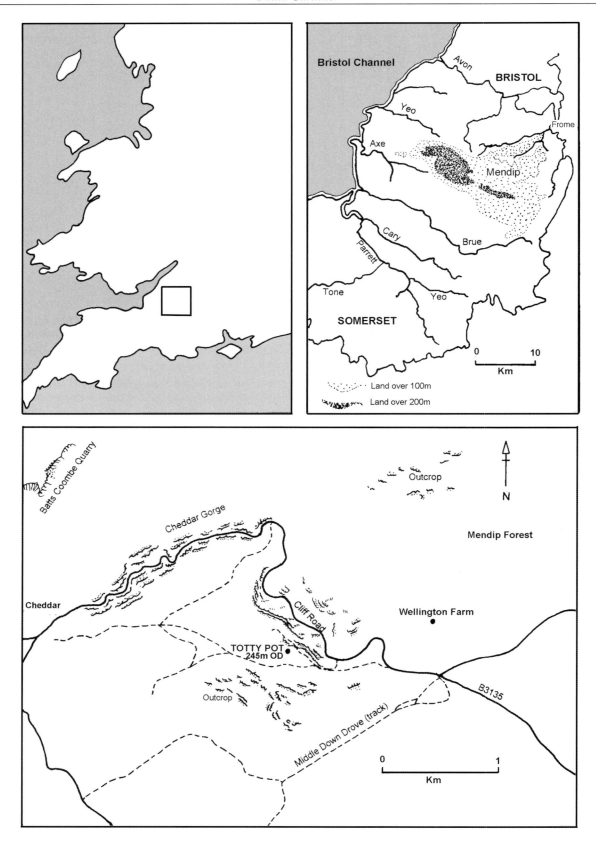

Fig. 2.5 Location map of Totty Pot, Mendip, Somerset (Gardiner 2001).

Shaft entrance

regarded as hunting losses. There still remains, however, a distinct late Mesolithic presence inside the swallet-hole and around the entrance. The tool typology suggests a late date for Mesolithic activity in the cave. The animal bone evidence from Totty Pot and from Charterhouse Warren Farm nearby, suggests that the hunting of aurochs on the Mendips continued from the Mesolithic into the Bronze Age (Burleigh and Clutton-Brock 1977; Gardiner, 2001).

It seems reasonable to suggest that the swallet-hole was used specifically for burial in the Mesolithic, with the environment around the site being used for hunting both in the Mesolithic and the early Bronze Age. The elevated and exposed position of Totty Pot cave with its dark and inaccessible chambers, presents itself as a burial site in the Mesolithic. The radiocarbon dates from Aveline's Hole close by, suggests that both caves were used in the later Mesolithic. Whether the microliths from Totty Pot can be regarded as grave goods is debatable without further excavation inside the chambers. The radiocarbon date from Totty Pot suggests burial in the cave by hunter-gatherers up to around 7050 cal BC (see Table 2.2).

No other Mesolithic sites in North Somerset have

Fig. 2.6 (left) Entrance to Totty Pot swallet hole.
Fig. 2.7 (below)The narrow shaft entrance which leads to the small chambers inside the cave.

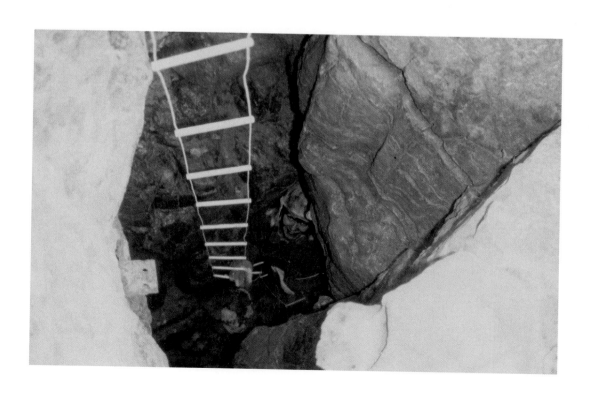

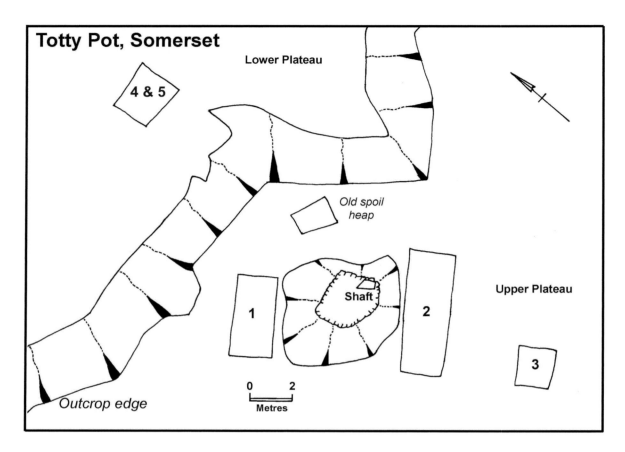

Fig. 2.8 Trench plan for the 1998 excavation.

Site	Lab Sample	Radiocarbon Years	Calibration 95%
'Cheddar Man'	BM-525	9080 ± 150	8700–7760 cal BC
	OxA-814	9100 ± 100	8610–7980 cal BC
Totty Pot	BM-2973	8180 ± 70	7450–7050 cal BC
Aveline's Hole	Gr-N-5393	8100 ± 50	7302–6864 cal BC

Table 2.2 Radiocarbon dates from the Mendip caves (Gardiner 2001; Schulting 2005).

been found that have the quantity and quality of flint on the scale of Birdcombe. However, there are similarities in tool typology between Birdcombe and other sites on Mendip (Figure 2.10). These include Totty Pot, Hay Wood Cave, Hutton (Everton and Everton 1972), Gorsey Bigbury (Jones 1938) and Rowberrow Cavern (Taylor 1920–21; 1924; 1926).

This suggests that the Mendip Hills may have been used for both hunting and/or burial by a group that had a more permanent base on lower ground at Birdcombe. Mendip is 25km from the Mesolithic coastline near Blackstone Rocks and hunting groups could move from the low lying ground in the area around Clevedon, through the Birdcombe valley and up on to the Mendip Hills for hunting. The higher ground around Charterhouse, Ebbor Gorge and further west towards Hay Wood cave, has evidence of Mesolithic finds and it is reasonable to suggest that this was the hunting territory used by a group who may have wintered at Birdcombe. This is an easily accessible seasonal round, with flint being brought in from outside the area and with hunting and burial within a day's walk of a more permanent site at Birdcombe.

Flint from C. J. Hawkes' Collection

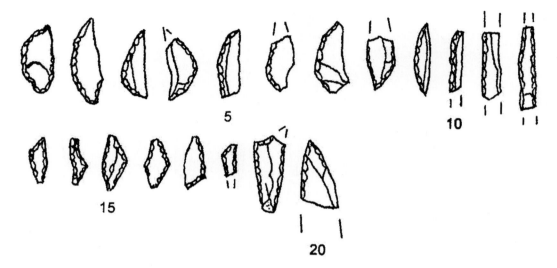

Microliths – 1998 Excavation

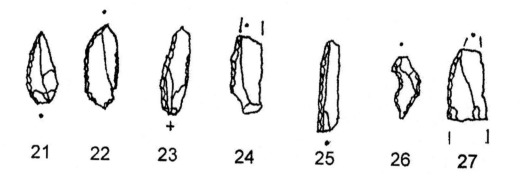

Scale 1:1
(C. Norman 2000)

Fig. 2.9 Microliths from the Totty Pot collection (Gardiner 2001, 111).

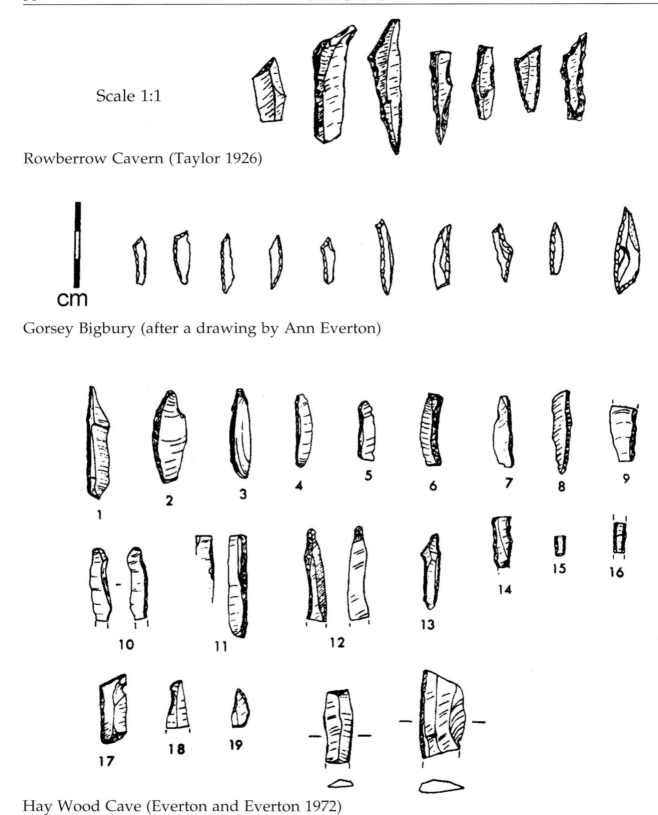

Scale 1:1

Rowberrow Cavern (Taylor 1926)

cm

Gorsey Bigbury (after a drawing by Ann Everton)

Hay Wood Cave (Everton and Everton 1972)

Fig. 2.10 Flint from Hay Wood cave, Gorsey Bigbury and Rowberrow cavern (Gardiner 2001).

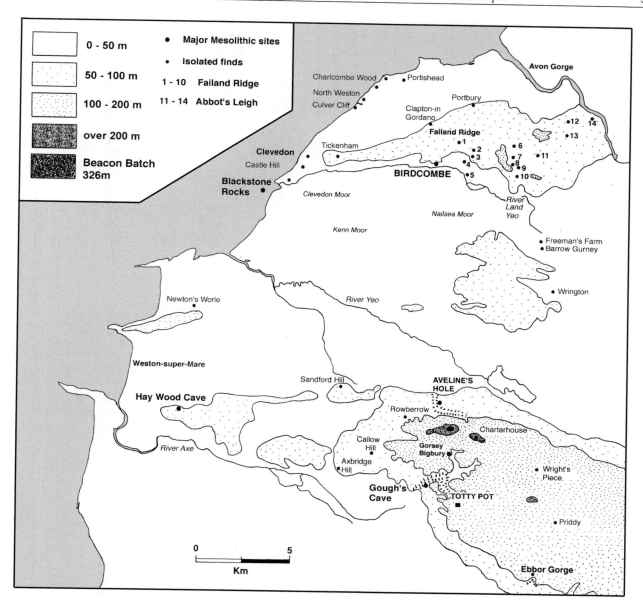

Fig. 2.11 Mesolithic sites on the Failand Ridge and Mendip Hills, Somerset (Gardiner 2001, 120).

Hawkcombe Head Case Study

Hawkcombe Head has been known as a late Mesolithic site for over fifty years due to the extensive collection of worked flint that has been recovered from the areas around the Hawkcombe and Ven Combe springs (SS844457) (Figure 2.12). The finds are held in the Wedlake Collection and at the County Museum, Taunton and contain hundreds of microliths from the late Mesolithic period, together with flint debitage in excess of around 6,000 pieces (C. Norman, pers. comm.). Three seasons of excavation (2002–4) by the author, the University of Bristol and the Exmoor National Park Authority, have revealed detailed evidence of hunter-gatherer activity around the spring-heads and established Hawkcombe Head as the earliest occupation site within the Exmoor National Park (Gardiner 2007).

The site takes its name from a springhead which rises at the top of a combe that drops down to Porlock Beach 3km away. It is situated on open moorland 420m above sea level, in an area known as Porlock Common (SS844457). In this area is a Neolithic/Bronze Age

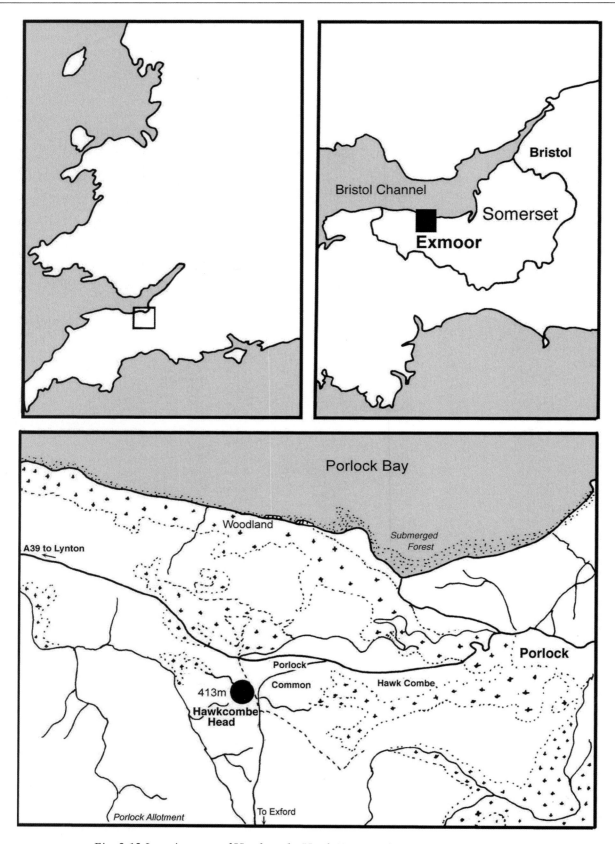

Fig. 2.12 Location map of Hawkcombe Head, Exmoor, Somerset (Gardiner 2007).

Fig. 2.13 *Aerial photograph of the areas excavated at Hawkcombe Head. (Reproduced by permission of English Heritage NMR 21521/32 2003).*

monument called the Whit Stones and just under a kilometre away are more stone monuments and Bronze Age hut circles (Riley and Wilson-North 2001). The Mesolithic site lies on open moorland and is crossed by the road from Exford to Porlock and by footpaths and tracks across the open moor. At Porlock Beach there is a submerged forest that is visible at low tide. In the nineteenth Century, worked flint was recovered from the submerged forest (Wymer, 1977) and more recently by the Exmoor National Park Authority (R.Wilson-North, pers. comm.). Palaeoenvironmental studies indicate that the area, which we know as a pebble beach today, was forested in the Mesolithic (Riley and Wilson-North 2001). There is a natural routeway from the beach that follows the combe cut by the Hawkcombe Head spring to the top of the moorland.

Three seasons of excavation at the site have revealed evidence of hearths, postholes and a temporary structure, together with 2500 pieces of worked flint, of which 490 are retouched or modified tools belonging to the later Mesolithic period. There is now in excess of 8400 pieces of worked flint recovered from Hawkcombe Head.

The Ven Combe area (Area B, Trench 3) (Figure 2.14) has a second springhead, which cuts a combe to Lynton. Around the springhead is a boggy area known as the flushing. Close to the western edge of the flushing is a temporary structure erected around a deliberately laid clay floor (303) measuring 2.0m × 2.2m (Figure 2.15, 2.16). It is thought that the clay for the floor may have been dug from the flushing and laid directly on to the ground surface. Within the floor were 84 pieces of flint debitage, including 22 retouched tools. The diagnostic pieces include microliths, micro-cores, awls and triangles. The position of the flint within the clay spread suggests that it became embedded in the surface of the floor as a result of flint knapping (Gardiner 2007).

Three shallow postholes (310, 318 and 914) surround the clay floor, together with two further postholes (916 and 908) are 2m to the west and south of it (Figure 2.17). These postholes appear to be associated with the floor, but they could represent a separate feature of their own. Two pebble tools, which show wear marks and a polished base, were also recovered from this trench. To the west of the flushing

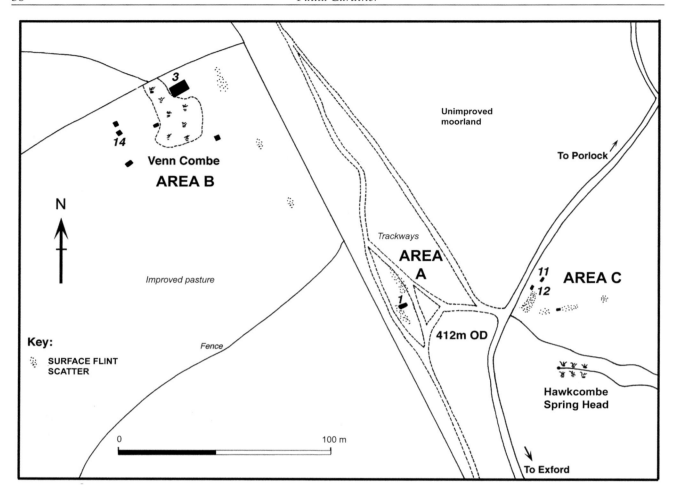

Fig. 2.14 Plan of trenches at Hawkcombe Head (Gardiner 2007).

a hearth in Trench 14 (Area B) contained a large quantity of charcoal, including oak (*Quercus*), hazel (*Corylus avellana*) and hawthorn (*Pomoideae*) (Figure 2.18, 2.19). The radiocarbon date from the hazel charcoal confirms the feature as late Mesolithic (see Table 2.3).

Area C on the moorland adjoining the Exford to Porlock Road, Trench 12 (1m × 2m) produced the greatest quantity of flint, almost a thousand pieces, of which 134 are retouched tools. A sealed posthole in this trench (12–08) contained one piece of flint waste, packing stones *in situ* together with holly (*Ilex aquifolium*) and oak (*Quercus*) charcoal. A sample of the holly charcoal has been radiocarbon dated to the late Mesolithic period (see Table 2.4). Four pebble tools similar to that found near the clay floor structure have been recovered from this trench and Trench 11 (Figure 2.20).

The raw material mainly derives from beach pebble

with a small quantity of Greensand Chert from the Blackdown Hills. Pebble flint is not found on Porlock Beach in any quantity as the shingle ridge that forms the beach today is Devonian Sandstone. Small pieces of pebble flint can sometimes be found on Porlock Beach, but it is too small to be knapped into tools. It is likely that the pebble flint found at Hawkcombe Head comes from further down the coast beyond Lynton (Chris Norman, pers. comm.).

At Hawkcombe Head there appears to be discrete areas of Mesolithic activity where flint knapping took place and temporary shelters were erected and fires were lit for warmth or cooking. It is unlikely, due to its height above sea level that the site was used in winter, but frequent visits were made by small local groups over a considerable period of time. The large number of tools suggest that it could have been small family units who were involved in hunting (Figure 2.22, 2.23) processing bone tools using flint blades and flakes

(Figure 2.24, 2.25), or skin working using borers and awls. Some of the microliths may have been used as composite tools for plant processing (Figure 2.24).

Hawkcombe Head is more than a short-stay hunting camp, as can be seen by the diversity of tools found on the site. It is not a 'transition' site, nor was it chosen for the availability of raw material, but it must be considered as a frequently used *locale* within the Hawkcombe Head landscape (Gardiner 2007). Hunter-gatherers were moving between the coastal plain of Porlock and Lynton and up to the moorland for summer activities following the natural routeways cut by the combes. At the end of the Mesolithic, Hawkcombe Head went out of use and there is no archaeological evidence to suggest any later use of the site. It is difficult to see a direct link with the Neolithic or Bronze Age monument builders as it appears that hunter-gatherers had either abandoned Hawkcombe Head before the stone erecting groups came into the area, or they continued their lifestyle regardless of any monument building activities.

Fig. 2.15 Half-section of clay floor (303).

Fig. 2.16 Detail of clay floor (303).

Hawkcombe Head, Somerset   TRENCH 3

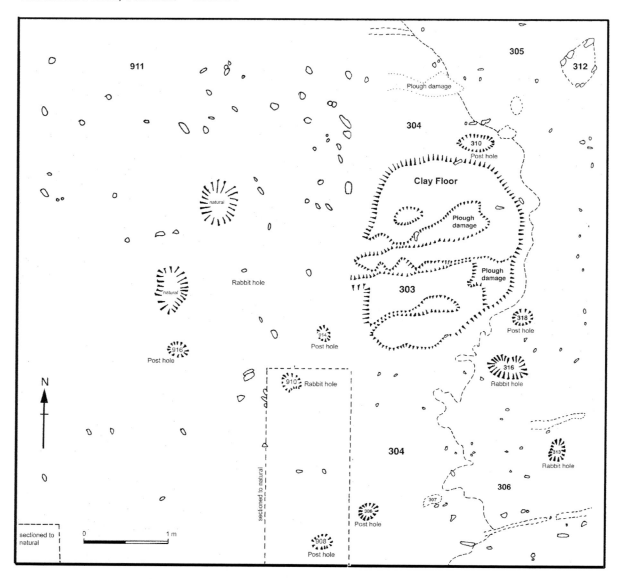

Fig. 2.17 Planning drawing of Trench 3 showing clay floor (303) and postholes (Gardiner 2007).

The Mesolithic-Neolithic Transition

The 'Wave of Advance' model

Ammerman and Cavalli-Sforza's model of *demic-diffusion* (1973, 344) claimed that the spread of farming resulted from population growth and displacement. The 'Wave of Advance' modelled the spread of colonists across Europe from the Near East and it was seen as a "slow, continuous expansion" of farmers bringing domesticates. The model measures this expansion using radiocarbon dates and is based on the existence of a 'farming frontier' at the head of the colonists who advanced across Europe.

The model has been criticised by Zvelebil (1986) on the grounds that Ammerman and Cavalli-Sforza have confused the understanding of the Neolithic in different areas of Europe, with the rate being too swift in the Mediterranean and too slow in the east and north, with no account taken of regional variations. Zvelebils's more recent research shows that in eastern

Fig. 2.18 Uncovering the hearth (14–04) in Trench 14. © Chris Chapman.

Lab Sample	Context	Material	Radiocarbon Years	Calibration 94.4%
SUERC-2970 (GU-11979)	14-04	Hazel	7420 ± 35	6390–6210 cal.BC

(Stuiver *et al.* 1998; OxCal v.3.8 Bronk Ramsey (2002))

Table 2.3 Radiocarbon date from the hearth in Tench 14 (Gardiner 2007).

Europe and the north European plain farmers that had contact with the indigenous population caused an extended delay in the initial take-up of farming, which was then rapidly followed by a shift in economy (Zvelebil 1986; 1995b).

It has taken a long time to throw off the idea of immigrating farmers moving uniformly across Europe and although the *diffusionist* theory still carries some weight, more recent studies have conflicted with this view (Dennell 1985; Rowley-Conwy 1983; 1997; 1998; Thomas 1999), suggesting that the indigenous population were capable of manipulating their environment to their own advantage and that the 'Neolithic package' might be more fragmented than was previously thought. It is against this background that the *indigenist* models have emerged.

The 'Availability' model

Zevelebil and others have used the 'farming frontier' as a "conceptual and cognitive construct" by which to model the process by which the transition to agriculture occurred in Europe (Zvelebil, 1986; 1995b, 127; Dennell 1985; Rowley-Conwy 1986). Using data from central Europe, Zvelebil suggests that it bridged the gap between the forager Bug-Dniester groups and the farming culture of the Cucuteni-Tripolye (Zvelebil 1995b) and allowed new, ideological and economical elements to be filtered between them.

The exchange of artefacts as shown in Figure 2.28 suggests some form of contact between different cultural groups in Europe. Examples can be found in Ertebølle pottery which contains plant tempering similar to that of the *LBK;* shoe-last adzes, T-shaped antler axes, bone combs and rings are found in Ertebølle sites in Denmark; domesticated cattle bones are found in small numbers on Mesolithic sites in Denmark, Scania, northern Poland (Zvelebil 1995b) and at Ferriter's Cove, Co. Kerry (Woodman *et al.* 1999). Dennell (1985) suggests that both Mesolithic and Neolithic groups would have a vested interest in an

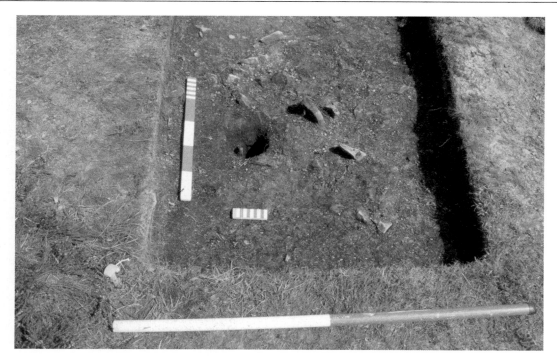

Fig. 2.19 Photograph of post-hole (12–08) in Trench 12. © P. Gardiner.

Lab Sample	Context	Material	Radiocarbon Years	Calibration 95.4%
SUERC-2968 (GU-11978)	12–08	Holly	7815 ± 40	6760–6500 cal.BC

(Stuiver *et al.* 1998; OxCal v.3.8 Bronk Ramsey (2002)).

Table 2.4 Radiocarbon date from the post-hole in Trench 12.

amicable relationship and early farmers would not necessarily be superior. Although there is palaeo-environmental evidence to support that idea that Mesolithic groups in Britain might be manipulating their environment (Simmons and Dimbleby 1974; Caseldine and Hatton 1993); Edwards 1993; Edwards and Hirons 1984; Simmons 1993; 1996), much of this evidence is not securely linked to the archaeological evidence that is needed to support it.

In support of *indigenism* Zvelebil and Rowley-Conwy (Zvelebil 1986; 1995b; Zvelebil and Rowley-Conwy 1986) have put forward a model for the transition to farming in Europe, where there is clear evidence of a symbiotic relationship between hunting and farming communities.

The model calls for the transition to have occurred in three distinct stages: an *availability* phase where material goods and information could be exchanged without groups losing their cultural identity and with no more than 5% of domesticates being found on hunter-gatherer sites; a *substitution* phase where hunter-gatherers may still retain some foraging activities, but with less than 50% of domesticates on site; a final *consolidation* phase when there is a complete shift to agriculture with domesticates making up to 100% of the evidence on site.

The 'Availability' model relies on identifying the differences between foragers and farmers and works particularly well with the eastern European evidence where the Mesolithic Bug-Dniester sites show evidence of these phases before they vanish from the archaeological record and are assumed to have become established within the Cucuteni-Tripolye culture (Zvelebil 1995b). The 'Availability' model creates a clear economic and cultural division between foragers and farmers, but does not allow for total resistance, or a long *availability* phase, as in the Ertebølle example.

It is very difficult to test the 'Availability' model on the British data. Deliberate deposits in pits and, more visibly, the erection of monuments are the first

Fig. 2.20 Pebble tool with wear marks, © S. Knight.

Fig. 2.21 Microcore, © S. Knight.

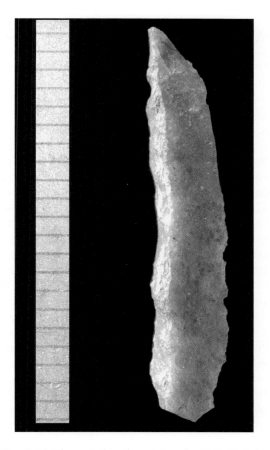

Fig. 2.22 Elongated scalene triangle, © S. Knight.

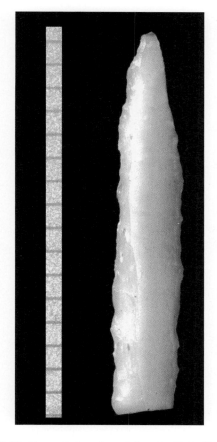

Fig. 2.23 Elongated scalene triangle, © S. Knight.

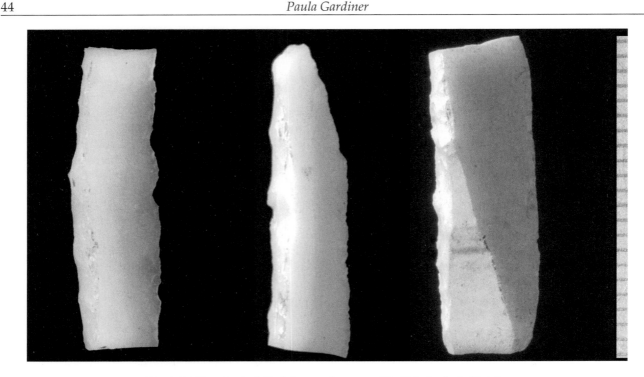

Fig. 2.24 Two backed bladelets and one modified blade, © S. Knight.

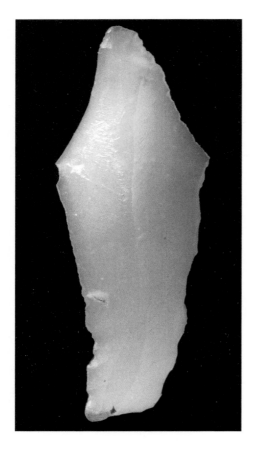

Fig. 2.25 Modified flake with notch at base, © S. Knight.

indication that there is a change in society, with only a hint of economic change in the deposits from the causewayed enclosures (Liddell 1935; Mercer 1980; 1981; Thomas 1999l; Smith 1965). If monuments are put into the *availability* phase, it would be a long one, with little or no evidence of *substitution* and with *consolidation* not being seen in the landscape until the Bronze Age, when more conclusive evidence of settlement and field systems can be seen in the landscape (Milles *et al.* 1989; Whittle *et al.* 1986). One might suggest that these are not valid comparisons as the evidence is drawn from different registers and although we can see differences between foragers and monument builders in the archaeological record, in Britain, hunter-gatherers remain a completely separate culture from early farmers, who themselves may not be fully-fledged at the point of *availability* (Gardiner 2001, 38). Without considerable modification there does not appear to be a way of successfully applying the 'Availability' model on the current British data, especially in the absence of a 'farming frontier' and the 'transition' sites which might show an overlap between the late Mesolithic and early Neolithic.

Monument building and hunter-gatherers in Britain

Radiocarbon dates have often been used to suggest an overlap between the late Mesolithic and the early Neolithic. This kind of exercise is fraught with

Fig. 2.26 Reconstruction of the Ven Combe area, © Christine Harrison.

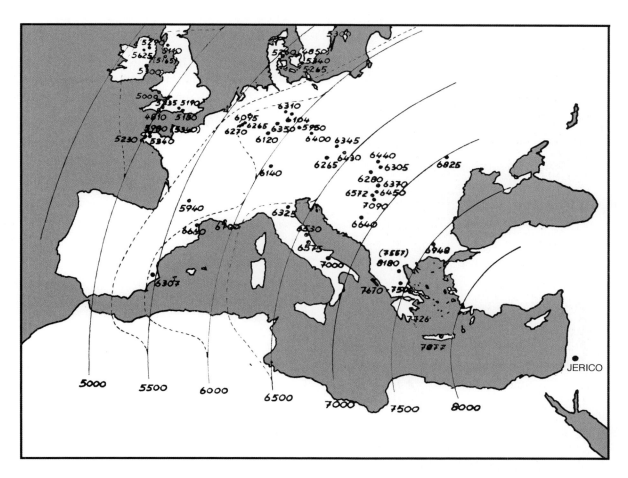

Fig. 2.27 The 'Wave of Advance' model showing radiocarbon dates in years BP; arcs indicate the expected position of the spread at 500 year intervals; broken lines take into account regional variation (Ammerman and Cavalli-Sforza 1971).

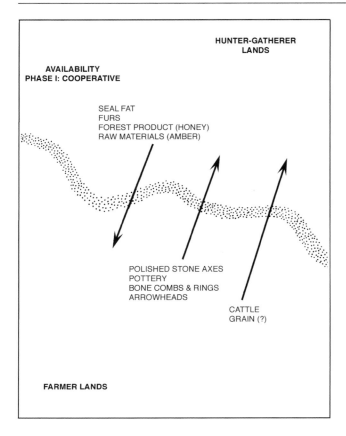

Fig. 2.28 Forager-farmer contacts expected during the co-operative part of the availability phase *(Zvelebi 1995b).*

problems, partly because of the security of some of the samples. Table 2.5 shows late Mesolithic sites *(shaded)* and early Neolithic dates from monuments in England after insecure samples have been rejected by Jacobi (pers. comm.) and Williams (1989) (Gardiner 2001, 142). Although the date for Ballynagilly has been included, it has more recently been regarded as being insecure (Woodman 2000). Table 2.5 has only included dates from Neolithic monuments, although Green and Allen (1997) have dated the layers containing microliths from the shaft in Fir Tree Field, Cranborne Chase, to 4300–4150 cal BC.

The results in Table 2.5 (excluding Ballynagilly) show that Birdcombe and Eskmeals (Mesolithic) overlap with Broome Heath (Neolithic). Birdcombe and the Whitwell long cairn are roughly contemporary, but then there is a steady and continuous phase of Neolithic monument building. The Post Track and the Sweet Track appear around the time of Eaton Heath, Abingdon, Hazleton and Carn Brea. Broome Heath is seen as the earliest open Neolithic site with the Whitwell long cairn and the Hembury causewayed enclosure as the earliest Neolithic monuments.

The archaeological evidence from both the later Mesolithic and the early Neolithic suggests there is no mixing of cultures, but the radiocarbon dates suggest that Birdcombe and Eskmeals overlap into the Neolithic. The latest date for Birdcombe suggests that hunter-gatherers were lingering well into the Neo-

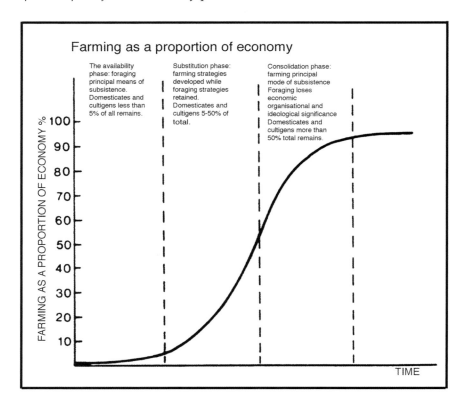

Fig. 2.29 The 'Availability' model of the transition to farming (Zvelebil 1995b).

Site	Code	Lab Sample	Radiocarbon yrs BP	Calibrated BC
Aveline's Hole	*AV*	*BM-471*	*9144 ± 110*	*8684 – 8028*
Aveline's Hole	*AV*	*Q-1458*	*9090 ±110*	*8554 – 7967*
Cheddar Man	*CH*	*BM-525*	*9080 ± 150*	*8686 – 7827*
Totty Pot	*TP*	*Unpublished*	*8320 ± 69*	*7541 – 7086*
Aveline's Hole	*AV*	*GrN–5393*	*8100 ± 50*	*7302 – 6864*
Culverwell	*CU*	*BM–473*	*7150 ± 135*	*6242 – 5730*
Culverwell	*CU*	*BM–960*	*7101 ± 97*	*6201 – 5774*
Westward Ho!	*WH*	*Q–672*	*6585 ±130*	*5726 – 5303*
Poldowrian	*P*	*HAR–4568*	*6450 ± 110*	*5618 – 5149*
Windmill Farm	*WF*	*HAR-4626*	*6160 ±150*	*5470 – 4718*
March Hill II	*MH*	*Q-788*	*5850 ± 80*	*4904 – 4499*
Stonewall rock shelter	*S*	*Q-1143*	*5770 ±100*	*4846 – 4362*
Ballynagilly	BN	UB-305	5745 ± 90	4800 – 4361
Thorpe Common	*TC*	*Q-1118*	*5680 ± 150*	*4897 – 4245*
Eskmeals	*E*	*UB-2712*	*5509 ± 54*	*4456 – 4249*
Broome Heath	BH	BM-679	5424 ± 117	4492 – 3979
Birdcombe	*B*	*Beta-147106*	*5420 ± 60*	*4358 – 4047*
Whitwell long cairn	W	OxA-4176	5380 ± 90	4433 – 3981
Hembury	HM	BM-138	5280 ± 150	4448 – 3714
Cannon Hill	CH	HAR-1198	5260 ± 110	4338 – 3798
Carrowmore	CM	Lu-1441	5240 ± 80	4318 – 3815
Beckhampton Road	BR	NPL-138	5200 ± 160	4350 – 3653
Ascott-under-Wychwood	A	BM-835	5198 ± 225	4488 – 3524
Poldowrian*	P	HAR-4323	5180 ± 150	4338 – 3653
Balbridie	BB	GU-1038	5160 ± 70	4218 – 3792
Eaton Heath	EH	BM-770	5095 ± 49	3980 – 3776
Abingdon	AB	BM-351	5060 ± 130	4220 – 3543
Hazleton North	HZ	OxA-910	5000 ± 150	4218 – 3382
Carn Brea	CB	BM-825	4999 ± 65	3960 – 3649
Eskmeals*	E	UB-2711	4925 ± 165	4042 – 3362
Lambourn	L	OxA-7693	4955 ± 45	3905 – 3645
Hazard Hill	HH	BM-149	4920 ± 150	4036 – 3368
Poldowrian*	P	HAR-4052	4870 ± 130	3960 – 3365
Hay Wood*	HW	OxA-5844	4860 ± 65	3773 – 3520
Hambledon Hill	H	NPL-76	4740 ± 90	3700 – 3351
Birdcombe	*B*	*Beta-147105*	*4700 ± 50*	*3637 – 3362*
Post Track				3838 (Dendro)
Sweet Track				3806/7 (Dendro)

(Stuiver *et al.* (1998); OxCal v3.4 Bronk Ramsey (2000))

shaded = Later Mesolithic sites
* = Mesolithic site with later Neolithic phase

Table 2.5 Late Mesolithic and early Neolithic radiocarbon dates for England after insecure samples have been rejected by Jacobi (pers. comm.) and Williams (1989) (Gardiner 2001, 145).

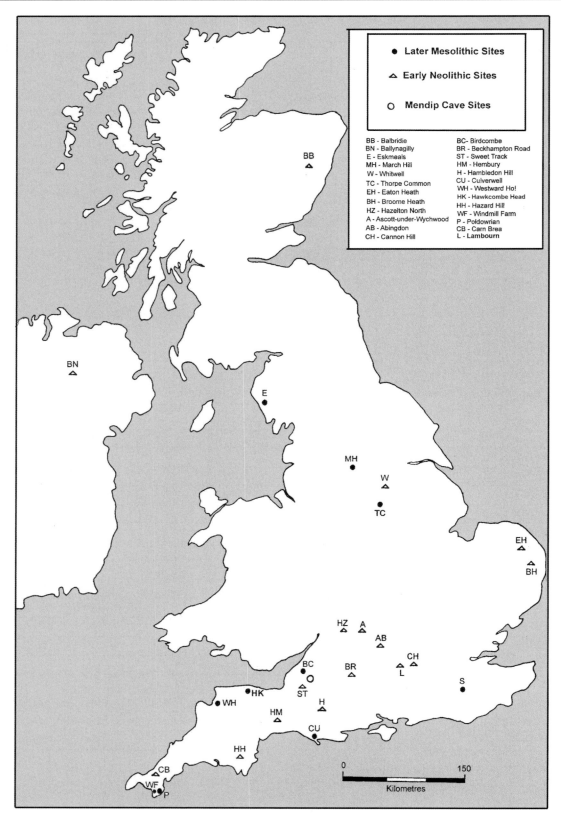

Fig. 2.30 Late Mesolithic sites (filled circles) and early Neolithic sites (open triangles) in England (adapted from Rowley-Conwy 1986).

lithic, but remain a distinct hunter-gatherer group, even though they must have been aware of changes in the landscape.

If the Mesolithic and Neolithic sites in Table 2.5 are analysed geographically, they bear little relation to one another.

The pattern represented in Figure 2.30 shows that the late Mesolithic and early Neolithic are separated geographically, often by hundreds of kilometres, but chronologically by perhaps a few hundred years. Early Neolithic sites are dispersed throughout southern England, with the addition of Broome Heath in East Anglia and the Whitwell long cairn in Derbyshire. Late Mesolithic sites are even more widely dispersed with Eskmeals in Cumbria, March Hill II and Thorpe Common in the Midlands, with Westward Ho! in Devon and the Stonewall rock shelter in Kent. Two Mesolithic sites that have later phases are Eskmeals and Poldowrian. There is approximately over 500 years between the Mesolithic at Eskmeals and the Neolithic phase (Bonsall *et al.* 1989) and at Poldowrian there is a gap of approximately 1700 years between the Mesolithic and Neolithic phases (Smith and Harris 1982). The closest sites geographically are Birdcombe and the Post Track and Sweet Track which are only 48 Km apart. Culturally there is nothing to link the Somerset trackways with the hunter-gatherers at Birdcombe, but chronologically there may be only a few hundred years between them. The artefacts found at the trackways are culturally Neolithic, but the timber used to build them comes from managed and coppiced woodland (Coles 1986). This suggests that the trackway builders must have been living in the area well before the trackways were built and begs the question of whether they were indigenous hunter-gatherers or early farmers.

Although we lack a comprehensive database, Figure 2.30 clearly shows that the late Mesolithic and early Neolithic are almost randomly dispersed throughout the south west peninsula, with Carn Brea (Neolithic) and Poldowrian (Mesolithic) being the closest geographically, but chronologically there is 1500 years between them (Mercer 1981; Smith and Harris 1982).

Discussion

In Britain at the end of the Mesolithic we have no evidence of a 'farming frontier' or the kind of 'transition' sites that might show contact and exchange between hunter-gatherers and early farmers or monument builders. A pattern of site abandonment by the late Mesolithic, before the onset of the Neolithic can be repeated throughout the south west. Microliths are rarely found, if at all, as part of a Neolithic assemblage,

although there may be earlier contexts on Neolithic sites. At the Hazleton North long barrow Saville (1990) found microliths in a pre-cairn context and within a Neolithic midden. Those found in the pre-cairn context are spatially separated from the Neolithic activity and there are no radiocarbon dates to link either contexts. Although Saville suggests that the Neolithic tomb builders may have had a Mesolithic ancestry, there is nothing stratigraphically to link these two very distinctive cultures together (Saville 1990). At the Hembury, causewayed enclosure microliths have been found scattered throughout the site (Liddell 1935; Berridge 1986), but it is probably coincidental that the Mesolithic and the Neolithic were using the same area, rather than the Neolithic specifically choosing a site previously occupied by earlier hunter-gatherers.

The late Mesolithic in the south west of England shows a general pattern of longer-stay sites on lower ground (Birdcombe), with the use of summer uplands for hunting (Hawkcombe Head). In Devon and Cornwall there is a pattern of cliff sites such as Trevose Head (Johnson and David 1982), Poldowrian (Smith and Harris 1982) and Gwithian (Berridge and Roberts 1986) where hunting tools have been produced from local beach pebble. Throughout the south west the Mesolithic and the Neolithic remain spatially separated and although we can plot distribution maps, this tells us little more than where sites are located. We just do not appear to have the 'transition' sites to be able to test the 'Availability' model successfully.

The evidence from southern England, albeit, incomplete, suggests that the Mesolithic came to an abrupt end around 4000 cal BC. At Birdcombe, hunter-gatherers lingered on into the Neolithic and may have been aware of monument building. If the indigenous population were involved in the construction of monuments, we cannot see it in the archaeological record, although the radiocarbon dates suggest in some cases that both hunter-gatherers and monument builders could have been using the landscape at the same time (Gardiner 2001). There is a distinct separation of cultures and there is no archaeological evidence to suggest contact or exchange.

The graphic representation in Table 2.6 of the calibrated radiocarbon dates discussed above, shows a steady progression through time of hunter-gatherer sites, but by the end of the Mesolithic this is slowing down. From around 4400 cal BC there is a marked clustering of early Neolithic sites appearing in the landscape. When they arrive, they do so sharply and abruptly throughout southern England.

We are unable to see the demise of hunter-gatherers in the archaeological record and do not know whether they were assimilated into a new farming culture as in

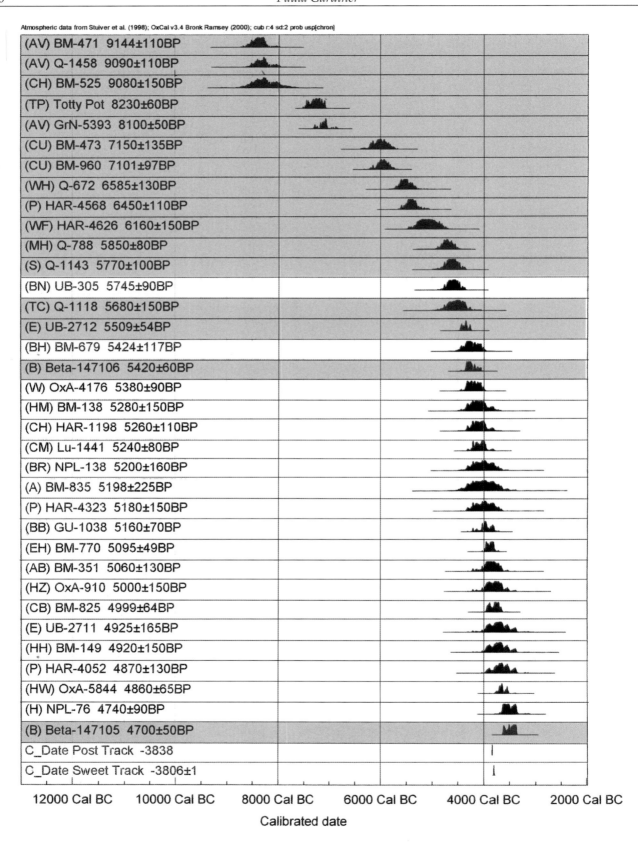

Atmospheric data from Stuiver et al. (1998); OxCal v3.4 Bronk Ramsey (2000); cub r:4 sd:2 prob usp[chron]

(AV) BM-471 9144±110BP	
(AV) Q-1458 9090±110BP	
(CH) BM-525 9080±150BP	
(TP) Totty Pot 8230±60BP	
(AV) GrN-5393 8100±50BP	
(CU) BM-473 7150±135BP	
(CU) BM-960 7101±97BP	
(WH) Q-672 6585±130BP	
(P) HAR-4568 6450±110BP	
(WF) HAR-4626 6160±150BP	
(MH) Q-788 5850±80BP	
(S) Q-1143 5770±100BP	
(BN) UB-305 5745±90BP	
(TC) Q-1118 5680±150BP	
(E) UB-2712 5509±54BP	
(BH) BM-679 5424±117BP	
(B) Beta-147106 5420±60BP	
(W) OxA-4176 5380±90BP	
(HM) BM-138 5280±150BP	
(CH) HAR-1198 5260±110BP	
(CM) Lu-1441 5240±80BP	
(BR) NPL-138 5200±160BP	
(A) BM-835 5198±225BP	
(P) HAR-4323 5180±150BP	
(BB) GU-1038 5160±70BP	
(EH) BM-770 5095±49BP	
(AB) BM-351 5060±130BP	
(HZ) OxA-910 5000±150BP	
(CB) BM-825 4999±64BP	
(E) UB-2711 4925±165BP	
(HH) BM-149 4920±150BP	
(P) HAR-4052 4870±130BP	
(HW) OxA-5844 4860±65BP	
(H) NPL-76 4740±90BP	
(B) Beta-147105 4700±50BP	
C_Date Post Track -3838	
C_Date Sweet Track -3806±1	

12000 Cal BC   10000 Cal BC   8000 Cal BC   6000 Cal BC   4000 Cal BC   2000 Cal BC

Calibrated date

Table 2.6 Representation of calibrated radiocarbon dates for the late Mesolithic (shaded) and the early Neolithic.

Central Europe or whether they died out after a loss of their hunting environment. We do not know from sites like Birdcombe and Hawkcombe Head why the hunter-gatherer lifestyle was abandoned so abruptly and completely. Although it is possible that hunter-gatherers were interfering with their environment and may have been deliberately modifying the landscape at the end of Mesolithic, it is generally accepted that domesticated species were not native to Britain (Bell and Walker, 1992). The 'Availability' model does not fit neatly on to the British evidence and the arrival of the Neolithic, as it does in southern England, suggests that the idea of some form of *diffusion* should not be totally discounted. *Diffusion* and *indigenism* may not necessarily be mutually exclusive in Britain and with our diverse topography and wide-ranging environment the transition to agriculture may have included a combination of the two, but with a regionality and intricacy of its own that is not mirrored in Europe.

Acknowledgements

Michael Costen for including a prehistoric paper in a predominantly Medieval tribute to Mick Aston. English Heritage for their air photograph of Hawkcombe Head; Steve Knight for photographs of the Hawkcombe Head microliths; Christine Harrison for her reconstruction of the clay floor structure at Hawkcombe Head; Josh Pollard for reading and commenting on the text. The views expressed in this paper are entirely my own.

References

Ammerman, A. J. and Cavalli-Sforza, L. L. (1971) Measuring the Rate of Spread of Early Farming in Europe, *Man*, 674–688.

Ammerman, A. J. and Cavalli-Sforza, L. L. (1984) *The Neolithic Transition and the Genetics of Populations in Europe*. Princeton, University Press.

Barrington, N. and Stanton, W. (1970) *The Complete Caves of Mendip*, 112. Weston-super-Mare, Allens (Weston) Ltd.

Berridge, P. (1986) Archaeological Notes. Mesolithic Evidence from Hembury. *Proceedings of the Devon. Archaeological Society* 44, 163–165.

Berridge, P. and Roberts, A. (1986) The Mesolithic Period in Cornwall. *Cornish Archaeology*, No. 25, 7–34.

Bonsall, C. Sutherland, D. tipping R and Cherry, J. (1989) The Eskmeals Project: Late Mesolithic Settlement and Environment in North-West England. In C. Bonsall (ed.) *The Mesolithic in Europe. Papers presented at the Third International Symposium Edinburgh 1985*. Edinburgh, John Donald Publishers Ltd, 175–205.

Bronk Ramsey, C. (1995) Radiocarbon calibration and analysis of stratigraphy: The OxCal program. *Radiocarbon* 37(2), 425–430.

Burleigh, R. and Clutton-Brock, J. (1977) A Radiocarbon Date for *Bos Primigenius* from Charterhouse Warren Farm, Mendip. *Proceedings of the University of Bristol Spelaeological Society* 14(3), 255–257.

Caseldine, C. and Hatton, J. (1993) The Development of High Moorland on Dartmoor: Fire and the Influence of Mesolithic Activity on Vegetational Change. In F. M. Chambers (ed.) *Climatic Change and Human Impact on the Landscape*. London, Chapman and Hall, 119–31.

Childe, V. G. (1936) *Man Makes Himself*. London, Watts.

Clark, J. D. G. (1932) *The Mesolithic Age in Britain*. Cambridge, Cambridge University Press.

Clark, J. D. G. (1934) The Classification of a Microlithic Culture: The Tardenoisian of Horsham, *Archaeological Journal*, Vol. XC, 52–75.

Coles, J. and Coles, B. (1986) *Sweet Track to Glastonbury*. London, Thames and Hudson.

Davies, H. N. (1904) The Discovery of Human Remains under the Stalagmite Floor at Gough's Cavern, Cheddar. *Quarterly. Journal of the Geological. Society of London*, 60 (3), 335–48.

Dennell, R. W. (1985) The Hunter-Gatherer/Agricultural Frontier in Prehistoric Temperate Europe. In S. W. Green and S. M. Perlman, (eds) *The Archaeology of Frontiers and Boundaries*, 113–39. Orlando, Academic Press Inc.

Edwards, K. J. (1993) Models of mid-Holocene forest farming for north-west Europe. In F. M. Chambers (ed.) *Climate Change and Human Impact on the Landscape*, 133–45. London, Chapman and Hall.

Edwards, K. and Hirons, K. (1984) Cereal pollen grains in pre-elm decline deposits: implications for the earliest agriculture in Britain and Ireland. *Journal of Archaeological Science*, 11, 71–80.

Everton, A. and Everton, R. (1972) Hay Wood Cave Burials, Mendip Hills, Somerset, *Proceedings of the University of Bristol Spelaeological Society*, Vol. 13(1), 5–29.

Gardiner, P. (2000) Excavations at Birdcombe, Somerset: Mesolithic Settlement, Subsistence and Landscape Use in the South West of England. In R. Young (ed.) *Mesolithic Lifeways. Current Research from Britain and Ireland*. Leicester Archaeology Monographs No.7, University of Leicester, 199–207.

Gardiner, P. J. (2001) *The Mesolithic-Neolithic Transition in South West England*. Unpublished PhD Thesis, University of Bristol.

Gardiner, P. J. (2007) Mesolithic Activity at Hawkcombe Head, Somerset: Interim Report of the 2002–3 Excavations. In C. Waddington and K. Pedersen (eds.) *Mesolithic Studies in the North Sea Basin and Beyond. Proceedings of a Conference held at Newcastle in 2003*. Oxford, Oxbow. In press.

Green, F. (1996) Mesolithic or later houses at Bowman's Farm, Romsey Extra, Hampshire. In T. Darvill and J. Thomas (eds) *Neolithic Houses in Northwest Europe and Beyond*, 113–122. Oxford, Oxbow Monographs, 57.

Green, G.W. (1992) *British Regional Geology. Bristol and Gloucester region 3rd edition*. London, H.M.S.O.

Green, M. and Allen M. J. (1997) An Early Prehistoric Shaft on Cranborne Chase, *Oxford Journal of Archaeology*, 121–132.

Hillam, J. Groves, C.M. Brown, D. M. Baillie, M. G. L. Coles, J. M. and Coles, B. J. (1990) Dendrochronology of the English Neolithic. *Antiquity*, 64, 210–220.

Jacobi, R. M. (1978) The Mesolithic of Sussex. In P. L. Drewett (ed.) *Archaeology in Sussex to AD1500*. CBA Research Report No. 29, 15–21, London.

Jacobi, R. M. (1982) Ice Age Cave-dwellers, 12,000–4,000BC. In M. A. Aston and I. Burrow (eds), *The Archaeology of Somerset*, 11–13. Taunton, Somerset County Council.

Johnson, N. and David, A. (1982) A Mesolithic Site on Trevose Head and Contemporary Geography, *Cornish Archaeology*, No.21, 67–103.

Liddell, D. M. (1935) Report on the excavations at Hembury Fort, Devon. Fourth and Fifth Seasons, 1934 and 1935. *Proceedings of the Devon Archaeological Exploration Society*, 2, 135–75.

Mellars, P. and Dark, P. (1998) *Star Carr in Context*. Cambridge, McDonald Institute for Archaeological Research, University of Cambridge.

Mercer, R. J. (1980) *Hambledon Hill – a Neolithic Landscape*. Edinburgh.

Mercer, R. J. (1981) Excavations at Carn Brea, Illogan, Cornwall, 1970–73 – a Neolithic fortified complex of the third millennium bc. *Cornish Archaeology*, 20, 1–204.

Milles, A. Williams, D. and Gardner, N. (eds) (1989) *The Beginnings of Agriculture. Symposia of the Association for Environmental Archaeology. No.8*. BAR International Series, 496. Oxford, British Archaeological Reports.

Norman, C. (1982) Mesolithic Hunter-Gatherers 9000–4000BC. In M. A. Aston and I. Burrow, *The Archaeology of Somerset*,15–21. Taunton, Somerset County Council.

Pitts, M. W. and Jacobi, R. M. (1979) Some Aspects of Change in Flakes Stone Industries of the Mesolithic and Neolithic in Southern Britain. *Journal of Archaeological Science*, 6, 163–177.

Riley, H. and Wilson-North, R. (2001) *The Field Archaeology of Exmoor*. London, English Heritage.

Rowley-Conwy, P. (1983) Sedentary hunters: the Ertebølle example. In G. Bailey (ed.) *Hunter-Gatherer Economy in Prehistory*, 111–26. Cambridge, Cambridge University Press.

Rowley-Conwy, P. (1997) 'In sorrow shalt thou eat all thy days'. *British Archaeology*, No.21 February 1997, 7. London, Council for British Archaeology.

Rowley-Conwy, P. (1998) Cemeteries, Seasonality and Complexity in the Ertebølle of Southern Scandinavia. In M. Zvelebil, L. Domanski and R. Dennell (eds) *Harvesting the Sea, Farming the Forest. The Emergence of Neolithic Societies in the Baltic Region*.193–202. Sheffield, Sheffield Academic Press.

Rowley-Conwy, P. (1986) Between Cave Painters and Crop Planters: Aspects of the Temperate European Mesolithic. In Zvelebil, M. (ed.) *Hunters in Transition. Mesolithic Societies of Temperate Eurasia and Their Transition to Farming*, 17–32. Cambridge: Cambridge University Press.

Saville, A. (1990) *Hazleton North, Gloucestershire, 1979–82. The excavation of a Neolithic long cairn of the Cotswold-Severn group*. English Heritage Archaeological Report No. 13. London, HBMCE.

Schulting, R. J. (2000) New AMS dates from the Lambourn Long Barrow and the question of the earliest Neolithic in southern England: repacking the Neolithic package? *Oxford Journal of Archaeology*, Vol. 19 No.1, 25–35.

Schulting, R. J. (2005) '...Pursuing a Rabbit in Burrington Combe': New Research on the Early Mesolithic Burial Cave of Aveline's Hole. *Proceedings of the University of Bristol Spelaeological Society*, 23(3), 171–264.

Schulting, R. J. and Wysocki, M. (2002) The Mesolithic Human Skeletal Collection from Aveline's Hole: A Preliminary Note. *Proceedings of the University of Bristol Spelaeological Society*, 22(3), 255–268.

Simmons, I. G. (1993) Vegetation change during the Mesolithic in the British Isles; some amplifications. In F. M. Chambers (ed.) *Climate Change and Human Impact on the Landscape*. London, Chapman and Hall.

Simmons, I. G. (1996) *The Environmental Impact of Later Mesolithic Cultures. The Creation of Moorland Landscape in England and Wales*. Edinburgh, Edinburgh University Press for the University of Durham.

Simmons, I. G. and Dimbleby, G. W. (1974) The Possible Role of Ivy (*Hedera helix* L.) in the Mesolithic Economy of Western Europe. *Journal of Archaeological Science* 1, 291–296.

Smith, D. I. and Drew, D. P. (1975) *Limestones and Caves of the Mendip Hills*. Newton Abbot, David & Charles, 388.

Smith, G. and Harris, D. (1982) The Excavation of Mesolithic, Neolithic and Bronze Age Settlements at Poldowrian, St. Deverne, 1980. *Cornish Archaeology*, No.21, 23–60.

Smith, I. F. (1965) *Windmill Hill and Avebury*. Oxford, Clarendon Press.

Stringer, C. (1986) The Hominid Remains from Gough's Cave. *Proceedings of the University of Bristol Spelaeological Society*, 17(2), 145–152.

Stuiver, M. and Reimer, P. J. (1993) Extended 14C database and revised CALIB 3.0 14C Age calibration program, *Radiocarbon*, 35 (1), 215–230.

Stuiver, M. Reimer, P. J. Bard, E. Beck, J. W. Burr, G. S. Hughen, K. A. Dromer, B. McCorman, G. van der Plicht, J. and Spurk, M. (1998) INTCAL98 Radiocarbon Age Calibration, 24000–0 cal BP, *Radiocarbon*, 40 (3), 1041–1083.

Sykes, C. M. and Whittle, S. L. (1960) The Birdcombe Mesolithic Site, Wraxall. *Proceedings of the Somerset Archaeological and Natural History Society*, 104, 106–122.

Taylor, H. (1926) Fifth Report on Rowberrow Cavern. *Proceedings of the University of Bristol Spelaeological Society*, 2(3), 190–210.

Thomas, J. S. (1988) Neolithic explanations revisited: the Mesolithic-Neolithic transition in Britain and south Scandinavia. *Proceedings of the Prehistoric Society*, 54, 59–66.

Thomas, J. (1999) *Understanding the Neolithic*. London, Routledge.

Tratman, E. K. (1977) A further radiocarbon date on human bone material from Aveline's Hole, Burrington Combe, Mendip. *Proceedings of the University of Bristol Spelaeological Society*, 14(3), 261–262.

Waddington, C. (2007) Rethinking Mesolithic Settlement and a Case Study from Howick. In C. Waddington and K. Pedersen (eds) *Mesolithic Studies in the North Sea Basin and Beyond. Proceedings of a Conference held at Newcastle in 2003*. Oxford, Oxbow. In press.

Whittle, A. Keith-Lucas, M. Milles, A. Noddle, B. Rees, S. and Romans, J. C. C. (1986) *Scord of Brouster. An Early Agricultural Settlement on Shetland. Excavations 1977–1979*. Oxford, Oxford University Committee for Archaeology Monograph No.9.

Williams, E. (1989) Dating the introduction of food production into Britain and Ireland. *Antiquity*, 63, 510–21.

Woodman, P. (2000) Getting back to basics: transitions to farming in Ireland and Britain. In T. D. Price (ed.) *Europe's First Farmers*, 219–259. Cambridge, Cambridge University Press.

Woodman, P. Anderson, E. and Finlay, N. (1999) *Excavations at Ferriter's Cove, 1983–95: last foragers, first farmers in the Dingle Peninsula*. Bray, Co. Wicklow, Wordwell Ltd.

Wymer, J. J. (1977) *Gazetteer of Mesolithic Sites in England and Wales*. London, Council for British Archaeology, Research Report: 20.

Zvelebil, M. (ed.) (1986) *Hunters in Transition. Mesolithic Societies of Temperate Eurasia and Their Transition to Farming*. Cambridge, Cambridge University Press.

Zvelebil M. (1989) On the Transition to Farming, or What was Spreading with the Neolithic: A Reply to Ammerman, *Antiquity* 63, 379–83.

Zvelebil, M. (1995a) Hunting, Gathering, or Husbandry? Management of Food Resources by the Late Mesolithic Communities of Temperate Europe. *MASCA Research Papers in Science and Archaeology* Vol.12 Supplement (1995), 79–104.

Zvelebil, M. (1995b) Neolithization in Eastern Europe: A View from the Frontier. In *Porocilo o raziskovanju paleolitika, neolitika in eneolitika v. Sloveniji* 22, 107–151.

Zvelebil, M. and Rowley-Conwy, P. (1984) Transition to Farming in Northern Europe: A Hunter-Gatherer Perspective, *Norwegian Archaeological Review*, Vol. 17, No. 2, 104–127.

Zvelebil, M. and Rowley-Conwy, P. (1986) Foragers and farmers in Atlantic Europe. In Zvelebil, M. (ed.) *Hunters in Transition. Mesolithic Societies of Temperate Eurasia and Their Transition to Farming*, 67–94. Cambridge, Cambridge University Press.

Chapter 3

Keeping the Faith: the Physical Expression of Differing Church Customs in Early Medieval Britain

Teresa Hall

Introduction

From the very beginnings of Christianity the church fathers spent a great deal of time defining Christian beliefs. Following the acceptance of Christianity as the state religion of the Roman Empire in 313, these definitions were promulgated through Ecumenical Church Councils. No sooner was one question resolved than another would arise to the extent that each point of orthodox doctrine had at least one attendant heresy. The debates themselves did not generally affect the Christian laity – they took place amongst the educationally elite – usually the bishops. Having been adopted as a state religion, politics became enmeshed with Christianity – Constantine himself was involved in hearing the case of the Donatists, a schismatic group in North Africa (White 2000, 727). Christianity, as with other religions, was a very potent political tool and heresies associated with particular rulers or peoples sometimes engendered splits or schisms with the formation of separate churches.

The major heresies were mostly concerned with the nature of Christ and his position within the Trinity. Arianism denied the true divinity of Christ and was condemned at the Council of Nicaea in 325; Monophysitism proposed that Christ had a single divine nature and was not man; whereas to the Nestorians, Christ had two separate distinct natures (Livingstone 1977, 32–3, 343, 354). Perhaps the heresy which is most relevant to us in the British Isles is Pelagianism, as Pelagius appears to have been of British or Irish origin. (Herren and Brown 2002, 23). This heresy centred on the nature of man, rather than God and it gripped the Mediterranean world for just over a century, from about 400 to 529, when the less fundamental version, semi-Pelagianism, was finally pronounced heretical at the Council of Orange.

Technically, heresy can be one of two types – material heresy or formal heresy. Material heresy is

where a person or group holds the wrong belief in ignorance of the Church's position and this involves neither 'crime nor sin' (Livingstone 1977, 237). In formal heresy, however, the Church's position is known, but the heretic continues to hold the erroneous belief – the punishment for which was excommunication and exile. Schism is defined as 'formal and wilful separation from the unity of the church' but it is not doctrinal in basis (Livingstone 1977, 461).

Martin Carver has pointed out that heresy need not always be reflected in material culture, but that it can be. Excavations in North Africa in the 1930s identified the schismatic Donatist church in Algeria through inscriptions connected with their particular viewpoint (Carver 2003, 5; Frend 1996, 230).

At the other end of the scale, the Catholic Church took every opportunity to reinforce orthodox teaching not only in the written word, but also in architecture and iconography. An example of this was the construction of the Lateran baptistery in Rome by pope Sixtus III (432–440), who included an inscription of six verses detailing the nature of baptism and the necessity of grace to reinforce the Church's position following the Pelagian heresy (McBrien 1997, 72). Sixtus III was also pope when the Nestorian heresy was condemned at Ephesus in 431. At this council it was officially agreed that Christ was God and one of the consequences of this was that Mary was declared to be *theotókos* or Mother of God. Sixtus proclaimed this in his mosaics in the church of St Mary Major in Rome which show Mary surrounded by angels following the conception of Christ (Duffy 1997, 31).

The written word, such as Augustine's works on original sin and grace, disseminated correct doctrines to the literate, whereas pictorial representation, (obviously along with the spoken word) spread these ideas to the laity. They would not be expected to know the nuances of the debates; only to accept in good faith the teachings of the church. Thus, material culture in the form of writings, symbolism and pictorial representation, was used by the church to reinforce orthodox belief.

Heretical Beliefs in the British Isles in the Early Medieval Period

There is little written evidence for this period, but most of it suggests that the major heresies which were problematic across the rest of the Roman Empire did not affect the British Isles. However, Gildas suggests that Arianism had reached these shores – 'the Arian treason, like a savage snake, vomited its foreign poison upon us', and he implies that other heresies followed, – 'and as though there were a set route across the ocean there came every kind of wild beast, brandishing in their horrid mouths the death-dealing venom of every heresy, and planting lethal bites in a country which always longed to hear some novelty' (*DEB*, 12).

One heresy which Gildas does not mention, but which we know about from Bede and others, is Pelagianism. Pelagius was a native of Britain or Ireland who went to Rome in about 400 AD. His natural tendency was to believe that the human race had to put a lot of effort into the business of saving itself. He was deeply shocked when he came across Augustine of Hippo's words which implied that men and women were born in original sin and could only be saved through God's grace. To Pelagius this smacked of predestination and took away from humanity the onus not to sin. Pelagius considered Augustine's opinion on grace to be unorthodox. But Augustine and Jerome joined forces against him and he was condemned by Councils at Milevis and Carthage (Rees 1991, 3, 4). In 418, following the intercession of the Emperor Honorius, Pelagian beliefs were declared heretical and anyone with such opinions was sent into exile. Britain was already cut off from the Roman empire by this date, and it is possible that exiles fled to Britain, thus eliciting the visit of Germanus of Auxerre in 429 to counter the heresy (Charles-Edwards 2000, 203–204). Bede recounts two visits of Germanus concluding that the heretics were banished into the marchlands or no-man's-land at the edge of Britain (*HE* i.21). As Thomas Charles-Edwards has pointed out, this probably just displaced the problem rather than providing a solution, and it may well account for what Michael Herren and Shirley Ann Brown see as distinct Pelagian tendencies in the Insular church up until the renewed contacts between Ireland and Rome in 630 (Charles-Edwards 2000, 204; Herren and Brown 2002).

As well as describing the Pelagian heresy, Bede spent a great deal of time on the Easter controversy. Whilst we would not consider this a heresy in itself, it

arguable that it was being defined as such by Archbishop Theodore. The *Penitential of Theodore* has two sections relevant to this problem. Chapter V of Book One, deals with 'Those Who are Deceived by Heresy', and it classifies as heretics those who celebrate Easter using a calendar which meant that Easter occasionally coincided with the Jewish Passover. Book Nine of the *Penitential* deals particularly with the problem – 'Of the communion of the Irish and Britons who are not Catholic in Respect to Easter and the Tonsure' (McNeill and Gamer 1938, 188–189, 206).

For Bede, the British and the Irish had been advised of their erroneous customs back in the time of Augustine of Canterbury and his successor archbishop Laurence, so those who did not act to resolve the problem were wilfully defying the church. Bede never goes quite as far as referring to the British and Irish who have not mended their ways as heretics, but he repeatedly refers to their customs as unorthodox and contrary to the unity of the Catholic Church and he calls them faithless at one point (*HE* ii.2; ii.4, iv.2; v.18; v.19). As Bede draws his *Ecclesiastical History* to a close, he notes that the Britons still 'oppose …the whole state of the catholic Church by their incorrect Easter and their evil customs' (*HE* v.23). This was no insubstantial controversy – it was something which was current from before Bede was born, throughout the whole of his lifetime and beyond. It was pertinent for at least 150 years in one part of the British Isles or another and by the time of Archbishop Theodore (668–690) had come to be viewed as a heresy.

The acceptance of the Roman way of calculating Easter by the Insular Churches was, in some respects, a watermark of the tide of orthodoxy sweeping across the British Isles. Augustine arrived from Rome using the 19-year Easter calendar in 597. The southern Irish agreed to the new dating system in 629–30 at the Synod of Mag Lene; the Northumbrians conformed in 664; the Picts in 710; the Northern Irish were persuaded by Adomnan at some time around 690; and Iona finally in 716, twelve years after Adomnan's death. The recalcitrant Welsh did not change until 755 at Bangor, and 768 in south Wales, and were apparently still 'in a great tumult' on account of Easter when Archbishop Elvod died in 809 (Haddan and Stubbs 1964, 203–4).

Bede's antipathy towards the Insular churches which did not subscribe to Rome is apparent in other of his works than his *Ecclesiastical History*. Cubitt has shown that Bede takes the anonymous Life of Cuthbert and turns him from 'a figure whose sanctity was rooted in Irish practices to one whose *vita* could be used as a vehicle for Romanizing propaganda. The development of Cuthbert's cult emphasizes the deep rift within the Northumbrian Church caused by the rejection of the Irish Easter reckoning and other ecclesiastical practices' (Cubitt 2000, 30, 46).

Other customs were grouped with the dating of Easter as being in need of reform. Bede tells us that when Augustine met the British bishops, the British were celebrating baptism in an unorthodox manner (*HE* ii.2). Theodore's *Penitential* states that any British or Irish person who doubted their own baptism should be baptized again (McNeill and Gamer 1938, 207). Unfortunately, we cannot be sure where the problem with baptism lay. In all probability it was linked with Augustine's ideas on grace and original sin which were being formulated at about the time Britain ceased to be a part of the Roman empire. In Ireland, Augustine's ideas receive no mention before the renewed links with Rome in the 630s. After this the works of the Pseudo-Augustine appear in 655 – writings which disseminate Augustine's ideas, under his name (Herren and Brown 2002, 91–94).

The question of tonsure is not mentioned by Augustine of Canterbury as being a problem. By the Synod of Whitby, however, it had become an issue, and when Aldhelm wrote to King Geraint of Dumnonia, he linked the tonsure of the unreformed Irish and British with that of Simon Magus, 'the founder of the magical art' who tried to purchase spiritual powers with money (hence the term Simony) (Lapidge and Herren 1979, 157).

The other grievance of archbishop Laurence (Augustine's successor), was that some of the British and Irish had customs which precluded them eating with anyone who did not follow the strict customs they themselves followed. When Laurence wrote to the Irish bishops, he exhorted them to reform, commenting that, 'on becoming acquainted with the Britons, we still thought that the Irish would be better. But now we have learned from Bishop Dagan when he came to this island and from Abbot Columban [Columbanus] when he came to Gaul that the Irish did not differ from the Britons in their way of life. For when Bishop Dagan came to us he refused to take food, not only with us but even in the very house where we took our meals'. It is interesting that Laurence accused Columbanus of this type of behaviour, and the Irish in general of Pelagianism (*HE* ii.4; ii.19).

About 50 years later, Aldhelm complained to King Geraint that the Welsh bishops of Dyfed also behaved in this manner: they would not take communion or celebrate divine office with the English, or even eat at the same table as them; and should any English priest or monk go to them, they (the English) had to spend 40 days in penance before they could be admitted to the company of the Welsh clergy (Lapidge and Herren 1979, 140–143,155–160). What this does suggest is that the monasticism practised by some of the British and Irish had elements which were not considered acceptable to those in the main body of the Church.

The writings of Aldhelm, bishop of Sherborne, also imply that the Insular churches of Wales and South West England were considered heretical. When Aldhelm writes to King Geraint of Dumnonia, he accuses the British bishops and those of Dyfed of pride, superficial piety and secrecy. Aldhelm pleads that the bishops of Dumnonia should 'no longer detest with swollen pride of heart and scornful breast the doctrine and decrees of blessed Peter'. With respect to false piety he says of the bishops of Dyfed that they are, 'glorifying in the private purity of their own way of life' and he accuses them of concealing themselves behind clever interpretation of the Scriptures (Lapidge and Herren 1979, 158, 159, 160). Malcolm Lambert, in his work on medieval heresy, identifies pride, superficial piety and secrecy as the three main characteristics associated with heretics – pride, for setting themselves up against the teachings of the Church; the superficial appearance of piety; and secrecy, which is contrasted to the openness of Catholic preaching (Lambert 1992, 4).

John Cassian, Semi-Pelagianism and transformational monasticism

Was monasticism radically different in the Insular churches? One of the most noted contrasts by the seventh century was the emphasis on asceticism in the Insular church. Asceticism was an important element of the church in Gaul in the 5th century (for example Martin of Tours) but by the early 6th century the Gallic bishops were limiting the foundation of new monasteries and attempting to keep them near towns so that they could be adequately supervised. Monasticism was becoming institutionalized (Dunn 2003, 96, 98).

Ascetic monasticism, which was seen as a method by which the individual could attune his soul to God, was not confined to Christianity as a religion. All sorts of other religions in the Middle East practised self-transformation as a path to God. Because of this borrowing, heretical ideas tended to be absorbed with the method, and from its outset in Christianity, monasticism was constantly modified and refined to avoid heretical beliefs. The ideas of Antony, the father of desert monasticism, were based upon those of Origen who was later condemned at the Council of Alexandria in 400. Antony believed that by going out into the desert he was purifying his soul so that he could be united with God. Athanasius, bishop of Alexandria, Antony's biographer, used his *Life of Antony*, to promote an ideal eremetical life removed from towns and cities where he believed ascetics were dangerous because they produced heresies such as Arianism. Athanasius' manipulation of Antony's *Life* was, to quote Marilyn Dunn 'an attempt to ensure the continuance of an episcopally-directed asceticism within an orthodox church'. It was this text which was mainly responsible for the promotion of monasticism in the west (Dunn 2003, 2–10, quote at 10).

The most prolonged influences on western monasticism, however, were Augustine of Hippo and Jerome as their ideas were ultimately promoted by the church. Their understanding of monasticism differed from those who were seeking self-transformation through asceticism. For Augustine, monasticism was all about invoking the power of the grace of God and monks could not do this by themselves. His doctrine invalidated the idea of an individual person transforming themselves by their actions and placed emphasis instead, on living in a community under a rule, in obedience to a superior (Dunn 2003, 67).

All was not immediately lost for transformational monasticism, however. John Cassian, founded two monasteries in Marseilles before 420, where he became part of an influential monastic network. He attempted to steer a line between Pelagius on the one hand and Augustine on the other as he believed that the views of both were too extreme on grace and free will (Rees 1991, 6). One of his works on monasticism, the *Conferences*, is dedicated to Honoratus (amongst others), the founder of the island monastery of Lérins off the Mediterranean coast of France (Dunn 2003, 74). Knight points out that the Lérins school should more correctly be termed anti-Pelagian but Cassian's teachings were, nonetheless, declared semi-Pelagian and thus heretical at the council of Orange in 529 (Knight 1981, 56; Livingstone 1977, 190, 369; Rees 1991, 6). The period between Cassian's death in 435 and the Council of Orange in 529 was sufficiently long, however, for his works to become widely disseminated in the west and they were a particular favourite of the Irish church, and of Columba himself (Herren and Brown 2002, 117; Dunn 2003, 81; Rees 1991, 7). Cassian had lived in Palestine and Egypt among the monks and his works include many references to this period. For Cassian the eremetical life was superior to the coenobitic but it had to be preceded by a period of training in a *coenobium*. This aspect (which might take years and could not be achieved by everybody) enabled the monk to move out to become a hermit as part of a group of hermits still attached to the monastery (Frank 1997, 427–432). Cassian believed that a true hermit associated with others and was subject to the tradition of the elders (Chadwick 1950, 49). The connection with Cassian and his teachings may well be one of the

reasons for the accusation of Pelagianism levelled at the Irish and British Churches.

In about 590, there arrived on the continent, the Irish monk Columbanus, deeply influenced by Cassian and the idea of self-transformation (Stevenson 1997, 216; Herren and Brown 2002, 24). Columbanus's monasticism was severe, but he was a great believer in community. Within a very short time of his death, Columbanus's monasteries at Luxeuil and Bobbio had abandoned the rule of their Irish founder and had become centres of Benedictinism. One explanation for this, is that it may have been as the result of changes brought about at the Synod of Mâcon in 626/7 because the Burgundian bishops were hostile to Columbanus and the Irish aspects of his monasticism (Charles-Edwards 2000, 364–5, 385).

The great monastery at Lérins also reformed at about this time. Its monks had lived under a rule (Cooper-Marsdin, 1913, 47) based on Cassian's ideas until about 600, when one of their abbots had introduced Columbanus's rule. In 660, shortly before Benedict Biscop became a monk there (Lapidge 2001, 60) the community introduced the Rule of St Benedict (Cooper-Marsdin, 1913, 47–8). The continent was not alone in preferring the communal Rule of St Benedict at this time. Back in Northumbria, Wilfrid's biographer, Stephanus, wrote that Wilfrid introduced the Rule of St Benedict in order to reform Irish monasticism in the last quarter of the seventh century (LOW 47).

There was generally across Europe in the seventh century a move away from self-transforming monasticism. It became far less common for monks to leave the main community to struggle by themselves in the 'desert'. Enclosed communities came to be seen as the norm, where the emphasis was on charity and co-operation within the community itself. Perfection of the soul was to take place through charitable interaction with others, not through isolation and personal deprivation.

Possible effects on material culture

Having established that the differences in practice between the Insular church and the rest of western Christendom as described by Bede and others were a real problem, we have to ask the question, are they apparent in the archaeology as well as in the literature? This may seem to be a difficult, even potentially fruitless question, as we have such problems identifying even obvious elements of Christianity such as monasticism in the early medieval period, without having to differentiate between differing aspects of belief. However, the possibility of finding such evidence should not be dismissed and we should be aware of how the different factions within the church might manifest themselves in the archaeological record.

It is well to state at the outset that because of the piecemeal nature of the acceptance of Rome as the ultimate authority on questions of orthodoxy, evidence may well differ in each of the kingdoms or subdivisions of the British Isles. The problem was current in different places at different times and the severity with which it was treated depended to a certain extent on its political context.

There are two different facets to the problem. Firstly, evidence may exist which indicates the differing beliefs of the two factions; and secondly, there could be material differences which may be construed as propaganda – i.e. those which indicate that the orthodox Church sought to emphasize correct belief symbolically in its material culture.

Within the first group of indicators, the two main areas in which we might expect to find differences are in baptismal provision, and in monasticism itself. As already noted, we do not know where the problem with baptism lay, but it may have been associated with pre-Augustinian ideas on grace and original sin. Pelagius believed that infants who died without baptism would not be deprived of heaven (Evans 1968, 76). A hint of this difference may be found in the laws of King Ine of Wessex which state that all infants must be baptised within 30 days (Attenborough 2000, 37). Its position at the head of Ine's laws may indicate that it was a measure designed to overcome a semi-Pelagian (or pre-Augustinian) British attitude to baptism.

A change to include infant baptism would engender certain changes in material culture. If children were baptised in infancy, within a generation or two, the whole population would be Christian. Large fonts into which adults could step would no longer be required. Infant baptism also raises the question of distribution of baptismal places. Converts were generally baptized at Easter and Pentecost, quite often at the cathedral by the bishop, (or even in streams and pools before churches were built). Because Ine's law puts the onus on the parents to seek baptism within 30 days, they would have had to take the baby to a baptismal place reasonably close at hand. In Wessex at this time, this would have entailed a visit to the local minster church which was located within a distance of 5–8 kilometres (Hase 1975, 2; Hall 2000, 79). We should, therefore, expect by the 8th century, the minsters to have administered baptism and to have the artefactual evidence associated with it.

It seems quite possible that the differences apparent in monasticism would reveal themselves in the arch-aeological record. The problem of tonsure can be passed over quickly in this section as it is not something which would be apparent in the archaeological record (unless there were some very inept barbers amongst the monks who managed to slice through to the bone!). As noted already, the Irish and British churches retained a strong element of asceticism in their monasticism which is apparent in the sixth and seventh centuries in Scotland, Northumbria and on the continent as well as in Ireland itself, as at Skellig Michael. Indeed it is partly this element which made Insular monasticism so charismatic and popular with the laity as it moved out from Ireland across Europe.

A different layout of the monastic landscape might be implied in those monasteries following the ascetic ideal. One of the most copied models of ascetic monasticism was Lérins in the south of France. Arranged as a central monastery with outlying hermitages, Aston has suggested that this form was copied in Ireland and Britain, citing as examples; Kilmalkedar in Galway; St David's in Pembroke; Beckery a hermitage of Glastonbury in Somerset amongst other places (1993, 25; 2003, 36). Following a rigorous training, monks would eventually move out from the central monastery to live singly or in small groups in inhospitable places which equated with the desert. Dark draws attention to the growth in large monasteries and the decline of small religious foci in Wales in the eighth century and suggests that this is as a result of the renewed contacts with Rome, presumably following the acceptance of the Roman system of calculating Easter (1994, 222–223). This may represent the decline of the Lérins-type monastic establishment with hermitages.

Within the English church monasticism seems to have taken a different form. There is very little evidence that Augustine or Theodore included any eremitic element within their monasticism and the canons instituted by Theodore repeatedly urge monks not to wander about but to remain within their monasteries (Cubitt 1995, 9). Like their episcopal colleagues on the continent, Theodore and Hadrian were anxious to supervise monasticism to ensure orthodoxy of belief. This would produce a monastery consisting of a single enclosed unit, from which priests might go out into the landscape to minister to the laity, but they would return to the monastery.

As well as the layout of the landscape the differences could be reflected in types of artefacts made on site. Herren and Brown have suggested that from the 5th century until contact with Rome in the 630s there are no contemporary religious artefacts produced in Ireland or Britain (other than simple inscribed stones). This, they suggest, is a conscious decision following the Pelagian and semi-Pelagian ideas against making representations of God, a rule reinforced in the works of Cassian (Herren and Brown 2002, 187, 190).

In the second category, we might expect to find evidence which supports the theology of the Roman church following the acceptance of the ideals of Augustine. Under this category belongs the use by the English Church of all things associated with Rome and the Roman Empire. When Augustine of Canterbury arrived from the continent his remit was to establish two archbishoprics one in London and one in York. Because of the political circumstances he had to make do with establishing his base in the Roman walled town of Canterbury. Eric Cambridge has suggested that the layout of the early churches in Canterbury replicates what was present in Rome at the time (1999, 211). Indeed many of the early churches established in Kent and beyond, under Augustine's influence were placed within Roman shore forts and associated with Roman remains (Blair 1992, 235–246). Stocker has drawn attention to the reuse of Roman stone in the churches of Anglo-Saxon England and points to its iconic nature in some instances (1990, 93–8). Eaton picks up on this point but assigns the motive to the 'imperial 'ambitions'' of the patrons, suggesting that the Church was creating a position of authority by reminding the English 'that *it* was the natural successor to the Roman empire' (2000, 134). However, what is surely being emphasized is the orthodoxy of the church of Rome.

Later in the seventh century, Wilfrid, the main proponent of the Roman faction in Northumbria, was responsible for a distinctly Roman style of church architecture in his principle churches of Hexham and Ripon where the surviving crypts replicate the burial chambers or catacombs of Rome (Crook 2000, 91–93). Wilfrid also reintroduced the use of square Roman capital-letters for inscriptions, a style emulated in the foundation inscription at Jarrow (Charles-Edwards 2000, 324). We know from Bede that building in stone was considered to be part of the package of allegiance to Rome. In 710, Nechtan, king of the Picts, sent to Monkwearmouth and Jarrow to ask for instruction in keeping Easter at the right time. He also requested help to build a stone church in the Roman style (*HE* v.21). Here we have an instance of the building style being linked with the practice of celebrating Easter in the orthodox way. The 'stone church' was for Nechtan, as it had been for Wilfrid, the visible confirmation of the change in religious practice. Nechtan was convinced that the way forward lay with Rome and to this end he expelled the monks of Columban persuasion from southern Pictland (this act may well have been a major deciding factor in persuading the

monks of Iona to change to the Roman system – they held out until their conversion by Ecgberht in 716) (Charles-Edwards 2000, 410). This change in practise also heralds the move from Class I to Class II Pictish stone monuments. The Class II stones include Christian themes – another hint that the Irish Church had been opposed to the use of images (beyond the use of simple linear crosses) whereas the Catholic Church was not (Herren and Brown 2002, 188–9).

What we know of the Saxon conquest of Wessex suggests that the West Saxons originally supported what Christianity they found in the region at places such as Glastonbury and Sherborne. It is probable that Aldhelm's own monastery of Malmesbury was an Irish foundation as there are references in his letters to him having been taught by Irish monks.

However, following his prolonged re-education with Abbot Hadrian and Theodore in Canterbury, Aldhelm's writings take on all the fanaticism of the newly converted. In letters to Wihtfirth and Heahfrith he castigates people for going to Ireland to study when they could go to Canterbury. He equates Irish monasteries with 'briny muddy waters in which a dark throng of toads swarms in abundance and where croaks the strident chatter of frogs', as opposed to the 'clear waters flowing from [the] glassy pools' of Canterbury (Lapidge and Herren 1979, 154–5, 160–4).

It is against this background that the system of minster churches was established in western Wessex (Hall 2000). The rectilinear layout around many of the minsters can be interpreted as an aspect of this *Romanitas*. It is linked with a change from building monasteries and hermitages in isolated places, which could equate with the 'desert', to building minster churches in flat accessible locations. Some British sites can be shown to have become dependent chapelries of the newly founded minsters. In Devon, the British monastery of Landkey (or Lantocai) became a dependent chapel of the bishop's church at Bishop's Tawton. In Dorset, the British site of Lanprobus, on the island in the swamp at Castleton, became a dependent chapel of the nearby bishopric of Sherborne; in Somerset, there was a move from the islands and marshes of the levels to the abbey site at Glastonbury; and at Congresbury, from the hillfort to the present site of the church beside the river (Hall 2003; 2005; forthcoming).

Further afield, an example of the change of plan can be seen at Whithorn in Galloway where Peter Hill's excavation showed a change from curving boundaries to rectilinear layout at a date following the Northumbrian conquest of the area and the installation of Pecthelm, a former pupil of Aldhelm, as bishop (Hill 1997, 36, 44).

Within different parts of the British Isles, evidence

for the Insular Churches and the English Church may well reflect the divergent practices which initially beset them. In Wessex, because the British Church came to be seen as unorthodox, it was reformed. Through the period when the controversy with the British church raged, the sites of the non-conformists were demoted and made dependent on newly founded minster churches. We should not, therefore, expect to find circular or oval sites within the areas of purely 'Roman' influence such as Kent. Bampton, in Oxfordshire, has been described as being curvilinear, but perhaps should be classified as rectilinear – it does not have the classic oval shape associated with the Insular churches but is more rectangular with rounded corners (a shape which would naturally occur if the boundary was a ditch). It is conceivable that there may have been some Irish influence in the area of chalkland stretching from the Marlborough Downs across into Berkshire. Malmesbury was reputedly founded by an Irishman, Maeldubh; Katherine Barker has suggested that Lambourn has a curvilinear form (Barker 1982, 97); and the church at Blewbury sits within a curvilinear boundary (and has a large 'cowbell' in the church which looks remarkably like the bells associated with Irish saints). Areas of the country which had British or Irish influence but were reformed, such as western Wessex, are more likely to have British curvilinear sites surviving as lesser churches.

Conclusions

Within this debate it has to be borne in mind that the real issue is not whether the Irish and British were heretical – the fact that they were perceived as such (if only temporarily) is the important point. However much we may disagree with the reasoning behind the accusation, to deny its existence is to hinder our understanding of the Insular churches of the British Isles. As Herren and Brown point out, people generally do not knowingly set out to be heretical. When their error is pointed out most mend their ways and conform (Herren and Brown 2002, 12). The Irish would have been shocked to have been told that they were out of step with the continent. It was not something easily accepted and they immediately sent a contingent to Rome in 631 to check the details for themselves (Walsh and O Croinin 1988, 6–7). As Cummian then writes to Abbot Segene of Iona, 'you ought to consider which are the dissenters of which I spoke, whether they are the Hebrews, Greeks, Latins and Egyptians who are united in their observance ....or an insignificant group of Britons and Irish who are almost at the end of the earth, and, if I may say so, but pimples on the face of the earth' (Walsh and O Croinin 1988, 72–75).

Bede's obsession with the Easter question was not unfounded prejudice and it is unfair to accuse him of exaggerating the problems. The Roman faction, and the Irish and British, were all passionate about their beliefs, and equally convinced that they were orthodox. As Thomas Charles Edwards (2000, 415) has reminded us, these were men who were practised in the art of exegesis (the detailed analyses of scripture), accustomed to reading symbolic meanings into even the smallest details of scripture. Bede states his point of view time and again because he feared for the souls of those whose belief he saw as being wilfully unorthodox. To quote Lambert, 'Heresy was not thought to be the product of the individual speculative intelligence....heresy was the work of the devil' (1992, 4). Following the arrival of Theodore as archbishop in 668 (before Bede was born), those who had not reformed were considered heretics, 'Those who have been ordained by Irish or British bishops who are not Catholic with respect to Easter and the tonsure are not united to the Church...Further, we have not the liberty to give them, when they request it, the chrism or the eucharist, unless they have previously confessed their willingness to be with us in the unity of the Church'. (McNeill and Gamer 1938, quote at p.206; Charles-Edwards 2000, 410).

The pivotal point of Bede's *Ecclesiastical History* is the Synod of Whitby which occurred in 664, a decade before Bede was born. However, the problems which were addressed at Whitby were still ongoing throughout Bede's lifetime and as archaeologists we should be aware that they may well be reflected in the archaeology of the early medieval church.

Abbreviations

DEB – *De Exicidio Britonum*, see Winterbottom
HE – Bede, Colgrave and Mynors
LOW – Life of Wilfrid, see Colgrave

References

Aston, M. (1993) *Monasteries*, London, Batsford.
Aston, M. (2003) Early monasteries in Somerset – models and agendas. In M. Ecclestone, K. Gardner, N. Holbrook and A. Smith (eds), *The Land of the Dobunni*, 36–48. Oxford, Parchment.
Attenborough, F. L. (2000) *The Laws of the Earliest English Kings*. Felinfach, Llanerch.
Barker, K. (1982) The early history of Sherborne. In S. M. Pearce, *The Early Church in Western Britain and Ireland: Studies presented to C. A. Ralegh Radford*, 77–116. BAR British Series 102. Oxford, British Archaeological Reports.
Blair, J. (1992) Anglo-Saxon minsters: a topographical review. In J. Blair and R. Sharpe (eds), *Pastoral Care Before the Parish*, 212–266. London, Leicester University Press.
Cambridge, E. (1999) The architecture of the Augustinian mission.

In R. Gameson, *St Augustine and the Conversion of England*, 202–236. Stroud, Sutton.

Carver, M. (2003) Introduction: Northern Europeans negotiate their future. In M. Carver (ed.) *The Cross Goes North: Processes of Conversion in Northern Europe, AD 300–1300*, 3–13. Bury St Edmunds, York Medieval Press.

Chadwick, O. (1950) *John Cassian: A Study in Primitive Monasticism*. Cambridge, Cambridge University Press.

Charles-Edwards, T. M. (2000) *Early Christian Ireland*. Cambridge, Cambridge University Press.

Colgrave, B. (ed. and trans.) (1985) *The Life of Bishop Wilfrid by Eddius Stephanus*. Cambridge, Cambridge University Press.

Colgrave, B. and Mynors, R. A. B. (eds) (1969) *Bede's Ecclesiastical History of the English People*. Oxford, Clarendon Press.

Cooper-Marsdin, A. C. (1913) *The History of the Islands of the Lérins: The Monastery, Saints and Theologians of S Honorat*. Cambridge, Cambridge University Press.

Crook, J. (2000) *The Architectural Setting of the Cult of Saints in the Early Christian West c.300–1200*. Oxford, Clarendon Press.

Cubitt, C. (1995) *Anglo-Saxon Church Councils c.650–850*. London, Leicester University Press.

Cubitt, C. (2000) Memory and narrative in the cult of early Anglo-Saxon saints. In Y. Hen and M. Innes, *The Uses of the Past in the Early Middle Ages*, 29–66. Cambridge, Cambridge University Press.

Dark, K. (1994) *Civitas to Kingdom: British Political Continuity 300–800*. London, Leicester University Press.

Duffy, E. (1997). *Saints and Sinners: A History of the Popes*. Yale, University Press.

Dunn, M. (2003) *The Emergence of Monasticism: From the Desert Fathers to the Early Middle Ages*. Oxford, Blackwell.

Eaton, T. (2000) *Plundering the Past: Roman Stonework in Medieval Building*. Stroud, Tempus.

Etchingham, C. (1999) *Church Organisation in Ireland AD 650 to 1000*. Naas, Co Kildare, Laigin Publications.

Evans, R. F. (1968) *Pelagius: Inquiries and Reappraisals*. London, A and C Black.

Frank, K. S. (1997) John Cassian on John Cassian. In *Studia Patristica* 33, 418–433.

Frend, H. C. (1996) *The Archaeology of Early Christianity*. London, Chapman.

Haddan, A. W. and Stubbs, W. (1964), *Councils and Ecclesiastical Documents Relating to Great Britain and Ireland*, volume 1. Oxford, University Press.

Hall, T. (2000) *Minster Churches in the Dorset Landscape*. British Archaeological Report, British Series 304. Oxford, Archaeopress.

Hall, T. (2003) The reformation of the British Church in the west country in the 7th century. In M. Ecclestone, K. Gardner, N. Holbrook, A. Smith (eds.) *The Land of the Dobunni*, 49–55. Oxford, Parchment.

Hall, T. (2005) Sherborne: Saxon Christianity *be Westanwuda*. In K. Barker, D. Hinton and A. Hunt (eds) *Saint Wulfsige and Sherborne*, 133–148. Oxford, Oxbow Books.

Hall, T. (forthcoming) Identifying British Christian Sites in Western Wessex. In N. Edwards (ed) *The Archaeology of the Early Medieval Celtic Churches*.

Hase, P. (1975) The development of the parish in Hampshire, particularly in the eleventh and twelfth centuries. Unpublished PhD thesis. University of Cambridge.

Herren, M. W. and Brown, S. A. (2002) *Christ in Celtic Christianity: Britain and Ireland from the Fifth to the Tenth Century*. Woodbridge, Boydell.

Hill P. (1997) *Whithorn and St Ninian: The Excavations of a Monastic Town 1984–91*. Stroud, Sutton.

Knight, J. (1981) *In Tempore Iustinti Consulis*: contacts between the British and Gaulish churches before Augustine. In A. Detsicas, *Collectanea Historica: Essays in Memory of Stuart Rigold*, 54–62. Maidstone, Kent Archaeological Society.

Lambert, M. (1992) *Medieval Heresy: Popular Movements from the Gregorian Reform to the Reformation*. Oxford, Blackwell.

Lapidge M. and Herren M. (1979) *Aldhelm: The Prose Works*. Ipswich, Brewer.

Lapidge, M. (2001) Benedict Biscop. In Lapidge *et al.*, (2001), 60.

Lapidge, M. Blair, J. Keynes, S. and Scragg, D. (eds) (2001) *The Blackwell Encyclopaedia of Anglo-Saxon England*. Blackwell, Oxford.

Livingstone, E. (1977) *The Concise Oxford Dictionary of the Christian Church*. Oxford, Oxford University Press

McBrien, R. P. (1997) *Lives of the Popes: the Pontiffs from St Peter to John Paul II*. San Francisco, Harper.

McNeill, J. T. and Gamer, H. M. (1938) *Medieval Handbooks of Penance: A translation of the principal libri poenitentiales and selections from related documents*. New York, Columbia University Press.

Rees, B. R. (1991) *The Letters of Pelagius and His Followers*. Woodbridge, Boydell.

Stevenson, J. B. (1997) The monastic rules of Columbanus. In M. Lapidge (ed.) *Columbanus: Studies on the Latin Writings*, 203–216. Woodbridge, Boydell.

Stocker, D. (1990) Rubbish recycled: a study of the re-use of stone in Lincolnshire. In D. Parsons, (ed.) *Stone: Quarrying and Building in England AD 43–1525*, 83–101. Chichester, Phillimore.

Walsh, M., and O Croinin, D. (eds) (1988) *Cummian's Letter* De Controversia Paschali *and the* De Ratione Conputandi. Toronto, Pontifical Institute of Medieval Studies.

White, L. M. (2000) Architecture: the first five centuries. In P. F. Esler (ed.) *The Early Christian World*, Volume 2, 693–746. London, Routledge.

Winterbottom, M. (ed. and trans.) (1978) *Gildas: The Ruin of Britain and other works*. London and Chichester, Phillimore.

Chapter 4

Anonymous Thegns in the Landscape of Wessex 900–1066

Michael Costen

Introduction

The thegns of late Anglo-Saxon England have been studied by many scholars over the years. The focus of the earlier part of the period, the tenth century particularly, has been upon the thegns as warriors and their place in the late Anglo-Saxon military world has been much debated. The long tradition of warrior households, depicted in Beowulf projects a very powerful image and long after the Norman Conquest, into the twelfth century, great men especially kings and princes had their military household of landless knights grouped around them. Conquering and alien kings, such as Cnut and later William and his sons certainly needed such a household. Although these households could be very large the number of thegns within them was small compared with the numbers who lived on the land, and in the late Anglo-Saxon world the thegns were certainly rooted in the land-scape, whatever service they performed for the king. Wulfstan, (Archbishop of York 1002–23), in the *Geþyncðo* assumed that in his ideal world the thegn had an estate of five hides – indeed that was how you judged his status as a thegn (Whitelock 1979, 431–5).

> And if a ceorl prospered so that he had fully five hides of his own land (agenes landes), church and kitchen, bell house and burh-geat, seat and special office in the king's hall, then he was thenceforward entitled to the rank of thegn.

In the minds of some contemporaries at least he was therefore primarily defined as a landed proprietor, a man with bookland and a direct relationship to the king. The Archbishop was probably describing a real group of people at the beginning of the eleventh century and there are plenty of men in the Domesday Book who also fit his description. John Blair has commented that; 'We are witnessing the creation of the English country gentry: a new class of small resident proprietors for whom manorial fragmentation provided an economic base' (Blair 1994, 133). They are, he thinks, and I agree, a part of the growth of the manorial regime of the high middle-ages, along with nucleated villages and open-fields.

However, the trajectory this group followed may not be as smooth as implied above. Katherin Mack has argued forcefully for a catastrophic upheaval among the aristocracy as a result first of the many years of war in Æthelræd's reign and then during the earlier years of Cnut. She suggests that there is evidence of the break-up of aristocratic estates and the re-appearance of some of this land in the hands smaller proprietors by 1066 (Mack 1984, 375–87). The implica-tion of her argument is that the families of the richer thegns were impoverished by deaths and their legal rights attacked during a period of political and social instability. This is an entirely plausible scenario, given the uneasy nature of Cnut's rule and the ruthlessness with which he asserted his authority, both against Danes and English in order to hold onto his new kingdom. However, it is difficult to see how the lesser men would have benefited from such a situation. Although probably much less affected by the political upheavals, it is hard to see where they would have found the money necessary to purchase estates from their betters, especially given the weight of taxation in Cnut's reign. And even at a time when the greater thegns found their influence diminished, it is hard to see how anything but money would have got their inferiors the bookland they undoubtedly held by 1066.

Other modern writers have been concerned to discuss the thegn as part of a group of what was essentially a 'gentry' but which was also to become, by the twelfth century, to quote Professor John Gillingham, the class of the *'strenuus miles'*, the active knight, who possessed the basic knight's equipment and weaponry and knew how to use it (Gillingham 1995, 129–153, 129). The same writer has also seen the thegn, as part of the machinery of the late Anglo-Saxon state and of the mechanism which governed the countryside through its hundred and shire courts. Professor James Campbell has also suggested that much of the explanation of what an eleventh century thegn was, lies in his relationship to the king and the likelihood that he usually had some obligation of office, delivering the king's writs, being an usher in his hall – jobs which in the post-Conquest world were fulfilled by sergeants (Campbell 1987, 201–218). For all these writers and for others before them, although they are willing to entertain the notion of 'thegns' who hardly fit these criteria, it is upon the thegn with five hides that they concentrate. However the reality is that such men, important as they were at local level, were probably outnumbered by others who were much less well-off.

Domesday Book demonstrates that many of the men described as thegns had much less than five hides of land and they are hardly likely to have been the possessors of a church and a bell tower. In practice, as Ann Williams has remarked, the distinction between a thegn and the ceorl, who was also a free man and might well fight alongside his more aristocratic neighbours, is not easily drawn (Williams 1992, 221–240). Was it the case that any man who regularly went off to serve in the army as part of his tenure was described as a thegn by his neighbours? Was he sometimes really just a ceorl with a mail coat, a shield and a sword? Was he called a thegn because he fought, rather than because he owned bookland, as a thegn ought? How little bookland might you own to still be regarded as a gentleman and a cut above your neighbours? Jean Scammell has pointed out that the *miles* of the tenth century could easily be an unfree man and that his arms and equipment could come from his lord, rather than from his own resources. She cites a number of examples of the low status of the knight in Gaul in the eleventh century, though we should not be too ready to transpose conditions in a rather different polity to Anglo-Saxon England (Scammell 1993, 591–636). It may be that the distinction was between those who held some bookland, however small, or held on a lease for lives and were thus thought of as 'gentlemen' and the ceorl, who held by a servile tenure. Clearly the thegns of the monasteries did not own their lands, but they were still described as thegns. Professor Christopher Dyer, writing about the Bishop of Worcester's estates has pointed to the extensive services provided by the retainers the bishop had planted on his lands, services concerned with escort duties, hunting services and administration, though it is hard to imagine that they were not also expected to fight for the bishop when called upon (Dyer 1980, 43). Such services were not menial, but part of the activity which brought such men into contact with the great and the important in late Anglo-Saxon society and sometimes the entrée to greater things (Gillingham 1995, 129–153).

So it is with the Domesday Book that this paper commences in its attempt to place these lesser thegns in the landscape of Wessex. If we can see how numerous they were, how well-off they may have been and identify some of their lands perhaps we might gain some insight into what place they and their estates had in the social structure and the landscape of the tenth and eleventh centuries.

Estates and Landowners in the South-West

Although there were many manors in Somerset which were of five, six or seven hides in extent those were not typical holdings. Only 76 estates in Somerset were of ten hides or greater but those 76 estates accounted for nearly 45% of the assessed hides in the shire. If we add in the King's unassessed lands, the bulk of which were in very large estates, the large holdings of 10 hides or more must have accounted for well over 50% of the land in the shire. This is important, because although the king and the church held relatively few estates, since those estates were large, they contained

Fig. 4.1 The study area.

a great deal of land. It is very difficult to make a consistent estimate of the holdings of King Harold as they were when he first became King. The core estates of the royal family, being ancient demesne were not hidated. However we do know their sizes in ploughlands. If we assess the King's estates at 68.77% of the ploughlands to obtain the hidage, the 417 ploughlands unassessed comes to 287 hides. This figure is achieved by taking a random sample of 97 estates from the Domesday Book for Somerset (Thorn and Thorn 1980). The ratio of hides to ploughlands of these 97 estates gives the ratio applied to the king's estates. To this must be added all the lands held by Edward's Queen and by Harold's relations as well as Harold himself. The grand total is about *657* hides. That represents over 22% of the total known hidage of the shire (Darby 1986, 336). Adjusting for the king's added hides the crown's holding still comes to 18% of the hidage. In addition the holdings of the church in Somerset in 1066 amounted to 25% of the hidage. Thus the king and the church together, held about 43% of all the land in the shire and what is more held it in large estates, for it was to this group of privileged landholders that the large estates predominantly belonged. The other secular landholders shared the remaining 57% of the shire's hidage between the remaining 857 separate estates which are enumerated. Darby (1986, 336) gives a total of 622 settlements, but I am here concerned with owners and their estates. Many of the named estates in Domesday Book have sub-units which were described separately. This gives the 857 estates. The average size of individual estates, outside the privileged group, was therefore very small and this was a strong characteristic of secular holdings in 1066. No less than 297 estates were of one hide or less. There was therefore a major divide in the shire between the court and the church with their extensive estates in large holdings on the one hand and the rest of the population of landowners on the other.

In Wiltshire the king and the church were again the dominant landowners. Of the 4032 hides in Wiltshire in 1086, 51 estates of twenty hides and over accounted for 1806 hides of land. Only 127 hides of these 1806 were outside royal or church ownership. Forty-five per cent of all land was therefore in the king's or the Church's control. In Dorset the king's lands are very difficult to assess, but consisted of a minimum of 227 ploughlands. If these are treated arbitrarily as hides and added to those of King Harold and the lands of the churches then about 1060 hides were held by that group, out of a total of 2357 hides in the shire. About a third of the shire was in estates of ten hides or more, with church holdings predominating. Devon was a shire which did not conform to the general pattern of

its eastern neighbours. Hidage was very low at 1142, despite the large modern acreage of the shire. As a result it is common to find estates with very low assessments in hidage but clearly very large in area and population. A random example would be Croyde, which was assessed at 1 hide, but had land for ten ploughs and had ten villeins and nine bordars. Lord and men had nine ploughs between them (Thorn and Thorn 1985, 15, 41). Clearly the tax assessment was very low. The number of ploughlands may well be a better estimate of its real potential and of the size of estates. One hundred and fourteen estates out 1164 had ten ploughlands or more and they accounted for 4398 of the shire's 7934 ploughlands, that is 55 per cent. By this measure Devon conforms to our general picture for the south-west. The court and the church owned about 27 percent of the shire, again defined in terms of the ploughlands. The official connection with the area was much less strong than further east, but still powerful. Again, the official estates were large. Queen Edith, for instance, owned North Molton with an assessment of 100 ploughlands, while Gytha had Hartland with 110 (Thorn and Thorn 1985, 11, 27.1, 30).

From the evidence in the Domesday Book as it covers the south-west, it is apparent that we cannot know much about the relationships between the landholders at all levels recorded there in 1066. There is little indication of how many men held their estates as bookland and so were alloidal landholders and who could sell or let their land without reference to some superior lord. The term 'alloidal' would have been familiar to men from Normandy and elsewhere in Gaul as a description of land which was held in full ownership and which could be freely bought and sold. I use it here although the term was not in use among the English, except in the south-east, to emphasize the completeness of ownership. The fact that failure to perform certain duties to the state or to pay the geld could lead to loss of property did not make the ownership any the less complete in practice (Williams 1987, 37–38).

Amongst the most important men; did they own their estates or were they holding land from the King on terms; did they do both? Regrettably, the Domesday Book in the south-west rarely tells us the status of a landholder in 1066. However, if we look outside the south-western circuit of the Domesday Book, it is possible to see a pattern which might also be applicable to the shire. Hampshire is in the south of England and was part of Wessex, but it was surveyed in a different circuit from the western counties, and so the questions asked and answered were probably worded a little differently. The Hampshire survey does indicate the lord of each manorial tenant (Munby 1982). A random sample of a hundred manors not held from the Church shows that eighty-five of them were held directly from the King. The manors were not chosen because of the high social standing of their owners. On the contrary many were very small and belonged to men of low social status. Forty-two of those who held from the king had manors described as allods. That is to say, these men were people who had commended themselves to the king but the land they held was their own and not his. They owned it as bookland which they could sell or bequeath as they pleased. One estate was held from the king on a lease. The remaining fifteen per cent were held from the Queen, Earl Harold and Earl Godwin, with two leased from the Bishop of Winchester. Two English landowners seem not to have had lords at all. Thus the king was the lord of the bulk (eighty-five percent) of the landholders in Hampshire who did not hold from the church, and most of whom them owned their estates as bookland. Returning to Somerset, if we were to transfer the same scheme, we would have to conclude that more than half of all estates were owned outright by the people named in the Domesday Book. The King would have been the personal lord of most of those small landowners. The other forty to forty-five per cent of small estates would have been held by men who were the *fideles*, mostly of the king, but also of other great men. They were living on estates which had been alienated on a lease of some kind, but which were not bookland. The land was held in return for service. Apart from the king it is likely that the most influential lords were great ecclesiastical owners, particularly the Abbeys of St Peter at Bath and St Mary at Glastonbury and also the Bishops of Wells and of Winchester. The influence of other great men was relatively small in any formal sense, perhaps confined to lordship of a few men who held estates from them and perhaps from others lords as well, and to closer control over a number of thegns who were tenants. All men were supposed to have a lord and men probably did not divide their allegiance very often, at least not in the south of England. Each man had only one lord.

Among the 1066 owners and holders of estates there were many who were either not named, or whose names were recorded in the Exeter Domesday and were omitted from the final Exchequer version. The most likely reason for this omission was their low social status. Where the occupiers were not named they were almost always described as 'thegns'. There were some 295 of them in Somerset. Many were on Church estates and they were clearly in a subordinate position, since very frequently we are told that they could not leave the lord. That is they could not seek a

new lord and retain their estates. They were lease-holders, probably for lives. Forty-eight of these thegns are to be found on Glastonbury abbey estates. It is clear also that the average holding of each of these men was very small, if we assume that they each held only the one estate. (It seems likely that if a man had held several estates and thus a substantial acreage, he would have been named). Thus on the Glastonbury estates they amounted to an average of about *1.5* hides a head. This is far from the 5 hides which the early eleventh century *Geþyncðo* suggested as the correct minimum holding (Whitelock 1979). It seems likely that these men were soldiers, or the descendants of soldiers who had been settled on small estates by the abbey as a way of meeting its military obligations to the Old English Kings as well as to perform other services (Abels 1988). The burden placed upon the church was also shared by secular landowners, and it seems likely that they also resorted to the same expedient in the course of the tenth century. It is probable that some at least of the other tenants of Glastonbury Abbey, who were named, were also thegns holding by lease, though whether they all did military service for their estates is doubtful. One such was Edmer Ator who held Cranmore in 1066 (Thorn and Thorn 1980, 8, 32). He also had estates at East Chinnock and at Odcombe, at Aldwick and Mudford and at Dinnington (from Glastonbury), as well as extensive lands in Devon and Dorset which were not held from Glastonbury (Thorn and Thorn 1980, 19, 44. 19, 47. 37,5. 37, 12. and Thorn and Thorn 1985, 15,12–13. 15, 14–30) He was clearly a tenant of the Glastonbury estate, but the owner of many other estates. As such his status was far above that of his nameless contemporaries and doubtless his relations with the abbey were different too. He was part of a much more aristocratic network of relationships which provided the abbey with influential local supporters and offered spiritual benefits to the laymen in return.

In Dorset there is more evidence of the nature of the landholding of many of these lesser men. In 1086 the Count of Mortain held 71 separate estates which were surveyed (Thorn and Thorn 1983, chap. 26). Few of them were of any size. Gussage was a fifteen hide estate and Bryanston ten hides, but otherwise they were mostly of three hides or less. The count's new holding had been constructed by the aggregation of many estates belonging to lesser landowners. Alward had been relieved of 4 estates totalling twelve and a half hides. Edmer had lost six estates, a total of thirty-seven hides. Otherwise most of the losses had been suffered by the ubiquitous anonymous thegns, with estates of one or two hides each. Thus the Dorset fee of the most powerful of secular land-owners after the king himself, was made up of a rag-bag of properties, although it may be that if we could go deeper into their make-up we might well find some link of lordship which connected these men. What we also know about these estates was that they were all held freely, since this is explicitly stated at the end of the Count's chapter. If that pattern was to be repeated throughout Dorset it seems likely that most of the estates which passed to laymen were lands owned by the thegns and that they owed only personal service to a lord, while those thegns on church estates held in return for service and were not the owners of their lands.

In Dorset there were 330 anonymous thegns in 1066, in a shire which contained 2357 hides altogether. They were a numerous group but were even poorer than their neighbours, with only 0.85 hides per thegn. Finally in Devon with 1142 hides, the far fewer 143 thegns had 0.18 hides each. However, we certainly ought not to see the Devon thegns as necessarily significantly poorer than their neighbours. It is clear that in Devon hides are not to be regarded as the only way to measure the wealth of the shire. If we use ploughlands as a measure, the Devon thegn with 1.01 ploughlands is ahead of his Dorset neighbour with 0.71 ploughlands and behind Somerset thegn with his 1.67 ploughlands. However, what is clear is the rather anomalous situation in Dorset, where a relatively small shire had so many lesser thegns compared with Devon or Wiltshire and proportionately more than Somerset, a much larger area.

Dependent or lesser thegns tended to be clustered together on their holdings. Although there were many estates held by one thegn alone, the normal pattern was for these men to have their holdings grouped together and this was another sign of their lowly status. Thus in Somerset, there were four thegns on the estate at Chaffcombe with 5 hides 1 virgate between them (Thorn and Thorn 1980, 5, 2), while no less than seven thegns held Sock Dennis in 1086, with a mere 3.5 hides between them (Thorn and Thorn 1980, 19,85). Clearly, either estates had been split up for the benefit of these men, or else on occasions they jointly occupied an estate which continued to run as a unit. This was not a system which had developed in the period immediately before the Norman Conquest, but over more than a century. Thus some dependent thegns probably occupied well developed estates, complete with their own field systems, villages, churches and manorial organisation. Such men may have been well established as the sons or grandsons of the original dependent thegns, while others, especially those who held small portions of undivided estates,

along with other men of the same status were probably first generation soldiers, with no long established tenurial rights.

In Wiltshire again the landholdings of the anonymous thegns were very small at 1.39 hides per thegn. As in Somerset thegns were common on church lands and the Abbey of Glastonbury had used parts of its large estates to support dependent thegns. At Damerham the 52 hide estate included three units held by thegns, one of five hides, one of 1 hide and 8 acres and one of three hides. The holders before 1066 'could not be separated from the church' (Thorn and Thorn 1979, 7, 1). Similarly at Deverill a thegn held 1.5 hides and could not be separated from the church and at Christian Malford two holdings, one of half a hide and the other a virgate were also thegnland (Thorn and Thorn 1979, 73–4). At Durnford, originally a 20 hide estate, four hides belonging to Wilton Abbey had been held by three men, two of whom paid the abbey a rent of five shillings each and the other served as a thegn (Thorn and Thorn 1979, 13,3; 32,1). It may be that they were brothers who had divided a holding or the three may have been in partnership to farm the estate and perform the service due between them.

In all four shires, the anonymous thegn usually held only a small plot of land. Although he was often at least three to four times as wealthy as his villein neighbour, with his virgate, it was by no means certain that the distinction between the two was significant. In Dorset the mode for thegns was that they would hold between a quarter and half a hide. Ninety-nine individuals fell into that category. Such men were likely to be twice as wealthy as the average villein, and of course they did no labour services and paid little in the way of rents, but if they needed to maintain a horse for riding and their armour and weaponry, the burden would have been considerable. For a proportion of the least well endowed thegns the chief distinction between themselves and their villein neighbours was one of status, not wealth.

It is important not to allow the averages to obscure the situation of individuals. In each shire there were of course, thegns who held much less than the average. At Marten in Wiltshire two thegns jointly held a small estate of one hide in 1066 (Thorn and Thorn 1979, 68, 10). The population was recorded as two slaves and two cottars. Presumably the thegns worked the land themselves, as well as using the slaves and the services of the cottars. We do not know in detail what services were expected of these two men other than those connected with warfare, but it may well have involved them in escort duties for the abbot and for abbey officials when they travelled in the case of thegns tied to a monastic lord, and perhaps similar duties towards the shire reeve and his officials for those men who had the king as their lord.

Devon, Somerset and Dorset are alike in that in all three the minor thegn was a common figure in the shire and they must have been the men who filled places on juries and crowded the shire court. If they were mostly dependents of the king they would have made a political counterweight to the followers of other great men, and indeed to the abbots and bishops. In Wiltshire the situation was a little different. Here there were only 52 thegns and many of them were dependent upon the church. The administration of the shire would have been much more easily dominated by the bishop and other churchmen as well as the other great landowners.

The Thegns in the Landscape

The other strand of evidence about these men comes from the landscape in which they lived. In two parts of Dorset it may be possible to reconstruct landscapes within which holdings of thegns were common. Both in the area to the west of the Weymouth to Dorchester road and in the Isle of Purbeck there are signs of large scale landscape planning (Figure 4.2). Near Dorchester, running north to south across the grain of the country-side, which tends east-west are a large number of parallel roads, tracks and boundaries which cross parish and manorial boundaries and which are often followed by the medieval and modern boundaries of parishes and manors, and on a smaller scale by field boundaries and footpaths (Figure 4.3). The pattern is on a large scale and appears to be set off from the Roman road from Dorchester towards Axminster in Devon. However, it crosses the Roman road which runs from Dorchester to Radipole which respects the alignments. This might suggest that the landscape was planned around the road and was laid out in the late Roman period or afterwards. To the west the pattern runs into the eastern part of Abbotsbury, after which the landscape becomes too broken for it to persist. To the north-west, in the parishes of Little Bredy, Kingston Russell and Long Bredy the pattern may also appear, though interrupted in places by difficult terrain.

The existence of such a landscape should not be too surprising, since similar areas have been noted else-where in the southwest. As long ago as 1970 Christopher Taylor pointed out the extant pattern of

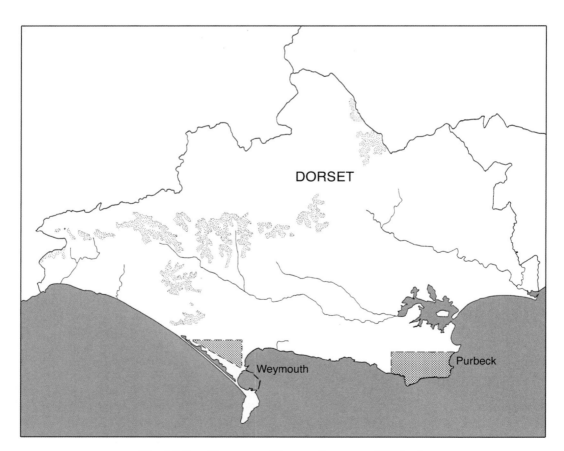

Fig. 4.2 Location map – Weymouth area and Purbeck.

Anglo-Saxon estates in Purbeck, where more than 50 separate settlements can be identified (Taylor 1970, 60–63). Professor Michael Aston looked at the landscape around Ilchester and across to South Cadbury in Somerset and concluded that there was an underlying pattern of north-south alignments (Aston 1985, 146–

48). Very recently, looking more closely at the landscape around South Cadbury, John Davey has identified large areas of aligned, rectangular field systems, which cross parish boundaries and which he regards as being of at least late Roman origin (Davey 2004). Dr Davey's reconstructions are very reminiscent

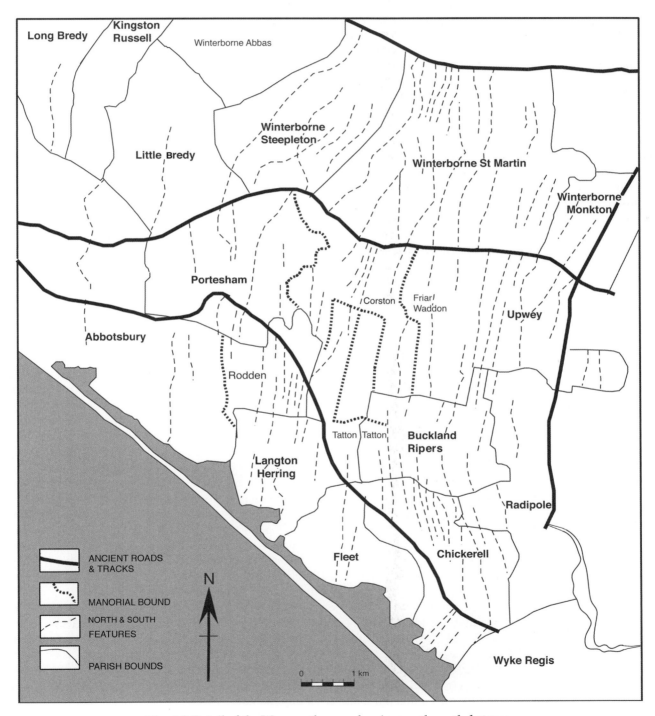

Fig. 4.3 Detail of the Weymouth area, showing north south features.

of the landscapes proposed for Norfolk and Suffolk by Dr Williamson (1987, 419–431). The landscapes of South Dorset do not demonstrate the same co-axial features. They look much more as if they were formed by using long parallel boundaries, often running for many kilometres across the grain of the country.

The landscape near Dorchester/Weymouth pre-dates the division of the landscape into the much later parishes, and must also predate any Anglo-Saxon estate construction, at least in the later, ninth/tenth century period, since although small estates, described in the Domesday Survey, fit within it, so do other larger units present in 1066, some of which have high-medieval open-field plans which also fit into the pattern (see Figure 4.2). Thus it is a large scale landscape, into which are fitted a number of smaller units, in many cases much smaller than the later parishes. Some of these units can be identified from their names, some of which are late Anglo-Saxon in origin, mostly tenth century. However because the names are of that date we cannot definitively state that the settlements had their origins in that period also. They may be much older and the name may record a significant moment in the history of the estate, a point at which not only ownership, but the nature of ownership changed fundamentally. Such a moment might be if the estate was granted to someone on a permanent basis, rather than it remaining in the hands of a great magnate, to be granted on a temporary basis.

To the east of Portesham lies a group of manors recorded in the Domesday Book: Waddon, Corton, Friar Waddon, East and West Shilvinghampton and the two Tattons. It is possible to trace the boundaries of all but the eastern Tatton through tithe, enclosure and estate maps of the eighteenth and nineteenth centuries. All but the eastern Tatton lay in the parish of Portesham in the middle ages. Part of this parish appears as an estate of the nearby monastery at Abbotsbury in 1042, in the charter S 961, of AD 1024 (Sawyer 1968. Hereafter charters are quoted by their 'Sawyer' numbers), if the reconstruction of the bounds is correct (Morris 2002, 9 and pt. 2, appendix. 2.1). However, Friar Waddon, although part of the medieval parish of Portesham, was not part of the Anglo-Saxon charter estate of 1042. Whether Corton and the rest of the manors were is unclear, although they lay outside the medieval demesne of the Abbey.

There are two possible explanations for this state of affairs. The first is that Friar Waddon, which in 1066 was held by three thegns and was a six hide estate, had been divided from the Portesham charter area before 1042 when the charter was granted. If that were so, then Friar Waddon would have no connection with Abbotsbury, and would have been joined to Abbotsbury for ecclesiastical purposes at a comparatively late date. An alternative explanation is that the charter boundary is not actually of 1042, but later, made after the division of the primitive estate, at the time when these estates were either being set up or granted to thegns for the first time. If that were the case, then the whole document may be a re-written copy of an earlier document, made between 1042 and 1066. This argument is supported by the Domesday entry for Friar Waddon which tells us that the three thegns had paid customary dues to Abbotsbury of six acres of harvest, two acres for each thegn and three church dues, one per man, up to 1066 (Thorn and Thorn 1983, 23,1). There is no suggestion here that they were leasing the land, but a tenurial commitment of some kind had clearly been made. The payment of church dues to Abbotsbury points to a more ancient situation, where the church at Abbotsbury had rights over people in a *parochia* of which Portesham and Friar Waddon may have been parts. Tatton also was divided in parochial status in the later middle ages. One Tatton, which later was part of Portesham parish was held on a lease from the abbey of Cerne in 1066 and was rated as a two hide estate (Thorn and Thorn 1983, 49, 10. 55, 23). The other Tatton also Cerne property, lay in Buckland Ripers parish for ecclesiastical purposes.

By 1066 the area seems to have been polarised between two great landholders. The first of these was the king and the largest royal estate was at Wyke and Portland (Thorn and Thorn 1983, 1, 1). Portland was the first of the king's estates enumerated in the Dorset Domesday Book, suggesting its importance. It may be that much of the land in the Weymouth hinterland was royal originally and that there were two phases of dispersal. The first was possibly the granting away of substantial lands to monasteries, by means of a gift to favoured servants who then were able to gain prestige by using the gift to found a monastery. In this case, in 1023 Cnut granted his *huscarle* Orc, the land at Portesham (Sawyer 1968, S961) which Orc and his wife subsequently used to endow a church at Abbotsbury. By 1058–66 Orc's widow, Tole, had permission to bequeath her lands and possessions to St Peter's Abbotsbury (Sawyer 1968, S1064). Thus the lands on the westward edge of the area passed into monastic possession and although the monastery never rivalled the king as a landowner it did form the second great corporate presence in the area. Other lands were held by a variety of smaller owners by 1066, and also by a large number of thegns. The appearance of so many of these men may well mark another important phase in the dispersal of royal property as well as the lands of the monastery.

Tatton will serve as an example which helps to

demonstrate further the process as it affected the monasteries. In the Domesday Book the entries are:

> *Aiulf holds Tatton himself. A thegn held it before 1066 from Cerne Church, he could not be separated from it. It paid tax for 3 hides* (Thorn and Thorn 1983, 49, 10).

> *The woman (wife of Hugh son of Grip) holds 2 hides in Tatton herself which were part of the lordship of the Abbey of Cerne. Before 1066 2 thegns held them by lease* (Thorn and Thorn 1983, 55, 23).

The entries show that Tatton had once been a single unit of five hides, which was part of the lands of Cerne Abbey and had been parcelled out in order to support thegns who were *fideles* of the abbey and were tied to the estates. There are now two parts of Tatton, one of which has identifiable bounds, the other of which lies in Buckland Ripers parish and for which the bounds are not completely defined (Figure 4.4). The name Tatton means the *tun* of 'Tata' and suggests a single

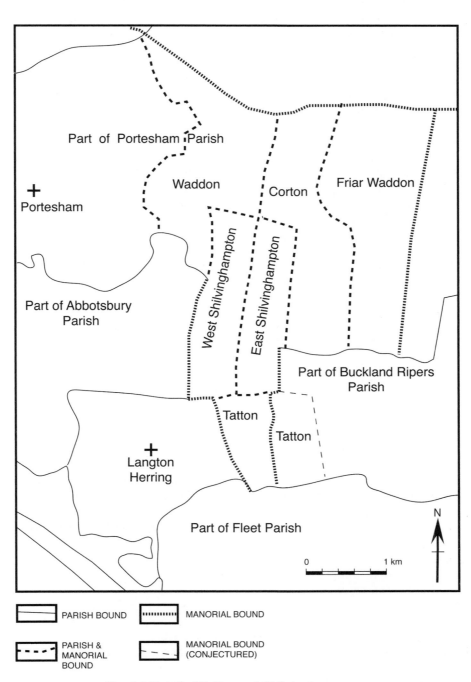

Fig. 4.4 Detail of Tatton and Shilvington manors.

estate granted out to or owned by an individual and probably named in the tenth century. Cerne Abbey may have created the two Tattons at any time up to 1066, but this division must have come after the monastery's refoundation, with the division of a thegn's classic five hide holding between three tenants.

Similarly, at Waddon (Friar Waddon) we get a hint of the relationship between the thegns and their lord, the Abbey of Abbotsbury (Thorn and Thorn 1983, 23, 1 and General Notes, 23, 1). As noted above, there were 3 thegns on six hides of land and a note in the Domesday Book entry indicates that the thegns each paid a customary due in kind of 2 acres of harvest – presumably two acres of crop, and a church tax. Another two hides of land at Little Waddon was held by Brictwin in 1066, suggesting that an estate of 8 hides had been dismembered to make the arrangement, perhaps after the foundation of Abbotsbury in 1042 (Thorn and Thorn 1983, 56, 23). Another view might be that an important church with a substantial land-holding already existed and that Orc and Tole simply took it over, sponsored the reform of its structure and granted it extra endowments. Whatever the reality, all these arrangements suggest that the new monastery found it necessary to create these small estates with their thegns in order to provide themselves with the secular and military followers they needed.

Other similar small estates may well have been created by the king in order to increase the number of thegns he too could command. Buckland Ripers has a place-name of a familiar form. The first element is Old English *bocland*, 'land granted by charter'. The king granted most charters, and although no record of this one has survived, it seems likely that the estate was granted in this way, probably in the ninth or tenth centuries. It must have been granted as a single block but in 1066 it was held jointly by four thegns as a four hide estate (Thorn and Thorn 1983, 55, 4). It was clearly regarded as a single unit for taxation purposes prior to 1066, though that would not preclude there being distinct agricultural units within the manor, but does point to it having existed as a single unit of jurisdiction in the tenth century. That four thegns should have each held a hide in 1066 seems too neat for the processes of inheritance and it is most likely that the land returned to the king for some unknown reason and was re-granted or leased to the four thegns in return for service, on the basis that each needed a hide for his support.

At Shilvinghampton there were already three holdings by 1066. One belonged to the Abbotsbury Abbey and was held by a priest in 1086. Before 1066 it paid tax for 5 virgates of land. The second part of Shilvinghampton had been held jointly by three thegns

in 1066. It was taxed at 1 hide 1 virgate. The final part of Shilvinghampton had belonged to a named individual and paid tax for 2.5 hides. Thus we actually have a five hide estate which has been divided into three parts. One might speculate that the abbey at Abbotsbury once owned the whole estate and had sold or granted parts away for service, though by 1066 the thegns and the holder of the 2.5 hides – Alwy – were alloidal owners, not tenants.

In the earlier Old English the king was the dominant landowning and juridical force in the area, based on his control of Dorchester, Wyke and the Island of Portland. By the eighth or ninth centuries the area was already divided into subunits, such as the Winter-borne, Bredy and Wey districts. These were all groups of river valley settlements and the difficulty of distinguishing the later settlements from the Domesday Book entries suggests that their separate identities were still in the process of establishment in the mid-eleventh century. The 'Wey' manors in particular, with their heavy complement of thegns cannot have been much like the later traditional unified agricultural units, normally with a single lord, so frequent in the south-west, and it may well be that the tenurial upheavals of the Conquest provided the opportunity for a radical restructuring of these places into a more normal manorial shape.

Other parts of the region followed a slightly different pattern. Some areas were granted to monastic houses. In the case of Abbotsbury the land close to the monastery became the demesne of the abbey, while outlying possessions were granted or leased initially to laymen in return for service. The land thus parcelled out, could already have existed as units tied into the ancient landscape patterns, or have been laid out anew to provide arable based estates for warrior dependants. Since some of these existed as separate manors, unlike the thegns' holdings in the Wey units, they were described in detail as manors in Domesday Book, and survived to be recognizable today. Some other small estates were created by the king, either by sale or gift during the tenth century or early eleventh century across other parts of his lands. Again they were created inside the existing large scale pattern, which probably made the process of delineation easy. In all these case, royal subdivision of fairly large estates already existing, – 'Wey', the 'Winterbornes' – or creation of smaller units such as Buckland Ripers or Langton Herring, or monastic creation of the Tattons, Shilvinghamptons, Cortons and Roddens, the purpose was probably the same, to plant dependant thegns in the landscape and draw from them service, especially military service and commendation. To do this both king and monastery were prepared to break up existing estates into smaller units, many of which were to become recognisable agricultural entities. This, then was not a landscape of planned settlements with open-field systems set up around them, or if it was the dominant lords were prepared to mutilate that system in order to accommodate their dependents.

A very similar pattern emerges in Purbeck. The model proposed would be of a landscape laid out on a large scale. This planned layout was regular and as rectangular as the topography allowed (Figure 4.5). It covered the whole of the regular and reasonably level area of the Isle of Purbeck. It is worth noting here that the place name 'Swanage' is a 'wic' name, meaning 'the peasants wic' (Mills 1977, 53). All three modern authorities (Ekwall 1960; Mills 1977; Watts 2004) see this as *wic*, 'a dairy farm', but it is possible that we should look beyond this meaning for somewhere so close to the sea. The possibility exists that this was originally a seaside trading site. Swanage itself was part of Worth Matravers parish until the beginning of the sixteenth century (Hutchins, vol. 1, 656). In 1373 Langton Matravers was described as a chapel

dedicated to St George, while Worth Matravers itself, with a dedication to St Nicholas is unlikely to have had a church at an early date, since this saint was not popular in England until the very end of the eleventh century and the church there dates from c. 1100 (RCHM 1970, pt.2, 410). The same is true of Kingston, a chapelry of Corfe, also dedicated to St Nicholas. Professor Hinton has argued very plausibly that Corfe, Kingston, Worth Matravers, Langton Matravers and Swanage all formed part of a *parochia* centred at Corfe in the Anglo-Saxon period and that this area may have been a southern part of a larger Wareham based unit (Hinton, 1994, 11). This southern *parochia* almost certainly reflected the existence of a royal estate which covered the whole area. As with the region between Portland and Abbotsbury the break up of the area is signalled by grants to monasteries and to laymen, here documented by charters, S534, of AD 948, a grant of 8 hides of land in Purbeck to a religious woman, Ælfthryth, S573, of AD 956, a grant to Wihtsige by King Eadred of 16 hides of land at Corfe and Blashenwell and S632 of AD 956, a grant of 7 hides at

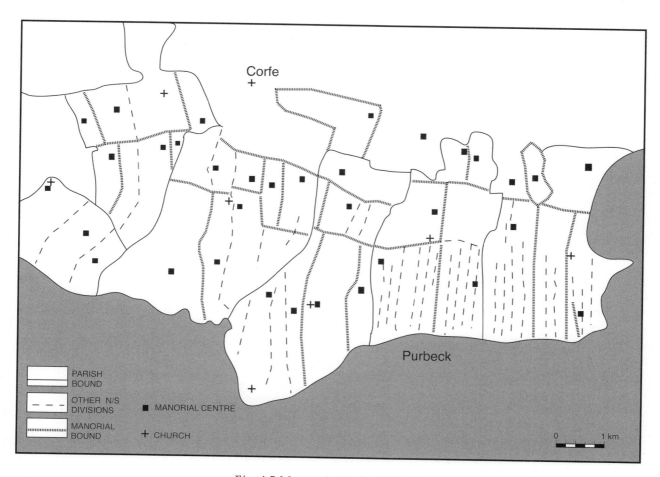

Fig. 4.5 Manors in Purbeck island.

Corfe and Blashenwell by King Eadwig to Wihtsige. Kelly (1996) considers this last charter a conflation of the two earlier ones and therefore certainly a forgery. The attempt by Professor Hinton to trace these bounds was not conclusive.

As mentioned above, a pattern of north south alignments certainly covers the three modern parishes of Swanage, Langton Matravers and Worth Matravers and extends into Kingston, Church Knowle and Kimmeridge, although here it is not as prominent, probably because the topography made it more difficult to lay out. It would seem to cover at least the whole of the ancient *parochia* of Corfe, at least to the south of the Purbeck ridge, pointing to its antiquity. The existence of such a pattern tells us little about its dating except to suggest that it predates the break up of the royal landholding and the creation of the minor estates within it and must therefore be Anglo-Saxon at the latest. Professor Hinton (1991 187–90) discussed some elements of the landscape of Worth and con-

cluded that each of the four known Iron Age and Roman sites in southern Worth parish, are found in constituent estates. He points out that the western boundary of Rempstone over-runs the Celtic field system on Kingston Down and suggests that therefore complete continuity is unlikely. It may be therefore that this is part of a planned landscape perhaps set up in the aftermath of the assimilation of eastern Dorset into the early West Saxon polity. Recently John Blair has argued very forcefully for the early minsters as major forces in the orgnisation and exploitation of these seventh and eighth century landscapes, which would certainly fit with the existence of a minster at Wareham and might also point to a role for the minster at Dorchester (Blair 2005)

What limited analysis is possible suggests that later open field systems were laid out inside this elongated rectangular plan. This is particularly clear for the manor of Swanage, known as 'Sandwic', where a vestige of a very regular open-field system still existed

Taken from D65/E2 of 1823 (Dorset Record Office)

Fig. 4.6 North-South detail in east Purbeck.

in 1823 (D65/E2, 1823) (Figure 4.6) and to the west in Herston manor there was also a trace of open-field furlongs, again within the north/south alignments within the larger pattern (RCHM, pt2, opposite p. 297).

By the time of Domesday the pattern of small units was well established (Taylor 1970, 60–3). At Orchard the 1.5 hide estate was held by four thegns in 1066 (Thorn and Thorn 1988, 55, 47). They could go to any lord they pleased and were therefore free owners of the land. Only after 1066 was this estate divided into two units, when a hide was given by Hugh son of Grip to Cranborne Abbey and his widow kept the other half hide.

Similarly Wilkswood (now in Langton Matravers parish) was an estate of just over four hides of which one estate contained over 3.5 hides and the half hide was held freely by 2 thegns in 1066 (Thorn and Thorn 1983, 55, 40 and 48). Here we cannot tell when the half hide estate was created, but we can see that the process of subdivision had stopped at that point. The two thegns do not seem to have divided it physically. Perhaps with such a small unit, that was not easy to do.

Rollington, an estate of 2.5 hides, to the north-east of Corfe, was held in 1066 by nine thegns. By 1086 it had been granted to a single occupier (Thorn and Thorn 1983, 47, 10). How or if this estate had been divided before the Conquest is unclear, but it could still be distinguished as a unit in the early nineteenth century (D/RWR/P3, 1803). Herston, now part of Swanage parish was held as two units in 1066 (Thorn and Thorn 1983, 47, 12. 57, 22), half a hide belong to a man called Her and one virgate held by Godfrey Scullion's father. Thus an estate of only three-quarters of a hide had been subdivided before the Conquest and continued in the same state in 1086.

In other parts of the region the small thegns are to be found in landscapes which are again ancient relict areas of late Roman development (Davey 2004, 106–8). Around South Cadbury Castle there are a number of small land units which have been identified, some of which were recorded as estates in Domesday Book. Woolston, in 1086 part of North Cadbury, had been divided into two parts, one of one hide and one of three hides and one and a half virgates, held by three thegns (Thorn and Thorn 1983 19, 55). Here it is much less easy to discern a pattern of large scale planning, followed by subdivision. It may well be that surviving units were redeveloped and in the case of Woolston, subdivided in the late Anglo-Saxon period (Figure 4.7).

However, by no means all the very small estates were created within an already planned landscape. Kingcombe in Dorset (Thorn and Thorn 1983, 32, 3. 56,61) is now distinguishable as two settlements, Higher and Lower Kingcombe, in the parishes of Hooke and Toller Porcorum respectively. In 1066 Kingcombe, perhaps already two units was held by a total of 15 thegns on only two hides. The unit had been subdivided unevenly as one hide and three parts of 1 virgate and three virgates and the fourth part of one virgate. There is nothing now to suggest a previously planned landscape or how the land was utilized by its holders before 1066. These men can have been no more than very minor warriors, distinguished from the peasantry only by their duty as soldiers. At Yatton Keynell, Wiltshire, the estate was divided between three landowners. In 1066 Leofnoth held 2 hides and three virgates, identified as Yatton Keynell (Thorn and Thorn 1979, 6,1), while two thegns held another part of the same manor as a five hide unit and 'an Englishman' held a single virgate (Thorn and Thorn 1979, 25,27. 32,14). The thegns may well have held West Yatton, which was still distinguishable in 1279 (Gover, Mawer and Stenton 1939, 114) and which still has a manor house of its own, but may not have physically divided it between them. Clearly a large estate of eight hides had been divided to give a five hide unit, which had then been subdivided again.

Conclusion

The process which produced these thegns, too obscure to have their names recorded in Domesday Book was clearly a pragmatic one. In two cases in Dorset there is some landscape evidence to suggest that landscapes created on a large scale, perhaps by the kings of Wessex after the seventh century, were first divided into large estates and then subdivided and tiny holdings created for dependents, at a late date in the Old English period. Elsewhere in Wessex new estates were created by the re-division of existing large units into smaller planned estates, some of which were then granted to dependent thegns. Such a process can be seen on the Glastonbury estates, where the greater Shapwick had been sub-divided before 1066. Part of the divided estate, Sutton Mallet, Edington, Chilton Polden and Catcott, each a five hide unit, were held by fourteen thegns. It certainly looks as if re-planned estates originally intended as grants of standard five hide units for followers had then been re-assigned to thegns of lesser status, with smaller potential incomes. However, it is not now possible to discern distinct units within these estates which might have been utilized by individuals. This may be because a planned open-field village of pre-conquest origins was never subdivided or because when the estates passed into the hands of a single individual after 1066 a single farming system was re-introduced. Whatever decision was taken at the time, it seems that the pressures which brought about such

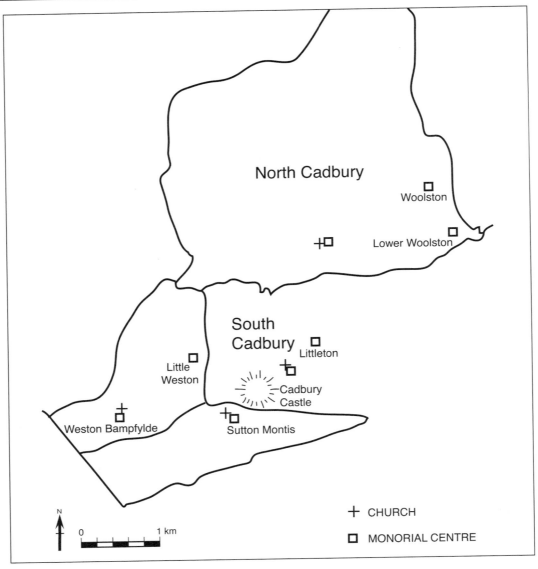

Fig. 4.7 Manors around Cadbury Castle.

creations were pressing and grave. By sub-dividing their estates landowners were in danger of losing revenue and perhaps impoverishing themselves. Domesday Book gives us an account of part of this process by detailing the pattern which existed in 1066. As far as can be seen, it was only ecclesiastical landowners who leased rather than sold or granted their lands. Otherwise small landowner-thegns were mostly bookland owners and at least nominally independent. In return for fidelity these men had in some cases been granted small estates which had become their free property. Others had received their lands on leases and the division between secular and religious practice looks fairly clear here. That service

included military service, though it is hard to imagine that the man with half a hide doing the service of a man with five hides. He might however, be like the famous account in the Berkshire Domesday Book.

> If the king sent out an army anywhere only one thegn went from each five hides, and for his sustenance or pay 4s for 2 months was given him from each hide. (Williams and Martin 2002, 136, col.2)

Each man would need to have his arms and his horse, ready to go, but might expect to serve his turn in the king's army only occasionally, perhaps at every fifth or sixth callout. This would make being a soldier much easier, but no doubt confer some degree of status upon a man who otherwise might be regarded as only a rather well-to do farmer. The pity of it from the point of view of the English, was that the Norman conquest not only destroyed the English aristocracy, it also largely removed this class. Those who didn't die fighting at Hastings, or in rebellions disappear from the record. By 1086 their land was usually held by someone with a Norman French name and in many cases the tiny estates had been re-grouped to make larger units. Some must have been displaced into the ranks of the unfree peasantry. It is romantic, but probably wrong to imagine that some few made the journey to Byzantium and helped form part of the Greek Emperor's foreign Legion, the Varangian Guard.

References

Manuscripts

D/MOW/E2, 1823, Dorset Record Office, Sale Catalogue of the Swanage Estate of the Mowlem family of Swanage.

D/RWR/P3, 1803, Dorset Record Office. Map of Rollington and farms in the Isle of Purbeck, belonging to John Calecroft Esq. Drawn by James Asser.

S 961 This charter exists as a single sheet charter in the Dorset County Record Office, D124.

Printed books

Abels, R. P. (1988) *Lordship and Military Obligation in Anglo-Saxon England*. London, British Museum Publications.

Aston, M. A. (1985) *Interpreting the Landscape*. London, Batsford.

Blair, J. (1994) *Anglo-Saxon Oxfordshire*. Stroud, Alan Sutton Publishing.

Blair, J. (2005) *The Church in Anglo-Saxon Society*. Oxford, Oxford University Press.

Campbell, J. (1987) Some Agents and Agencies of the Late Anglo-Saxon State, In J. G. Holt, (ed.), *Domesday Studies*, 201–218. Woodbridge, The Boydell Press.

Darby, H. C. (1986) *Domesday England*. Cambridge, Cambridge University Press.

Davey, J. (2004) *The Roman to Medieval Transition in the Environs of South Cadbury, Somerset*. Bristol, (unpublished PhD thesis).

Dyer, C. (1980) *Lords and Peasants in a Changing society. The estates of the Bishopric of Worcester, 680–1540*. Cambridge, Cambridge University Press.

Gillingham, J. (1995) Thegns and Knights in Eleventh-Century England: Who Was Then The Gentleman? *Transactions of the Royal Historical Society, sixth series, V*, 129–153; 129.

Gover, J. E. B., Mawer, A. and Stenton, F. M. (1939) *The Place-Names of Wiltshire*. [EPNS vol. XVI], Nottingham, English Place-Name Society.

Hinton, D. A. and Peacock, D. P. S. (1991) Worth Matravers. *Proceedings of the Dorset Natural History and Archaeological Society*, 113, 187–90.

Hinton, D. A. (1994) Some Anglo-Saxon charters and estates in South-East Dorset. *Proceedings of the Dorset Natural History and Archaeological Society*, 116, 11–20.

Hutchins, J. (1861–70) *The History and Antiquities of the County of Dorset*, 3rd ed. 4 vols. W. Shipp and J. W. Hodson (eds), Dorchester.

Kelly, S. E. (ed.) (1996) *The Charters of Shaftesbury Abbey*, Anglo-Saxon Charters, V. Oxford, Oxford University Press.

Mack, K. (1984) Changing thegns: Cnut's Conquest and the English Aristocracy. *Albion*, 16, 375–87.

Mills, A. D. (1977) *The Place-Names of Dorset, part 1. [EPNS vol. 52]*. London, English Place-Name Society.

Morris, P. (ed.) (2002) *Abbotsbury Historic Landscape Research Project: Synthesis Report No. 1*. privately prepared for the Ilchester Estates.

Munby, J. (1982) *Domesday Book, 4, Hampshire*. Chichester, Phillimore.

Royal Commission on Historical Monuments, England (1970), *An Inventory of Historical Monuments in the County of Dorset, vol. 2, South-East, pts 1–3*. London, HMSO.

Sawyer, P. (1968) *Anglo-Saxon Charters: An annotated list and bibliography*. London, Royal Historical Society.

Scammell, J. (1993) The Formation of English Social Structure: Freedom, Knights and Gentry, 1066–1300. *Speculum* 69, 591–636.

Taylor, C. C. (1970) *Dorset*. London, Hodder & Stoughton.

Thorn, C. and Thorn F. (eds) (1983) *Domesday Book, 7, Dorset*. Chichester, Phillimore.

Thorn, C. and Thorn F. (eds) (1979) *Domesday Book, 6, Wiltshire*. Chichester, Phillimore.

Thorn, C. and Thorn F. (eds) (1980) *Domesday Book, 8, Somerset*. Chichester, Phillimore.

Thorn, C. and Thorn F. (eds) (1985) *Domesday Book, 9, Devon* (2 vols.). Chichester, Phillimore.

Watts, V. (ed.) (2004) *The Cambridge Dictionary of English Place-Names*. Cambridge, Cambridge University Press.

Whitelock, D. (ed.) (1979) *English Historical Documents c. 500–1042*, 2nd ed. London, Eyre Methuen.

Williams, A. (1992) A Bell-house and a Burh-geat: Lordly Residences in England before the Norman Conquest. In C. Harper-Bill and R. Harvey, (eds) *Medieval Knighthood IV; Papers from the fifth Strawberry Hill Conference, 1990*, 221–240. Woodbridge, Boydell Press.

Williams, A. (1987) How land was held before and after the Norman Conquest. In A. Williams, (ed.) *Domesday Book, Studies*. London, Alecto.

Williams A. and Martin, G. H. (eds) (2002) *Domesday Book: A Complete Translation*. London, Penguin Books.

Williamson, T. (1987) Early Co-axial Field Systems on the East Anglian Boulder Clays. *Proceedings of the Prehistoric Society* 53, 419–431.

Chapter 5

Strategy, Symbolism and the Downright Unusual: The Archaeology of Three Somerset Castles

Stuart J. Prior

Introduction

Traditionally, the study of castles has been dominated by militaristic themes. Architectural historians have examined castles as functional structural entities, concentrating upon their fabric, design and construction, in order to assess their defensive military potential. The key element in their argument was that the architectural evolution of the castle was the product of a continual struggle between increasingly sophisticated techniques of attack and progressively more scientific methods of defence, whilst military historians have examined their martial significance, operational capabilities and role in medieval warfare. During the last decades of the twentieth century however, there was a reaction against the traditional military approach, principally focussed upon the later medieval period, but increasingly applied to the eleventh and twelfth centuries (Liddiard 2003, 7). As castellologists expanded their repertoires to include an ever-widening array of sites, source materials, methodologies and fresh technologies, new questions began to be asked of castles, and consequently new agendas for research developed.

In 1967, Davidson challenged the notion of the Norman origin of English castles – following a survey of mottes in Normandy which failed to date any to before 1066 (Davidson 1969). Davidson's work, although inconclusive, fired archaeological interest in earthwork castles, and Higham and Barker's book *Timber Castles* (1992) placed them firmly on the castle studies agenda. In 1990, Pound's book on the medieval castle opened up debate on the social and economic roles of castles. Architectural castle studies have recently witnessed a move away from 'military functionalism' towards 'iconographic symbolism', with Coulson (1979 onwards) placing increasing emphasis upon the defensive shortcomings of many castles in an attempt to transport castle-building into

the realms of aristocratic chivalric culture, where status and social competition become the more dominant characteristics, whilst Dixon (1990, [and with Marshall] 1993) and Heslop (1991) have explored the social functions of castles, highlighting the sophistication of domestic planning to the detriment of military design.

In 1984, Austin argued that castles needed to be studied within a wider historical framework, and his work on Barnard Castle was instrumental in demonstrating the importance of the castle's landscape setting (Austin 1984). This led to an explosion in castle landscape studies, and as a result, there has been a move away from seeing castle landscapes as purely functional environments (Creighton 1998 onwards; Hughes 1998; Liddiard 2000 and 2003). The most recent approach applied to the study of castles though is the phenomenological. Castellologists are becoming increasingly concerned with the ways in which landscapes were perceived and experienced by past societies, and with the impact of the castle 'monument' upon the human senses (O'Keeffe 2000; Marten-Holden 2001; Johnson 2002; Wheatley 2004). Today then, castellologists interpret castles and their landscapes in a variety of different ways. In addition to the military role of castles, aspects such as lordly display, peaceable power, aesthetics, iconography and symbolism are frequently considered, and castles are often studied in their wider administrative, social, economic and political contexts.

Between 1067 and 1202, the Normans founded twenty-seven castles in Somerset (Figure 5.1). This paper examines recent archaeological work on three of these castles, Cary, Montacute and Downend. As well as focusing upon the more traditional topics of dating, morphology and military functions – in keeping with current research agendas in castellology – the paper examines the varying roles, perceptions, iconographic and symbolic aspects of these castles. The castles of Cary, Montacute and Downend were chosen as the focus for this paper for two reasons, firstly each one has a particularly interesting story to tell, and secondly each one has, at one time or another, been studied by and played an important role in the work of Mick Aston.

Cary Castle

Cary Castle is located in south-east Somerset (ST 6411 3214), on the south-eastern edge of a small market town of medieval origin called Castle Cary. The village's name derives from the river which rises there

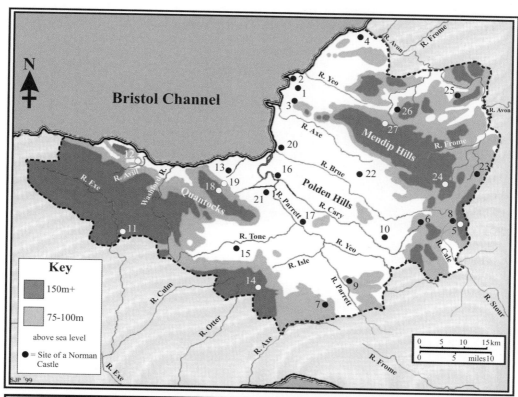

Castles shown on the map

1	Castle Batch	15	Taunton Castle
2	Swallow Cliff Mound	16	Down End Earthworks
3	Locking Head Castle	17	Burrow Mump
4	Portbury Mound	18	Over Stowey Castle
5	Ballands Castle	19	Nether Stowey Castle
6	Cary Castle	20	Edithmead
7	Crow Castle	21	Bridgwater Castle
8	Cockroad Wood Castle	22	Fenny Castle
9	Montacute Castle	23	Hales Castle
10	Wimble Toot	24	Breach Wood Castle
11	Bury Castle	25	Culverhay Castle
12	Dunster Castle (Torre)	26	Stowey Castle
13	Stogursey Castle	27	Richmont Castle
14	Castle Neroche		

Fig. 5.1 Somerset's Norman castles.

Fig. 5.2 Aerial photo of Castle Cary – Looking west (Photo courtesy of Mick Aston).

(the Cari or Cary) and the Norman castle. The castle itself comprises a partial ringwork and a large, strongly embanked bailey, side by side on the point of a sloping ridge (Figure 5.2).

A castle at Cary is first mentioned in 1138 when attacked and taken by King Stephen (Potter 1955), and this has led many to assign a twelfth century date to the site (Meade 1856, 1877–8; King 1983, ii, 442; Fry 1996, 134). However, the finding of a succession of ditches, and of tenth to eleventh century pottery, during recent archaeological excavations on the site (Leach and Ellis 2004) appear to indicate an earlier date of foundation and, more impressively, the form of this early fortification. During excavations in 1999, ditch F707 – the west side of deeply cut linear feature – was discovered (Figure 5.3). The feature was interpreted as the remains of a massive ditch, further excavation demonstrating that it curved away to the south-west. In addition, the layers and features associated with it contained a significant proportion of tenth to eleventh century material.

According to Domesday Book the first Norman lord to hold *Cari* was Walter of Douai (Williams and Martin 2002, 261), and it can be argued that the holding dated back to the Conquest. It is likely that Robert of Mortain, in the absence of William who had returned to Normandy in 1067, led a planned offensive into

Somerset shortly after the Conquest, and that the Normans came prepared to meet resistance, bearing in mind that King Harold himself had formerly been Earl of Wessex (Prior 2006). Resistance in Somerset, Devon and Cornwall did not end in January 1068, when Exeter fell to William shortly after his return. Harold's sons returned to the West Country from Ireland on two occasions in 1068 and 1069 to wage war, and Robert of Mortain's stronghold at Montacute was attacked in a separate incident in 1069 (Bradbury 1998, 229).

Apart from Robert, two other Norman lords stand out for their active involvement in the initial campaign in Somerset: William de Mohun and Walter of Douai. The latter was the most prolific of the Norman castle builders in Somerset and his sphere of influence was the north and east of the county. Here Walter was responsible for the construction of three early Norman castles – Edithmead, Batch and Cockroad Wood – and two others may also be attributable to him – Stowey and Hales; of these five castles, four are ringworks (Prior 1999, 17–18). The topography of the site at Cary and the location of the ditch (F707) and other early features suggest that primary Norman occupation on the site may have been in the form of an oval-shaped ringwork; a type that compares favourably with the others known to have been constructed by Walter.

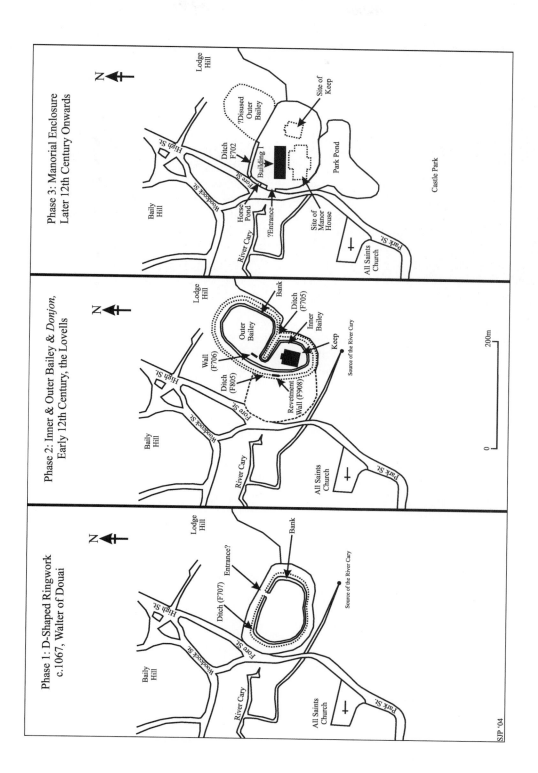

Fig. 5.3 Suggested stages of development for Castle Cary.

The castle is situated upon the lower north-west facing slope of Lodge Hill, and the suggested ringwork is seen as occupying a natural spur extending south-west from the foot of the hill overlooking the source of the River Cary (Figure 5.3 – Phase 1). Tactically speaking this site is ideal, as it is naturally defensible, occupies an area of higher ground providing good all round visibility, affords an elevated escape route along a ridge to the north-east, and enables ready access to a potable water supply. It has been suggested that the higher ground to the south-east of the site could compromise its tactical viability (Somerset Heritage Record PRN.51803), but this ground is approximately 400m away, placing the ringwork well outside of the range of weapons of the period.

Tactical considerations alone were seldom influential enough to dictate that a fortification should be erected however. The decision to build invariably deriving from the wider strategic importance of the location. The decision to construct a ringwork at Cary probably came from two such strategic considerations. Firstly, it was important to guard and control the county's borders and Cary is situated only 6 miles from the Wiltshire border and 6½ miles from the Dorset border. The ringwork, acting in concert with Walter of Douai's other castles in the region, could have formed part of a chain of linked sites around the north of the county. Secondly, if the Normans' campaign in Somerset was to succeed, it was essential that they gained control of the county's systems of transport, communication and supply. The ringwork was positioned to completely dominate the source of the River Cary, was only 1 mile from a navigable stretch of the River Brue and 2½ miles from the source of the River Cale. But more significantly, 7 miles downstream from the ringwork, at the point where the River Cary became navigable, was the small motte of Wimble Toot, and 19 miles further downstream again, at the point where the Cary ends, was the motte and bailey of Downend. Thus, working in concert with other castles in Somerset, the Cary ringwork could have formed part of a strategic network designed to afford the Normans control of the county's river systems.

Cary Castle clearly played a part in the Norman's military strategy in Somerset, but the story no longer ends with tactics, strategies and the practical advantages of the site. Norman castle builders, whilst making use of existing features, were also frequently aware of the symbolic importance of the sites they chose. This combination of motives can be seen in the region with the re-use of prehistoric earthworks, such as Castle Neroche (Davidson 1972), Old Sarum (King 1983) and Malmesbury (Haslam 1984). It can be argued

that the Cary ringwork was located at a site of some significance to the Saxons, because of its close association with the source of the River Cary, and there is perhaps even a link to a continuing religious tradition dating from at least the Roman period. During the recent excavations on the castle (Leach and Ellis 2004) a heavily leaded bronze figurine was recovered. It came from the interior of a 3rd century limekiln, and appeared to have been a deliberate deposit made at the time of the limekiln's destruction. The stance and arm action identify the subject as a *lar* (Figure 5.4). *Lares* generally came in pairs, and were deities who served different symbolic purposes in Britain; protecting households, crossroads, districts of towns and sometimes even fields and springs. The discovery of the *lar* appears to indicate that the hill at Cary held a special significance during the Roman period, and this significance may well have continued into later periods.

Returning to the castle, ringworks were relatively quick and easy to erect and provided adequate protection in a campaign situation, but such fortifications were hardly luxurious, and generally once the initial danger had passed they were often revamped to provide the lord with a dwelling befitting his status. Thus all of the ringworks that Walter erected in Somerset were subsequently modified and updated. Castle Batch became a ringwork and bailey, Cockroad Wood developed into a motte with two baileys, Stowey Castle developed into a motte and bailey, whilst Hales Castle became a ringwork and bailey (Prior 2004). The ringwork at Cary appears to have undergone similar changes (Figure 5.3 – Phase 2). The work was doubtless carried out by Walter's successor Ralph Lovell, who held Cary from early in the twefth century (Potter 1955, 44–5; Dunning 1995, 32). In all probability, the first stage of these alterations was the erection of a great tower, or *donjon*, inside the existing fortifications of the ringwork (Gregory 1890). The large quantity of construction debris present (formed from Doulting stone chippings), the thickness of the walls, and the fact that the tower remains include a cross-wall, indicate that it was a fairly substantial and impressive structure. The 'concrete like' deposit of chippings recorded in excavations in 1890 would have been formed as a result of working stone on site to build the tower (Gregory 1890, 172), and is directly paralleled at Ascot-under-Wychwood (Ascot Doilly), Oxfordshire (Jope and Threlfall 1946–7, 1959; Bond 2001). Following the construction of the great tower the excavation evidence suggests that the existing ringwork defences were slighted (Leach and Ellis 2004), and the western half of the ringwork went out of use, its ditch (F707, Phase 1, Figure 5.3) being backfilled.

Fig. 5.4 Lar *figurine recovered during recent excavations at Cary Castle (Photo courtesy of Peter Leach).*

took on the outward appearance of a motte. Any medieval lord worth his salt owned a motte and bailey castle and Ralph Lovell, who obviously aspired to own one, appears to have intentionally manipulated the landscape in an effort to create one. The great keep on its landscaped mound would have been clearly visible from across the plain to the west, serving as an impressive symbol of status and lordly power.

Once the landscaping was complete, the digging of the hollow continued on a north-west to south-east alignment at a shallower level, forming a V-sectioned cross-ditch separating the inner and outer baileys (Figure 5.3, F705, Phase 2) (Aston and Murless 1978; Leach and Ellis 2004). The earth dug out of this ditch formed a rampart on its south side which would have continued right around the perimeter of the inner bailey (visible today as the crescent-shaped bank to the east). The soil for the rampart derived from ditches cut to further define and enhance the inner bailey earth-work (a section of this ditch is still visible today beyond the crescent-shaped bank). The inner bailey appears to have been further defined by the addition of a revet-ment wall (Figure 5.3, F908, Phase 2) seen running parallel to the defensive ditch (Leach and Ellis 2004).

The combination of excavation results thus suggests that at Cary in the early twelfth century a second stage of development took place (Phase 2). A great tower was constructed, the original ringwork was reduced in size to form an inner bailey – with the outward appear-ance of a motte – and an outer bailey was constructed, probably housing a variety of stone and timber buildings. During this construction period, according to historic sources, the castle was attacked twice. Ralph Lovell ravaged the surrounding countryside in 1138, as Stephen laid siege to Robert of Gloucester's castle at Bristol. The records indicate that Stephen 'lost no time in besieging Cary, and pressing the siege with vigour; throwing, by his machines, showers of missiles and fire, without intermission, among the garrison and reducing them to starvation; so that at last he forced them to surrender on terms of submission and alliance' (Potter 1955, 168–74). It seems likely, following the siege, that Ralph Lovell, having sworn oaths of submission and alliance to Stephen, was allowed to retain his castle. Ralph later declared in favour of Matilda, and in 1147, following the death of Robert, Earl of Gloucester, Cary Castle was again besieged on behalf of Stephen. Henry de Tracy erected a siege castle on Lodge Hill to the south-east of, and overlooking, Cary Castle, the remains of which are still in evidence today. But William, the new Earl of Gloucester, 'arrived suddenly with a mighty host, levelled to the ground what Henry had begun, and compelled him and his men to a shameful retreat' (*ibid.*).

Contemporaneously with the slighting of the ringwork defences, the area immediately surrounding the great tower appears to have been landscaped and a new set of defences constructed. Nineteenth century excavations revealed that the area around the great tower had been covered with many tons of soil, 'of a sandy nature…mixed very largely with dust of Doulting stone, with here and there amongst it small bits of charcoal' (Gregory 1890, 173). The vast majority of this soil appears to have been dug out of the natural hollow to the north-east of the tower. This landscaping seemingly served two purposes. First, on a practical level, it covered the mass of construction debris, thereby removing the necessity to transport the waste material away from the site. Second, on an aesthetic level, by digging away soil from the hollow, raising the height of the ground around the tower, and reducing the size of the perimeter, the inner bailey

There is no mention made of a castle at Cary after the twefth century and it is possible that it was demolished, along with many other baronial strongholds, following the Anarchy. Norman military use of the site can therefore be suggested to have comprised first a ringwork, constructed immediately after the conquest. After which, in the early twefth century, the ringwork ditches were entirely remodelled. The earlier ditches were backfilled, and a new circuit cut. Within the new circuit a stone tower was erected, and its immediate surroundings were landscaped to sharpen the natural slopes beneath it to give the outward impression of a motte, and to further enhance the appearance of the stone tower. Following the sieges of the Anarchy the stone tower was either abandoned or demolished, the defensive ditches were infilled, and the lord's dwelling was shifted to a new location downslope from the tower (Figure 5.3 – Phase 3). The old castle buildings no-doubt being quarried over a long period to provide material for the new manorial centre.

The recent excavations at Cary have thus provided tangible evidence for the existence of an early castle upon the site (*c*.1067), and have demonstrated the form that this early fortification took (an oval-shaped ringwork). In addition, the results, in combination with other archaeological and historical evidence, allow the various stages of the castle's development to be accurately determined and tentatively dated. Evidence also suggests that the castle was probably intended to function in a predominantly military capacity, as its position was tactically and strategically ideal, although the castle does appear to embody some symbolic aspects.

Montacute Castle

Montacute Castle is located in south Somerset (ST 4935 1699), in the centre of the ancient parish of Montacute, 4 miles west of Yeovil, on an isolated conical hill called St Michael's. The hill has been scarped to form a large oval shaped motte, with an outer terrace around three sides, and a bailey on the south-east slopes (Figure 5.5).

A castle at Montacute is first mentioned in 1069, when it was attacked by the men of Somerset and Dorset (Ord. Vit. iv, cap.5, ii.193). According to Domesday Book the first Norman lord to hold Montacute was Robert, Count of Mortain, William the Conqueror's half-brother. Domesday book states 'The Count holds Bishopstone himself, in lordship. His castle, called Montacute, is there' (Williams and Martin 2002, 253). It is likely that the castle was constructed between 1067 and 1069; Domesday Book, by the

Fig. 5.5 Aerial photo of Montacute Castle, 1948 – looking south (copyright English Heritage).

inclusion of the word 'himself', implied that Robert made considerable use of the castle, probably as a permanent residence.

Strategically, the castle at Montacute is reasonably well positioned. It is situated upon the edge of a vast ridge of limestone that scribes a line between the uplands of Dorset and the lowlands of Somerset. It is situated only five miles from the Dorset border, to the south, and 19 miles from the meeting point of the Somerset, Wiltshire and Dorset borders, to the north-east: an important military location, as the greensand escarpment in Selwood Forest is the only place where a large army can easily descend from the uplands of Wiltshire. The castle is also close to the Fosseway running down to Exeter and, as it is only a few miles south of Ilchester, it was within easy striking distance of the routes through Sherborne to Crewkerne and from Ilchester south to Dorchester (Costen 1992, 160). In addition, the castle overlooks the modern A303 road, which is known to have been an important route-way from prehistory onwards (Hollinrake 1991). It is also directly adjacent to another minor road that is almost certainly of Roman origin, which heads south from Ilchester into Dorset (Prior 2000).

Robert's castle at Montacute, like Walter's castle at Cary, clearly played an important role in the Norman's campaign strategy in Somerset. Unlike the castle at Cary however, in terms of its tactical location, the castle at Montacute was very poorly positioned indeed. The castle is hemmed in from south-east to south-west by a curving area of high ground. To the west it is overlooked by the heights of Hedgecock Hill. The castle's bailey extends all the way to the foot of the hill in the south-east, affording it very little protection. There is no elevated escape route, and the nearest potable water supply is 120m south-east of the bailey. Fletcher, discussing the castle at Montacute, states that 'its position, apparently partially obscured by Ham Hill, suggests that it had both a limited impact and significance as a prominent feature in the landscape' (Fletcher 2000, 1). This is all the more puzzling considering that the castle is situated only 500 metres away from one of the largest Iron Age hillforts in England, Ham Hill. Ham Hill was continually occupied from the Mesolithic period until the end of the Roman period due to its strategic importance and natural defensibility, the Romans building first a fort and later a villa in its interior. The ideal position for a castle in this locale was therefore, unquestionably, upon Ham Hill. Strange then that the Normans chose to ignore the strategically significant, tactically superior, hillfort as a site upon which to erect their castle, opting instead for a location that was far less suited to their purpose.

The origins of the settlement at Montacute lay in the estate known as *Logworesbeorh*, *Lodegaresberghe* or *Logderesdone*, in the 7th century. The name probably derived from the personal name '*Logor*', whom William of Malmesbury links to one of the twelve original monks of Glastonbury when St Patrick arrived (Dunning 1974, 212), and the Old English word '*beorg*' meaning 'a hill'. No documents relating to this estate survive from the tenth or first half of the eleventh centuries, but the *Cronica* states that William the Conqueror himself seized *Lodgaresburgh* from Glastonbury Abbey (Townsend 1985). The evidence that Glastonbury Abbey ever held this estate is questionable though, as the documentary evidence is conflicting and cannot be properly substantiated, and other independent evidence survives which seems to indicate that during Cnut's reign Montacute was in the hands of Tovi, the Sheriff of Somerset (Abrams 1996, 160). In Domesday Book the estate is called *Bishopstone* and Robert of Mortain is recorded as holding nine hides there in 1086, which Athelney Abbey held in 1066, Robert obtaining this land in exchange for the manor of Purse Caundle (*Candel*), Dorset. Nothing survives to suggest how the estate might have come to belong to Athelney Abbey. What can be agreed upon nevertheless, is that either William or Robert considered the estate to be of some importance, and took steps in the period immediately following William's coronation to obtain it. The question that needs to be addressed here is why?

The Saxon word '*beorg*' is generally taken to mean 'a hill', it can equally apply to artificial works however, and is often confused with '*byrig*' or '*burh*', 'a fort' or 'stronghold'. The name may therefore suggest some form of pre-Norman defensive works. Significantly, the surviving earthworks of the motte and bailey appear to support this argument. 'St Michael's Hill…has recognisably been carved into a motte or castle mound with a bailey on its ESE side and a wide terrace on the remaining sides, but whether this terrace constituted a lower bailey is not certain…a bank around the base of the motte on the W side appears to be continued as a perimeter feature by terrace works within the bailey; these are incompatible with the bailey and…could suggest an original ?ring-work, possibly pre-Norman' (Somerset Heritage Record PRN.54297). Furthermore, John Leland, Henry VIII's antiquarian, who travelled through the region between 1535 and 1543, recorded the tradition of a Saxon stronghold here. Possibly the reason why Ham Hill was ignored as an ideal castle location, and the reason why either William or Robert was so quick to secure the estate after the coronation, was that St Michael's Hill itself was a place of significance to the West

Saxons. This notion is further supported by the fact that the hill was considered important enough to be given an individual Saxon name ('*Logworesbeorh*'), and was of sufficient merit to warrant claim by the abbeys of Glastonbury and Athelney, and by Tovi, the Sheriff of Somerset.

Why was St Michael's Hill significant, and why did the Saxon's choose to protect it by building a defensive structure of some kind upon its summit? The answer may lie in a manuscript entitled *De Inventione Sanctae Crucis Nostrae* that was written by a canon of Waltham Abbey in the twefth century. The manuscript recounts that in year 1035, during the reign of Cnut, a local blacksmith found a 'miraculous holy cross' buried on top of St Michael's Hill after it was revealed to him in a vision (Pooley 1877). The cross was presented to Tovi, Lord of Montacute and Sheriff of Somerset, who carried the sacred relic by oxen cart to Waltham in Essex where he also owned land, and built a church to house it (Warbis 1900, 9). When Tovi died the church and the cross passed to Harold Godwinson, the future King of England. Harold set great store by the cross, and believed himself to have been miraculously cured of sickness through its powers. He set about enlarging Tovi's church which, in time, grew to become Waltham Abbey. Later, Henry II further enlarged it, as part of his penance for the murder of Thomas à Becket, making it one of England's most powerful abbeys (Adkins 1992).

The Holy Cross, or Holy Rood, became an object of popular veneration and pilgrimage, and Harold apparently believed that its powers would help him in his struggle against the Vikings and the Normans. The manuscript records that Harold prayed before the cross on the eve of the Battle of Hastings, and on the day itself, and that while he lay prostrate on the floor praying for victory the Abbot noticed the head of the Christ bent down instead of up, and because of this ill omen two priests accompanied Harold onto the battlefield (Dean 1973, 5). 'Holy Cross' was the battle cry of Harold's armies both at Hastings and Stamford Bridge, and when Harold was killed at Hastings his body was taken to Waltham Abbey where he was buried; a plain stone slab is believed to mark his grave. 'As for the holy cross, it remains shrouded in mystery. Despite its apparent failure at Hastings, it continued to work miracles and made Waltham Abbey a place of pilgrimage right up to the dissolution of the abbey in 1540' (Adkins 1992, 25); after such times its fate is unknown.

It is feasible then that the hill known as *Logworesbeorh* was a place of immense religious significance to the Saxons, and this may have led to their building some kind of defensive or protective structure upon its summit. Later, the significance of the hill did not escape the attention of the Normans, and by 1068 Robert of Mortain had constructed a substantial motte and bailey upon the site. Phenomenologists have recently argued that some castles functioned iconographically as symbols of Norman power and influence; a role which sometimes transcended their military importance (Johnson 1996, 122–2; Lewis *et al.* 1997, 231; Creighton 2002, 65). The castle at Montacute appears to fall into this category, as its military importance was apparently surpassed by its function as a symbol of Norman dominion. The erection of a castle upon the very spot where the legendary fragment of the 'True Cross' had been found must have inflicted a serious blow to the morale of the defeated Saxons; which was almost certainly the reason for the castle's construction.

It could be argued that the castle perhaps served its purpose a little too well however, as the men of Somerset and Dorset were so enraged by the construction of the castle that in 1069 they rose-up and attacked it – making Montacute one of the few castles in England to ever see military action at the hands of the Saxons. As Trask so poetically stated, 'It was around the walls of this castle on the peaked hill that Englishmen dealt the last blow for the freedom of the western shires…[and] it was there that the last patriotic rising was crushed by the heavy hand of Bishop Geoffrey of Coutances, with the help…of the English forces of the shires and cities which were already conquered' (Trask 1898, 30). Robert's castle at Montacute thus stands in direct contrast to Walter's castle at Cary. Cary Castle was purposefully erected in a position that was both tactically and strategically ideal. Montacute Castle, on the other hand, was constructed in a location that was strategically questionable and tactically poor, the location chosen instead for the negative psychological impact it would have upon the Saxons; the castle, on completion, serving in a symbolic capacity as an emblem of Norman lordship, power and dominion.

Downend Castle

Downend Castle is located in the heart of Somerset (ST 3092 4135), at the extreme western end of the Polden Ridge, between the mouths of the Rivers Parrett and Brue, 1 mile north-east of Bridgwater. The castle itself consists of a motte and bailey (Figure 5.6). The motte was formed by cutting a trench across the terminus of the ridge and scarping what remained into an elliptical mount, and in an adjacent roughly circular field to the north there are three large earthen banks, one of which comprised the defences for the bailey (Figure 5.7).

Fig. 5.6 Aerial photo of Downend Castle – looking east (Photo courtesy of Mick Aston).

A castle at Downend is first mentioned in 1505, with reference to a ditch between 'Pylecherd and Le Baly' (PRO SC2/175/31), but by this date the castle would have been abandoned for centuries. Fortunately, the site was the subject of a small-scale excavation in 1908 (Chater and Major 1910), and pottery from the excavation can be matched to similar Norman wares found at Castle Neroche, nr. Taunton; suggesting a *c.*1100 date for the construction of the castle by the De Columbers family. The De Columbers are credited with establishing the medieval borough of Caput Montis at Downend before 1159 (Aston and Leech 1977, 39).

The association between the castle at Downend and Somerset's rivers was mentioned in the discussion on Cary Castle, above. The navigability of the River Parrett was unquestionably the reason for the erection of the castle at Downend. The Normans recognised early on in their campaign the strategic significance of the gap between the western end of the Polden Hills and the River Parrett; 'the junction of the north-south routes with the sea and river traffic, and the east-west Polden ridgeway' (Aston and Leech 1977, 39). Tactically the site was also ideal, situated between the confluence of two rivers, the Parrett and Brue, and additionally defended north and west by a stream, it was highly defensible. It was also supplied with its own source of potable water (a spring erupts at the foot of the motte). Unsurprisingly, with such a well-positioned castle, once military tensions lessened, the agriculturally rich environs were exploited for their economic potential and a 'New Town', with thriving river port, developed.

It was suggested above that the Normans often made use of existing features when constructing their castles. At Downend the Normans appear to have made use of some existing earthworks when constructing their castle, and in this instance these earthworks constitute the 'downright unusual' mentioned in the title of this paper. It is very uncommon to find evidence for Viking activity in the West Country, but at Downend there does appear to be some.

In 'Bally Field' (Bailey Field), the roughly circular field adjacent to the motte, there are three large earthen banks. One of these banks forms the defences for the bailey, the other two form a large D-shape; a shape not normally associated with Norman castle baileys. The two banks are also out of proportion to the rest of the castle. Significantly, a recent geophysical survey of the site (Figure 5.8) seems to support this argument, as it shows the motte and bailey as a compact unit in the south-east corner and appears to show a continuation of the largest bank, well away from the castle, in the south-west corner of the field. It is feasible then that these earthworks pre-date the Norman castle – the motte and bailey being a later addition.

Viking armies over-wintering in England needed to

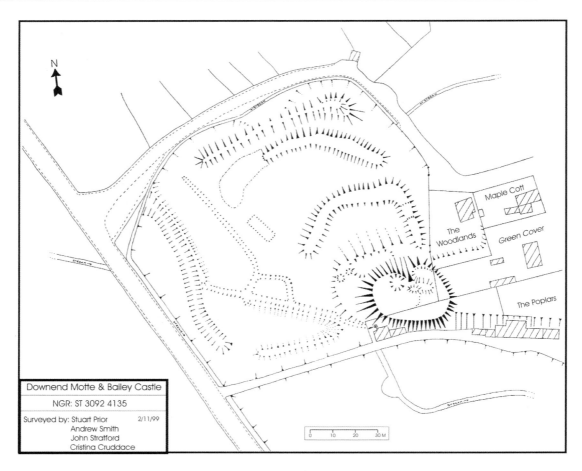

Fig. 5.7 Plan of the motte and bailey castle at Downend, Somerset.

camp in a defensible location. At first they tended to make use of natural islands such as the Isle of Sheppy and Thanet, but from the ninth century there are a number of references in the Anglo-Saxon chronicle to purpose built-fortifications. These forts were probably fairly rudimentary, comprising an earthwork bank-and-ditched enclosure, perhaps with a timber palisade. The chronicle references suggest that the Vikings preferred to make use of the sea or a river or marsh to protect them on one side (Richards 1994, 23). At these sites one might expect to find a D-shaped enclosure.

A study of modern maps covering the Downend area, or a visit to the site, would lead to the misconception that there is no nearby river to complete the proposed Viking D-shaped enclosure. However, the course of the River Parrett was altered in 1677 to make it easier for larger ships to sail into Bridgwater Port (Williams 1970, 93); prior to this the river ran right past the base of the motte, on its southern side, and was therefore in exactly the right position to form the spine of the proposed fortification. Interestingly,

the map which documents the alterations to the river's course also names the area immediately adjacent to the castle – *Viking's Pill.*

It is just possible then that the site at Downend, due to its location on the River Parrett, was attractive to raiders and settlers from a very early period. The Anglo-Saxon chronicle entry for AD845 informs us that 'in this year ealdorman Eanwulf with the men of Somerset and Bishop Ealhstan and ealdorman Osric with the men of Dorset fought against a Danish host at the mouth of the Parrett, and made great slaughter there and won the victory' (*The Parker Chronicle,* Garmonsway 1990, 64). The earthen banks at Downend may then be remnants of a Viking fortification dating from this historic event.

Conclusion

Castellology is currently a thriving discipline, and one that will undoubtedly continue to evolve and develop in years to come. Its new interdisciplinary approach,

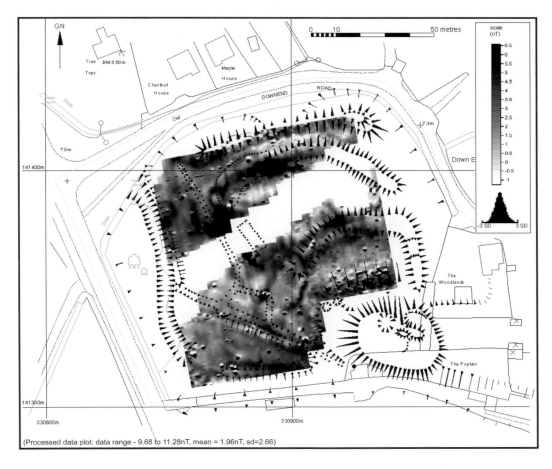

Fig. 5.8 Gradiometer survey of the Downend motte and bailey castle, NGR ST 3092 4135.

methodologies and theories are currently opening up many new avenues for research and as a result, much is being learnt about castles and their place in the medieval world. The castles of Somerset still hold many secrets and future castles studies will surely uncover them, and in doing so will enrich our understanding of the society that created these fortifications and the people that lived in their shadow. Such developments and insights would not be possible however, without the Mick Astons of this world.

Between 1974 and 1978, Mick Aston was the first County Archaeologist for Somerset. During his time there, he set up the county's Sites and Monuments Record, making the task of identifying and analysing Somerset's surviving archaeological remains a manageable task. He was also actively involved in getting many of Somerset's castles listed, in order to conserve and protect them for future generations – Cary and Downend were two such sites. Following this, during his 20 or so years at Bristol, he was instrumental in developing landscape archaeology as a discipline, and meticulously researched and published a vast amount of material on many aspects of medieval archaeology, including monasteries and planned settlements. All of which has greatly added to our knowledge and understanding of the medieval period. To paraphrase Isaac Newton, 'if we see further, it is by standing on the shoulders of giants'.

References

Abrams, L. (1996) *Anglo-Saxon Glastonbury*. Woodbridge, The Boydell Press.

Adkins, L. and Adkins, R. (1992) Mons Acutus and the Miraculous Cross. *The Somerset Magazine*, Oct. 1992, 22–25.

Aston, M. and Leech, R. (1977) *Historic Towns in Somerset*. Tiverton, Somerset.

Aston, M. and Murless, B. (1978) Somerset Archaeology. *Proceedings of the Somerset Natural History and Archaeological Society*, 122, 128.

Austin, D. (1984) The Castle and the Landscape. *Landscape History*, 6, 69–81.

Bond, J. (2001) Earthen castles, outer enclosures and the earthworks at Ascott d'Oilly castle, Oxfordshire. *Oxoniensia*, 66, 43–69.

Bradbury, J. (1998) *The Battle of Hastings*. Woodbridge, The Boydell Press.

Chater, A. G. and Major, A. F. (1910) Excavations at Downend, near Bridgwater, 1908. *Proceedings of the Somerset Natural History and Archaeological Society* 56, 162–174.

Chibnall, M. (ed.) (1969) *The Ecclesiastical History of Oderic Vitalis*, vol. II, Oxford, Clarendon Press.

Costen, M. (1992) *The Origins of Somerset*. Manchester, Manchester University Press.

Coulson, C. (1979) Structural Symbolism in Medieval Castle Architecture. *Journal of the British Archaeological Association*, 132, 73–90.

Coulson, C. (1982) Heirarchism in Conventual Crenellation: An Essay in the Sociology and Metaphysics of Medieval Fortification. *Medieval Archaeology* 26, 69–100.

Coulson, C. (1991) Bodiam Castle, Truth and Tradition *Fortress* 10, 3–15.

Coulson, C. (1992) Some Analysis of the Castle of Bodiam. *Medieval Knighthood* 4, 79–83.

Coulson, C. (1996) Cultural Realities and Reappraisals in English Castle-Study. *Journal of Medieval History* 22.2, 171–208.

Coulson, C. (1998) The Sanctioning of Fortresses in France: Feudal Anarchy or Seigneurial Amity? *Nottingham Medieval Studies* 42, 38–104.

Coulson, C. (2003) *Castles in Medieval Society: Fortresses in England, France and Ireland in the Central Middle Ages*. Oxford, Oxford University Press.

Creighton, O. H. (1999) Early Castles in the Medieval Landscape of Rutland. *Leicestershire Archaeological and Historical Society Proceedings* 73, 20–33.

Creighton, O. H. (1999) 'Early Castles and Rural Settlement Patterns: Insights from Yorkshire and the East Midlands. *The Medieval Settlement Research Group's Annual Report*, 14.

Creighton, O. H. (2000) 'Early Castles in the Medieval Landscape of Wiltshire. *The Wiltshire Archaeological and Natural History Magazine* 93, 105–19.

Creighton, O. H. (2002) *Castles and Landscapes*. London, Continuum.

Creighton, O. H. (1998) *Castles and Landscapes: an Archaeological Survey of Yorkshire and the East Midlands*. Unpublished PhD Thesis, University of Leicester.

Creighton, O. H. and Higham, R. (2003) *Medieval Castles, Shire Archeological Series*, 83, Aylesbury, Shire Publications.

Davidson, B. K. (1972) Castle Neroche: an abandoned Norman fortress in south Somerset. *Proceedings of the Somerset Natural History and Archaeological Society* 116, 16–58.

Davidson, B. K. (1969) Early Earthwork Castles: A New Model. *Château-Gaillard* 3, 37–47.

Dean, D. (1973) *The Legend of the Miraculous Cross of Waltham*. Waltham, Waltham Abbey Historical Society.

Dixon, P. (1990) The Donjon of Knaresborough: The Castle as Theatre. *Château-Gaillard* 14, 121–39.

Dixon, P. and Marshall P. (1993) The Great Tower in the Twelfth Century: The Case of Norham Castle. *Archaeological Journal* 150, 410–33.

Dunning, R. (1995) *Somerset Castles*. Tiverton, Somerset Books.

Dunning, R. (ed.) (1974) *Victoria County History of the County of Somerset*, Volume 3. Oxford, Oxford University Press for the University of London, Institute of Historical Research.

Fletcher, M. (2000) *An Archaeological Survey of St Michael's Hill, Montacute, Somerset*. Exeter, Unpublished English Heritage Report.

Garmonsway, G. (ed.) (1990) *The Anglo-Saxon Chronicle*. London, J.M. Dent & Sons Ltd.

Gregory, R. R. C. (1890) Notes on the Discovery of the Site of Castle Cary Castle. *Proceedings of the Somerset Natural History and Archaeological Society* 36, 168–74.

Haslam, J. (1984) *Anglo-Saxon Towns in Southern England*. Chichester, Phillimore.

Heslop, T. A. (1991) Orford Castle, Nostalgia and Sophisticated Living. *Architectural History* 34, 36–58.

Higham, R. and Barker, P. (1992) *Timber Castles*. London, Batsford Books.

Hollinrake, C. and Hollinrake N. (1991) *Wincanton by-pass report*. Unpublished DBA and excavation report, No. 12. Somerset County Council.

Hughes, M. (1989) Hampshire Castles and the Landscape 1066–1200. *Landscape History*, 11, 27–60.

Johnson, M. (1996) *The Archaeology of Capitalism*. Oxford, Blackwell.

Johnson, M. (2002) *Behind the Castle Gate – From Medieval to Renaissance*. London, Routledge.

Jope, E. M. and Threlfall, R. I. (1946–7) Recent Mediaeval Finds in the Oxfordshire District: The 12th Century Castle at Ascot Doilly, Oxon. 1946. *Oxoniensia*, 11–12, 165–7.

Jope, E. M. and Threlfall, R. I. (1959) The Twelfth Century Castle at Ascot Doilly, Oxfordshire; Its history and excavation. *The Antiquaries' Journal*, 39, 219–70.

King, D. J. C. (1983) *Castellarium Anglicanum* (2 vols). New York, Kraus International Publications.

Leach, P. and Ellis, P. (2004) Roman and Medieval Remains at Manor Farm, Castle Cary. *Proceedings of the Somerset Archaeological and Natural History Society*, 147, 80–128.

Lewis, C. Mitchell-Fox, P. and Dyer, C. (1997) *Village, Hamlet and Field: Changing Medieval Settlements in Central England*. Manchester, Manchester University Press.

Liddiard, R. (2000a) *Landscapes of Lordship – Norman Castles and the Countryside in Medieval Norfolk, 1066–1200*. BAR, British Series (no.309), Oxford, Archaeopress.

Liddiard, R. (2000b) Castle Rising, Norfolk: A 'Landscape of Lordship'? *Anglo-Norman Studies* 22, 169–186.

Liddiard, R. (2000c) Population density and Norman castle building: some evidence from East Anglia. *Journal for the Society of Landscape Studies* 22, 37–46.

Liddiard, R. (ed.) (2003) *Anglo-Norman Castles*. Woodbridge, The Boydell Press.

Marten-Holden, L. (2001) Dominion in the Landscape: Early Norman Castles in Suffolk. *History Today*, 51(4), 46–52.

Meade, Rev. P. (1856–7) Castle Cary. *Proceedings of the Somerset Archaeological and Natural History Society* 7, 82–99.

Meade, Rev. P. (1877–8) History of Castle Cary. *Proceedings of the Somerset Archaeological and Natural History Society* 24, 50–2.

O'Keeffe, T. (2000) *Medieval Ireland – An Archaeology*. Stroud, Tempus Publishing Ltd.

Pooley, C. (1877) *A Historical and Descriptive Account of the Old Stone Crosses of Somerset*. London, Longmans Green.

Potter, K. R. (ed. and trans.) (1955) *Gesta Stephani, the Deeds of Stephen*. Nelson's Medieval Texts, London, Nelson.

Pounds, N. J. G. (1990) *The Medieval Castle in England and Wales: A Social and Political History.* Cambridge, Cambridge University Press.

Prior, S. J. (2006) *The Norman Art of War: a few well positioned castles.* Stroud, Tempus Publishing Ltd.

Prior, S. J. (1999) *The Role of the Norman Castle in the Conquest and Subjugation of Somerset.* Unpublished BA Dissertation, University of Bristol.

Prior, S. J. (2000) *Early Castles in the West Country Landscape – Strategy or Symbolism?* Unpublished MA Dissertation, University of Bristol.

Prior, S. J. (2004) *Winning Strategies – An Archaeological Study of Norman Castles in the Landscapes of Somerset, Monmouthshire & Co. Meath, 1066–1186.* Unpublished PhD Thesis, University of Bristol.

Richards, J. (1991) *Viking Age England.* London, English Heritage & Batsford Books.

Somerset Fry, P. (1996) *Castles of Britain and Ireland.* Newton Abbot, David and Charles.

Townsend, D. (1985) '*Chronica Sive Antiquitates Glastoniensis Ecclesie*'; *The Chronicle of Glastonbury Abbey.* An Edition, Translation and Study of John of Glastonbury's… Woodbridge, Boydell Press.

Trask, C. (1898) *Norton Sub-Hamdon.* Taunton, Barnicott and Pearce.

Warbis, A. T. (1900) *Fragments of South Somerset – Montacute.* Yeovil, The Viking Press.

Wheatley A. (2004) *The Idea of the Castle.* Woodbridge, York Medieval Press, Boydell and Brewer.

Williams, A. and Martin, G. H. (eds) (2002) *Domesday Book – A Complete Translation.* London, Penguin Books.

Williams, M. (1970) *The Draining of the Somerset Levels.* Cambridge, Cambridge University Press.

Chapter 6

The Premonstratensian Canons in South-Western France: A Preliminary Survey

James Bond

Introduction

Attempting to investigate an aspect of medieval monasticism in south-western France from a base in north Somerset is fraught with difficulties. The task might almost have been easier in the high middle ages, when Gascony and Guyenne were in English hands and ships plied regularly between Bristol and Bordeaux! The following discussion makes no pretence at being a product of systematic research; it is merely an opportunistic reflection of a personal interest, based upon exploratory tours in 1993 and 2003 (undertaken without any anticipation of publication at the time), and upon a very limited investigation of the secondary literature. There has been no opportunity to revisit the sites discussed to study them more thoroughly, no archival work has been undertaken in France, and even access to French academic publications and adequate large-scale maps has been problematic.

In normal circumstances publication of the following text would have to be regarded as premature, but I would plead two extenuating reasons for offering it at this stage. The first relates to the special purpose of the conference at which this paper was delivered, to honour Mick Aston, an inspirational colleague who has also been a great friend for nearly forty years. In acknowledgement of Mick's huge contribution to landscape archaeology and monastic studies, I wanted to attempt something which would reflect both his long-term francophilia and his interests in the geographical spread of the monastic orders. Mick and I were both strongly influenced in the 1960s by one of our tutors in the Department of Geography at the University of Birmingham, Robin Donkin, who had already then published many scattered papers on the European impact of the Cistercian order, though the consolidation of his work in book form did not appear until some years later (Donkin 1978). Mick has follow-ed Donkin in stressing the pan-European nature of medieval monasticism and the importance of the continental perspective in understanding developments in England; and some of the products of his legendary tours of French monastic sites in his van have appeared in his own published works, most conspicuously in his paper on the Carthusian order in the *festschrift* for Philip Rahtz edited by Martin Carver (Aston 1993), and in his discussion of the new monastic orders in Europe after the eleventh century, which appeared in the volume *Monastic Archaeology* which he edited with Graham Keevill and Teresa Hall (Aston 2001).

My second justification, and my particular reason for exploring the impact of the Premonstratensian canons, is that, by comparison with the Cistercians, and even with Mick's Carthusians, this important order has still, as yet, attracted only limited attention (cf. Kirkfleet 1943). The standard historical work on the order in England (Colvin 1951) is over half a century old, though this has recently been reinforced by a thorough and valuable study of the English houses in the later fifteenth century (Gribbin 2001); and, while important excavations have been reported from several sites (e.g. Streeten 1983), there has been no synthesis on the architecture of the order since Clapham (1923), and only a few scattered works on the estates of individual houses (e.g. Colvin 1939; Seymour 1977). Apart from a handful of works on individual sites (e.g. John 1953; Caviness 1990) hardly anything has yet been written in the English language on the order's role in France, or, indeed, on any other part of the continent. So great has been the neglect by English writers of this topic that even the most superficial of contributions is a small step forward. For these reasons I offer to Mick this preliminary exploration of the Premonstratensian settlements in a part of France which he knows so well.

The Premonstratensians in Europe

The Premonstratensians were an order of regular canons who followed a modified version of the rule of St Augustine of Hippo. They became one of the most successful of the new religious groups to emerge out of the ferment of reform which swept through the church in western Europe during the eleventh and twelfth centuries. The order was founded by St Norbert of Xanten, who settled his first community at Prémontré near Laon in 1120. During the following 130 years they established a network of houses extending from Ireland to the Holy Land and from Scandinavia and the Baltic to Spain and Italy (Bond 1993). Like the monks of the near-contemporary Cistercian reform, by whom they were strongly influenced, they preferred to settle in remote places (at least in western Europe), and were often cast in the role of pioneer farmers, clearing woodland and draining marshland.

Hugh de Fosses, Norbert's successor at Prémontré, was a capable administrator and legislator, who ensured the integrity of the order by persuading its autonomous abbots of the need for a centralised organisation with an annual general chapter meeting, arrangements for visitations, and a system of filiation on the Cistercian model. Normally each mother-house retained supervisory responsibility for its own colonies. Occasionally independent houses of some other order became affiliated to the Premonstratensians, and they too were slotted into place in the filiation structure (Figure 6.1).

As the Premonstratensian order expanded across Europe, it organised its houses into about 30 provinces called *circaries*, each under the charge of a vicar-general. The circaries, which often spanned contemporary political divides, provided a basis for visitation and for the appointment of representatives to attend the order's general chapters at Prémontré. The modern area of France was covered by about ten medieval circaries, half of which also included houses then and now in neighbouring states.

The distribution of Premonstratensian houses in France is most strongly concentrated in the north and north-east, in Artois, Picardy, the Ile de France, Champagne and Lorraine. By comparison with the Cluniacs and Cistercians they made relatively little impact in the centre, south and west of the country. There is, however, an isolated concentration in the south-west, between the Garonne and the Pyrenees, which formed the basis for the Gascon circary (Figure 6.2).

Until recently the only modern gazetteer of Premonstratensian houses across Europe was that published in Latin by Fr Norbert Backmund (Backmund 1949, 1952, 1956). Since 1993, however, the historical and bibliographical information available on the houses in France has greatly been enhanced by the gazetteer of Fr Bernard Ardura. Much of what follows has drawn very heavily from his invaluable work.

The Circary of Gascony

The Gascon circary contained about a dozen abbeys, roughly the same number of small dependent priories and three nunneries, though it is difficult to provide precise figures, for reasons which will become apparent. Of the houses within the circary, only eleven lay within the bounds of Gascony proper, mostly concentrated in the southern half of the duchy and extending into the Basque country (Lalanne 1992). Two more houses lay to the north of the Gironde estuary in the Saintonge, another four lay to the east in the county of Toulouse and one lay beyond the Rhône in Provence (Figure 6.2). The Gascon circary also extended over the Pyrenees into the medieval kingdoms of Navarre, Castile and Aragon, where there were at least half a dozen more houses, perhaps as many as ten, now in Spain; but limited space will exclude much consideration of the houses south of the Pyrenees in this paper.

Eleanor of Aquitaine's marriage to Henry Plantagenet in 1152 brought Aquitaine and Gascony under English rule, and their son, Richard, created Duke of Aquitaine in 1169, did establish a small Premonstratensian foundation at Génétouze near La Roche-sur-Yon in the Vendée. In 1196, as King Richard I, he supplemented its endowments in thanks for his release from captivity at the hands of Leopold of Austria; as a result of its increased wealth it was promoted to abbatial status, and two years later the community moved to a new site on the edge of the coastal marshes at Lieu-Dieu-en-Jard (Ardura 1993, 347–51). However, none of the Premonstratensian houses in the Gascon circary were actually of English foundation, though many of them lay in territories which fell under Plantagent rule. Subsequently some of them found themselves passing from English to French controlled territory and then back again with the fluctuating fortunes of the Hundred Years War.

The precise status of some houses is hard to ascertain, and status was sometimes liable to change. Several of the early abbeys (La Casedieu, Béhaune and possibly also Pleineselve) seem initially to have been double houses containing both canons and nuns; this practice was discouraged after 1137 when the general chapter issued the first of several decrees that the sisters should be removed to separate convents of their

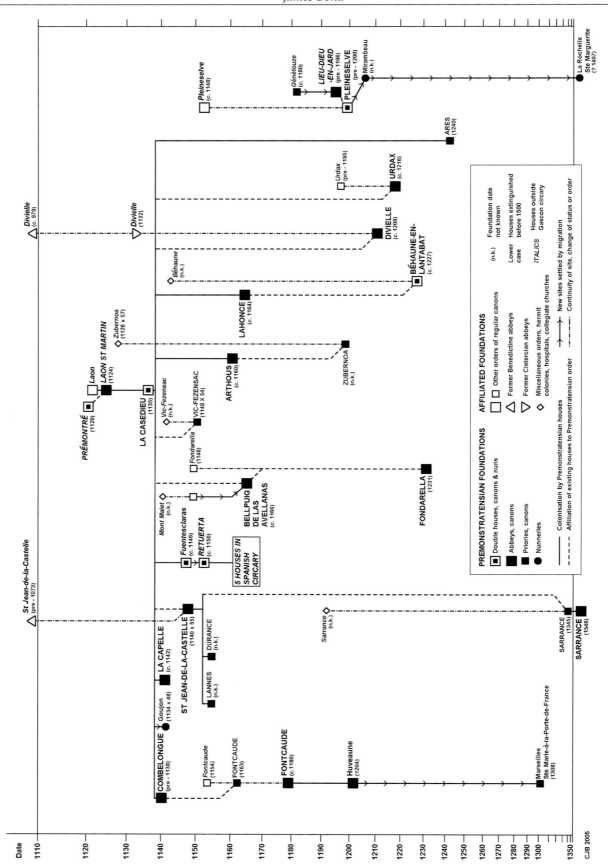

Fig. 6.1 Premonstratensian houses in the Gascon circary: filiation table.

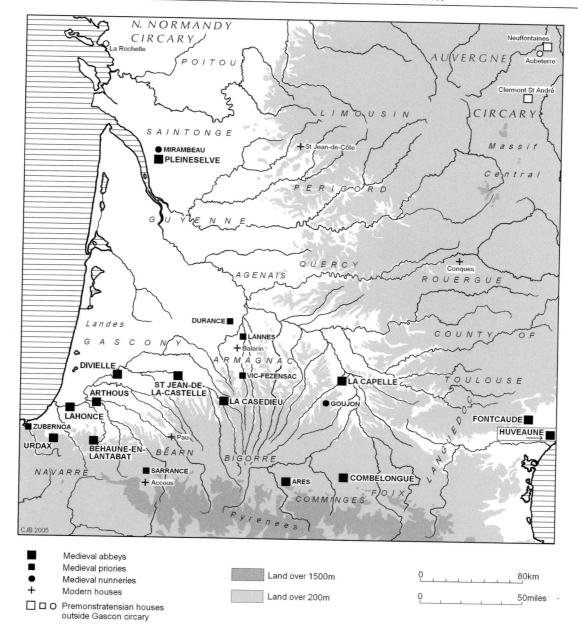

Fig. 6.2 Location of Premonstratensian houses in south-western France.

own. A couple of the smaller priories were subsequently promoted to the status of abbeys: Fontcaude gained its independence from Combelongue in about 1180, while Sarrance nominally became an abbey in 1546, though in practice it continued to be administered from La Castelle, the abbot of which assumed the title of 'abbot of St Jean and Sarrance'. At the lower end of the scale, some priories such as Durance never seem to have contained more than one or two canons,

and in effect were little more than granges. The priories of Sarrance, Vic-Fezensac and Zubernoa, were associated with hospitals or pilgrim chapels on the routes to Santiago de Compostela.

In several instances the Premonstratensians took up residence on a site previously occupied by some other order: St Jean-de-la-Castelle had been founded as a Benedictine house before 1073, but this was derelict by about 1140–55, when the land was given to the canons. Divielle had initially been founded for the Cistercians, Fontcaude and Pleineselve for Augustinians, while Vic-Fezensac had initially been a collegiate church. In other cases the Premonstratensian presence was itself relatively short-lived: the nuns of Goujon, under Premonstratensian regulation for little more than two decades, had adopted Cistercian customs by 1165.

The Premonstratensian Campaigns Against Heresies

On several occasions during the decades which followed the settlement of Prémontré, the episcopal authorities found it expedient to encourage Norbert and his followers to direct their energies not just against the pagan frontier, but also against perceived enemies within the church. In 1124, Bishop Burchard of Cambrai had appealed to Norbert for assistance against the deviant doctrines of the preacher Tanchelm of Antwerp, who had gained considerable support in the Low Countries through his attacks upon clerical privileges and property. Tanchelm himself had been murdered by a priest wielding an axe in 1115, but his views continued to attract a popular following, and the provost and canons of the collegiate church of St Michael in Antwerp had come under his influence. Bishop Burchard removed them, and Norbert travelled to Antwerp with a dozen canons of Prémontré to take over the church and restore the regular celebration of the Eucharist.

The Premonstratensians were first brought to the south of France to help to counter the influence of another heretic preacher, Pierre de Bruis. Most of our knowledge of the life of this man comes from a treatise condemning his teaching, issued by Peter the Venerable, abbot of Cluny (1122–56). Pierre de Bruis began his career as a radical village priest in the Cottian Alps. Having been ejected from his parish shortly before 1120, he spent a decade in relative obscurity, preaching in the mountain settlements around Embrun in the upper valley of the Durance. By the 1130s, however, he was becoming a more dangerous figure, touring through the County of Toulouse, attacking many of the ceremonies and traditions of the established church. He accepted the authority only of the Gospels, rejecting the rest of the New Testament and the Old Testament in its entirety. He preached against the validity of the Eucharist, infant baptism, and offerings of prayers for the dead. He claimed that God had no use for churches, and would respond just as readily to prayers from a market-place, stable or tavern, so long as they were deserving. In particular, he rejected the veneration of the Cross as the symbol of the torture and death of Christ, and called upon his followers to break up and burn crucifixes wherever they found them. He and his followers were reported on occasions to have dragged monks from their monasteries, and to have defied the church's strictures on fasting by ostentatiously eating meat on Good Friday. His influence spread southwards to Arles and Narbonne and westwards into Gascony.

Pierre de Bruis met his end some time between 1131 and 1140 at St Gilles in Languedoc. The church had brought great prosperity to this town, since it was both a significant pilgrimage centre in its own right and an important station on one of the routes to Santiago de Compostela. Some of the citizens of St Gilles became so incensed when Pierre urged them to burn all their crucifixes that they pushed him into his own bonfire and burnt him alive (Fearns, ed. 1968; Brooke 1975, 63–6, 140–42; Brooke and Brooke 1984, 63–4,103; Lambert 1992, 47–9). However, Pierre's doctrines continued to be promoted in modified form by Henri of Lausanne, a former Cluniac monk, who drew large crowds in towns throughout Aquitaine, Gascony and the county of Toulouse. The Petrobruisian heresy was finally stamped out when Bernard of Clairvaux undertook a preaching tour through the same region in 1145.

However, the south of France continued to provide fertile ground for challenges to the authority of the catholic church. Although the early evangelical zeal of the Premonstratensians was generally giving way to a more settled, contemplative way of life, individual abbots continued to play a prominent part in the struggle against later heresies. Bernard, first abbot of Fontcaude (1177–88) was the author of a tract against the Waldensians, another group of wandering preachers whose influence had spread from Lyon, their place of origin, down the Rhône valley into the Languedoc (Verres 1955). In the following century the growing popularity of the Cathar heresy posed an even more serious threat to the established church. Navarre d'Aqs, Premonstratensian abbot of Combelongue, became bishop of Couserans in 1208 and, unlike many of his episcopal colleagues in the Languedoc, he was a fervent and active campaigner against the Cathars. So, too, was Jean, abbot of La Capelle. Although the baton was soon to be handed on from the canons to the new order of Dominican friars, St Dominic himself had stayed several times at La Capelle, and had been inspired to borrow from the statutes of Prémontré when drafting those of his own Order of Preachers.

The Abbeys of La Casedieu and Pleineselve

The first Premonstratensian settlement in the south of

France was the abbey of Notre-Dame at La Casedieu, on the borders of the counties of Bigorre and Pardiac, 23 miles north of Tarbes, near the confluence of the Rivers Boués and Arros. In 1135 Guillaume d'Andozille, Archbishop of Auch, hindered in his attempts to reform his diocese by the lingering influence of the Petrobruisians, and knowing of Norbert's success against the followers of Tanchelm, prevailed upon Abbot Gauthier, the prior-general of the order, to despatch a group of canons from St Martin's at Laon. Gauthier had been appointed to the abbacy of Laon in 1124 by Norbert himself, and the abbey of St Martin's ranked second only to Prémontré in the hierarchy of the order. Archbishop Guillaume further enlisted the support of Pierre, Count of Bigorre, and land for the new abbey was provided by Bernard of Troucens, lord of Peyrusse, Tourdun and Juillac.

Fig. 6.3 The abbey church of Ste Marie-Madeleine at Pleineselve (Dép. Gironde, Dioc. Bordeaux): the Romanesque east end.

The first canons of Laon to arrive in Gascony were led by one Bernard, who ruled for 13 years as abbot at La Casedieu (1135–48). The first church was consecrated in 1157. The number of canons grew, from 22 in 1298 to at least 30 by 1340, but this was the zenith of its fortunes (Gaubin 1904; Backmund 1956, 171–4; Ardura 1993, 163–6).

All but one of the remaining houses of Premonstratensian canons in the Gascon circary were regarded as daughter-houses of La Casedieu. The exception was the abbey of Ste-Marie-Madeleine at Pleineselve in the Saintonge (Figure 6.3), which is located within a straggling village amongst woods and vineyards on the low hills east of the Gironde estuary. This was founded in about 1148 by Godefroid de Louroux, archbishop of Bordeaux, himself an Augustinian canon, and it may initially have been an Augustinian house, or perhaps a hospital serving the main western pilgrimage road to Santiago de Compostela. Premonstratensian canons had been introduced there before 1200, and some sources suggest that it was colonised directly from Prémontré itself, though at a later date there is some evidence that it was treated as a dependency of Lieu-Dieu-en-Jard in the circary of North Normandy. The abbey became moderately prosperous, but internal corruption led to the deposition of Abbot Ayquelin Ayroud in 1327 and the dispersal of the canons around other houses of the circary, and it never fully recovered from this blow (Backmund 1956, 191–3; Peyrous 1982; Ardura 1993, 420–22)

Daughter-houses of La Casedieu

Like other early Premonstratensian foundations, La Casedieu initially housed both canons and sisters, but the nuns were soon removed, probably to Goujon (see below). Within a century La Casedieu had sent out colonies to establish seven daughter-houses, and had also taken four other pre-existing houses under its wing as dependencies.

The first daughter-house of La Casedieu, recorded as such in 1143, was at Combelongue in the Couserans (Figure 6.4), 45 miles south of Toulouse, an isolated site near the head of the River Baup in the wooded foothills of the Pyrenees. According to tradition this was founded shortly before 1138 by Arnaud de Austeia, Count of Pailhas; another of his family, Antoine, became its first abbot (Backmund 1956, 175–7; Ferras 1992; Ardura 1993, 195–9).

The second, La Capelle, was founded in about 1142 by Bernard Jourdain de l'Isle, whose son, Jourdain, confirmed and added to its endowments. This lay within the commune of Merville, about 10 miles north-

Fig. 6.4 The abbey church of St Laurent at Combelongue (Dép. Ariège, Dioc. Couserans, now Pamiers): view from the northeast.

west of Toulouse, an isolated site in flattish open country not far from the confluence of the River Save with the Garonne (Backmund 1956, 168–70; Ardura 1993, 160–63).

The priory of Notre-Dame in the small town of Vic-Fezensac, about 15 miles east of Auch, originated as a hospital on one of the pilgrimage roads to Santiago de Compostela. It was administered by a master or provost, assisted by lay brothers and perhaps one or two canons. Its early history is obscure, but it was given to the abbey of La Casedieu some time between 1148 and 1154. Its church was made available for parochial use, and by 1456 the abbey had made provision for up to 12 canons there (Bacqué 1914; Backmund 1956, 203–4; Ardura 1993, 568–9).

The abbey of Arthous occupied an isolated site on the edge of wooded hills on the southern side of the Gaves valley, about 20 miles east of Bayonne (Figure 6.5). It was founded in about 1160 by Martin Sancho de Domezain, and it soon acquired a modest prosperity through donations by the bishops of Dax, the viscounts of Béarn and other local noble families (Backmund, 1956, 159–61; Lambert, 1956; Peyrous, 1972; Ardura, 1993, 81–3).

La Casedieu's next daughter-house was St Jean-de-la-Castelle, yet another isolated site, in the Adour valley, 4 miles below Aire sur l'Adour (see Figure 6.17,

below). A Benedictine monastery, founded here before 1073, had been abandoned by the early twelfth century. Although there is no authentic documentation relating to the Premonstratensian house before 1227, it appears that the lands of the abandoned Benedictine monastery were used by Pierre, count of Bigorre, co-founder of La Casedieu itself, and his wife Beatrice, for the endowment of the new abbey some time between about 1140 and 1155. Further substantial endowments came from the viscounts of Béarn and Marsan and from the bishops of Aire, which resulted in St Jean-de-la-Castelle becoming the most prosperous abbey of the circary (Légé 1878; Backmund 1956, 194–6; Ardura 1993, 476–80).

In contrast with the relative remoteness of the other daughter-houses of La Casedieu, the abbey of Lahonce (Basque *Lehonza*) (Figure 6.6) is within a loose-knit village set amidst rolling wooded hills and orchards in the Basque country, on the south bank of the River Adour, about 4 miles east of Bayonne. Its origins are far from clear, but the necrology of La Casedieu attributes its foundation to Bertrand, viscount of Labourd, in about 1164. There is no authentic contemporary record of its existence before 1227. Although it had the status of an abbey, its income was small, and it never seems to have had many resident canons (Backmund 1956, 187–9; Biard 1992; Ardura 1993, 315–9).

Fig. 6.5 *The abbey church of Notre-Dame at Arthous (Dép. Landes, Dioc. Aire et Dax): view from the south-east.*

Fig. 6.6 *The abbey of Notre-Dame at Lahonce (Dép. Pyrénées-Atlantiques, Dioc.Bayonne) from the east, showing the cloister corbels of the west range and the bellcote and apsidal east end of the church.*

The abbey of Divielle stands alone amidst an area of dispersed settlement in flat, partly wooded country on the River Louts just above its confluence with the Adour, about 7 miles east of Dax. Tracing its history is difficult because of the loss of its archives. According to tradition the first monastic house was founded in the late tenth century. In about 1132 the Cistercians acquired the site, but failed to recruit sufficient numbers to establish a working community, so handed it over to the Premonstratensians. Navarre d'Acqs, former abbot of Combelongue, then bishop of Couserans, was the son of Arnaud-Raymond, viscount of Dax, and it seems to have been through his intervention that a group of canons was eventually sent from La Casedieu to take possession of the site in about 1209. With the support of donations from local aristocratic families, the abbey rapidly achieved some prosperity, with a community of about ten canons (Degert 1924a, 1924b; Backmund 1956, 177–80; Ardura 1993, 217–20).

La Casedieu also had three or four dependencies in northern Spain. In about 1146 it sent out a colony to Fuentesclaras, which soon moved to Retuerta near Valladolid in Old Castile and subsequently established several daughter-houses of its own. In Aragon a group of canons occupying a former hermitage on Mont Malet near Vilanova del Sol had already established a colony at Fondarella in 1148 before moving themselves to Bellpuig de las Avellanas soon after 1166, at which time they were placed under Premonstratensian rule. Then, in about 1216, a pilgrim hospital at Urdax in Navarre (Basque *Urdazubi*), probably formerly served by Augustinian canons, became incorporated into the Premonstratensian order as a priory affiliated to La Casedieu. Two years later it gained its independence

as the Abbey of San Salvador, and became an important and influential house (Ardura 1993, 534–8).

The last of the daughter-houses of La Casedieu lay near the head of the Garonne in the central Pyrenees. In 1240 Pierre de Malavicina gave land at Ares or Arros to the abbot of La Casedieu on condition that divine office be regularly celebrated there, failing which the donation would revert to him or to his successors. A small priory dedicated to St Anne was established, but little is known of its history, and even its site seems uncertain. Backmund (1956, 205) located it at Arros in the Valle de Aran on the Spanish side of the border, whereas Ardura (1993, 80–1) has placed it in the Pyrenean foothills 17 miles to the north, on the Col des Ares in the commune of Cazanous in Comminges.

Daughter-houses of Combelongue, Arthous, St Jean-de-la-Castelle and Lahonce

Five of the daughter-houses of La Casedieu in due course either adopted or generated further dependencies of their own. The first to do so was probably Combelongue, which in 1164 took over responsibility for the priory of Fontcaude in the Languedoc, about 12 miles north-west of Béziers (Figure 6.7). This site is isolated amidst scrubland in the commune of Cazedarnes, but with vineyards and arable land

Fig. 6.7 The abbey of Notre-Dame at Fontcaude (Dép. Hérault, Dioc. Narbonne, now Montpellier): the dormitory range and apsidal east end of the church.

nearby. Ten years before, the church of this place had been given by Bernard and Arnould de Clairmont to the Augustinian canons of Valcros for the foundation of a new priory. Dissatisfied by its progress, the founders decided in 1163 to transfer the endowments to the canons of Combelongue, and Pope Alexander III confirmed Fontcaude as a Premonstratensian house the following year. Some of the canons of Valcros, attracted by the stricter rule and finding opposition to reform in their own community, seem to have decided to move to Fontcaude. The increase in numbers led to Fontcaude being promoted to the status of an abbey in about 1180, and it retained a dozen canons in 1276 (Backmund 1956, 181–4; Vignes 1976; Barthes 1979; Ardura 1993, 256–60).

In 1204 the bishop of Marseilles decided to establish a Premonstratensian priory in the southern suburb of the city, near the mouth of the River Huveaune, from which it took its name. The foundation charter names two men, Amans and Guillaume, as founders; Amans became the first prior and Guillaume succeeded him as first abbot in 1230. Abbot Marc of Fontcaude appended his seal to the charter, but the bishop reserved numerous prerogatives to himself. In the early catalogues of the order Huveaune was not included among the houses of the Gascon circary and administratively was treated as a daughter-house of Prémontré; but in 1249 the General Chapter confirmed the rights and duties of the abbot of Fontcaude there. Completion of the buildings was long delayed, and the canons suffered frequent harassment from pirates and brigands. For this reason, in 1308 the abbot petitioned the pope for consent to transfer his community inside the walls of Marseilles, to occupy premises alongside the church of Ste Marie-à-la-Porte-de-France (Dailliez 1967; Ardura 1993, 294–6).

The hospital of Zubernoa or Subernoy was located at Hendaye, where the Santiago pilgrimage road crossed from the duchy of Gascony over the River Bidassoa into the Basque territory of Guipuzcoa. A charter of 1305 attributed its foundation to King Alfonso VII of Castile (1126–57). Initially it seems to have been served by a Spanish military order, the Order of the Red Sword, then by the Hospitaller Order of the Holy Spirit; finally it became incorporated with the abbey of Arthous and administered by the Premonstratensian canons there and at Lahonce (Nogaret 1930; Ardura 1993, 576–7).

The abbey of St Jean-de-la-Castelle was responsible for three dependent priories, all of obscure origin. Lannes is an isolated site surrounded by plum orchards amongst rolling hills about 20 miles south-west of Agen (Figure 6.8 and see Figure 6.15), while Durance is even more isolated in a small clearing

Fig. 6.8 The priory church of Lannes (Dép. Lot-et-Garonne, Dioc. Agen) from the south-west.

within the eastern margins of the vast Landes forest, just north of the small bastide of the same name. In neither case has any record of their foundation survived, and, despite the presence of substantial buildings, Durance may never have been more than a grange (Backmund 1956, 189–90, 206–7; Ardura 1993, 319–20, 232). Sarrance is a small village in Béarn in the northern foothills of the Pyrenees, where the valley of the River Aspe provides access towards the Somport Pass (Figure 6.9). Not only was this on one of the main roads to Compostela, in addition a statue of the Virgin discovered by a spring there had long been a pilgrimage venue in its own right. A church and pilgrim hospital already existed when in September 1314 the viscount of Béarn arranged for Abbot Sanctius of St Jean to enter into possession and to despatch a priest there to provide daily masses. Under Premonstratensian control, the ancient hospital flourished, a regular priory developed, and pilgrim visitors included Gaston Phoebus, viscount of Béarn, Charles II of Navarre, Pedro IV of Aragon and Louis XI of France. In 1445 Pope Eugenius IV offered plenary indulgences to those who made the pilgrimage to Sarrance (Menjoulet 1859; Dubarat 1892–1901; Backmund 1956, 196–8; Ardura 1993, 496–9).

Finally, in the small village of Béheaune-en-Lantabat in the rolling hills of the Basque country

about 25 miles south-east of Bayonne, there was an ancient independent mixed community not attached to any regular order. In about 1227 Pierre Arnaud, baron of Luxa, Ostabaret and Lantabat, supported by his nephew, Arnaud de Luxa, the local lord, decided to convert this to a regular Premonstratensian house and placed it under the supervision of the abbot of Lahonce (Figure 6.10).

Houses of Premonstratensian Nuns

Two medieval nunneries were founded within the Gascon circary. Both were a product of the removal of nuns from an earlier dual house, and neither was of much importance. The first was established some time between 1134 and 1148 at Goujon, an isolated site located in wooded hills about 18 miles west of Toulouse. The founder, Bernard, abbot of La Casedieu, seems to have resettled the sisters of his own abbey there, assisted by a benefaction from the seignurial family of Bonrepos-sur-Aussonelle, 3 miles away. The community remained under Premonstratensian regulation for little more than 20 years, then lapsed, probably due to the practical difficulties of support from a parent abbey 45 miles away, if not its outright indifference. Some time around 1165–7 Goujon passed under the control of the Cistercian abbey of l'Oraison-

Fig. 6.9 The village and priory of Notre-Dame at Sarrance (Dép. Pyrénées-Atlantiques, Dioc. Oloron-Ste-Marie, now Bayonne).

Fig. 6.10 The priory church of St Pierre at Béhaune-en-Lantabat (Dép. Pyrénées-Atlantiques, Dioc. Bayonne): the south wall, showing the cloister corbels.

Dieu near Muret; later, in 1454, it became incorporated with the Cistercian abbey of Gimont as a dependent priory of monks (Fonds 1860; Gabent 1895; Leblanc 1954; Ardura 1993, 282–3).

The second nunnery, at Mirambeau in the Saintonge, is known only from a mention of its prioress, Petronilla de Flayaco, in a letter of Pope Urban V in 1373 (Laurent, ed. 1854, ii, 1054, no.621). From its proximity to the abbey of Pleineselve it seems likely that it was founded for sisters removed from that house. In 1407 Pleineselve was wrecked during the Hundred Years War, and the nuns may have taken refuge in La Rochelle, since the nunnery of Ste Marguerite there, otherwise of undocumented origin, originally belonged to the Gascon circary. In 1538 the general chapter of the order placed the sisters of Ste Marguerite under the authority of the abbey of Lieu-Dieu-en-Jard, and it was transferred to the North Normandy circary (Ardura 1993, 330–32, 377).

Churches and Claustral Buildings

The survival of medieval Premonstratensian buildings in Gascony is, predictably, patchy. Some of the medieval churches survive, at least in part, having been converted to parochial or agricultural use. The rebuilding of the domestic ranges to a greater standard

of comfort in the seventeenth or eighteenth centuries, as occurred at Prémontré and at many of the grander abbeys in northern France, appears less common in the south. Much damage occurred during the religious wars of the later sixteenth century, and even more was destroyed during or after the French Revolution.

Some of the greater Premonstratensian churches built in northern France after 1150 were heavily influenced by the austere style of their Cistercian counterparts, and adopted the squared-off east ends and transeptal chapels of the so-called Bernardine plan (Clapham 1923; Clark 1984). However, the order itself enacted no legislation on church plans. Across Europe as a whole, Premonstratensian churches show little uniformity. Generally the canons simply adopted the building conventions of the localities where they settled, though a few local types emerged, for example, the long, narrow, aisleless naves found in several English houses, such as Bayham and Egglestone. The Premonstratensians were among the least ambitious of monastic planners, and their claustral buildings display little uniformity either.

No systematic recording of churches and claustral ranges in the Gascon circary has yet been possible, so comparative plans of surviving buildings and precincts cannot be provided here. The most comprehensive survival of church and claustral buildings survives at Fontcaude, at Arthous and at Lannes. At Fontcaude the apsidal-ended chancel and choir-aisles of the twelfth-century Romanesque church survive, with blocked arches on the western side facing the site of the vanished nave. There are also ruins of some of the thirteenth-century claustral buildings on the southern side of the church, of which the dormitory range to the east is the best preserved (see Figure 6.7). The cloister capitals have been the subject of a study by Vignes (1977). Some excavation has taken place here (Giry 1973).

At Arthous the twelfth-century church consists of a long, barn-like unaisled nave, north and south transepts with apsidal eastern chapels and a short chancel also terminating in a semicircular apse (see Figure 6.5). The roof-eaves of the apses are richly decorated with Romanesque corbels (Figure 6.11). Internally the church was formerly stone-vaulted and partitioned by a wall separating the canons' part from the area used by local lay people (Figure 6.12) (Cabanot 1978, 292–319). Around the north-side cloister the west range has a timber-framed upper storey resting upon square stone pillars (Figure 6.13), the north range is stone-built and converted in part to a tall four-storey dwelling, while only portions of the east range survive (Figure 6.14).

The small priory of Lannes is now a farm called 'La Grangerie'. A small rectangular gothic church survives, now used as a *chais* for Armagnac (see Figure 6.8). Again the cloister is on the north side, and all three ranges of farm buildings which enclose it show evidence of medieval windows. Both the north range and the north side of the church have lean-to structures which preserve the general alignment of the cloister walk, and the east range retains a row of corbels for the roof of the alley on that side (Figure 6.15).

The twelfth-century Romanesque church at Lahonce, consisting of a long, aisleless nave leading into an apsidal-ended chancel, survives intact, and is now in parochial use. The west end of the nave terminates in a prominent stone and timber-framed bellcote (Cabanot, 1978, 33–4). The cloister lay on the south side, and a small portion of the east range and the whole of the west range survive, the latter with a row of corbels marking the line of the cloister walk roof (see Figure 6.6).

At Combelongue the Romanesque church is brick-built with a polygonal apse at the east end (see Figure 6.4), and it seems likely that the adjoining domestic and farm buildings to the south and east preserve something of layout of the earlier claustral buildings.

Most of the buildings of Pleineselve were demolished after the suppression in 1790. Only the square-ended chancel and the north chancel aisle of the twelfth-century church survives in parochial use, with a heavily buttressed Romanesque east end of some

Fig. 6.11 Romanesque corbels around the apse of the south-east chapel of the abbey church of Arthous (Dép. Landes, Dioc. Aire et Dax).

architectural pretensions (see Figure 6.3). Blocked arches on the west and south sides reflect the positions of the vanished nave and south chancel aisle

At Béhaune-en-Lantabat too only the church survives, a small whitewashed building with a square tower. High semicircular-headed windows and a row of corbels along the southern side of the building betray the former presence of a cloister walk (see Figure 6.10).

The abbey of Divielle has had the unluckiest fate. Enough survived of its buildings as late as 1870 for them to be reoccupied by a Trappist community from Melleray; but the Trappists failed to maintain recruitment and abandoned the site in 1936. Subsequently it fell into the hands of lay owners, who embarked upon a systematic programme of demolition, dynamiting the church. Only incoherent ivy-clad ruins of two of the claustral ranges survive.

Elsewhere, at Durance there appears to have been a substantial church, but the evidence for claustral buildings is less clear, and it is by no means certain that regular conventual life was maintained here; perhaps this was no more than a grange. At Vic-Fezensac the much-altered Chapel of Ste Marie and some remains of medieval domestic buildings survive. At Goujon a private house incorporates some

Fig. 6.12 (left) Interior of the abbey church of Notre-Dame at Arthous (Dép. Landes, Dioc. Aire et Dax): view east.

Fig. 6.13 The cloister garth of the abbey of Notre-Dame at Arthous (Dép. Landes, Dioc. Aire et Dax): the church and west range.

Fig. 6.14 The cloister garth of the abbey of Notre-Dame at Arthous (Dép. Landes, Dioc. Aire et Dax): the north and east ranges.

Fig. 6.15 Remains of the cloister garth, refectory and dormitory ranges of the priory of Lannes (Dép. Lot-et-Garonne, Dioc. Agen).

medieval fabric, but this relates to the later Cistercian occupation. At La Rochelle the walls of the medieval church of Ste Marguerite and two fifteenth-century precinct gates survive.

Few Premonstratensian houses in the south were able to afford much major rebuilding in later periods. The priory of Sarrance, unusually, experienced a period of relative prosperity in the later seventeenth century. Its church and domestic buildings were comprehensively reconstructed, the church gaining a three-stage baroque west tower with six incurved sides surmounted by a lantern, and a richly-decorated interior veneered with Pyrenean marble, the claustral buildings being rebuilt as two-storey ranges (Figure 6.16 and see Figure 6.9,) (Evans 1964, 82–3, pl.489–91).

At St Jean-de-la-Castelle the medieval buildings were largely destroyed by the Protestants in 1568–70. Between 1583 and 1675 four successive members of

Fig. 6.16 The late seventeenth-century cloisters and church of the priory of Notre-Dame at Sarrance (Dép. Pyrénées-Atlantiques, Dioc. Oloron-Ste-Marie, now Bayonne).

the Lompagieu family served as abbots and restored the buildings; but in 1728 the premises were again gutted by fire, and further reconstruction had to be undertaken by François de Lavelle, the penultimate abbot, between 1731 and 1760. The church and the south and east ranges of the cloister were demolished in 1832, only the gate and one wing surviving. The rest of the buildings were transformed into a small chateau (Figure 6.17).

Some houses have left little or no trace in the present landscape. The abandoned church of Huveaune had enjoyed a brief popularity as a place of pilgrimage, but it was destroyed in 1747, and even its exact site is now forgotten. Its successor, the church of Ste Marie-à-la-Porte-de-France in Marseilles, was destroyed soon after the suppression of the house in 1405. All the buildings of La Capelle were comprehensively destroyed soon after 1790.

The most regrettable loss of all has been the head house of the circary, La Casedieu. The first church of this abbey was consecrated in 1157, but it came to serve as the mausoleum of the noble families of Bigorre, Pardiac and Armagnac, and this apparently encouraged its reconstruction on a more lavish scale, since it was reconsecrated in 1489 (Ardura 1993, 163–4). Many of the buildings of La Casedieu were still standing into the early nineteenth century (Caneto 1840), and an illustration of that period shows a gatehouse with a chamber and attic storey over, a large roofless building which is probably the church, a small tower with a pyramidal roof, and several other buildings (reproduced in *Beaumarchés* 1988, 21); but the church was destroyed in 1853, and, although some recent descriptions speak of fragments of walls and of one of the gates and of the stump of a tower (*Beaumarchés* 1988, 22; Loubès 1990, 38), little was seen in 2003 in the vicinity of the isolated dwelling 'La Cazedieu' which preserves the name. A stone pulpit from the abbey has been moved to the parish church of Ladevèze-Ville, and there are scattered reused fragments elsewhere (Loubès 1990, 38).

The Estates and Properties of Premonstratensian Houses

By comparison with the larger Benedictine and Cistercian abbeys of southern France, the landed endowments of most of the Premonstratensian houses were relatively modest. Nevertheless, individual studies have demonstrated that the Premonstratensian canons in France, as in England, were developing granges on the Cistercian pattern (Higounet 1959). Rarely do these estate farms appear to have been pioneer settlements on virgin lands; for the most part

Fig. 6.17 Eighteenth-century gate at the abbey of St Jean-de-la-Castelle (Dép. Landes, Dioc. Aire et Dax).

they were created by the consolidation of holdings formerly worked by and for peasant cultivators, and not infrequently they superseded older villages and hamlets. Fournier (1950) has shown how the canons of St André in Clermont in the Auvergne circary developed a grange in place of the village of Gergovie in the Puy de Dôme, gradually accumulating lands through purchase and exchange until they owned the entire property.

Little research seems yet to have been undertaken on the estates of Premonstratensian houses further south, and one can only see fragments of a complex pattern. A papal bull of Pope Celestine II in 1143 confirmed and listed the possessions of the abbey of La Casedieu (Gaubin 1903). Among its extensive properties were a vineyard near Boes and a mill at Esplanque (quoted in part in *Beaumarchés*, 22) and the grange of Ribaute and the church of Ste Quitterie, with the freehold, mill, tithes and dependencies (Lagors n.d. 2). Its abbots exercised seignurial rights over the towns of Beaumarchés, Marciac and Plaisance. St Jean-de-la-Castelle, the most prosperous of the Gascon houses, had a grange nearby at Bordères, and more distant agricultural properties at Grioux, St Macaire, Pouy and Ste Colombe, along with mills at Renung, St Jean-de-Priam and Cazères. In 1492 the small abbey of Lahonce acquired a grange at St Sauveur d'Orthecole at Urt, a few miles to the east.

The possession of urban property as such appears to have been relatively unimportant, though in their capacity as landholders some abbeys were able to take an income from bastides planted on their lands (see below). The abbey of Huveaune had a property in the centre of Marseilles, the *Maison d'Huveaune*, while the priory of Lannes had a house in Mézin, both of which may have served as small hospices or refuges. By the sixteenth century the abbey of La Casedieu had established a small college at the University of Toulouse (Ardura 1993, 295, 319, 164).

A significant element of Premonstratensian income usually came from their possession of churches. The abbey of St Jean-de-la-Castelle had a particularly large number of appropriated churches, including Lasbezeilles (Duhort), Aurandet, Cournet, Le Vignau, Bordères, Cazères, Lacquy, Maillères, Juliac (with St Julien and Créon), Piétat, Priam, Renung, Cabrious, St Macaire, Ste Colombe de Miradox, St Pierre de Buzet (Fontclaire) and Ste Marthe de Pujos at Vianne. Vic-Fezensac was endowed by the archbishop of Auch with the parishes of Sarambat, Caillavet and St Jean-Poutge with their dependencies of Leviac, Tabaux, Phéhout and Lugugnan, while the count of Armagnac gave the chapels in his fortified dwellings at Vic, Auch and Lavardens and the abbot of La Casedieu added the parishes or granges of Vic-Fezensac, Martéret, Bourgos and Mourède. The abbeys of Divielle, Lahonce, La Casedieu, La Capelle and Arthous all had between eight and five churches, and many of the remaining houses had at least two or three.

Bastides on Premonstratensian Lands in Gascony

A striking feature of the economic geography of south-western France during the second half of the thirteenth century and the first half of the fourteenth century was the plantation of *bastides*. These were a distinctive type of new town, many of them laid out with an orthogonal plan incorporating a rectangular market-place surrounded by arcades, and some of them possessing defences.

The founders of bastides had diverse motives. Earlier investigators (e.g. Higounet 1948) viewed them as a product of dynastic rivalries, emphasizing their strategic role as strongholds along the shifting frontier between English- and French-held lands. This view was countered by Trabut-Cussac (1954), who pointed out that the majority of bastides were founded over a period in which Anglo-French relations were relatively cordial, that their foundation charters reveal little evidence of any military purpose, that two-thirds of all Gascon bastides lacked castles or town walls; and, moreover, that where defensive works did occur, they were often not part of the original plan, but were added during the fourteenth century, a time of increasing conflict and insecurity. While some bastides did occupy sites with strong natural defences, many more lay in areas of subdued relief, approachable from any direction. Political and administrative motives may have played a more significant role, as the French and English crowns, the counts of Toulouse, and other local lords attempted to stamp their authority over areas where their rule was fragile, to build up local reservoirs of loyalty, and to develop common interests with local partners.

Commercial interests were also prominent. All bastides were expected to yield a seignurial income from rents and market tolls, and many of them were located alongside important trade routes. The promotion of new markets stimulated local agriculture generally; but it also encouraged the development of specialisation, particularly after Louis VIII's successful invasion of Poitou in 1224, which resulted in the vineyards which had traditionally supplied the English market, falling into the hands of the French. To compensate for this loss there was a major increase in vine-growing in Gascony, the wine being exported to England through the port of Bordeaux. Progress towards vine monoculture meant that other necessities, including corn, hides and wool, had to be brought in from elsewhere, so the development of a network of small local market centres was vital (Beresford 1967, 361–72). Further east the devastation of the Languedoc during the Albigensian Crusade in the early thirteenth century had led the new count of Toulouse, Alphonse of Poitiers, brother of King Louis IX, to initiate a programme of economic recovery, in which the creation of bastides played a significant part:

for example, between 1246 and 1271 Count Alphonse and his seneschals were involved in 16 bastide foundations in the Agenais (Beresford 1967, 352).

Monastic houses contributed significantly to this form of urbanisation, though usually in a passive role as landholders. Between 1252 and 1325 at least 44 bastides were planted in the Garonne basin, a very high proportion of them on land held by Cistercian abbeys. The foundations were engineered through partnership contracts (*paréages*) between Cistercian landholders and royal or comital promoters, both French and English (Higounet 1975). The *paréages* specified how the new towns should be organised, and how authority over them and income from them should be shared, while charters defined their customs and liberties. Bastides created through partnerships between Cistercian and secular authorities were settled almost exclusively on land which had previously been used as granges: for the secular partners this considerably simplified the process of foundation, since the Cistercians had gone a long way towards eliminating the interests of other proprietors; while for the abbeys it provided an opportunity to reorganise the management of their estates, increasing their income from their least productive lands, and permitting them to concentrate their dwindling and increasingly expensive agricultural labour resources on the more profitable parts of their properties (Berman 1998).

The Premonstratensian canons contributed in a similar way to the creation of bastides, though never on quite such an extensive scale. The abbey of Combelongue provided land for four such promotions, La Casedieu and St Jean-de-la-Castelle three each, while the abbeys of Arthous and Urdax (the latter formerly in Navarre, now in Spain) were each involved in single foundations (Figure 6.18).

The earliest foundation with which the Premonstratensians were associated was the small bastide of Aïnhoa in the Basque country. This was settled in about 1230 in pastureland in the northern foothills of the Pyrenees by the local lord, Juan Pérez de Baztan, commander-in-chief of the army of the kingdom of Navarre. The abbey of San Salvador at Urdax contributed to the foundation, providing parochial services and establishing there a way-station on one of the pilgrimage routes to Santiago (Altuna and Garric 1997, 6–7). Aïnhoa consisted of little more than a single main street with back lanes, with a triangular market-place at its northern end (Figure 6.19).

Next came the four bastides of Combelongue, all founded between 1246 and 1272, and all within a 16-mile radius of the abbey in the Couserans. The largest and the most northerly, Montesquieu-Volvestre, was founded on the abbey's land in the Arize valley in

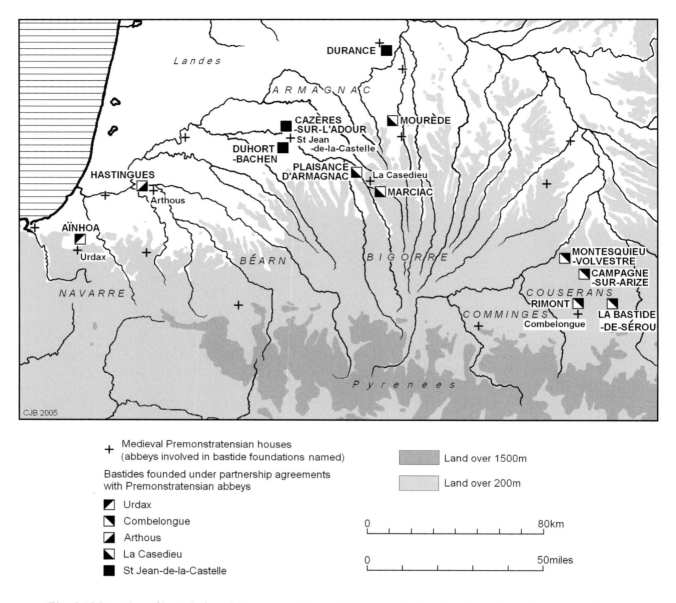

Fig. 6.18 Location of bastide foundations associated with Premonstratensian abbeys in south-western France.

1246 by Count Raymond VII of Toulouse. This was a much more ambitious promotion, though still not wholly regular, with a ladder plan of five parallel streets, several cross-lanes and a market square which is entered, characteristically at its corners, by two of the main streets and one of the cross-streets (see Figure 6.19). A semi-fortified fourteenth-century brick-built church with a tower of sixteen sides faces one side of the square. Its walls have been destroyed entirely, but their alignment is preserved by avenues of trees (Gisclard and Prat 1993, 14–19).

La Bastide-de-Sérou lies amidst rolling hills towards

the headwaters of the Arize, 8 miles east of the abbey. The castle of Montesquieu-de-Sérou had been built on a hilltop overlooking the north bank of the river in about 1250. The site lay on the borders of the county of Foix, and in 1252 Count Roger IV of Foix acquired a charter of customs for the new bastide, which was followed in 1255 by a tripartite *paréage* involving the count, the Premonstratensians of Combelongue and the Benedictines of Le Mas d'Azil. The small town was laid out below the eastern side of the castle. The market-square is entered at its corners by two streets which are not quite parallel, and there is further

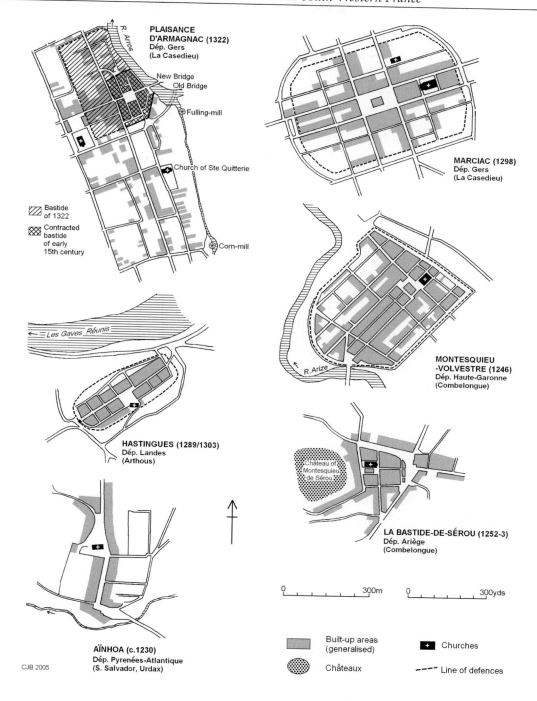

PLAISANCE D'ARMAGNAC (1322)
Dép. Gers
(La Casedieu)

New Bridge
Old Bridge
Fulling-mill
Church of Ste Quitterie

Bastide of 1322

Contracted bastide of early 15th century

Corn-mill

MARCIAC (1298)
Dép. Gers
(La Casedieu)

Les Gaves Réunis

HASTINGUES (1289/1303)
Dép. Landes
(Arthous)

R. Arize

MONTESQUIEU-VOLVESTRE (1246)
Dép. Haute-Garonne
(Combelongue)

Château of Montesquieu de Sérou

LA BASTIDE-DE-SÉROU (1252-3)
Dép. Ariège
(Combelongue)

AÏNHOA (c.1230)
Dép. Pyrénées-Atlantique
(S. Salvador, Urdax)

CJB 2005

0   300m   0   300yds

Built-up areas (generalised)

Châteaux

Churches

Line of defences

Fig. 6.19 Plans of bastides in south-western France founded in partnerships with Premonstratensian abbeys.

evidence of orthogonal planning, but on a smaller scale than at Montesquieu-Volvestre (see Figure 6.19). Fragments of walls survive with one gate, and two other gates are recorded (Rumeau 1882; Gisclard and Prat 1993, 10–11). The bastide of Campagne-sur-Arize, 8 miles upriver from Montesquieu-Volvestre, was

another foundation under a *paréage* between Roger IV of Foix and the abbey of Combelongue, dated 1255. The final foundation, Rimont, was on the higher ground immediately north of the abbey itself. This was a product of a *paréage* dated 1272 between the abbey and Eustace of Beaumarchés, the new seneschal of

Toulouse, one of the most active figures in bastide creation (Gisclard and Prat 1993, 30).

King Edward I had actively promoted the foundation of new towns in the English-held parts of Gascony, particularly during the 1280s, when over 30 bastides were established there (Beresford 1967, 354–61). Among them was Hastingues on the Gaves, at the extreme southern end of the Landes, not far from the frontier with Navarre. This was founded as a result of a *paréage* agreement concluded in February 1289 between the abbey of Arthous and John Hastings (from whom the town took its name), lord of Abergavenny and seneschal of Gascony, representing the English king. The abbey owned land at a place previously called *Auriamala* on a hilltop south of the river, where the bastide was planned. A later petition recalled that its purpose was to protect local commerce from bandits and cross-border raiders who plundered the abbey's lands. The initial agreement was stillborn as a result of Philip IV of France's attempt to confiscate Edward's fiefs in Gascony in 1294, which resulted in the outbreak of a war which dragged on until 1303. Only then could the construction of the bastide be resumed. The plan consisted of a row of chequers along a single main street with back lanes on either side, the main street entering the western corner of the market square and departing from its north-eastern flank (see Figures 6.19 and 6.20). Initially progress was

slow: in 1315–16 only half a dozen towns in the sparsely-populated Landes contained sufficient wealth to be worth taxing, and Hastingues produced the lowest assessment of all, £8. Then, in 1321, Edward II granted to the bastide of *Haurihastinggs* (*Auriamala* + Hastings) customs modelled upon those of Bonnegarde-en-Chalosse, the bastide on the frontier of English Gascony, 22 miles to the east, where his father had been staying when he drew up the first agreement with the canons of Arthous; at the same time, Edward II gave it a grant of tolls for ten years to help finance the construction of town walls and of a bridge over the town moat. The only substantial part of the defences to survive is the west gate, a rectangular machicolated tower of three stages equipped with arrow embrasures and pierced by a vaulted gate-passage with a portcullis (Figure 6.21); but vestiges of the walls and of a second gate can also be traced. Thereafter it enjoyed a modest prosperity: it had 240 inhabitants in 1330, and in 1343 Edward III licensed it to be a river-port, serving ships making passage between the Gave de Pau and the port of Bayonne. In 1453 Hastingues submitted to King Charles VII of France and finally passed out of English control (Beresford 1967, 131–2, 186, 200, 270, 604; Dezelus 1986; Altuna and Garric 1997, 11–13).

The large bastide of Beaumarchés lay only three miles from the abbey of La Casedieu, and the abbey

Fig. 6.20 The square in the bastide of Hastingues (Dép. Landes), founded on land of the abbey of Arthous.

Fig. 6.21 The west gate of the bastide of Hastingues (Dép. Landes).

certainly exercised some seignurial rights there, but the *paréage* of May 1288 names only King Philip IV of France and the count of Pardiac, and there is little indication that the abbey played any part in its development (*Beaumarchés* 1988). However, La Casedieu was involved in three other bastide foundations between 1286 and 1322. The first, Mourède, founded in partnership with Count Bernard VI of Armagnac (Dubourg 2002, 359), awaits further study. Marciac, founded through a tripartite *paréage* of August 1298 involving the abbot, the count of Pardiac and the seneschal Guichard de Marciac (from whom the place took its name), was among the most extensive and regularly-planned bastides in Gascony. The centrepiece of the town plan is the large arcaded rectangular market place, about 250ft × 500ft (Figures 6.22 and 6.23). Pairs of parallel streets enter each corner of the market square from each direction, while further chequers are defined by back lanes. The fourteenth-century parish church lies in the north-east quarter of the town. Marciac appears to have been walled from

the outset, and the course of the defences is very clear on the town plan (see Figure 6.19) (Dubourg 2002, 312; Cursente and Loubès 1991, 88).

Plaisance d'Armagnac was founded in 1322 as a result of a *paréage* between the abbot of La Casedieu and Count John I of Armagnac. It superseded the grange and earlier village of Ribaute, the church of which, Ste Quitterie, survived to become the parish church of the town from 1322 to 1863. The bastide was laid out to the north of this church, and was based upon a roughly cruciform street pattern with a rectangular outline of ditched defences initially covering some 25 acres. However the timing and location were unpropitious, since it was laid out during a period of population decline within 9 miles of the pre-existing bastides of Marciac and Beaumarchés. Some of the lots were never taken up, and Plaisance was dealt a further blow by the ravages of the Black Prince's army in 1338 and 1355 and the impact of the Black Death, disasters which resulted in the abandonment of much of the town. A survey of the early fifteenth century shows that some recovery had taken place, but the new walls enclosed only 6 acres in the south-eastern quarter of the old bastide, and the occupied area was reduced to nine blocks of buildings around the market-square. Renewed expansion took place in the nineteenth century, during which the rectilinear street system of the fourteenth-century foundation was recolonised and extended (see Figure 6.19) (Lagors 1976, n.d.; Cursente and Loubès 1991, 92, 106).

Finally, the abbey of St Jean-de-la-Castelle was involved in three bastide foundations during the second, third and fourth decades of the fourteenth century. Two lay little more than a mile away from the abbey, on opposite sides of the Adour valley. Cazères-sur-L'Adour, to the north, was founded in 1313 or shortly afterwards under a partnership agreement between the abbey, Marguerite of Béarn and the viscount of Marsan. The plan of the small town includes an arcaded square and a perimeter lane which reflects the circuit of the defences (Meyranx 1874). Duhort-Bachen, to the south, was founded in 1331 through a partnership with King Edward III of England. Each corner of its square is entered by a single road in alignment with one side. The third foundation, Durance, lay nearly 40 miles to the north-east, about half a mile south of the abbey's grange. Today this lies in a small clearing in very gently undulating country in the midst of the vast forests which extend eastwards from the Landes. In 1320, when it was founded in partnership with King Edward II of England, the site was much more open, but the infertile soil was of limited value except for sheep pasture. Although

Fig. 6.22 The square in the bastide of Marciac (Dép. Gers), founded on land of the abbey of La Casedieu.

Fig. 6.23 The arcades of the bastide of Marciac (Dép.Gers).

Fig. 6.24 The bastide of Durance, view to the south gate (Dép. Lot-et-Garonne).

several rectangular blocks were laid out on either side of the axial main road, and defences were built (of which some remains of the walls, ditches, towers and gates survive) (Figure 6.24), the bastide failed to prosper (Beresford 1967, 132, 617–8).

From the Late Middle Ages to the Revolution

Most of the Premonstratensian houses in the region entered a period of stagnation after the fourteenth century. Discipline declined and the number of canons dwindled. The first casualty was the Provençal community of Huveaune: having moved within the walls of Marseilles, by 1382 it consisted only of an abbot and a single canon, without sufficient resources to survive. The abbot petitioned successfully for a merger with the hospital of SS Jacques and Lazarus outside the walls, but this failed to improve matters, and in 1405 the Antipope at Avignon, Benedict XIII, effected the suppression of the house, annexing its meagre endowments to the Augustinian sisters of St Paul's Abbey (Ardura 1993, 295).

The passage of rival armies during the Hundred Years War impoverished the countryside and sometimes effected serious damage to monastic property. English armies can be blamed for the burning of several Premonstratensian abbeys elsewhere in western France, including Lieu-Dieu-en-Jard in Poitou and Lieu-Restauré in Valois. However, in Gascony and Guyenne the greatest havoc was wrought by the *routiers*, free companies nominally serving the king of Navarre and the counts of Armagnac and Foix, but having to support themselves by living off the land during periods of truce. The abbey of Divielle suffered particularly badly during this time. The troops of Louis of Orléans wrecked the buildings of Pleineselve during the sieges of Blaye and Bourg in 1407. The abbey of Combelongue was reduced to ruin in 1446, a time of nominal peace, and the canons were forced to abandon it, taking refuge for a time in La Bastide-de-Sérou.

Calvinism had spread rapidly in France during the 1540s, and conflicts between Catholics and Calvinists or Huguenots during the later sixteenth century caused even greater damage. The buildings of Vic-Fezensac were burned down in 1559 and lay abandoned for four years before communal life could be restored. The crisis came to a head in the late 1560s, when several Premonstratensian abbeys were attacked and sacked by the Huguenots – Fontcaude in 1567, St Jean-de-la-Castelle in 1568, Divielle, Combelongue, Sarrance and Fontcaude again in 1569, La Casedieu and La Capelle in 1571. A protestant army led by the baron of Arros sacked the villages of the Aspe valley in 1569 and devastated the priory of Sarrance. St Jean-de-la-Castelle was again invaded in 1570 by a protestant force led by Montgomery, lieutenant of Jeanne d'Albret, and in the following year his followers almost annihilated the community at Arthous.

None of the Gascon houses ever fully recovered from these disasters. Many of the canons of St Jean-de-la-Castelle had been killed, their archives and library had been burned, and the premises reduced to a shell. At Combelongue the conventual buildings had been left uninhabitable in 1569, and there were plans to move the community to Rimont, though this was never done; despite limited repairs in 1672, the claustral ranges collapsed, never to be rebuilt; and after 1724 the few remaining canons were forced to celebrate the offices behind the high altar, since the rest of the chancel had become unusable. At Sarrance the statue of the Virgin was hastily concealed in a cave in 1569 and the priory and hospital lay abandoned for forty years. Lahonce had only two canons in 1618, and its chapter house was used as a *cave* for wine, while a single resident canon remained at Pleineselve.

One house did achieve a significant reversal of its fortunes during the seventeenth century. The ruined priory at Sarrance was recovered in 1605 by the abbot of St Jean-de-la-Castelle, and by 1609 he had re-settled half-a-dozen canons there. The restored priory was in a dangerous frontier zone after 1635 when France, concerned about the growth of Hapsburg power during the earlier part of the Thirty Years War, declared war on Hapsburg Spain, but the ending of that conflict by the Peace of the Pyrenees in 1659 reopened the pilgrimage route, and the priory of Sarrance enjoyed an Indian summer of prosperity, on occasions housing up to a dozen canons. As related earlier, the buildings were comprehensively reconstructed at this time. In the early eighteenth century, the bishop of Bayonne also achieved some revival at Lahonce, valuing a community of canons able to undertake pastoral duties in the Basque language.

Apart from the adverse effects of war, significant administrative changes were also taking place. During the fifteenth and sixteenth centuries, in place of regularly elected abbots, many houses passed under the control of commendators, relatives of the king or men appointed by the crown as a reward for services rendered. Few of these appointees had previously taken clerical orders, and in general their only interest in the community placed in their charge was as a source of income. While the daily routine of the ordinary canons was little affected, in the longer term the removal of positive leadership tended to undermine morale and discipline. Fontcaude, for example, was placed under a commendatory regime after 1437, and was unable to recover from the damage wrought during the religious wars, since the commendators

reserved to themselves most of its modest revenues. Eventually, in 1687, the General Chapter intervened to order the separation of the communal revenues from those of the commendator. From 1614 to 1635 three successive members of the de La Salle family held the abbey of Lahonce as a sinecure, one of them becoming commendator at the age of four. La Casedieu was intermittently ruled by commendators from 1473 to the final suppression, though the rule of regular abbots was briefly restored in 1483–1533 and 1673–93. St Jean-de-la-Castelle passed into the hands of commendators on several occasions after 1475, but here, unusually, through the intervention of Jean Despruets, one of its former canons who had risen to become abbot-general of the order at Prémontré (1573–96), it was served by regular abbots throughout the last two centuries of its existence. Elsewhere, once a commendatory regime had been introduced (as at Arthous in 1514, Lahonce in 1524, Combelongue in 1530 or Divielle in 1532) it normally continued up to the final suppression.

Suppression and Revival

The French Revolution resulted in the closure of all remaining monastic houses in 1790 and the expulsion of the canons, following which the buildings were sold (Lavagne-d'Ortigue 1991). There were only a few flickers of resistance. Despite the sale of the buildings of St Jean-de-la-Castelle in 1791, some of the canons were permitted to remain there until the following year, and even after their ejection a few refused to take the new constitutional oath and continued to exercise their ministry in secret.

The Premonstratensians have regained a foothold in southern France since the mid-nineteenth century, establishing new houses at St Michel-de-Frigolet in Provence (1856), Conques in Rouergue (1873), St Jean-de-Côle in the Dordogne (1877–80), Balarin in Gascony (1867–1904), and Pau and Accous in Béarn (1986) (see Figure 6.2).

References

Altuna, J. and Garric, J.-P. (1997) *Les Bastides du Béarn et du Pays Basque*. Toulouse, Privat.

Ardura, B. (1993) *Abbayes, Prieurés et Monastères de l'Ordre de Prémontré en France des Origines à nos Jours: Dictionnaire Historique et Bibliographique*. Nancy, Presses Universitaires de Nancy.

Aston, M. (1993) The development of the Carthusian order in Europe and Britain: a preliminary survey. In Carver, M. (ed.) *In Search of Cult: Archaeological Investigations in Honour of Philip Rahtz*, 139–151. Woodbridge, The Boydell Press.

Aston, M. (2001) The expansion of the monastic and religious orders of Europe from the eleventh century. In Keevill, G. Aston, M. and

Hall, T. (eds) *Monastic Archaeology: Papers on the Study of Medieval Monasteries*, 9–36. Oxford, Oxbow Books.

Backmund, N. (1949, 1952, 1956) *Monasticon Praemonstratense, id est Historia Circarium atque Canoniarum Candidi et Canonici Ordinis Praemonstratensis* (3 vols, Straubing vol.1, 2nd edn. Berlin and New York, 1983).

Bacqué, Z. (1914) Le monastère de Notre-Dame à Vic-Fezensac. *Bulletin de la Société Archéologique, Historique, Littéraire et Scientifique du Gers*,15, 55–65.

Barthes, H. (1979) *Histoire de l'Abbaye Sainte-Marie de Fontcaude, Ordre de Prémontré... et de ses Bienfaiteurs*. Albi.

Beaumarchés Anon. (1988) *Au Coeur de la Gascogne, Beaumarchés, Bastide Royale*. Beaumarchés.

Beresford, M. W. (1967) *New Towns of the Middle Ages: Town Plantation in England, Wales and Gascony*. London, Lutterworth Press.

Berman, C. H. (1998) Cistercian vernacular architecture in southern France: the question of bastides. In Lillich, M. P. (ed.) *Studies in Cistercian Art and Architecture*, vol.5 (Cistercian Studies Series no.167), 238–269. Kalamazoo, Michigan.

Biard, G. (1992) L'abbaye prémontré de Lahonce. *Actes du 17e Colloque du Centre d'Etudes et de Recherches de l'Ordre de Prémontré*. 105–110. Amiens.

Bond, C. J. (1993) The Premonstratensian order: a preliminary survey of its growth and distribution in Europe. In Carver, M. (ed.) *In Search of Cult: Archaeological Investigations in Honour of Philip Rahtz*, 153–185. Woodbridge, The Boydell Press.

Brooke, R. B. (1975) *The Coming of the Friars*. London, Allen & Unwin

Brooke, R. and Brooke, C. (1984) *Popular Religion in the Middle Ages: Western Europe, 1000–1300*. London, Thames and Hudson.

Cabanot, J. (1978) *Gascogne Romane*. La Pierre-qui-Vire, Zodiac.

Caneto, (1840) Eglise de Marciac et ruines de L'abbaye de Lacase-Dieu (Gers). *Bulletin Archéologique publié par la Comité d'Histoire des Arts et des Monuments*, vol.1, 338, 346.

Caviness, M. H. (1990) *Sumptuous Arts at the Royal Abbeys in Reims and Braine*, esp. Ch.3, Saint-Yved of Braine: "*Amplissima Ecclesia*". Princeton, New Jersey, 65–74.

Clapham, A. W. (1923) The architecture of the Premonstratensians, with special reference to their buildings in England. *Archaeologia*, 73, 117–46.

Clark, W. W. (1984) Cistercian influences in Premonstratensian church planning: Saint-Martin at Laon. In Lillich, M.P. (ed.) *Studies in Cistercian Art and Architecture*, vol.2 (Cistercian Studies Series no.69), 161–188, Kalamazoo, Michigan.

Colvin, H. M. (1939) Dale Abbey: granges, mills and other buildings. *Journal of Derbyshire Archaeological and Natural History Society*, 60, 142–155.

Colvin, H. M. (1951) *The White Canons in England*. Oxford, Clarendon Press.

Cursente, B. & Loubès, G. (1991) *Villages Gersois, ii: Les Bastides*. Auch .

Dailliez, L. (1967) L'abbaye Notre-Dame d'Huveaune à Marseille. *Marseille*, 93–4, 14–17.

Degert, A. (1924a) L'abbaye de Divielle: les origines. *Revue de Gascogne*, 19, 23–30.

Degert, A. (1924b) Les prémontrés à Divielle. *Revue de Gascogne*,19, 114–126.

Dezelus, R. (1986) *Hastingues, Village de Gascogne, 1304–1986*. Dax.

Dubarat, V. (1892–1901) Documents sur Notre-Dame de Sarrance. *Etudes d'Histoire Religieuse du Diocèse de Bayonne*, Vols.1, 2, 3, 5 & 11.

Dubourg, J. (2002) *Histoire des Bastides: les Villes Neuves du Moyen Age*. Luçon.

Evans, J. (1964) *Monastic Architecture in France*. Cambridge University Press, Cambridge.

Fearns, J. V. (ed.), (1968) Peter the Venerable, *Contra Petrobrusianos*.

In *Corpus Christanorum, Continuatio Mediaevalis*, X. Brepols, Turnhout.

Ferras, V. (1992) L'abbaye Notre-Dame et Saint-Laurent de Combelongue en Ariège (1131–1790). *Actes du 17e Colloque du Centre d'Etudes et de Recherches de l'Ordre de Prémontré*, 111–119. Amiens.

Fonds, V. (1860) L'abbaye de Goujon. *Mémoires de la Société Archéologique du Midi*, 7, 335–343.

Fournier, G. (1950) La création de la grange de Gergovie par les Prémontrés de Saint-André. *Le Moyen Age*, 4th ser.5, 56, 319.

Gabent. (1895) Goujon, abbaye et paroisse. *Revue de Gascogne*, 36, 407–506, 545–559.

Gaubin, J. (1903) Les possessions de La Casedieu. *Rapport au Congrès des Sociétés Savantes*, Bordeaux.

Gaubin, J. (1904) *Histoire de l'Abbaye de La Casedieu depuis sa Fondation (1135) jusqu'à nos Jours*. Toulouse.

Giry, J. (1973) Les fouilles archéologiques sur l'emplacement de l'ancienne abbaye de Fontcaude. *Bulletin de l'Académie de Science et Lettres de Montpellier*, new ser. 4, 79–80 .

Gisclard, P. and Prat, N. (1993) *Les Bastides du Comminges et du Couserans*. Toulouse.

Gribbin, J. A. (2001) *The Premonstratensian Order in Late Medieval England*. Boydell Press, Woodbridge.

Higounet, C. (1948) Bastides et frontières. *Le Moyen Age*, 54, 113–21.

Higounet, C. (1959) Les types d'exploitation cisterciennes et prémontrées du XIIIe siècle et leur role dans la formation d'habitat et des paysages ruraux. In *Géographie et historie agraires: Annales de l'Est*, mémoire no.21, 260–271. Nancy.

Higounet, C. (1975) Cisterciens et bastides. In *Paysages et Villages Neufs du Moyen Age: Recueil d'Articles de Charles Higounet*. 265–274. Bordeaux.

John, J. (1953) *The College of Prémontré in Mediaeval Paris*. Notre Dame, Indiana.

Kirkfleet, C. J. (1943) *The White Canons of St Norbert*. West de Père, WI, St Norbert's Abbey.

Lagors, A. (1976) Aperçu sur la bastide de Plaisance. *Bulletin de la Société Archéologique du Gers*, 229–47.

Lagors, A. (n.d.) *Les Etapes de l'Evolution de Plaisance au Moyen Age*. Auch.

Lalanne, V. (1992) Les abbayes prémontrées de la circarie de Gascogne: tout particulièrement celles du Béarn et du Pays Basque. *Actes du 17e Colloque du Centre d'Etudes et de Recherches de l'Ordre de Prémontré*. 85–104. Amiens.

Lambert, E. (1956) L'abbaye d'Arthous. *Etudes Médiévales*, 2, 133–147. Toulouse.

Lambert, M. (1992) *Medieval Heresy: Popular Movements from the Gregorian Reform to the Reformation* (2nd edn). Oxford, Blackwell.

Laurent, M. (ed.) (1954) *Lettres communes d'Urbain V*. Paris.

Lavagne-d'Ortigue, X. (1991) Les Prémontrés de France et la suppression des ordres monastiques, 1766–1792. *Analecta Praemonstratensia*, 67, 232–61.

Leblanc, G. (1954) L'église et L'abbaye de moniales de Goujon. *Mélanges Saint Bernard, Actes du 24e Congrès de l'Association Bourguignonne de Sociétés Savants*, Dijon, 1953, 350–358. Dijon.

Légé, J. (1878) *Monastère et Abbaye Royale de Saint-Jean de la Castelle à Duhort*. Bordeaux.

Loubès, G. (1990) *Le Gers Monastique: Abbayes et Monastères*. Auch.

Menjoulet, J. (1859) *Chronique de Notre-Dame de Sarrance*. Oloron.

Meyranx, L. B. (1874) *La Bastide de Cazères-sur-Adour*. Dax.

Nogaret, J. (1930) L'abbaye d' Arthous et Le prieuré de Subernoa. *Bulletin de la Société de Sciences, Lettres, d'Arts et d'Etudes Régionales de Bayonne*, 52, 218–246.

Peyrous, B. (1972) Les Prémontrés à Arthous (1160–1791). *Analecta Praemonstratensia*, 48, 291–307.

Peyrous, B. (1982) Les Prémontrés à Pleineselve. *Les Cahiers du Vitrezais*, 11, 55–62.

Rumeau, R. (1882) *Monographie de la Bastide-de-Sérou.* Toulouse.

Seymour, D. (1977) *Torre Abbey: an Account of its History, Buildings, Cartularies and Lands.* Torquay, The Author.

Streeten, A. (1983) *Bayham Abbey.* (Sussex Archaeological Society, Monograph 2).

Trabut-Cussac, J.-P. (1954), Bastides ou forteresses ? *Le Moyen Age,* 60, 81–135.

Verres, L. (1955) Le traité de L'abbé Bernard de Fontcaude contre les Vaudois et les Ariens. *Analecta Praemonstratensia,* 31, 5–36.

Vignes, C. (1976) L'abbaye de Fontcaude, étude historique. *Analecta Praemonstratensia,* 52, 142–55.

Vignes, C. (1977) Les chapiteaux du cloître de L'abbaye de Fontcaude. *Bulletin Monumentale,* 135, 181–93.

Chapter 7

Angevin Lordship and Colonial Romanesque in Ireland

Tadhg O'Keeffe

I met Mick Aston for the first time as recently as 1995 when he and I were part of the small but memorably free-spirited Anglo-Irish delegation at the inaugural Ruralia conference in Prague. We have been close friends since then, and over the years Margaret and I have had the pleasure of his company, and Theresa's, on very many occasions, both in Bristol and in Dublin. Long may it continue. Colleagues and friends of Mick's will agree that life has few more pleasurable passages than an evening in his company in Farthings Hermitage, talking archaeology, glass of red wine in hand, and complaining about establishments. I am delighted to contribute this essay on Ireland – Mick is a committed and knowledgeable Hibernophile – to this *festschrift* in recognition of his scholarly and popularising contributions to archaeology, and more especially as a small token of deep personal affection.

The appearance of the word *Romanesque* in my title probably raises the expectation that this is a paper about churches, a field of interest that Mick and I share (although rarely is either of us inside a church unless it is in ruins!). The terms *Angevin* and *colonial* raise the expectation that this is about church archaeology, probably monastic archaeology, in the post-1169 period of Irish history; indeed, he and I, with Mark Horton, investigated a Carthusian monastery in County Galway that was founded by a scion of a family that came to Ireland during the phase of Angevin colonisation. But this paper is mainly about castles. Mick knows more than a little about these monuments, as he does about so many things, but has generally resisted their charms. I have tried to convert him in the field to no avail; this paper is my final effort!

Introduction

We can probably forgive ourselves for assuming that whenever reference is made to the presence somewhere of Romanesque architecture or sculpture it is with respect to an ecclesiastical context. Churches of all grades – private, parochial, priory/abbey, cathedral – are the places in which we are most accustomed to seeing Romanesque, wherever we travel in Europe. Occasionally we are reminded that secular buildings of the same eleventh- and twelfth-century period could also be canvases for the display of the stylistic forms which constitute Romanesque. If the appearance of Castle Hedingham rather than of one of the great cathedrals on the dust-cover of a recent book on England's Romanesque (Fernie 2000) makes the point with an almost sly innuendo, trips to a Chauvigny, with its intimidating and jaw-droppingly spectacular cordon of twelfth-century Romanesque towers (Figure 7.1), or a Cluny, with its extant Romanesque houses, forcefully drive the point home. The preferential treatment of ecclesiastical contexts is entirely understandable, as churches are the most numerous to remain from our period. Contemporary castles, however, suffer on the double: not only is their number significantly lower, thereby pushing them to the edges of our thinking about Romanesque, but more than a century of castellology – the study of castles – has type-cast them in a military mould, despite the evidence of the combined formal/structural/iconographic qualities of their architecture.

Turning specifically to the Insular context, the incastellation of Ireland in the late 1100s and early 1200s by mercenaries-turned-conquistadores from south-west Britain – people whom we describe customarily as Anglo-Norman although one might raise the technical objection that 'Norman' is no longer appropriate after 1154 – has considerable *a priori* interest to castellologists and specialists in medieval architectural history. First, the processes of conquest and colonisation on the island required immediate incastellation in order to be successful, and our inheritance is a landscape, at least in eastern Ireland, with very large numbers of earth-and-timber castles

Fig. 7.1 One of the Romanesque donjons *at Chauvigny.*

(Figure 7.2), mainly dated to within a fairly short period (O'Conor 1992; McNeill 1997, 56–74; Sweetman 1999, 3–32). Second, the new stone castles of the more powerful among the Angevin lords who came to Ireland were precisely that: new. There were no older castles onto which new parts had to be grafted, Chepstow-like, thereby necessitating some compromise in planning. Rather, the new colonial castles were generally sited on virgin sites, or on sites from which the traces of earlier or existing native occupation could be cleared away, thus allowing the builders relatively free rein within the boundaries of their resources to design what they desired. So, if we want to understand the nature of 'the castle' in the Angevin territories in general (which was virtually all of Britain, most of Ireland, and the whole west side of France) in the decades before and after 1200 we cannot avoid a careful consideration of Ireland. There is a greater number of royal and baronial castles built *ab initio* in Ireland during this period than anywhere else.

The special interest of that period of *c.*1200 lies in the claim, made with an almost mantra-like insistence, that those decades were a period of experimentation, driven less by stylistic adventurism than by a desire for the optimal, scientifically-assessed, fortress architecture (see, for example, Toy 1955). The 'proof' resides in *donjons* of unusual plan, designed to alleviate perceived problems of defensibility in traditional square or rectangular *donjons*, and in enclosure castles in which the idea of a *donjon* is simply dispensed with and the defensive emphasis placed on the curtain wall instead. It also resides indirectly in the successful insinuation of Edward I's enormous castles in north Wales, like Harlech and Caernarvon, that they represent the high-point of medieval castle-planning in Europe. Thankfully, we are now growing out of this phase of exclusive military determinism with its tiresome privileging of the views of fighting men (see Coulson 1996 and Johnson 2002 for England, and O'Keeffe 2001 for Ireland). Sandy Heslop's paper on Orford Castle, for example, one of the first to illuminate a revisionist path for the period of interest to us (Heslop 1991), shattered the myth that the plan of this particular *donjon* was intended 'to avoid the weakness at the corners inherent in a rectangular keep' (Prestwich 1980, 49, caption to photograph), thus demonstrating the potential for scrutinising castle architecture as we would ecclesiastical architecture, and for developing a discourse about castle architecture which is as rooted in aesthetic theory and even phenomenology as it is in conventional style-history (see also Heslop 1994 for a further demonstration of this).

This paper attempts speculatively to build on this project with respect to Angevin castles in Ireland dating from the first half-century or so after the so-called 'invasion' of 1169. It does not offer any radical reinterpretations of long-studied buildings but is simply a work-in-progress effort which aims, first, to attach the adjective Romanesque (as conventionally understood) to a small selection of castles or parts of castles, and second, to promote an approach to their study which combines the customary sensitivity to their inherent symbolic qualities with an awareness of their *layout as performative spaces.*

Romanesque Castles/Royal Complexes in Pre-1169 Ireland

The contexts in which we encounter Romanesque architecture and sculpture in Ireland are mainly ecclesiastical, and mainly pre-date 1169, at least in southern and eastern Ireland. In describing the Romanesque works of that period as 'ecclesiastical', which they indisputably were, we should not forget

Fig. 7.2 The half-sectioned motte at Castlegrace, Co. Carlow.

the role of *secular* powers in their patronage, and we should be cognisant of the possibility that a display of Romanesque detail on a church communicated ideas among contemporary spectators about the secular power which facilitated it or maybe even paid for it (O'Keeffe 2003; 2006). In fact, we know enough about secular lordship and its relationship with the Church to believe that pre-'invasion', twelfth-century, secular power in Ireland was articulated by Romanesque forms on its high-status sites, *at least in some parts of Ireland*, even if there is as yet relatively little supporting archaeological knowledge.

Somewhat ironically perhaps, the best historical evidence for sites of secular power in this period is in the lands of the powerful ua Conchobhair kings in the west of Ireland, where Romanesque (as conventionally defined by certain recurring motifs) was not really popular until the end of the twelfth century, by which time much of the rest of Ireland has been enfolded into Angevin lordship. Briefly, there were places or monuments in this western region that were described in native sources in the twelfth century as 'castles' (for references and discussion see Graham 1988; Flanagan 1996; O'Keeffe 1998). We know very little about the archaeology of such places. Some may have been of stone: Ruaidhri Ua Conchobhair, for example, *de facto* national king at the time of the 1169 'invasion', had a *caislén ingantach* (a large castle) erected in 1164 in Tuam, Co. Galway. Tuam was the dynastic capital and the centre of western Ireland's archepiscopal province, so it probably had a stone 'castle'. Indeed, a very small and insignificant part of a stone building is celebrated in the town as the remains of this castle. But there is a strong possibility that many of these Connacht 'castles' were of earth-and-timber type; two places in the ua Conchobhair lands of which this can be claimed confidently are Caistél Dúin Leódha at Ballinasloe, Co. Galway, which was extant in the eighteenth century when an antiquarian described it in a manner that suggests it was a classic motte (Nicholls 1982, 389), and Dún Mór (now Dunmore), also in Co. Galway, which is a motte on which a later, thirteenth-century, tower now stands (Graham 1988, 115).

Contemporary, secular, buildings or building-complexes which undoubtedly existed at the small number of power-centres of comparable rank with Tuam, principal among them being Killaloe, Co. Clare, and Cashel, Co. Tipperary, were not described explicitly as castles in the twelfth century but might well have been. Here too the evidence for twelfth-century non-ecclesiastical architecture, Romanesque or otherwise, is missing. In the case of Cashel, it is possible, using careful metrological analysis of and around the two extant twelfth-century buildings, the Round Tower and Cormac's Chapel, to locate the probable site of the original twelfth-century cathedral and to suggest tentatively that there was another, presumably palatial, building (of stone?) standing to its west and facing it. The site of that latter, putative, structure is where stands now the mainly fifteenth-century residental tower at the west end of the thirteenth-century Gothic cathedral. The reconstruction of this overall plan is tentative, but even if I am incorrect in thinking that the later medieval residental tower occupies the actual site of an earlier tower, it is certainly tempting to envisage early twelfth-century Cashel having four structures which were paired in very particular spatio-political relationships, explicitly homologous of the relationship between 'church and state' in early twelfth-century Ireland (the metrological analysis and a wider discussion of the Romanesque architecture on the summit at Cashel are presented in O'Keeffe 2003, Chapter 4). In such a conceptualisation it seem inconceivable that a palace building at Cashel would not have been Romanesque.

Ireland Incastellated, 1169–1200

I made the point above that the Irish lordship gave Angevin castle-builders an opportunity to build what they wished within their resources. Two categories of resource interest us here, one financial, one labour. Apropos of the first, the men who settled in Ireland and had their captured Irish lands legitimised *post facto* by Henry II (for a summary see Frame 1995, 35–9) did not have vast estates in England or Wales from which they could siphon money for elaborate programmes of castle-building. Excluding the king himself, who intervened in Ireland to maintain control over his subjects as they spilled across the island, not one of the great landowners of the English lowlands had a significant stake in late twelfth-century Ireland. Revenue issuing from the newly-formed (or still forming) Irish estates aided the island's new baronial aristocracy as it engaged in castle-building in stone, but there must be a suspicion that the corpus of fairly modest buildings which remains from this period reflects the limitations of the fiscal environment. Turning to the matter of labour, the new colonists depended on native hands, and this may help explain the alacrity with which the colony was filled out with motte-castles (and possibly ringwork castles), but the native labour force had relatively little experience, as far as we know, of large-scale stone buildings, and this must have been an impediment. Moreover, there were relatively few stone buildings from which substantial amounts of stone could be pilfered, and there were probably very few open quarries.

Beyond the issue of resources are the larger questions of formal style. The Anglo-Norman arrival in Ireland around 1170 is slightly too early – note the date of Canterbury's new east end – to expect Gothic work to be a significant feature of the very earliest colonial horizon in church-building or castle-building. So, regarding churches, we find that within the infant colony the Romanesque style was still favoured in some significant building projects, such as the transepts of Holy Trinity (now Christ Church) Cathedral in Dublin (Stalley 2000; O'Keeffe 2000) and

the since-altered parish church of St Nicholas in Carrickfergus, Co. Antrim, dated by McNeill (1980, 47–50) to *c*.1200 but probably better regarded as a decade or two earlier in date (given that Gothic work is present in Anglo-Norman Ulster in the 1180s).

After about 1200 an English-style version of Gothic spread fairly widely, the impetus coming from some major building works such the vaulted nave of Holy Trinity or the vaulted presbytery of Duiske Cistercian abbey in Graiguenamanagh, Co. Kilkenny. By contrast, in early colonial castle architecture the Romanesque style seems to have had a longer currency, stretching into the 1200s. Castle-builders of this era may, knowingly, have been more conservative than church-builders: their understanding of 'castle' as an architectural type seems to have been rooted in the twelfth-century English model, and it took the increasing use of Gothic for the churches – always the first settings in the middle ages in which the most up-to-date styles were executed and displayed? – to break down that conservative trait.

That survival of Romanesque in castle architecture in Ireland is manifest in an extremely limited repertoire of sculptural forms: roll-moulded corners or chevron-decorated arches. One could argue, perhaps, that it is also manifest in the round-arched openings of undressed voussoirs, and in the use of lag-boards for vault centering, both very common in pre-1250 Irish castles, even if applying the label Romanesque to such relatively non descript features has its hazards. The shallow pilasters which are a feature of a small number of later twelfth and thirteenth-century Irish castles might also be described as Romanesque given their obvious pedigree in English twelfth-century hall/ *donjon* architecture: in the late twelfth-century *donjon* of Carrickfergus, for example, they appear in combination with classic, later twelfth-century, round-arched twin-light windows (Figure 7.3). Perhaps we might also regard some basic architectural design conceptions as Romanesque manifestations: in the case of the Carrickfergus *donjon*, for example, the third-floor room with a gallery above it is sufficiently similar in conception to what we now know of *donjons* like Hedingham (Dixon and Marshall 1993) for us to suggest that such uses of space are fundamentally Romanesque, notwithstanding their actual stylistic or structural attributes.

Some Castle Buildings

I want now to discuss a small selection of Anglo-Norman Romanesque castle-buildings: the halls of Adare Castle, Co. Limerick, and Ballyderown Castle, Co. Cork, the *donjon* of Nenagh Castle, Co. Tipperary,

Fig. 7.3 Carrickfergus Castle.

each of which has Romanesque decorative features, and the *donjons* Trim Castle and Maynooth Castle, in counties Meath and Kildare respectively, both of which can be understood as belonging within the English Romanesque *donjon* tradition.

Adare

The castle at Adare, founded by Geoffrey de Marisco after 1199 when he was granted the cantred of Adare and Croom, preserves three important thirteenth-century buildings, at least one of which – identified by all writers as a hall, and identified in Figure 7.4 as Hall I – belongs to the very start of the century.

This is a difficult castle complex to read. Its basic ground plan has an arrangement which is seen in different versions at many castles of the twelfth century and later in Britain: a core of roughly circular plan defined by a curtain wall and fosse and an outer bailey to one side of it which contains buildings. Although many phases of growth and alteration are represented at sites of this character, the origin of this type of lay-out – the template which suggested to successive generations that this was the 'right' way to allow a castle develop – can probably be found in motte-and-bailey castles. What makes Adare difficult to work out is partly that phases of construction are especially fugitive in the sort of non-ashlar fabric which is so common in Ireland but more particularly

that its cluster of buildings is without parallel in Ireland and their functional interrelationships are not at all clear.

Hall I, a rectangular building with a length-breadth ratio of a little under 1:2, is dated by its first-floor fenestration – twin-light, roll-moulded, windows – to the very beginning of the thirteenth century. They have been paralleled with the so-called 'Transitional' – I prefer to describe them as 'Late Romanesque' – windows in the west end of the Cistercian abbey of Monasteranenagh, Co. Limerick, founded in 1148 and presumably finished by 1200 (Leask 1960, 35–8; Stalley 1987, 248–9). Their symmetrical arrangement, with two in each of the long walls and one in the east wall, is certainly consistent with a room for public use.

The hall's chronological and functional relationship with the damaged and altered tower in the inner court is uncertain. That tower – both McNeill and Sweetman avoid calling it a *donjon* – was originally two-storeyed, with a dark basement propping up a first-floor room. No features remain which help date it, but the shallow pilaster projections flush with the end walls locate it within a general twelfth-century tradition, even if its actual date of construction falls into the early 1200s.

Although McNeill assigns them to separate though closely-spaced phases, with Hall I indicated as the earlier, it is tempting to see these two buildings as a pair, a hall in the outer court and a chamber in the

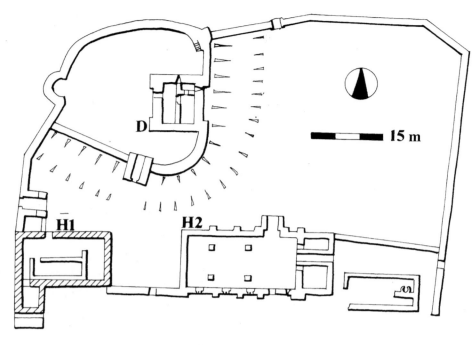

Fig. 7.4 Plan of Adare Castle showing Hall I.

inner. Later in the thirteenth century a new hall was constructed to the east of the original; it was a ground-floor hall with a porched entrance and paired service rooms of classic plan at its east end where it faced a kitchen. It is conceivable that the original hall was converted to a chamber – it had a garderobe turret added to it – at this stage, with the original chamber-tower in the inner court becoming an inner chamber and, later, being vaulted and heightened to better accommodate this more exclusive function.

Ballyderown

Another building which surely falls within our consideration is the sole extant remnant of the little-known (and, by comparison with Adare, minor) castle of the de Caunteton family at Ballyderown (O'Keeffe 1984). McNeill casts doubt on my dating of this rectangular block (Figure 7.5) to c.1200, writing that it is 'claimed' to be early but has 'a first-floor window in the west wall which appears to be much later, as does the thin walling' (1997, 238; Sweetman 1999, incidentally, makes no reference to it at all). But the early date is incontestable. The combination of its shape, its chamfered quoins in a soft, chalky stone which was quarried especially for the purpose, its mural stair with a plank-turned vault over it, its lack of main-space vaulting, and its base batter, are all consistent with a general late twelfth- or thirteenth-century date in an

Irish context, while the two massive round-arched windows (originally with two-light opening?) with fragmentary roll-mouldings in the extant short wall of its first floor (Figure 7.6) certainly belong within the Romanesque tradition, narrowing its chronology still further.

Ballyderown may only have been two storeys high originally; the fragmentary (and thin-walled, *pace* McNeill) third story is conceivably contemporary with a small garderobe turret which was added to one end of the building at a later date. It is not clear whether the original entrance was directly into that large upper room at first-floor level (with the surviving mural stair descending into the basement), or at basement level (with the mural stair ascending from there). If the large windows and their location opposite the stairs doorway suggest that the first-floor room was a hall, there must have a chamber-block of some nature elsewhere in the castle. It might even have been of timber, and its lack of durability may explain why in the later middle ages the hall was converted to more conventionally habitable space by the addition of a garderobe turret.

Nenagh

Nearly twenty cylindrical *donjons* (the number cannot be exact in the absence of a proper national survey) and at least three polygonal *donjons* survive from Anglo-Norman Ireland. The buildings of the latter

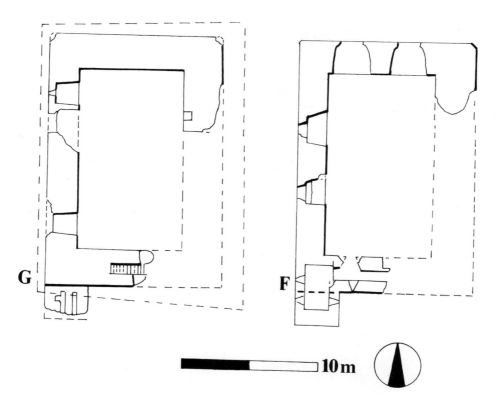

G   F   10m

Fig. 7.5 Ballyderown Castle. Suggested window reconstruction.

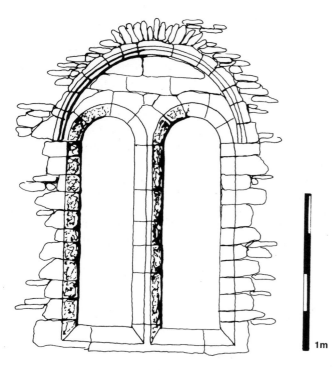

1m

Fig. 7.6 Window detail, Ballyderown Castle.

group, too fragmentary for discussion in this context, may include one late twelfth-century example at Castleknock, Co. Dublin. The cylindrical *donjons* are mainly of early thirteenth-century date. The finest of them is in the midlands at Nenagh (Figure 7.7, 7.8). Conventionally attributed to a date of *c.*1200, construction work on this castle probably began before that date, as Nenagh was the capital of the vast territory which had been granted to Theobald Walter by King John in 1185. Originally this was a three-storey tower with a basement, an entrance floor, and a second floor above; an additional storey was added around the middle of the thirteenth century and a new, highly-fenestrated, upper portion was built in the nineteenth century. The embrasure containing the stair at original upper floor level has a Romanesque opening facing into the room: the arch has intrados and extrados chevrons meeting to form lozenges on the arris, and the pattern continued down the jambs. A similar chevron-type can be seen, for example, on the reconstructed doorway of the smaller Romanesque church at Rahan, Co. Offaly, another midland Irish site. It is tempting to identify the Nenagh Castle arch as the work of a Gaelic-Irish mason. Exact dating for it is not

possible; in another context a date in the 1170s could be considered, but assuming it to be original to the castle and given that the castle cannot have been started before 1185 a date in the 1190s is likely, making it one of the last works in a Romanesque stone-carving tradition in the Irish midlands (O'Keeffe 1995).

Trim

We have already discussed the earth-and-timber castles of the first soldiers and settlers of the late 1100s in Ireland, noting both their proliferation and their permanence. With Trim we enter the Angevin lordship of Ireland in earnest (Fenlon and O'Brien 2002). Its builder was Hugh de Lacy, who had come to Ireland as part of Henry II's entourage in 1171. One of the king's trusted allies, Hugh was appointed Lord of Meath, constable of Dublin, and justiciar of the new colony, roles he maintained despite his frequent absenteeism. Trim was his choice of *caput* for the lordship of Meath, and he raised an earth-and-timber castle there almost immediately. He left Ireland in 1173 to serve with the king in France, after which the castle was wrecked by the Irish, and when he returned in 1175 he set about building a new stone castle. Much of that new castle, especially its *donjon* (Figure 7.9), remains to be seen today. To put it in the context of English castles, it post-dates Orford, and its earliest phases are contemporary with the end of construction at Newcastle-upon-Tyne and immediately precede the start of building work at Dover. In terms of Irish castle-building history it is the

Fig. 7.7 (above left) Nenagh Castle.
Fig. 7.8 (below) Plan of Nenagh Castle.

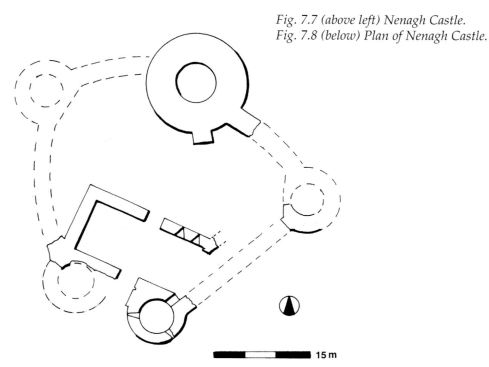

15 m

Fig. 7.9 The donjon at Trim Castle.

earliest substantially-sized colonial castle of stone surviving in Ireland. There was a stone building in Hugh's original pre-1175 castle, but there is no extant *major* stone construction associated with the unfolding conquest of Ireland prior to 1175; the island's other great *donjon* of the period, Carrickfergus, associated with John de Courcy's venture into Ulster, was not started until a few years later.

Recent excavation and conservation work has transformed our understanding of this great castle, but we must await the full publication before settling on an interpretation. The enclosure around the *donjon* (Figure 7.10) is mainly of two phases, that to the north of the *donjon* has squared-off features between stretches of straight wall and is later twelfth-century in date, while that to the south dates from the early 1200s and has a sweeping curve (possibly following the line of the enclosure of the old church site on which the castle was built) interrupted at intervals by outwardly-round towers. The gate-tower to the north-west of the *donjon* in the earlier curtain was built around 1180 to connect the castle with the adjacent borough (town) which was in the process of being developed at that time. Interestingly, it changes to a semi-octagonal shape at upper storey level; this has been identified as a change made in the thirteenth

century, but there are similar semi-octagonal shapes on late twelfth-century towers at Ludlow, another castle of the de Lacy family, and Carlingford, begun in the 1190s by Walter de Lacy's younger brother.

Recent conservation and restoration at Trim's *donjon* has revealed the complexity of its building history. It appears to have been built in three stages, the earliest starting in 1175 under Hugh's patronage, and the second and third under Walter de Lacy's patronage starting in 1194 and 1202 respectively. By 1205 it looked much as it does today. In brief, the sequence of building has been established as follows. In the first phase, dated between 1175 and 1180, the tower was laid out with its familiar Greek Cross plan but rose to only one floor above the basement. Entry was directly to first floor level through the projecting turret on the east side. This turret served, in fact, as one end of a forebuilding, the rest of which was formed from stone walls which survived from the pre-1175 castle on the same site; in the thirteenth century a more elaborate forebuilding was constructed on the same spot, complete with a rectangular room identified as a reception or waiting room. A cross-wall, inserted very early in the tower's history, divided the first-floor space into two compartments: a hall nearest the entrance and a chamber beyond. For a brief period of

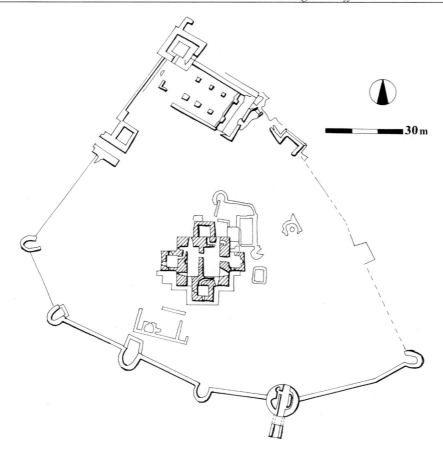

Fig. 7.10 Plan of Trim Castle.

time these two rooms served as the public and private epicentres of Meath power. In the 1190s the roofs of the hall and chamber were taken down and the tower was extended upwards to a second, also partitioned, floor. This too would have had parallel roofs over its hall and chamber parts, and the wall of the *donjon*, with its passages or galleries, would have risen over this. Finally, in the early 1200s the upper parts of the *donjon* were converted into a third floor, a great open chamber (not sub-divided until the late 1200s) which was serviced by those older passages or galleries.

Was it Hugh's intention to leave the *donjon* as it appeared at the end of the first phase, as a low, two-storey, block, almost as wide as it was high? Such *donjons* were not unknown in the twelfth century but by the time Trim was built it was fairly common for low *donjons* to be raised a bit more in height. In this respect, the best English parallel for Trim is probably the Romanesque *donjon* at Porchester. This was originally a two-storey building with a hall and chamber at upper, entrance, level; indeed Trim, minus its projecting turrets, is about the same size. When it was in the possession of Henry II in the early 1170s it was raised a further two storeys. So, it is conceivable

that Trim *donjon*'s appearance at the end of its second phase of construction is how it had always been envisaged: a three-storey block with a basement, an entrance floor, and an upper floor with galleries outside its roof-line.

The third phase at Trim – the making of the third floor with its great chamber – borders on caprice, so briskly did it follow the completion of the second phase. It suggests an almost instantaneous rethinking *c.*1200 of how the *donjon* could be made to reflect and service the prestige of the lordship of Meath. The positive benefit of this alteration at Trim was copious accommodation soaring into the Meath sky, but the entrance into the *donjon* below and the system of access once inside the building were not especially well equipped for the extra traffic. A visitor to the great chamber at the top of the *donjon* would have entered from the forebuilding, moved into the first-floor hall, turned sharply right to look for the short mural passage leading to the stairs, entered the stair well, ascended past the second floor (resisting the tempta-tion to get off the stairs at that level) to the third floor, left the stair well for another short mural passage before stepping down, ruffled and perspiring, into the great chamber. An enemy force could move far more effortlessly and effectively through Trim's labyrinthine mural passages and stairs than a distinguished visitor. If this reinforces our suspicion that Trim's *donjon* was not really designed to withstand an attack by a determined force, it equally suggests that Trim was not especially well equipped internally, especially after 1180, for the public rituals of lordship appropriate to the ranks of the de Lacys. One can only assume that, despite its inadequacies of scale and darkness, the first-floor hall originally set out by Hugh de Lacy remained the castle hall until a new hall was erected in the north-east corner of the castle enclosure in the second half of the thirteenth century.

Trim's *donjon* is quite a sophisticated piece of architecture, its various changes notwithstanding. Its plan's inherent Christian symbolism – the Greek Cross shape – was achieved by a clever reconfiguration of the more conventional and widely distributed square or rectangular plan-type of twelfth-century date; its four projecting turrets contain spaces which the builders of *donjons* elsewhere normally stuffed into mural chambers or created by partitioning. It also possessed a clever system of water collection and distribution. Even its alterations, decade after decade, seem to bespeak a growing confidence and authority as the fledgling colony became more firmly annexed to the Angevin core. Hugh's enjoyment of the king's ear, his familiarity with the trappings of royal (as distinct from seignorial) hegemony, and the geographical detachment from England of his constituency of power in Ireland, combine with the *donjon*'s imperfect system of internal access and lack of substantial hall space to suggest a particular interpretation of Trim's *donjon*: this was a building of outward display which was of almost 'pseudo-royal' character. An Irish equivalent of Orford, its projecting square turrets reflected, as at Orford, the square turrets of its outer enclosure. Its imagined spectators were not really the Irish, on whom such architectural cleverness was lost, but fellow Angevin lords, who might understand its message in the way the king presumably intended the Bigods of Norfolk to understood Orford's message. The king himself may have been among those whom the de Lacys hoped would see Trim. Given the nature of Dover's *donjon* Henry II would doubtless have found Trim to very impressive indeed.

Maynooth

Trim's history may parallel that of another Irish *donjon*, that at Maynooth (Figure 7.11), the key castle of the great FitzGerald family. Never having been studied in the detail it clearly deserves, its exact chronology is uncertain: it is normally assigned to a date of *c.*1200

but its stylistic relationship with Trim suggests that its construction may have begun as early as the 1180s. It was laid out using similar mathematics to Trim, and it further relates to Trim by virtue of having – as a variation on Trim's large mid-wall turrets containing large chambers – shallow mid-wall pilasters containing tiny chambers. There was some interval, or some change of circumstance, between the building of its basement and first-floor levels, since the nicely carved quoin-stones of the bottom part of the *donjon* stop abruptly at their junction, but the two lower storeys are certainly of a piece. The first-floor space, entered via a now-lost forebuilding of some size on the *donjon*'s east side, was partitioned longitudinally into a hall and chamber of equal size. Significantly, that partition was by an arcade rather than a solid wall: this follows the pattern of Trim's first-floor hall-and-chamber as it was originally designed in the later 1170s. One interesting feature of the Maynooth chamber is an original though defaced doorway in its north wall which opened out of the building and into what seems to have been empty space; a shallow corbelled platform on its exterior suggests that this was some type of spectator-oriel for the lord. The walls of Maynooth rose over 10 metres above the floors of this hall and chamber, and presumably the original roofs of the two parallel rooms were tucked under these high walls. Here too we see the same pattern as at Trim in its early phase. At Maynooth a second floor appears to have been inserted in place of these original roofs, thereby making it a three-storey tower like Trim, and, presumably at the same time, the outside walls of the *donjon* were raised by another 10 metres and provided with a mural gallery. The date of this alteration is possibly the first decade of the thirteenth century: the finish on what little remains of the parapet suggests that this building was to have a skyline somewhat reminiscent of that at Trim around 1205. Why was the Maynooth *donjon* extended upwards? Perhaps that skyline *is* the answer. Significantly, there was virtually no natural lighting for that newly-installed second-floor room, so it is difficult to see what function it had other than to prop up the new parapet and the mural viewing gallery immediately below it.

Conclusion

This paper has done nothing more than draw attention to a small number of interesting Irish castles of the period around 1200 and suggested, first, that the label Romanesque is appropriate for them, on account of either their architectural detail or their basic planning conception, and second, that their conservative Romanesque character stands in contrast to the

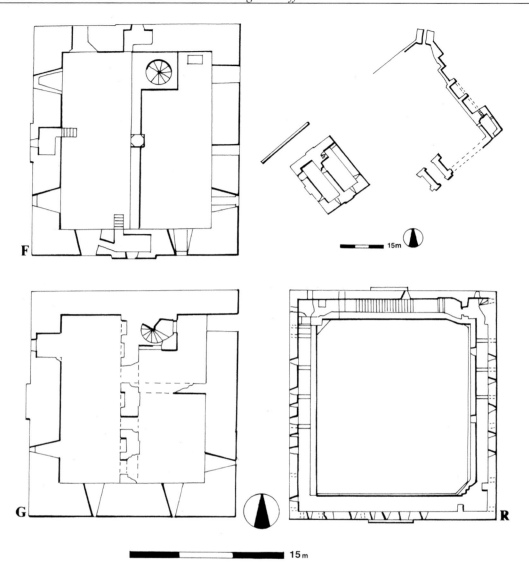

Fig. 7.11 Plan of Maynooth Castle.

contemporary embrace of Gothic among church-builders in Angevin Ireland. I want to finish by making two points, one factual, one meditative. First, it is interesting to note – but no more than that – that at the same time as these castles were being built in newly-colonised eastern Ireland the Gaelic-Irish Romanesque tradition was still alive in non-colonised parts of western Ireland, mainly in a small number of churches associated with the reformed orders and erected under the patronage of ua Conchobhair kings or their subordinates (Kalkreuter 2001). Second, when we look at Trim and Maynooth we are reminded that Roman-esque architecture was not just about physical space

and the treatment of the wall surfaces which defined it; the ways in which Romanesque architecture was used, either as spaces to be moved through and occupied, or as structures and surfaces intended to be seen and understood, were just as important. Perhaps the idea that Romanesque castles are elements within wider iconographically-charged landscapes, as Rob Liddiard has shown (2000), and that they sometimes have 'viewing platforms', as Maynooth's *donjon*, for example, seems to have had, suggests that the value of the adjective Romanesque extends beyond the physical entity of the architectural object itself into the land-scape. Romanesque landscapes – a novel idea!

References

Coulson, C. (1996) Cultural realities and reappraisals in English castle-study. *Journal of Medieval History* 22, 171–207.

Coulson, C. L. H. (2003) *Castles in Medieval Society*. Oxford, Oxford University Press.

Dixon, P. and Marshall, P. (1993) The great tower at Hedingham Castle: a reassessment. *Fortress* 18, 16–23.

Fenlon, J. and O'Brien, K. (2002) *Trim Castle*. Dublin: Dúchas, The Heritage Service.

Fernie, E. (2000) *The Architecture of Norman England*. Oxford: Oxford University Press.

Flanagan, M. T. (1996) Irish and Anglo-Norman warfare in twelfth-century Ireland. In T. Bartlett and Jeffery, K. (eds), *A Military History of Ireland*. Cambridge, Cambridge University Press, 52–75.

Frame, R. (1995) *The Political Development of the British Isles 1100–1400*. Oxford. Clarendon Press.

Gosling, P. (1995) Tuam. In A. Simms and Andrews, J. H. (eds), *More Irish Country Towns*. Cork, Mercier Press.

Graham, B. J. (1988) Timber and earthwork fortifications in western Ireland. *Medieval Archaeology* 32, 110–29.

Heslop, T. A. (1991) Orford Castle: nostalgia and sophisticated living. *Architectural History* 34, 36–58.

Heslop T. A. (1994) *Norwich Castle Keep: Romanesque Architecture and Social Context*. Norwich, Centre for East Anglian Studies.

Johnson. M. (2002) *Behind the Castle Gate: from Medieval to Renaissance*. London, Routledge.

Kalkreuter, B. (2001) *Boyle Abbey and the School of the West*. Bray, Wordwell.

Leask, H. G. (1960) *Irish Churches and Monastic Buildings* II. Dundalk, Dundealgan Press.

Liddiard, R. (2000) *Landscapes of Lordship: the Castle and the Countryside in Medieval Norfolk, 1066–1200*. Oxford, BAR British Series 309.

McNeill, T. E. (1980) *Anglo-Norman Ulster. The History and Archaeology of an Irish Barony 1177–1400*. Edinburgh, John Donald.

McNeill, T. (1997) *Castles in Ireland. Feudal Power in a Gaelic World*. London, Routledge.

Nicholls, K. (1982) Anglo-French Ireland and after. *Peritia* 1, 370–403.

O'Conor, K. (1992) Irish earthwork castles. *Fortress* 12, 3–12.

O'Keeffe, T. (1984) An early Anglo-Norman castle at Ballyderown, Co. Cork. *Journal of the Royal Society of Antiquaries of Ireland*, 114, 52–79.

O'Keeffe, T. (1995) The Romanesque portal at Clonfert Cathedral and its iconography. In C. Bourke (ed.), *From the Isles of the North*. Belfast: HMSO, 261–9.

O'Keeffe, T. (1998) The fortifications of western Ireland, AD 1100–1300, and their interpretation. *Galway Archaeological. Society Journal* 50, 184–200.

O'Keeffe, T. (2000) Architecture and regular life in Holy Trinity cathedral, 1150–1350. In S. Kinsella (ed.), *Augustinians at Christ Church: the Canons Regular of the Cathedral Priory of Holy Trinity, Dublin*. Dublin, Christ Church Cathedral, 23–40.

O'Keeffe, T. (2001) Concepts of 'castle' and the construction of identity in medieval and post-medieval Ireland. *Irish Geography* 34, 1, 69–88.

O'Keeffe, T. (2003) *Romanesque Ireland. Architecture and Ideology in the Twelfth Century*. Dublin, Four Courts Press.

O'Keeffe, T. (2006) Wheels of words, networks of knowledge: Romanesque scholarship and Cormac's Chapel. In D. Bracken and D. Ó Riain-Raedel (eds), *Ireland and Europe in the Twelfth Century: Reform and Renewal*. Dublin, Four Courts Press, 257–69.

Prestwich, M. (1980) Development and decline. In R. A. Brown *et al. Castles: a History and Guide*. Poole, New Orchard Editions, 44–61.

Stalley, R. (1987) *The Cistercian Monasteries of Ireland*. New Haven, Yale University Press.

Stalley, R. (2000) The construction of the medieval cathedral, c.1030–1250. In K. Milne (ed.), *Christ Church Cathedral, Dublin. A History*. Dublin, Four Courts Press, 53–74.

Sweetman, D. (1999) *The Medieval Castles of Ireland*. Cork, Collins Press.

Toy, S. (1955) *A History of Fortification from 3000 B.C. to A.D. 1700*. London, William Heinemann.

Chapter 8

The Peripatetic Life of the Medieval Bishop: The Travels of Salisbury and Bath and Wells

Naomi Payne

Mick Aston, with his great interest in medieval monasteries, supervised my doctoral research on the other great ecclesiastical landowners of the Middle Ages, the bishops. Under Mick's guidance, the focus of my doctoral thesis became the development of the estates of two of the medieval West Country bishoprics, Bath and Wells, and Salisbury, and in particular the archaeological reflection of these estates, in the form of manor houses or palaces, and the associated deer parks, fishponds and gardens.

This paper focuses on a particular aspect of the life of the late medieval bishop, his itinerant existence. The evidence for this takes a number of forms, historical, archaeological and architectural. The bishops' numerous residences were used to varying degrees through time and patterns of use are reflected in the investment made in the upkeep and aggrandisement of their residences, some of which survive, at least in part. The episcopal registers, which for most dioceses were kept fairly consistently from some point in the thirteenth century onwards, can provide information on the bishops' itineraries. More detailed information may sometimes be gleaned from household accounting rolls, which occasionally survive. The focus of this paper is the surviving documentary sources, including the bishops' registers and two household accounts, one from the bishopric of Bath and Wells dating from 1337 to 1338 (Palmer 1924) and one from the bishopric of Salisbury, dating from 1406 to 1407 (Woolgar 1992).

Medieval bishops were constantly on the move, within their dioceses and travelling to and from London. Every three years or so, they were in theory required to carry out visitations of the monasteries under their jurisdiction. The other episcopal duties of ordination, confirmation and the consecration of churches and holy oil would have also necessitated travel. Most medieval bishops had roles in government which involved their spending time in London,

and some spent almost all their time there, for example Bishop Henry Bowet, an early fifteenth century bishop of Bath and Wells, who came to his diocese only a handful of times during his six year episcopate (Holmes 1899). Some medieval bishops also had their own family property which they would visit. Travelling from one manor to the next might have been undertaken for practical reasons, to verify that the episcopal estates were being properly managed, and because manorial produce could be exploited at different locations in turn. However, in practice, the surviving household accounts show that at least in the later Middle Ages food and other resources were obtained from many of the other manors and elsewhere, particularly during prolonged sojourns (Dyer 1994, 259–60).

The Network of Residences

The extent of each bishopric's network of residences depended on its income and therefore its ability to build and maintain residences, the number and location of estates it owned, and the size and location of diocese. Residences went in and out of use. In the high medieval period, the bishops of Salisbury had the following residences available to them:

- The palace at Salisbury.
- A town house in Fleet Street in London.
- A mansion at Sonning, in Berkshire, between the diocese and the capital.
- A manor house at Lower Woodford, a short distance north of the cathedral city.
- Other manor houses at Ramsbury (which had formerly been the diocesan centre in the later Anglo-Saxon period), Potterne, both in Wiltshire and Chardstock on the Devon/Dorset border.
- A castle at Sherborne which was lost to the king by Bishop Roger in the twelfth century but regained by Bishop Wyvil in the fourteenth century.

As for the bishops of Bath and Wells, they had:

– The large mansion at Wells and the palace at Bath. The latter was probably used in the twelfth to fourteenth centuries, but went out of use by the bishop and was let out. It was then reused by one of the late fifteenth century bishops, Oliver King, for accommodation.
– A house in the Strand in London, Bath Inn.
– A mansion at Dogmersfield in Hampshire, which was a convenient stopping point on journeys between Somerset and London.
– A number of other residences within Somerset, several of which continued to be used into the late medieval period: Wookey, Banwell, Wiveliscombe, Chew Magna (which appears to have gone out of use for a century before coming back into favour in the very late fifteenth century and the early sixteenth century).
– Others which went out of use earlier: Blackford (demolished in the mid-fourteenth century), Claverton (not used from later fourteenth century), Evercreech (last used in the mid-fifteenth century)
– Various other manor houses which appear to have been used very occasionally for accommodation purposes by the bishop, and not later than the fourteenth century.

The maintenance and development of these residences was also affected by the agency of individual bishops who favoured particular residences, staying there more frequently and therefore investing larger sums of money in them.

Frequency of Movement

Frequency of movement will be illustrated using the following two case studies.

1. Simon of Ghent, Bishop of Salisbury (1297–1315)

The register of Bishop Simon of Ghent (1297–1315), the earliest to survive for Salisbury diocese, shows that this bishop was frequently on the move. He was often to be found travelling around the diocese, staying for a night or two at various locations, and perhaps signing some documents whilst on day trips from his manor houses. The bishop's register suggests that visits to the episcopal manor houses were sometimes fairly short, but he would stay for longer periods at Ramsbury, Potterne and Sonning in particular. The greatest percentage of time in the bishop's itinerary was spent at Ramsbury (about 27% of the total days probably spent in episcopal accommodation), closely followed by Sonning (25%) and then Potterne (21%).

The bishop also used the residences at London (15%), Chardstock (10%), Woodford and Salisbury (both just over 1%).

2. Thomas Langton, Bishop of Salisbury (1485–1493)

Thomas Langton resided in his official residence in London fairly often (16%), but when in the diocese he strongly favoured Ramsbury, with almost 61% of the known days spent there. Sherborne (10%), Sonning (8%), Woodford (3%) and Salisbury (2.5%) continued to be used occasionally, but must have been in decline. Langton signed one document at Chardstock in August 1490, but he may not have actually stayed the night at the residence.

Two years have been selected from the episcopates of Ghent and Langton to illustrate the change in frequency of movement and numbers of places visited by a bishop of the early fourteenth century and a bishop of the late fifteenth century (see Figures 8.1–8.4). As can be seen in these examples, the bishops reflected the general trend through the later Middle Ages, using a smaller number of houses, many of which were developed to a palatial scale, for longer periods, and moving around less frequently.

Practicalities and the Cost of Moving

It was very expensive to run and maintain so many households. At one point in the Middle Ages the Archbishop of Canterbury was asked to keep his travelling retinue to a maximum of fifty men and their horses because of the huge expenses involved in his lifestyle (Kershaw 1914, 107).

For the bishops of Bath and Wells and Salisbury it seems to have been a particular expense to spend time in their cathedral cities, as there they often had to cater for many more people. This may have been another reason why many of the bishops spent so little time at Wells and Salisbury, in addition to another explanation which is often cited, that there was too much risk of conflict with the cathedral dean's jurisdiction (Edwards and Owen 1975, xxxvi). London was also expensive in terms of the general cost of living (Palmer 1924, 170), which may explain why many bishops of Bath and Wells, and Salisbury favoured Dogmersfield and Sonning respectively, both close enough to the capital to be reached without an overnight stay.

In some circumstances the bishop's household might be split between two residences and when a prolonged stay was planned at a particular residence, horses would often be stabled at more than one location (Woolgar 1999, 191). Presumably it would have been easier to feed the horses using the stocks of

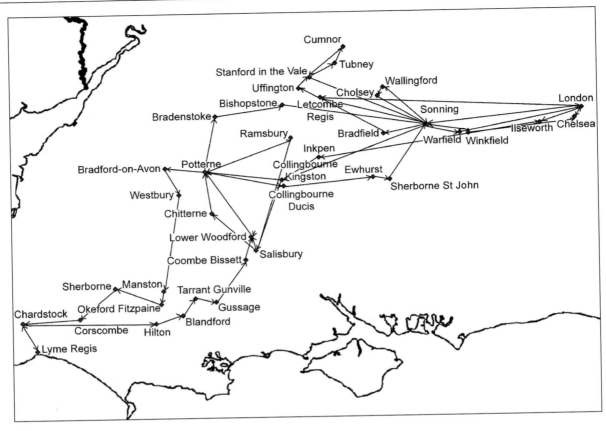

Fig. 8.1 The travels of Simon of Ghent in 1302.

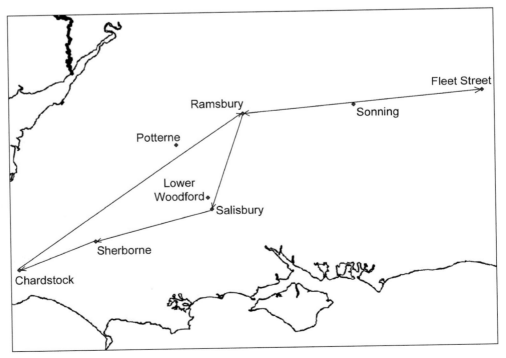

Fig. 8.2 The travels of Thomas Langton in 1490.

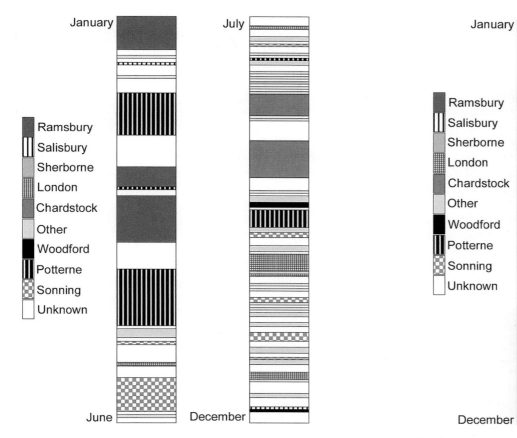

Fig. 8.3 Time spent at each residence by Simon of Ghent in 1302.

Fig. 8.4 Time spent at each residence, Thomas Langton in 1490.

more than one manor, hence the marshalsea chose to divide them up. In these circumstances, part of the household would also be stationed at the other residence, in order to look after the horses. This is known to have taken place in December 1337, when Ralph of Shrewsbury, bishop of Bath and Wells, was staying at Evercreech, during which time some of the horses were stabled at Wookey, along with part of the household (around 20 grooms and pages) who were on a detached duty. Two months later (in February and March of 1338), when Shrewsbury paid a visit to London, the horses he brought with him were stabled at Fulham, with 6 grooms and a page looking after them (Palmer 1924, 134–50).

During October 1406 when Bishop Mitford of Salisbury was staying at Woodford, some horses were stabled at Woodford, but a larger group were kept nearby at Salisbury palace between the 1st and 5th of October. The horses were then all moved to Woodford, but a group returned between the 19th and 25th of October, just before the bishop moved to his house at Potterne. On the 26th when the bishop made this journey, he was at Woodford for his midday meal and

at Horston, en route, for supper. Hay and bedding at Horston for 54 horses were required, at a cost of 5 shillings and 3 pence. A few days previously, on 20th of October, hay for 30 cart horses travelling from Sherborne to Potterne, 54 miles, was listed amongst the marshalsea's expenses, evidently in preparation for the lord's arrival at Potterne. Not long after arriving at Potterne, on the 16th November, a number of horses were moved to Ramsbury to be stabled there. The horses continued to be split between these two manors until three weeks after the bishop's death, when (on 27th of May 1407) the household moved to Salisbury in advance of his funeral. The average number of horses being stabled by the bishop during the period covered by the surviving diet account was 39, including an average of 5 hackneys.

Many of the medieval bishop's possessions, including furniture and linen, would have been carried from one place to the next, rather than being stored at each household, in order to keep the costs manageable. Everything in the household would have been transportable in two-wheeled carts or larger four-wheeled wagons (Woolgar 1999, 181). As no expenses are mentioned other than hay for the cart horses which carried some of Bishop Mitford's possessions to Potterne in mid-October 1406, it seems that the bishop had his own carts for transporting his effects whilst on the move.

The lifestyle was physically demanding for the bishops, many of whom became old and infirm during their episcopates. Elderly bishops often remained in one place for many months before their deaths, perhaps indicating that they were too ill to travel. For example, Richard Mitford was at Potterne from 27th of October 1406 until his death on 3rd of May 1407 (Woolgar 1992, 279–382) and there is no evidence that Bishop Ralph of Shrewsbury of Bath and Wells moved from the residence at Wiveliscombe at all between 23rd of August 1361 and his death on 14th of August 1363 (Holmes 1896). Shrewsbury held the bishopric of Bath and Wells for more than 34 years, and as most bishops were of mature age when appointed, he may well have been a very old man at the time of his death.

The bishops' itineraries show that the distances travelled on single days were not inconsiderable. For example, Potterne to Ramsbury and Woodford/ Salisbury to Potterne (around 25 miles by modern roads) seems to have been a standard single journey (the household were apparently at Potterne for their lunchtime meal and Salisbury for supper on 27th May 1407, according to the Mitford diet account) (Woolgar 1992, 396). The bishops would sometimes travel between Ramsbury and both Lower Woodford and Sonning, both journeys being about 38 miles by modern roads (e.g. Flower and Dawes, 565: Potterne to Ramsbury, 24th–25th of January 1298; 594 and 837: Ramsbury to Lower Woodford, 25th–26th of April 1299; 867 and 871: Sonning to Ramsbury, 18th–19th of September 1304). Likewise, the bishops of Bath and Wells would sometimes undertake the 40 miles from Wookey or Wells to Wiveliscombe in one journey (e.g. Holmes 1896, 2300 and 2304, 5th–6th of October 1349). Away from the principal routes, these journeys might take a little longer, but the fact that they appear in the itineraries show that they were feasible (Woolgar 1999, 187). The quality of roads must have been adequate for the transportation of a number of individuals on foot or on horseback, and the carts which held their possessions. The bishop and his *familia* (household) evidently planned their routes ahead because some register entries refer to arrangements made for certain dates and places.

The Itinerant Household

Surviving household accounts from other dioceses reveal that fifty to one hundred people might accompany the medieval bishop on his journeys, the bishop and senior officials on horseback, with furniture and supplies following in carts and most individuals on foot (Thompson 1998, 13). Those on horseback might reach their destination more quickly and some servants may have departed in advance in order to prepare for their lord's arrival. Other elements of the baggage train might take a little longer to arrive. During the journey made by Bishop Ralph of Shrewsbury from London to Dogmersfield in March 1338, the carts travelled half a day behind the bishop, with two household officials and three grooms (Woolgar 1999, 188).

The surviving diet accounts from the households of Ralph of Shrewsbury and Richard Mitford can be used to calculate a general estimate of the size of the bishops' households. The surviving fragment of Ralph of Shrewsbury's account contains data for 61 days during 1337 and 1338, over which time the average number of individuals provided for was 89. The total is broken down on two occasions:

	05/01/1338	09/03/1338
Free household (*libera familia*)	30	16
Household officers (*officales*)	21	17
Servants (*garciones*)	83	56

There is no mention of guests and their attendants, who must have been included in the totals above. The account from the episcopate of Richard Mitford contains data for 242 days during 1406 and 1407.

Average number of people of gentle rank	29
Average number of grooms and valets	44
Average total number of individuals provided with food	73
Average number of guests	29

The total number of individuals dining, minus the average number of guests was 44, so this would be the approximate number of people who would travel with the bishop from residence to residence, his own personal household. The totals may however include some temporary workers, who would not have moved on with the bishop. As well as individuals who worked at different levels in the offices of the household, the hall, the pantry, the buttery, the kitchen and the stables, there would have been men employed by the bishop to aid him in the administration of his diocese. In the fifteenth century, the diocesan staff of the bishops of Bath and Wells included the spiritual chancellor, the registrar, the apparitor-general, clerks of the writing office, notaries, domestic chaplains and temporal administrative staff (Dunning 1966, 25). It would have been necessary for many of these staff to travel with the bishop at times.

By the fourteenth century, the great household of a magnate like a bishop would receive individual visitors, sometimes with a select entourage, rather than having to accommodate another bishop or noble's household at their own expense (Woolgar 1999, 21). The 1406–1407 household account supplies some detail about the sorts of people who might be provided for at the bishop's residence (and sometimes might be accommodated). Bishop Mitford's sister and her entourage stayed at Potterne for a few days before and after his death on 3rd of May 1407. Various important lay people, minor gentry and others might be entertained, sometimes with their wives. Usually names are given, but sometimes these individuals' professions are given too, for example, the parker of Hampstead, two burgesses of Devizes, a knight and two clerks of the duke of York. Sometimes the bishop provided food for people of a more lowly standing, such as the customary tenants of a manor. There were also many ecclesiastical guests, such as the priors and prioresses of local monasteries, for example those of Amesbury and Ivychurch in Wiltshire (the bishop had jurisdiction over priories within his diocese), the bishop's suffragan (an assistant bishop who could perform episcopal duties), an Irish bishop, the dean of Salisbury and various lower clergymen (canons, chaplains, rectors, vicars and friars). The bishop of Winchester and an unspecified number of his household were apparently watered but not fed at Potterne on 29th of May 1407 (Woolgar 1992, 397).

Likewise the bishop might also go out to visit other people and dine with them. Ralph of Shrewsbury and his retinue had their midday meal with the rector of Curry Rivel on 13th of November 1337, then returned to Somerton, where they were staying temporarily, to eat supper (Palmer 1924, 96). This type of short-term journey may often be invisible in the registers, apart from in circumstances when an official document was created whilst at the other location.

Maintenance Expenses

The surviving account rolls make it clear that repair work of various kinds was necessary at every residence each year, whether or not the bishop had stayed there for any length of time or even at all. It is no coincidence that these sorts of repairs come up on all of the surviving account rolls. Considering the annual cost of maintaining so many houses, particularly during the episcopates of bishops who were often absent from the diocese, it is unsurprising that several of the residences of the bishops of Bath and Wells became disused. The types of repairs which commonly appear on the medieval account rolls include the lime washing of walls, tiling and thatching work and the repair of gates and doors. Surviving accounts for manors belonging to other dioceses tell a similar story. Nathaniel Alcock, for example, has examined the medieval accounts that concern the bishop of Exeter's manor at Bishop's Clyst, Devon, which show that "regular repairs had to be carried out on the roofs... the thatcher and tiler were employed almost every year on large jobs" (Alcock 1966, 142).

The Range of Other Locations Where the Bishop Might Stay

There are some interesting details in Bishop Bekynton's register which shed light on where exactly the bishop might stay when he could not use any of his diocesan residences. For example, at Glastonbury Abbey there was a "chamber commonly called the bishop's chamber", where the bishops presumably regularly rested when they had business at the monastery (Maxwell-Lyte and Dawes 1934, 929). When the bishop was in Bagshot (Surrey) in August 1445, he stayed "at the inn marked with the sign of the crown, at which... [he] was wont to lodge when travelling there." (Maxwell-Lyte and Dawes 1934, 138). In April 1448, Bishop Bekynton lodged at the house of Richard Page in Warminster (Wiltshire) and later the same year, he signed a document in "an upper chamber wherein the bishop was lodging in the house of the Augustinian Friars, Bristol." (Maxwell-Lyte and Dawes 1934, 333, 377). In July 1457, he passed a few nights at an inn in Salisbury, Wiltshire (Maxwell-Lyte and Dawes 1934, 1063). Bekynton's predecessors had presumably also employed similar accommodation for short periods, where and when necessary.

Conclusion

Despite the piecemeal survival of documentary evidence for the movements of medieval bishops, it is possible to discern the general trends of where and when they travelled during the late medieval period. As for any great magnate travel between houses and then the upkeep of these residences consumed and enormous amount of both time and resources. His duties in his diocese, as well as his position as an important figure in the king's administration inevitably led to a peripatetic lifestyle, if the bishop wished to maintain his influence. The houses between which they travelled reflected both their perculiar and superior status and their administrative activities as well as being the residences of wealthy men. The limited documentary evidence makes this an area ripe for further archaeology study, where so little survives of this particular stratum of building.

References

Alcock, N. W. (1966) The Medieval Buildings of Bishop's Clyst. *Transactions & Reports of the Devonshire Association*, 98, 132–153.

Dunning, R. W. (1966) The Households of the Bishops of Bath and Wells in the Later Middle Ages. *Proceedings of the Somerset Archaeological and Natural History Society* 110, 24–39.

Dyer, C. (1994) *Everyday Life in Medieval England*. London, The Hambledon Press.

Edwards, K. and Owen, D. M. (eds) (1975) *The Registers of Roger Martival, Bishop of Salisbury 1315–1330. Volume 4: General Introduction to the Registers and the Register of Inhibitions and Acts*. (Canterbury & York Society, volume 68). Torquay, The Devonshire Press.

Flower, C. T. and Dawes, M. C. B. (eds) (1934) *Registrum Simonis de Gandavo, Diocesis Saresbiriensis A. D. 1297–1315*. (Canterbury & York Series volume 40). Oxford, University Press.

Holmes, T. S. (ed.) (1896) *The Register of Ralph of Shrewsbury, Bishop of Bath and Wells 1329–63*. (Somerset Record Society vols. 9–10). Taunton.

Holmes, T. S. (ed.) (1899) *The Registers of Walter Giffard, Bishop of Bath and Wells, 1265–6 and of Henry Bowet, Bishop of Bath and Wells, 1401–7*. (Somerset Record Society vol. 13). Taunton.

Maxwell-Lyte, H. C. and Dawes, M. C. B. (eds) (1934) *The Register of Thomas Bekynton, Bishop of Bath and Wells 1443–1465, part 1*. (Somerset Record Society vol. 49). Taunton.

Maxwell-Lyte, H. C. and Dawes, M. C. B. (eds) (1935) *The Register of Thomas Bekynton, Bishop of Bath and Wells 1443–1465, part 2*. (Somerset Record Society vol. 50). Taunton.

Palmer, T. F. (ed.) (1924) *Collectanea I: A Collection of Documents from Various Sources*. (Somerset Record Society vol. 39). Taunton.

Payne, N. (2003) *The Medieval Residences of the Bishops of Bath and Wells, and Salisbury*. Unpublished PhD thesis, University of Bristol.

Thompson, M. (1998) *Medieval Bishops' Houses in England and Wales*. Aldershot, Ashgate.

Woolgar, C. M. (ed.) (1992) *Household Accounts from Medieval England Part 1: Introduction, Glossary, Diet Accounts (I)*. Oxford, Oxford University Press.

Woolgar, C. M. (1999) *The Great Household in Late Medieval England*. New Haven and London, Yale University Press.

Chapter 9

An Aristocratic Mausoleum at Grosbot Abbey (Poitou-Charente, France)

Mark Horton and Katharine Robson Brown

At the beginning of Mick Aston's classic book on monasteries, he enjoins us to consider the role they took as 'social and economic centres' and not simply in terms of their surviving architecture or individual histories (Aston 1993, 16). Shortly after the publication of that volume, and after we had joined him on the staff of the University of Bristol, he suggested that we should go to France to investigate Cistercian Abbeys in their landscapes. Mick had previously visited Grosbot Abbey in Western France, and identified it as a suitable site to work on.

Six seasons of survey and excavation at Grosbot between 1996 and 2002 were concentrated to the east of the main cloistral buildings in the area that would, by convention, contain the infirmary and monastic graveyard. A geophysical survey of this area had indeed indicated the remains of a large east-west rectangular building, and it was hoped that an excavation would reveal evidence of the outer features of the monastery, so often ignored in monastic archaeology (Aston 1993, 110). As often happens with archaeological excavations, the unexpected turns up, and here we offer to our colleague, Mick Aston, an unusual building that enlarges our understanding of monasteries as social and economic centres. We discovered a substantial mausoleum, accommodating the burials of the lay benefactors of the abbey and their family, which has wider implications for the study of feudalism in medieval France.

Grosbot Abbey

The abbey (known locally as L'abbaye de Grosbot) is located approximately 35km south-east of Angoulême, in an area of western France that remains heavily wooded; indeed, the place-name probably derived from the French *gros bois*, 'large wood or forest' (Besse 1905, 128; Larigauderie-Beijeaud 1998), rendered in Latin *Grosso Bosco*, and it was this name that

came to be adopted by the Cistercians. An earlier monastic foundation on the site was known as Fontvive or Fontaine Vive, after the substantial spring, located to the west of the abbey buildings, which flowed under the cloisters and church (Bell 1997, 339). The Cistercians dropped this name shortly after their acquisition of the site, between c.1160–1166. A nineteenth-century source gives 975 as the original foundation date for the abbey, 'par un seigneur de Marthon' (Vigier de la Pile 1846, 17), but the primary authority for this is unknown. There may have been monastic activity at this early date, but there is no archaeological evidence at present for it. If true, it connects the abbey from its beginnings to the local landowning families.

In the early twelfth-century the abbey seems to have come under Augustinian control, and was closely linked to the cathedral and canons at Angoulême (Anon 1900, 253). The *Historia Pontificum et Comitum* (Boussard, 1957, 57) claims that the well-known bishop of Angoulême, Gerald II de Blaye (1102–1135) began the construction of the abbey church, along with La Couronne and Bournet, 'in his time and with his kindness and aid'. In 1121, the abbot, Jean de Font-Vive was given lands and rights to build an oratory at Luquet (Larigauderie-Beijeaud 1998, 5–6). In 1155, Guillaume, the abbot, and his brother canons were given the church of St Pierre in Souffrignac by the bishop, suggesting that there were still links with Angoulême (Sainte-Marthe 1656). The transfer of the abbey into the Cistercian Order, as a daughter house of Obazine, took place between c.1160 and 1166; the formal acceptance in 1166 (Janauschek 1877, 155; Mondon 1895–7, 216; Nanglard 1894, 566) may represent the completion of the church and abbey buildings. Some use may have been made of the Augustinian buildings, and traces of an earlier phase of building survive in the south transept of the church and east cloister range (Figure 9.1). Most of the abbey

Fig. 9.1 Abbey Church of Grosbot, showing external south wall nave and south transept. It is likely that the church was largely rebuilt by the Cistercians in c.1160, but that the south transept contains sections of earlier work.

Fig. 9.2 Interior of the Abbey Church, with cupola domes over the crossing and east end, which are part of the regional architectural tradition.

and its cloisters were however rebuilt on a standard Cistercian plan, although showing some local stylistic influences, such as the use of domed vaults above the crossing and at the east end (Figure 9.2).

The abbey managed to build up extensive estates in the local area, through its early foundation (when it probably acquired the lands immediately around the abbey), and the subsequent donations especially by the Marthon / La Rochefoucauld family, whose nearby residences included the surviving twelfth-century castle at Marthon and probably another at La Rochefoucauld itself. The first firm documentation comes from 1147–8, when Robert of Marthon, and his two sons, Wido de la Roche and Fergans grant the grange of Mas Cordorz to Obazine, alone with exemption from tolls on their land, the rights for grazing pigs in the forest of Grosbot, and the wood in this forest for heating (Larigauderie-Beijeaud 1998, 5–6). This estate seems to have passed to the abbey, when it transferred shortly afterwards to the Cistercian order, as a daughter house of Obazine. There are surviving monastic remains of this grange at Mas Cordorz. Another donation is recorded in 1264, when Gerald Robert of Marthon and his son Peter Robert grant to the abbey the grange of Eyraudie, near Brouillac (Larigauderie-Beijeaud 1998, 13).

The abbey survived as a functioning religious unit until its sale in 1791 (Larigauderie-Beijeaud 1998, 89–90), although monastic life was disrupted, and probably interrupted during both the Hundred Years War and the Wars of Religion, which had a major impact in this area of France. In 1632 a detailed survey was made of the derelict buildings, and there is good documentation for the subsequent restoration under the authority of a commendatory abbot, a status it retained until the French Revolution (Larigauderie-Beijeaud 1998, 65–6). After the Revolution, the abbey become a farm and the church fell into disrepair. Since the early 1990's the claustral buildings have been subject to extensive restoration and conversion as a private residence.

Archaeological Excavations

The focus of the archaeological investigations was to the east of the conventual buildings, where the resistivity survey indicated surviving foundations below the ground surface (Figure 9.3). An approximately square area (26m by 25m) was excavated during a period of six summers, revealing a complex sequence of occupation (Figure 9.4). The upper levels comprised nineteenth-century garden deposits, sealing a robbed-out basin or pool that formed part of the formal gardens of the seventeenth-century (post

1632) abbey. This rested on, and partly robbed out a large rectangular hall-like building, aligned east west, which had been identified on the resistivity survey.

This building measured internally 18.5m by 6.4m (60 ft 9 in. by 21 ft). The function of this hall remains uncertain; its location would suggest that it was the monk's infirmary, although there were neither diagnostic features nor artefacts to confirm this identification. An alternative function might have been as a guest hall, although this would have been unusual to the east of the abbey buildings. The hall was internally divided into two halves by a wooden partition, with a different sequence of floor levels recorded on either side. A single construction level of mortar and plaster was found across most of the building, which was cut by a well-preserved and unusual bell-founders' pit (Horton 2004). This pit was dug within the newly constructed building, before it was fully commissioned, and the ceramics in the fill, including early Saintonge wares, are a useful dating indicator for building of the hall around 1300.

Its interior was covered by a plaster floor to the west, and sand bedding for a tile floor to the east. The plaster floor showed traces of an intense fire and the collapse of timber and masonry blocks onto it, which could possibly have been associated with the documented damage to the abbey during the Hundred Years War (Larigauderie-Beijeaud 1998, 39). The hall was later repaired in the fifteenth century; in the eastern half, the damaged plaster floor was covered by the sand bedding for a tile floor, and a fireplace added at the east end of the north wall. The building went out of use in the later fifteenth or early sixteenth century.

The Mausoleum (Figure 9.5)

This large hall, built around 1300, replaced a smaller but grander building lying immediately to the south. The sequence of layers between the two buildings indicated that the later hall directly succeeded it, as its south wall was built over the foundation of the north wall of the earlier building, and the construction spreads of the hall covered its floor levels (Figure 9.6).

This earlier building functioned as a private burial chapel or mausoleum. It was a large freestanding, buttressed two-celled structure that was designed specifically for the burial of high status individuals in either stone sarcophagi or purpose-built tombs. Its walls were made from finely dressed limestone ashlar blocks, with a mortared rubble core set on a slightly wider foundation of smaller stones, in mortar and rammed clay. The internal dimensions were 10.25m by 4.85m, with the east and west walls 1.25m thick and the north and south walls 1.00m thick. The exact

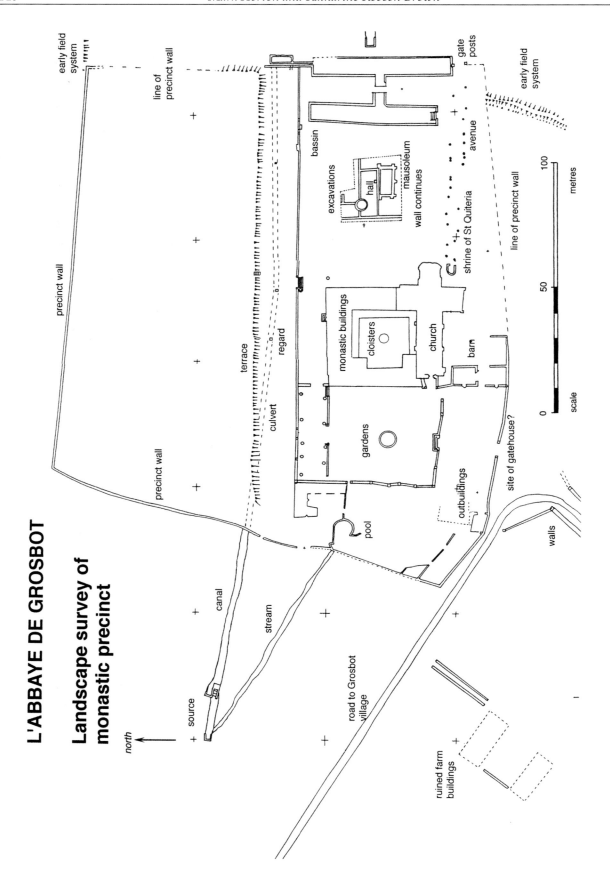

L'ABBAYE DE GROSBOT

Landscape survey of monastic precinct

north

source

canal

stream

road to Grosbot village

ruined farm buildings

walls

pool

site of gatehouse?

outbuildings

gardens

barn

church

cloisters

monastic buildings

shrine of St Quiteria

mausoleum

wall continues

hall

excavations

bassin

regard

culvert

terrace

line of precinct wall

avenue

gate posts

early field system

early field system

precinct wall

precinct wall

line of precinct wall

scale

0   50   100

metres

Fig. 9.3 The monastic precinct, showing the layout of the main cloistral buildings as they survive today, and the main excavation site to the east of the abbey church.

Fig. 9.4 General view of the excavations from the west. In the foreground are the walls and floors of the hall, with the later seventeenth century pool or garden feature overlying them. The mausoleum is on the right side of the photograph.

size of the building could be calculated, even though many of the ashlar blocks had been robbed out, because the edge of the internal plaster floor had survived (Figure 9.7). Foundations of a presumed central arch divided the building into two equal halves; while at each corner there were traces of an internal rebate that carried a vault, possibly a groin vault. Externally each corner has two clasping buttresses, 1.4m wide and projecting 0.8m with two further buttresses in the centre of the long sides, adjacent to the central arch, also suggesting the need to support a vault.

The internal floor levels survived best in the western half of the building. There were four floor levels with thin layers of silt or sand between each. At the east end, the floors had all been eroded away, with the exception of one small patch of mortar. This area was probably raised, and a single stone remained in position to indicate a step or platform at the eastern end. In the northwest corner, traces of a circular burn patch in the floor may indicate the location of a candle base or brazier.

Sealed below these floors were the original levelling layers and the foundation trenches for the walls, together with a number of sealed amorphous features (probably natural tree root holes and animal burrows), overlying the natural clay subsoil (Figure 9.8). These well-sealed deposits contained a small quantity of pottery, but significantly also clay roof tile. The tile was in sufficient quantity and in secure contexts to provide a *terminus post quem* date for the construction of the mausoleum. While the chronology roof tile usage has not been established in this part of France, dates from other Cistercian abbeys, as well as from sealed urban deposits and documentary evidence elsewhere in northern Europe, indicate a late twelfth or early thirteenth century for their introduction (Drury 1981, 130–1; Cherry 1991, 194). The building is most likely to have been constructed during the Cistercian ownership of the site, and was not a survival from the earlier Augustinians. This stratigraphic and dating evidence points to its use between c. AD 1200–1300.

A total of 35 burials or fragments of burials have been investigated, with at least a further 15 represented by charnel. These burials form three groups: burials within the mausoleum walls, burials in tombs and sarcophagi outside the mausoleum and either earlier or contemporary with it, and later burials, which were cut into the earlier burial horizon.

Burials within the Mausoleum

Within the mausoleum, there were five tombs (and a later child burial, dating to after the abandonment of the building), one of which was an elaborate double

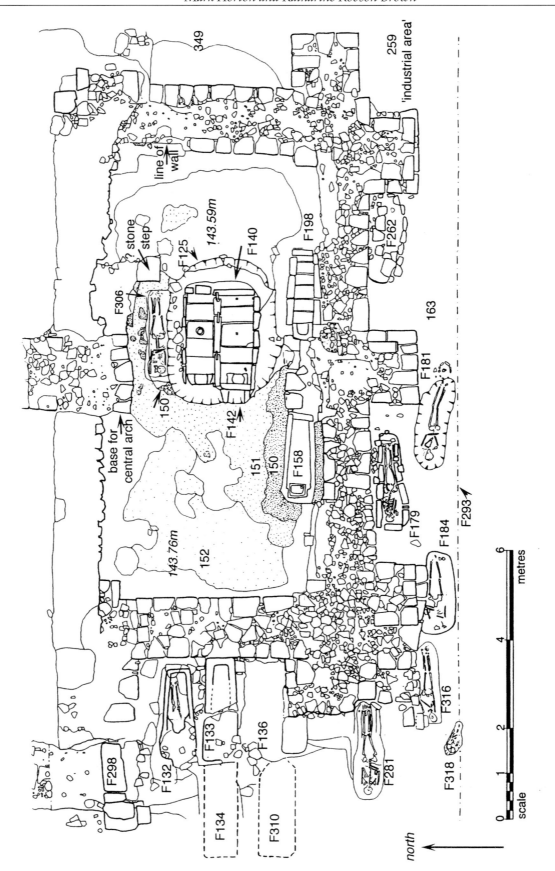

Fig. 9.5 Plan of the mausoleum, with the main excavated tombs, and internal floor levels.

Fig. 9.6 Photograph showing the stratigraphic relationship between the hall and the mausoleum. The south wall of the hall was built over the robbed-out foundations of the north wall of the mausoleum, and constructions spreads were found directly over the top floor of the mausoleum.

Fig. 9.7 General view of the mausoleum from the west, showing walls, internal floors and tombs. The external burials were exposed and robbed in the seventeenth century during the construction of a drain that ran north-south outside the building.

Fig. 9.8 The mausoleum fully excavated. The floors have been removed, exposing the foundation trenches for the walls, for the double tomb, and various amorphous features that are probably tree bowls.

tomb, located in the centre of the mausoleum. Unfortunately seventeenth-century robbing of the tombs took place when the sarcophagi were discovered during the digging of a drain for the garden feature (post-1632), and so in some cases the human remains were disturbed or incomplete.

The double tomb complex (F140) was the best-preserved tomb as well as the most elaborate (Figure 9.9). Its upper levels had been robbed out in the seventeenth century although there was no evidence that any of the actual tomb structure had been tampered with. The robbed back-fill contained some human bone, including two mature adults, two children and one neonatal individual. The main complex was made from finely finished limestone blocks, which had been laid very carefully to ensure that the tomb could be constructed on two levels, with a floor between. The blocks were clamped together using wrought iron clamps. On the bottom of each chamber, the floor had a stone that could be lifted up (there were remains of an iron handle) to gain access to the lower chamber (Figure 9.10). In both cases, the lower chambers were empty of deposits; the southern chamber contained a few small pieces of human bone.

The southern upper chamber contained a small number of bones, and some worked stone in the seventeenth-century disturbed deposit. There was

however an undisturbed primary fill that comprised a fine orange loam with no trace of burial. If there had been a burial in this southern chamber, it had been carefully removed prior to the seventeenth-century robbing. Indeed it likely that the covering stone had also been removed in the Middle Ages, as a later child burial (F367) was dug into the top of the tomb, where this cover would have been placed, after the building had been abandoned.

The north side of the double tomb preserved a third level, with a sarcophagus (F127) inserted into the top of the second-level tomb. This sarcophagus had been robbed in the seventeenth-century and there were again no finds in its fill or trace of its covering (Figure 9.11). The sarcophagus is of particular interest, as it appears to be a thick tomb cover that was reduced in length, and inverted, then hollowed-out to be converted into a sarcophagus. On its underside there was a cross, originally intended to be visible on the upper side. The arrangement left the sarcophagus open at its foot end, as the tomb cover was of insufficient length, and had to be closed with an extra stone.

This reused tomb cover/sarcophagus sealed an intact burial deposit in the second level of tomb chamber. This comprised a group of disarticulated human bones, of an adult male, and traces of a wooden box in which they had been placed (Figure 9.12). There

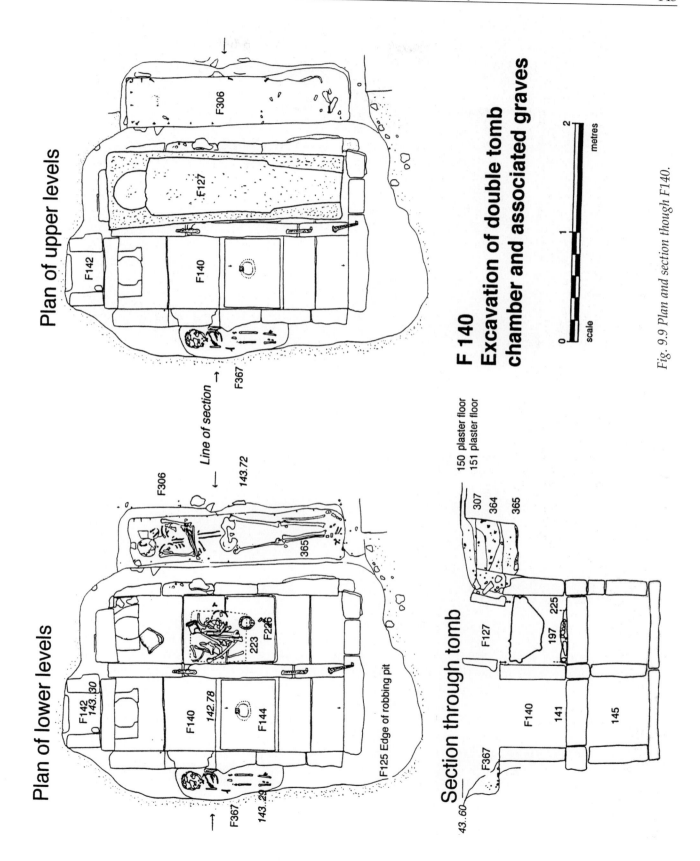

Plan of upper levels

F306

F127

F142

F140

F367

Line of section

143.72

Plan of lower levels

F306

F142
143.30

F140
142.78

F144

223 F226

F367
143.29

365

F125 Edge of robbing pit

F 140
Excavation of double tomb chamber and associated graves

scale metres
0   1   2

Section through tomb

307
364
365

150 plaster floor
151 plaster floor

F127

197
225

F140

141

145

F367

43.60

Fig. 9.9 Plan and section though F140.

Fig. 9.10 The double tomb, F140, showing it in its primary form. It was constructed from finely cut limestone slabs, held together with iron clamps. Two moveable slabs in the middle of each tomb opened to a lower chamber. They are visible with their iron rings.

Fig. 9.11 F140 as first excavated showing the robbed out lower southern tomb and the upper sarcophagus above the northern tomb, also robbed out. The water table is close to the surface, but this may be due to post medieval landscape changes.

were also traces of the iron lock and bindings for this box. The box was approximately 500mm square, and the bones had been carefully stacked within it. Over 90% of the bones from this burial (a male of 35–45+) survived, including many of the hand and foot bones, suggesting that they had been carefully curated before being placed in their box (Figure 9.13). There were also traces of knife marks on the long bones, possibly suggesting that the corpse had been cut up. At the head end of the tomb there was a complete (but empty) unglazed Saintonge ware ceramic jug (Figure 9.14), dating to the early to mid-thirteenth century (Brown 2002, 23, 27, no. 186; Platt and Coleman-Smith 1975, ii, 135–6, Figure 92, no. 1005, 1006; Anon 1975, 59).

An earth burial (F306) lay immediately to the north of the double tomb complex; the grave cut was cut by the foundation for it (Figure 9.15). The burial was first visible as a disturbed rectangular area in the third floor level. This may have been where a rectangular tomb-stone had been robbed from the floor surface, and a mortar trail suggested where the stone had been originally set. In the fill of the grave itself were regularly placed nails from a wooden coffin; there were three levels, with iron tacks marking the lowest level. This suggests that the coffin was made from two planks, with the bottom and top fixed to the sides. The nails were missing where the double tomb had cut the grave. The fill of the grave had numerous clay roof tiles. A layer of flat stones seems to have covered the main body. The skeleton was a male adult, laid supine, with arms crossed across the chest. The head had rolled over, but the jaw remained in position; the feet were slanted to the right. There was a small iron pin (most likely a shroud pin) by the right elbow.

A later stone tomb (F142) was placed above the southerly section of double tomb (Figure 9.16). Three slabs of limestone remained and were partly sealed by the two latest floors to the mausoleum. The rest of the tomb had been removed when the southern part of F140 was robbed out. The slabs form part of the head end of a typical slab-constructed tomb, which would have formed a pair with and at the some level as the upper sarcophagus. There were a few fragments of human bone in its fill comprising a young adult, but no trace of *in situ* burial, so we cannot be certain if this was the primary occupant.

Another example of the slab style of tomb was found against the south wall of the mausoleum. This tomb (F198) was probably associated with the first or second floor and built with well-shaped individual stones, set up on their sides, as well as a stone base of individual slabs. At the west end, there was a head inset, just like that found with F142. Unfortunately, this tomb was robbed in the seventeenth century, and no trace of the original burial was found.

The fifth tomb within the mausoleum was mono-

Fig. 9.12 F140, after the removal of the upper sarcophagus, with the burial and earthenware jug in position.

Fig. 9.13 Detail of burial within F140, showing the stacked human bone. The spread of bone represents approximately the original shape of the wooden box.

Fig. 9.14 Saintonge ware jug, found in F140. Early to mid thirteenth century in date, it has a typical parrot-beak spout, of this type of Saintonge whiteware and is unglazed.

Fig. 9.15 F140 fully excavated, showing the double tomb cutting the earth burial, F306, which lay to the north.

Fig. 9.16 Detail of F140, with upper sarcophagus (the sides have been removed for safety) and the later F142 lying over the head inset of the double tomb.

lithic stone sarcophagus (F158), made from oolitic limestone and set into the top floor of the mausoleum against the south wall, to the west of the central arch (Figure 9.17). The top of the tomb was higher than the earlier F198 to the east, and must have been one of the last tombs in the building. Unfortunately the burial was disturbed in the seventeenth century and the east end of the sarcophagus broken in the process. The loose fill excavated within the tomb contained a little human bone, and tile. However at the base of the tomb a thin layer of brown silt survived forming an oblong shape. This may be a surviving deposit from the burial, comprising a 'body-stain' from the pelvic area. It is possible that the burial was removed in the middle ages, before the tomb was later robbed in the seventeenth century.

There were sufficient relationships between the

tombs and the floor levels to indicate a broad sequence of burial activity within the mausoleum. It seems that the two earliest tombs lay around the sides of the building with F198 and F306. The double tomb F140 cuts F306 (but only marginally) may also be early, placed centrally in the building. The latest tomb was F158, a monolithic sarcophagus, with its contents removed and associated with the top floor level. The only dating evidence recovered was the sealed Saintonge jug, sealed in F140, which places the double tomb in the early or middle part of the thirteenth century. F306 contained much roof tile in its fill, again indicating a thirteenth century date.

No trace of the original covers for these tombs survived in position. With F306, a rectangular area was visible at the third floor level, and there may have been a stone cover, that was later moved when F140 was constructed. In the case of the double tomb, the third level only survived on the north side, and this sarcophagus may have been placed there after the construction and completion of the double tomb. There was no equivalent sarcophagus on the south side, although a slat constructed tomb, F142, was built at this level and virtually all removed in the robbing of the tomb. The third-level sarcophagus does not fit particularly well and probably was the original tomb cover that was inverted and hollowed out as a sarcophagus; its thickness would place its top slightly above the upper floor level.

Burials Outside the Mausoleum

In addition to these seven presumably 'high-status' tombs within the mausoleum, there were a whole series of tombs and graves to the west and south of the building (Figure 9.18). Many of these graves were heavily disturbed in the seventeenth century; parts of the sarcophagi were used to build the garden drain (Figure 9.19), while others were lifted complete from the ground, and may well be represented by sarcophagi moved into the cloisters. However, sufficient remained to provide an indication of the range of burials, to include adult males and females, as well as infants.

As with the burials within the mausoleum, the earliest were of slab construction with head insets. Four examples were found, (F298, F351, F405, F312) interestingly all aligned slightly more to the southeast, and at a lower level than those directly associated with the mausoleum, and possibly part of a pre-mausoleum burial area (Figure 9.20).

Three of these formed a line. The most westerly was F351. This was directly below a massive monolithic sarcophagus F119, which had to be moved in

Fig. 9.17 Stone sarcophagus, F158, showing foot end smashed in the robbing process.

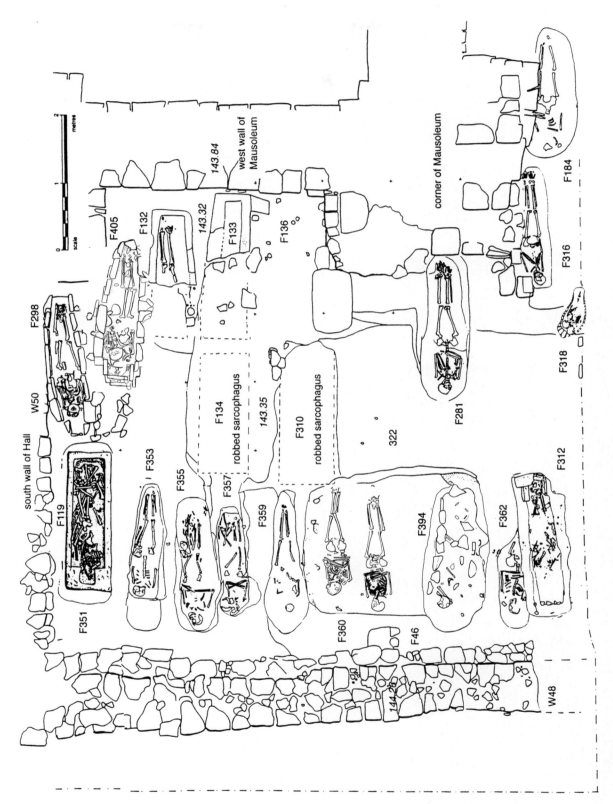

Fig. 9.18 Plan of excavated burials and tombs to the west of the mausoleum.

Fig. 9.19 (above) Area to the west of the mausoleum with post medieval drain removed to expose the partly robbed sarcophagi and burial deposits.

Fig. 9.20 (left) Three early tombs, F351, F298 and F405, with a similar construction of flat slabs of stone. F351 contained little human bone, and was sealed below the stone sarcophagus F119, which is this photograph has been rolled to one side to enable excavation.

order to excavate. F351 had lost its covering, and comprised flat slabs, forming the tomb shape and head inset. The main body had been almost entirely removed excepting for a few foot bones at the east end. The next in line (F298) survived largely intact (Figure 9.21). The capping comprised large limestone blocks, bonded by a gritty grey mortar that rested over three flat stones, set on the tops of the walls of the tomb. This was made from limestone blocks set vertically along the side of the grave cut (Figure 9.22). There were fourteen of these stones, with a crude head inset at the west end. The footstone was slightly higher than the other stones, so the cover stones abutted it. The base of the tomb was earth. There was only one burial within this grave, that of an adult male. The grave had been void for a considerable time, allowing for the skull and pelvis to have been displaced, possibly by animal action. Consequently the fill of the tomb was fine silt that had percolated through water action. The body was laid supine, but in a very

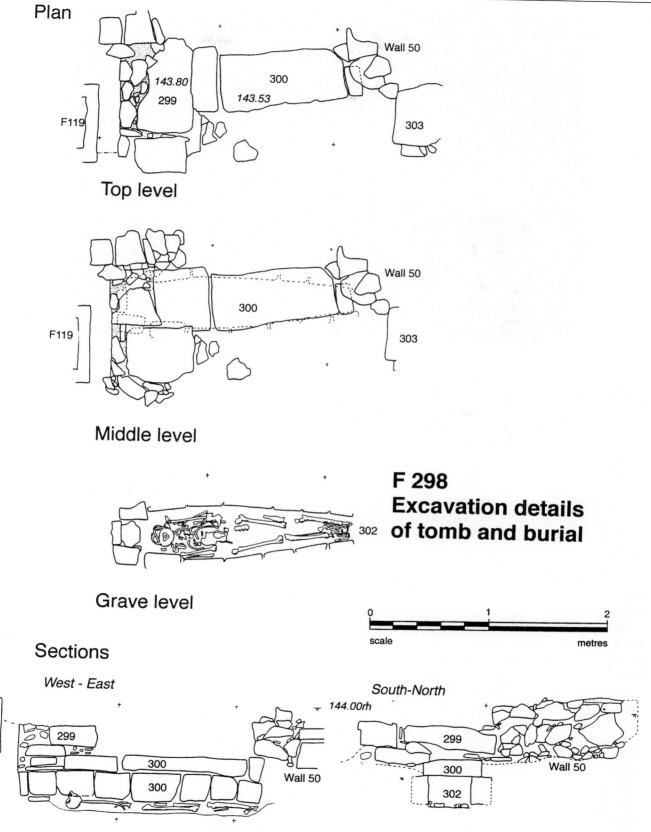

Fig. 9.21 Plan of F298, showing details of its construction.

Fig. 9.22 F298, showing the superstructure of the tomb before excavation.

unnatural position, suggesting that the corpse had been placed in the grave post rigor mortis. The feet were bent over the lower legs, and the right arm bent backwards upwards to the shoulder, the left arm was also bent back, with the fingers buried below the shoulder blade.

The third, F405, showed the clearest stratigraphic location, as it was partly sealed below a later stone sarcophagus, F132 (Figure 9.23). This burial in a constructed stone tomb, of vertical slabs, with eight covering stones with the same gritty mortar, survived because the tomb lay just below the base of the garden drain. It contained an adult male, although very disturbed by animal action inside the tomb.

The last example of an early tomb was F312 and this was positioned south of the others. It was constructed in a similar manner, but much more heavily disturbed. Only the stones at the foot end survived, and part of the lower leg bones, of an adult male. The tomb was later reused, for the burial of charnel and there was no trace of its covering.

Contemporary with the mausoleum were a series of monolithic sarcophagi made from oolitic limestone (Figure 9.24). Fragments of three were found in position, although there were probably originally five lined up in two rows outside the west wall, although all had been damaged or disturbed in the construction of the garden drain. The most northerly was F132, where the tapering foot end survived together with

part of the original cover stone, an undecorated oolitic slab in two pieces. Within, the lower legs and feet of an adult burial escaped robbing. This burial was unlikely to have been the first in the sarcophagus, as it was covered in a deposit of charnel containing at least two individuals – a young adult male and an adult female.

The foot end and base of an oolitic limestone sarcophagus (F133) was adjacent to F132, and contemporary with it. It had no surviving original deposits but there was considerable quantity of disarticulated human bone in the adjacent drain backfill from one adult individual that may have come from the original burial. The shape of the sarcophagus could be ascertained from the imprint of the mortar bedding (it tapered towards its foot end, as with F132). The third in the row (F136) had been completely robbed, but there remained the imprint of where the sarcophagus had rested.

The next row out comprised of two imprints of robbed sarcophagi (Figure 9.25). The more northerly (F134) had been removed at the time of the construction of the garden drain. The line of the cut included a wider cut on the south side, indicating that levers had been inserted on this side. The size of the pit suggests that this sarcophagus could either have been the fragment found in the construction of the drain, or the sarcophagus that is now in the cloisters of the abbey. The second imprint (F310) was a little

different as this feature contained a fill that was very distinctive, containing late medieval pottery as well as human and animal bone. Bones found in an adjacent layer may have come from this sarcophagus. The removal of this sarcophagus probably took place in the fourteenth or fifteenth century. One theory is that it was reburied 3m to the north, where an intact sarcophagus was found (F119, Figure 9.26), buried in a late medieval layer, containing a large quantity of disarticulated human bone representing a minimum of five individuals, of which two were female, and one possible male, and two indeterminate.

The next group of graves comprised tombs and graves on the south side of the mausoleum, buried up against its walls or buttresses (see Figure 9.5). Each burial lies directly against the building or its foundations, suggesting that there was merit in the burial actually touching the structure itself. The most easterly was F262, formed by setting seven stones in a line, and by laying three flat stones on the ground in the angle of the buttress and south wall of the mausoleum. The tomb was heavily robbed, but there was a finger bone, foot bones and two ribs, in their approximately correct position. This seems to be an example of a deliberate

Fig. 9.23 (left) F405, detail showing the arrangement of the main body and parcels of charnel.
Fig. 9.24 (below) F132, with lower leg bones in position, with a parcel of charnel.

Fig. 9.25 General view of the western area of the excavation, showing the earth burials and the partly excavated F360 pit, with its multiple inhumation.

Fig. 9.26 F119, stone sarcophagus with multiple charnel. This has probably been moved from one of them robbed sarcophagus pits, and reused to rebury disturbed bone in the fourteenth century.

medieval removal of remains. The next was F181, where four flat stones marked the grave, and grave cut (Figure 9.27). To the east was a post marker. On excavation an adult burial was discovered, laid supine, with its right arm laid across the body, and the left hand holding the right arm. The head lay to the right, but had probably been displaced, as the jawbone was in the correct position. The skeleton only just fitted into the grave cut, and the head was placed against the west end.

The most elaborate of this group was F179, where five flat stones lay on the ground-surface, sealing the early type of stone tomb comprising vertical limestone slabs, on which they rested (Figure 9.28). It was positioned very close to the south wall of the mausoleum. At the west end, outside the tomb, but associated with it, was a dense pocket of charnel, that may have comprised the original inhabitant of this particular tomb. On excavation, the fill comprised fine silt that must have filled the original void of the tomb, passing through the gaps in the stones and included one piece of small vessel glass. The burial itself was a complex one, with a substantial deposit of charnel overlying the main skeleton. In this charnel was a pelvis, with both sides intact, suggesting re-deposition before the ligaments had decayed, and thus shortly after the original burial. There were at least two individuals in this charnel deposit, a mature male and mature female. At the foot end of the tomb, there was another pocket of charnel, with at least two adults represented. The main burial comprised a male mature adult, laid supine, with head turned slightly to the left, and the arms upturned and crossing on the shoulders. The feet were also up-turned as the tomb was not quite long enough to accommodate the burial. It is likely that the tomb was reused for this burial, and the original occupants comprised the charnel inside and outside the tomb.

The next three graves were apparently unmarked. F184 had no stone marker or sides, and seems to have been placed in the ground, with the body placed supine, with the head to the west. It lay immediately against the south buttress to mausoleum. The burial was of a mature or elderly female of 45 years or more. F316 was similarly located hard against the foundations, and comprised a mature adult female. F218 was a very robust male, with the foot end against the foundation.

Fig. 9.27 Grave coverings for F179 and F181. F179 was a slab-constructed tomb, but F181 was an earth burial; however their surface coverings were identical.

Fig. 9.28 F179, showing main body and charnel.

Burials Post-Dating the Mausoleum

The last group of burials may post-date the mauso-leum, and form an outer row, running due south from the south wall of the hall. They are dug into a layer containing late thirteenth or fourteenth century pottery. These were all unmarked earth graves, and all of females or infants (Figure 9.25). Six (F353, 355, 357, 359, 362, 394) formed a neat row. Over the main body of F355 was a deposit of charnel including a crushed skull and 5 long bones stacked neatly on the north side of the main body. At the foot end of F357 was a large dump of charnel, including a jaw still attached to the skull and long bones laid on the north side of the main body. Three fragments of a scallop shell were found in this deposit of charnel (Figure 9.29). F360 was somewhat different. This formed part of the row, but was a single pit with two burials, both adult females, laid out at the same time, side by side (Figure 9.30). The fill of the burial pit contained a thin layer of lime that lay in the base of the pit and around the burials, suggesting that it had been added as part of the internment process. F394 cut into the large pit of F360, and differed from the other graves, by having a rough stone lining to the grave edge; it was heavily disturbed, and like the others, also contained charnel. It was clearly intrusive, and its construction may have removed other burials in F360.

In addition to this group of female burials, there were also infant burials, in addition to the child burial already noted in an upper level of the mausoleum (Figure 9.31). The burial of a baby (F293) up to 2–3 months old was located in the south side of the excavation comprising two large curving roof tiles set together with the body placed between them (Figure 9.32). Two newborn babies (F318) were found buried together, in a single grave. The northerly burial was slightly larger than the southerly burial. It seems likely that these were twins, who died in childbirth.

Fig. 9.29 Scallop shell reused as a pilgrim badge, found in the charnel associated with F357.

Fig. 9.30 F360, oval pit with two contemporary burials, placed in a layer of lime. F394 is a later burial that cuts into this pit, and may have removed further burials, as the pit is much larger that was needed for the two inhumations.

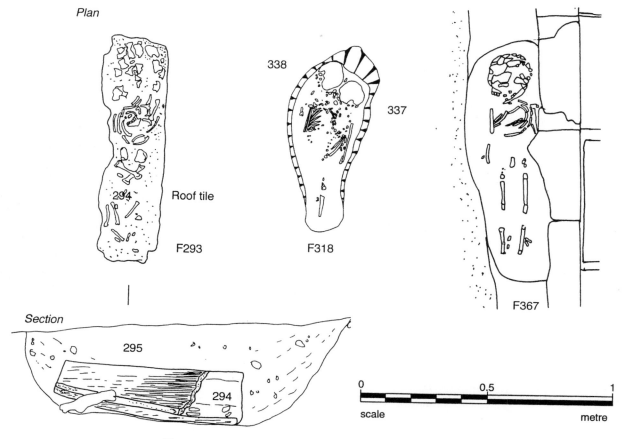

Fig. 9.31 Plan of the child burials excavated on the site.

Fig. 9.32 F293 showing the burial of an infant, between two roof tiles.

Burial Rites

These burials, numbering about 40 individuals including charnel were either within the mausoleum, or located outside to the south or west of the mausoleum. None were found on the north or east side, suggesting that south and west were the preferred areas. One group of four slab graves may be part of an early use of the site for burial (possibly pre-dating the mausoleum), but most date to either the period of the mausoleum's use during the thirteenth century or the continued use of the area for burial probably during the fourteenth. The early burials include both males and females, while the post-mausoleum burials are predominantly female or children. Given the rather elaborate burial rites, the use of stone coffins and the gender and age mix, it is very unlikely that any of these are the burials of Cistercian monks in a formal sense, but rather form a lay cemetery associated with the abbey.

Many of the tombs were reused, quite possibly on several occasions, and the original occupant(s) replaced over the later burial as loose charnel. Where burials cut through earlier burials, at least some of the bone was curated and reburied, either inside, or alone the side of the grave. The respect for the human bone, and its curation was especially marked in the monolithic sarcophagi, where several phases of bone depo-

sition can be deduced from the surviving charnel. Even the post-mausoleum burials carefully conserve the bones that were disturbed during the grave digging process, carefully replacing the disturbed bones back into the grave fill.

The double tomb was constructed on two levels. The purpose of the bottom level may have been for the curation of bone, even though very little bone was actually found in either chamber. The intention to reuse the tomb on multiple occasions, placing the earlier occupants in the lower chambers, seems to have been clear when it was constructed. We have already seen this pattern in the stone sarcophagi, where reuse may be deduced from the contents of the charnel, two or even three times, but in these cases, it may have been a pragmatic solution to use an existing stone tomb. The special feature of the double tomb was that reuse was clearly part of its original plan, even though in practice, no human remains were actually placed in the lower chamber, and instead, a third level of burial was placed on top of the primary internments. A parallel to this practice can be found in the nearby Cluniac abbey of Ronsenac (Montigny 1992), where a tomb was excavated at the entrance to the chapter house, where the upper level comprised stone bars, on which presumably the corpse was laid out and the process of decomposition allowed to occur; the defleshed bones could be collected later for burial elsewhere.

The human remains in the box at Grosbot were of a mature adult male. Virtually every bone had been collected, suggesting that the bones had been carefully moved from elsewhere. Knife marks suggests that death might have occurred elsewhere (possibly overseas), and that the body was dismembered and defleshed, a practice that has been reported elsewhere in medieval Europe (Gilchrist and Sloane 2005, 80; Weiss-Krejci 2001, 770–775) where it was known as the *mos teutonicus* (the German custom), and involved boiling the dismembered body in wine or vinegar to remove the flesh. The cleaned bones were placed in a box or locked casket for transportation and this is also attested archaeologically elsewhere (Gilchrist and Sloane 2005, 116). The practice of careful curation of the mortal remains was not limited to saints, but also to apparently high status individuals, who were often moved repeatedly over the succeeding centuries (Weiss-Krejci 2001).

Particular importance was attached to the actual human remains, presumably because it was believed that loss would jeopardize the ultimate resurrection process, and forms part of a widespread pattern across northern Europe (Gilchrist and Sloane 2005, 194). Indeed the fact that some of the tombs were empty on excavation, also points to the careful translation of some of the human remains, quite possibly into the abbey church, when the mausoleum is demolished.

The inclusion of an empty pottery vessel inside the burial is not unusual in this part of France; indeed at least one of the tombs of the bishops of Angoulême has an almost identical vessel, and examples are known from Angers, Nantes, Rouen (Cochet 1857). These vessels must have contained either holy oil or water for purification, and this use is borne out in a medieval descriptions (Madsen 1983, 179).

Because of the later disturbances, the thirteenth-century ground level has been lost. It was likely that the mausoleum was entered from the west, although there was no direct architectural evidence for this. If that was the case, the tops of the stone sarcophagi would have been just below ground level, leaving enough space for stone cover slabs (which in the case of F132 did survive), over which anyone would have walked to gain entrance. There was no space for a pathway between the tombs, leading to the presumed west doorway; this does suggest that the entrance to the mausoleum was infrequent, and that the whole of the western area in front of the building was given over to burial. Lifting a few small stones gained access to the underlying sarcophagi and old burials could

have easily been replaced with new ones, placing the charnel to one side.

Identifying the Dead

It seems likely that these were lay burials, although clearly of a somewhat special nature. The most likely users were the lay benefactors of the abbey, and there is some documentary evidence to indicate that members of the House of La Rochefoucauld did indeed use Grosbot as one of their burial places during the thirteenth century. In 1241, a donation is recorded to the abbey by the family, in exchange for the right be to buried in the monk's cemetery (Mondon 1895–7). This must refer to the mausoleum, as it lies directly adjacent to the likely location of the monks' cemetery.

Only three members of La Rochefoucauld family are actually recorded as being buried at Grosbot. In 1295, Gui V1 (who may have died as a monk) was buried at "next to his father and mother". His father was Aimery, who died c.1255, and his mother was Létice de Parthenay (Vigier de la Pile 1846, 27). It is tempting to suggest that the double tomb in the mausoleum is that of Aimery and Létice, and that Guy was buried in the tomb on the third level (along with his wife in the adjacent tomb F142), in the reused tomb slab that was turned into a sarcophagus. When the building was taken down shortly afterwards, his burial, his wife and presumably his mother were translated into the abbey church, but the bones of his father, Aimery, were left where they were. Unfortunately there is no record of where Aimery died to explain why his remains had been carefully prepared and buried in their wooden box.

The tomb slab belonging to Létice, or another of the family may still survive, although its present whereabouts is unknown. It was moved from the abbey to the châteaux in Charras in the nineteenth century and was then sold in 1990, and we have been unable to locate it. It shows a woman in a Cistercian habit, with the La Rochefoucauld arms at its foot. In the seventeenth century *Gallia Christiana*, this tomb was recorded in the transept of the abbey, showing 'a women dressed in a nuns habit, with the noble pedigrees of the distinguished families of La Rochefoucauld, where only the cover is removed' (Sainte-Marthe 1656). In the nineteenth century it was in the cloisters, covering a large sarcophagus (the sarcophagus still remains, and probably comes from one of the robbed-out tombs outside the mausoleum).

It is possible to suggest at least some of the mausoleum burials at Grosbot from their recorded genealogy (Turton 1928, 9; Figure 9.33). The mausoleum may have been built for Gui IV (1120– c.1170) but this is

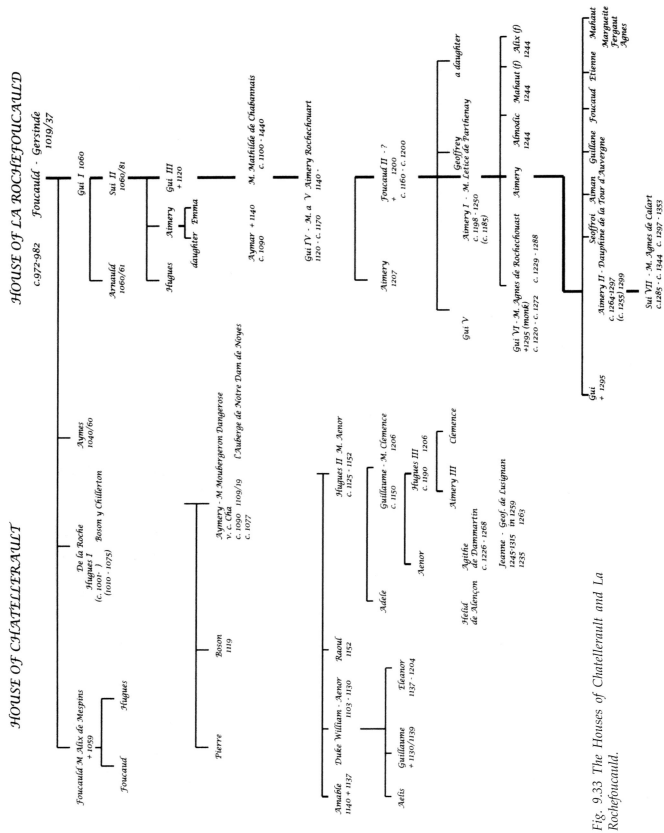

Fig. 9.33 The Houses of Chatellerault and La Rochefoucauld.

probably too early on the archaeological evidence, and it is more likely to have been for his son, Foucaud II (c.1160– c.1200). Gui had one recorded brother Aimery, who was alive in 1201. The two early central burials (F198, F306) may be of Foucaud and Aimery, one of a lower status than the other. The next generation comprised Gui V, (about whom very little is known) who was succeeded by Aimery I (c.1198–c.1255) and Létice (1190– ?), who we have already suggested may have been buried in the central double tomb. Aimery had two other recorded siblings, Geoffroi and an unnamed sister, possibly buried in the external sarcophagi. The next generation comprised Gui VI (c.1220–1295), who married Agnes de Rochechouart (c.1229–1288). Gui VI, we have suggested, was buried above the tomb of Aimery and Létice, while Agnes may have been buried in the adjacent F142. Gui VI had four recorded siblings (Aimery, Almodic, Mahaut, Alix), some of who may have been buried outside the building. Gui VI had eleven children (Gui, Aimery II (c.1264–c.1297), Geoffroi, Aimar, Guillaume, Foucaud, Etienne, Mahaut, Marguerite, Fergant, Agnès), some of who predeceased him, and Aimery II six children (Gui VII, Geoffroi, Aimery, Agnès, Marguerite, Létice). The last burial inside the mausoleum, F158, might be ascribed to Aimery II, before the whole structure went out of use around 1300, although burial continued outside.

We will never know exactly who was actually buried there, but it may be possible through the study of the surviving ancient DNA, to test directly the hypothesis that this was indeed the family mausoleum. It is clearly impossible to suggest correspondence between all the burials and individuals. Between 1200 and 1350, there are 29 known individuals whose deaths occurred in the immediate family. In addition there may be other members of cadet branches about which we know very little, but presumably included Gerald Robert and Peter Robert de Marthon, who are recorded granting lands to the abbey in 1264. Given the incomplete nature of the record the 40 or so estimated burials from the site would adequately include most of the family during this period.

Historical Context

If this group of burials do indeed belong to a single extended family, then it is interesting that they choose to be buried in and around a purpose-built free-standing mausoleum. Such structures are practically unknown in the twelfth and thirteenth centuries, as most lay cemeteries in monasteries were located within clearly demarcated areas, away from the monks

cemetery, or within the church or occasionally the cloister (Gilchrist and Sloane 2005, 31–4, 56–60). The normal pattern was for dynastic families to enrich parts of church, which could then act as the family mausoleum. A lay mausoleum, east of the abbey church raises many questions, not least how the burials were conducted, implying that the dead (including women and children) were taken through the monks' quire and precinct.

The Cistercians had strict legislation as to who could be buried and where within the monastery (Kinder 2002, 365–6) and it is especially surprising that these burials were located around a special building immediately to the east of the Abbey Church. Free-standing buildings are known in cemeteries, but these often have undercrofts, date in general to the four-teenth century onwards, and were charnel houses to store the disturbed dead (Gilchrist and Sloane 2005, 39). The very rare examples of detached burial chapels recorded in England are all from non-Cistercian houses and include Abingdon abbey (Allen 1990, 76) and St Augustine's Abbey, but reusing an earlier Saxon building, (Gem 1997). Norton Priory has a burial chapel of this date, but attached to the north east corner of the abbey church (Greene 1989, 10–12).

A possible link to an early medieval past might be suggested for the freestanding mausoleum at Grosbot. Mausolea were used to bury kings and other high status figures in northern Europe. St Denis contained the burials of the Merovingian kings of France, but around 1260, Louis IX commissioned a series of effigies of these early kings (Erlande-Brandenburg 1975, Steane 1993, 43), for St Denis, to create a royal mausoleum including a place of his own burial. Edward I intended Westminster Abbey to contain royal burials at a single location, in this case linked to the burial and cult of Edward the Confessor, which had already been developed by Henry III (Steane 1993, 45–6; Binski 1995). In both cases however, these developments date to after the construction of the Grosbot mausoleum.

Louis and Edward may have drawn part of their inspiration from the activities of their great grand-mother, Eleanor of Aquitaine (Steane 1993, 42–4), and here there may be another connection with Grosbot. Royal and aristocratic families were founding abbeys in the twelfth century, acting in a more general sense as mausolea for these families. Perhaps the best-known example is Fontrevault, which later became the burial place of the Angevin kings starting with Henry II in 1189, but also crucially the place of retirement for female members of Royal family, including of course Eleanor of Aquitaine herself who was buried there in 1204, as well as the burial place of Richard and Jeanne in 1199. Eleanor may have planned the development of Fontrevault, in the words of Charles Wood (2003, 414) as, "a royal necropolis, one in which the shrewd placement of tombs could help the living to foster a dynamic cult by demonstrating their own line of descent from the dead". The burial of Henry II at Fontrevault may have been largely by chance (he intended to be buried at Grandmont), but Eleanor's hand was clearly detected in the later royal burials at the abbey at the end of the twelfth century. Eleanor's own travels around Europe may have been the inspiration for the creation of a royal necropolis at Fontrevault; earlier examples include Las Huelgas, founded in 1187 as a Cistercian convent and the burial place of the Castilian royal family (Nolan 2003, 387), and the Cistercian Abbey of Heiligenkreuz for members of the Babenberg dynasty (Weiss-Krejci 2001, 772).

The construction of the Grosbot mausoleum fits closely with these developments at Fontrevault, Las Huelgas and Heiligenkreuz at the end of the twelfth century. It is quite possible that the House of Rochefoucauld intended a similar dynastic burial place for their own members. It might seem presumptuous for a family of only regional importance set out to emulate contemporary royal practice. However it is particularly interesting that there was dynastic connection between the La Rochefoucauld and Eleanor herself (Weir 1999,13), which would have been fully appreciated by her contemporaries, and this may explain the presumption.

The traceable genealogy of the House of La Rochefoucauld (or La Roche) extends to the early part of the eleventh century when they become distinct from the Lusignans (Turton 1928, 9). Foucaud (born c.972–82) was the son of Joscelin de Lusignan (died c.1015). He married Gersende and they had four recorded children, Gui, Aymer, Gerberga and Foucaud; their descendants comprised the "House of La Rochefoucauld". The descendants of Gui I the senior branch of the family claimed the title of Lord of La Roche, adding Verteuil around 1140 and Marthon and Blanzac around 1170; Aimery (m. Létice of Parthenay), and Gui VI who were buried at Grosbot were the eldest and direct descendants, six and seven generations later respectively.

The other branch of the family of which much is known descends from Gerberga (died 1092), who married Hugues (?1010–1075) Viscount of Chatellerault (in some versions of the genealogy, Hugues is one of the sons of the Foucaud, and acquires the Chatellerault title through his marriage). In 1115, William IX, Duke of Aquitaine, had a passionate and very public affair with Dangerosa, wife of Aimery I, who was the grandson of Hugues and Gerberga (Painter 1955, 379–81; Costen and Oakes 2000, 34).

Dangerosa had two sons, Hugh and Raoul and a daughter, Aenor, through her marriage to Aimery, and it was her daughter Aenor, who married Duke William's son (later William X) around 1121 and gave birth to Eleanor in 1122. Eleanor of Aquitaine was therefore directly part of the La Rochefoucauld line through her mother (Weir 1999, 13–15).

In our reconstruction, we suggest that the mausoleum was built around 1200, at exactly the same time that Eleanor was devising Fontrevault as the dynastic burial place of the Plantagenet's. The La Rochefoucauld family, who would have seen themselves as the senior branch, must have been aware of the increased status of the Chatelleraut branch through their association with Eleanor, and may have planned the Grosbot mausoleum as response. The choice of Grosbot may have been influenced by the tradition (or knowledge) that their remote ancestors founded the abbey in the late tenth century, when they became a distinct branch from the Lusignans. Remarkably, they choose to construct a freestanding building, not to use the abbey church itself, as was normal practice, and anticipated the link with an earlier medieval past, that was developed by Kings Louis and Edward on a much grander scale at St Denis and Westminster sixty year later.

Finally, it is perhaps worth observing how our findings from the excavations of the Grosbot mausoleum might throw light on the nature of feudal society in thirteenth century Poitou. There has been considerable debate about the conflicting loyalties imposed by the state, the feudal overlord and the family during this period (Bloch 1961, 123–142). The aristocratic families of Poitou, such as the Lusignans, Chatellerault, Parthenay, Thouars and Rancon, as well as La Rochefoucauld, played a disproportionate role in the affairs on twelfth and thirteenth century Europe, through their dynastic marriages, their role in the Crusades, and their connections to the royal families of both France and England (Painter 1955, 1956, 1957). The importance of the aristocratic family was underlined by the practice among some (most notably Parthenay) of the *droit de viage*, where a man's possessions were inherited by all his sons in order of birth, before passing to the sons of the eldest son. In a study of charters and grants by these families, it was found that a remarkable 80% of ecclesiastical documents mention the wider family, and not just the senior member (Hajdu 1977, 129). The mausoleum represents the same family solidarity, which includes not only the male heirs but also the wider family that includes women and children, and was above all a material statement of the identity and longevity of the family in thirteenth-century Poitou.

Acknowledgements

The project at Grosbot was undertaken as part of the summer excavations of the University of Bristol, Department of Archaeology. We are very grateful to owners of the Abbey, Anne and Jonathan Clowes, for allowing us to undertake the research and for helping the project in so many ways. We are especially grateful to Service Regional de l'Archéologie Poitou-Charentes for granting us an excavation license, and to the Association des Archéologues de Poitou-Charentes for financial assistance towards the project.

References

Allen, T. (1990). Abingdon vineyard redevelopment. *South Midlands Archaeology* 20, 73–9.

Anon. (1900) *Cartulaire de l'eglise de Angoulême*, Angoulême, Chasseignac.

Anon. (1975) *Potiers de Saintonge. Huit siècles d'artisanat rural.* Exhibition catalogue, 22 Nov 1975 – 1 March 1976 Paris, Musée National des Arts et traditions populaires (Exhibition catalogue, 22 Nov 1975 – 1 March 1976).

Aston, M. (1993) *Monasteries*. London, B.T. Batsford.

Bell, D. N. (1997) An Eighteenth-Century Book-List from the Abbey of Grosbot. *Cîteaux: Commentarii Cistercienses*, 48, 339–370.

Besse, D. J. M. (Dom Beaunier) (1905) *Abbayes et prieures de l'ancienne France*. Paris, Picard.

Binski, P. (1995) *Westminster Abbey and the Planagenets; kingship and the representations of power, 1200–1400*. New Haven, Yale University Press.

Bloch, M. (1961) *Feudal Society*. Chicago, Univeristy Chicago Press.

Boussard, Jacques (ed.) (1957) *Historia pontificum et comitum Engolismensium*. Paris Libraire d'Argences.

Brown, D. H. (2002) *Pottery in Medieval Southampton c.1066–1510*. York, Council for British Archaeology Research Report 133.

Cherry, J. (1991) Pottery and tile. In J. Blair and N. Ramsey (eds) *English Medieval Industries*, 189–209. London, Hambledon Press.

Cochet, M. l'Abbé J. B. D. (1857) Sépultures Chrétiennes de la périod Anglo-Normande trouvées à Bouteilles, près Dieppe en 185. *Archaeologia* 37, 32–8, 258–66.

Costen M. and Oakes, C. (2000) *Romanesque Churches of the Loire and Western France*, Stroud, Tempus books.

Drury, P. (1981) Brick and tile in medieval England. In D. E. Crossley (ed.) *Medieval Industry*, 143–150. London, Council for British Archaeology.

Elande-Brandenburg, A. (1975) *Le roi est mort:etude sur les funérailles, les sepultures et les tombeaux des rois de France jusqu'à la fin du XIIIe siècle*. Geneva, Droz.

Gem, R. (1997) *St Augustine's Abbey, Canterbury*. London: Batsford.

Gilchrist, R. and Sloane, B. (2005) *Requiem, the Medieval Monastic cemetery in Britain*. Oxford, Oxbow Books and Museum of London Archaeological Service.

Greene, J. P. (1989) *Norton Priory: the archaeology of a medieval religious house*. Cambridge, Cambridge University Press.

Hajdu, R. (1977). Family and Feudal Ties in Poitou, 1100–1300. *Journal of Interdisciplinary History*, 8.1, 117–139.

Horton, M. (2004) A bell-founders pit at the Cistercian abbey of Grosbot. In T. N. Kinder (ed.) *Perspectives for an architecture of solitude. Essays on Cistercian art and architecture in honour of Peter Fergusson*, 253–260. Turnhout, Brepols/Cîteaux: Commentarii cistercienses (Medieval Church studies 11, Studia et Documenta 13).

Janauschek, P. Leopoldus, (1877) *Originum Cisterciensium*, Vienna, Vindobonae, vol 1, (repr. Ridgewood, NJ, Gregg Press, 1964).

Kinder, Terryl (2002) *Cistercian Europe. Architecture of Contemplation* Kalamazoo, Cistercian Publication.

Larigauderie-Beijeaud, M. (1998) Abbaye cistercienne Notre-Dame de Grosbot, Charente. Recueil de Textes (1121–1791). *Bulletin pour la sauvegarde et l'étude du patrimoine religieux de la Charente, 8.*

Madsen, P. K. (1983) A French connection: Danish Funerary pots – a group of medieval pottery. *Journal of Danish Archaeology*, 2, 171–183.

Mondon, A. (1895–7) *Notes historiques sur la Baronie de Marthon en Angoumois*, Angoulême, Chasseignac.

Montigny, P. (1992) Ronsenac. *Archéologie Médiévale*, 22, 463–4.

Nanglard, J. (1893–4) *Pouillé historiques de Diocese de Angouléme*. Angoulême, Chasseignac.

Nolan, K. (2003) The Queen's Choice, Eleanor of Aquitaine and the tombs of Fontrevaud. In B. Wheeler and J.C. Parsons, 2003, 377–406.

Painter, S. (1955) The Houses of Lusignan and Chatellerault 1150–1250. *Speculum* 30 (no 3), 374–384.

Painter, S. (1956) Castellans of the Plain of Poitou in the eleventh and twelfth centuries. *Speculum* 31 (no 2), 243–257.

Painter, S. (1957) The lords of Lusignan in the eleventh and twelfth centuries. *Speculum* 32 (no 1), 27–47.

Platt, C. and Coleman-Smith, R. (1975) *Excavations in Medieval Southampton 1953–1969*, 2 vols. Leicester, Leicester University Press.

Sainte-Marthe, S. de, (1656), *Gallia Christiana*, 4 vols. Paris, Edmundi Pepingué.

Steane, J. (1993) *The Archaeology of Medieval English Monarchy*. London and New York, Routledge.

Turton, W. H. (1928) *Plantagenet Ancestry*. London, Phillimore and Co.

Vigier de la Pile, F. (1846) *Histoire de l'Angoumois*, Paris, 1846 (repr. Marseille, Laffitte, 1976).

Weir, A. (1999) *Eleanor of Aquitaine*. London, Jonathan Cape.

Weiss-Krejci, E. (2001) Restless corpses: 'secondary burial' in the Babenberg and Habsburg dynasties. *Antiquity* 75, 769–80.

Wheeler, B. and Parsons, J. C. (eds.) (2003) *Eleanor of Aquitaine, Lord and Lady*. New York, Palgrave Macmillan.

Wood, C. (2003) Fontrevaud, Dynasticism and Eleanor of Aquitaine. In Wheeler and Parsons 2003, 407–422.

Chapter 10

Not All Archaeology is Rubbish: the Elusive Life Histories of Three Artefacts from Shapwick, Somerset

Christopher Gerrard

Introduction

This paper examines three artefacts, each of a different period and fashioned from a different material. The first is of antler, the second of bronze and the third of shell. All three were recovered during the course of the Shapwick Project, in which Mick Aston played such a pivotal role. Working backwards from the moment of their discovery, my aim is to reconstruct their individual biographies and, in so doing, to illustrate some of the ways in which the study of artefacts can open up novel lines of historical and archaeological enquiry.

For those readers who are not familiar with the Shapwick Project, this was an investigation into the archaeology, history and topography of a single parish in Somerset (Figure 10.1). The Project began in 1989 as a study of the evolution of early and late medieval settlement patterns but soon became something of a laboratory for landscape research (Aston and Gerrard 1999). Conventional methods of archaeological investigation such as field-walking, standing building recording and aerial photography were all applied extensively and more novel techniques such as soils analyses, botanical and invertebrate surveys, shovel-pitting, garden bed collections and test pits were also evaluated. The combined results from these surveys were at least as important as the 66 excavations undertaken at sites of prehistoric to nineteenth century date across the parish which, needless to say, produced artefact assemblages that were both voluminous and wide-ranging. Field-walking alone produced nearly 100,000 finds, an average of 14 finds per 25m of walked line and, as for excavation, there are few rural assemblages in Britain with which Shapwick can be matched. The pottery assemblage alone numbers 48,000 sherds and metalwork is represented by some 6,600 fragments. It is therefore something of a luxury to select just three artefacts and spend a short time developing their individual stories.

An Object Out of Time: A Broken Roman Antler Rake

My first object, a very ordinary one, was found by excavators from Somerset County Council in an unexpected context at a site known as Shapwick Sports Hall (Webster 1992). It is a Y-shaped tool of antler with an oblong hole driven through its middle, presumably to hold a short wooden shaft (Figure 10.2). The two 'points' of the antler have been shaped, cut to a point and then polished by frequent use. Identical examples are known from other sites in Britain and the Low Countries (MacGregor 1985a, 178–179), including Wroxeter in Shropshire, where they are usually identified as rakes or hoes for breaking up the soil. The natural form of the antler and the compact, hard tissue from which antler is formed make this an ideal fork-like tool. The shapes of antlers from roe, fallow and red deer are distinctive and in this case the antler is from a red deer, the tool being formed from the two upper tines. All of the known examples are Roman in date. This one, however, was found in a medieval pit which contained nothing other than late twelfth or early thirteenth century coarseware pottery. To add to the puzzle, the tool had been broken, split straight through the middle of the hafting hole.

This then is a simple utilitarian agricultural tool which is at least 800 years outside its expected chronological context. Perhaps the tool was discovered by a medieval villager at a Roman site somewhere close by and taken home. Since the blunt base shows signs of it being used as a hammer, it may have been adapted for a use for which it was never intended, broken and discarded for a second time. This seems plausible enough, except that it suggests our medieval finder was ignorant of the qualities of antler as a craft material, something which might seem odd given that objects of antler like combs and 'pin beaters' used in weaving were routinely in circulation in the medieval village. Moreover, only a little way to the north of the

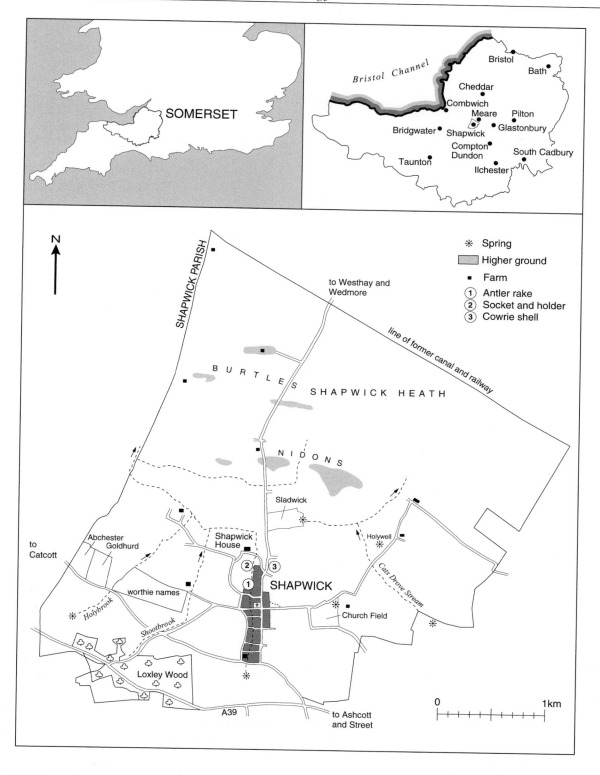

Fig. 10.1 Shapwick. A location plan showing main sites mentioned in the text. Map created by Alejandra Gutiérrez.

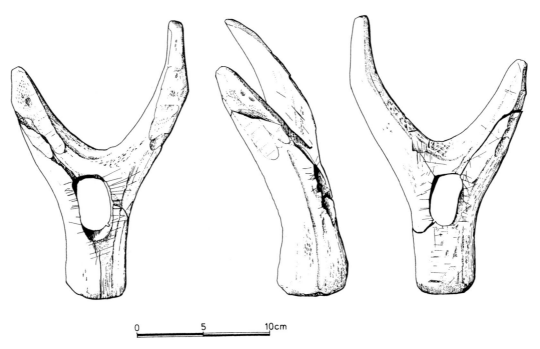

0   5   10cm

Fig. 10.2 Roman antler rake excavated at Shapwick Sports Hall, Shapwick. Drawn by Liz Indunni.

site where the antler tool was found, another excavation at Shapwick produced an incised bone rough-out, perhaps marked out to cut smaller objects from such as dice. It too may be twelfth century in date and so perhaps there was even local expertise in bone working. In this context, it seems rather surprising then that our medieval finder made such inappropriate use of his newly acquired Roman tool.

Other than how and when it was re-cycled, there is, of course, another unusual thing about this object. The rake was found in two parts and can be re-fitted back together to make a complete object. Was the rake broken for burial in the pit or buried because it was broken? Archaeologists, particularly prehistorians, have long been familiar with the idea that some of the deposits they excavate are placed there intentionally and one possibility is that this artefact has been deliberately 'killed'; broken in two and then deposited. Not only is this practice well attested in prehistory (Grinsell 1960; for other references see Chapman 2000) but some other medieval artefacts such as pilgrim badges were certainly deliberately mutilated before being disposed of 'as if to take them out of circulation' (Spencer 1998, 18). Chapman (2000, 37–39) cites several medieval examples of mutilated objects, including the snapping of staffs of office to symbolize the end of a feudal bond and the deliberate breakage of objects at the death of an individual. In this case, the crispness of

the break between the two halves of the rake suggests that the object was deposited in the pit soon after it was broken and the same seems to be true of most of the pottery found there. Most of the 550 sherds of pottery from the pit could be re-fitted into four complete globular jars, something which is unique among the many hundreds of later medieval contexts excavated at Shapwick (Gutiérrez forthcoming). Taken together, the assemblage seems unusual, these are not objects broken accidentally during use, they have more of a feel of a house clearance which might have occurred at a change of tenancy or at the death of the occupant. The act of destruction may therefore be understood as a deliberate ending of the life-cycle of the pottery and the rake, the rupture of any connection with a particular individual or place. Repugnance at re-use and a desire to avoid association with the property of the deceased are two of the reasons given by Grinsell (1960) in his explanation as to why prehistoric objects might be broken prior to deposition.

The Roman antler tool is not the only material culture from Shapwick to be found 'out of context' in this way. Two perforated Roman coins, both 4th century in date, were recovered from Shapwick. Coins like this are usually associated with early Anglo-Saxon burials, often in association with beads, where they are thought to have an amuletic function (Stoodley 1999, 20). In this case, however, the coins were found in sealed contexts dating to the late twelfth–early thirteenth century and, like the antler rake, they are well outside their expected context and may also have been chance finds. An event of just this kind is probably commemorated in the fieldname 'Nuthergoldhurd' (in 1313; Costen forthcoming) to the west of the village. Coins are very portable, of course, and they also would have been a recognisable artefact type to the finder, even if the coins themselves were exotic and unusable. Given that they were pierced they must also have been suspended and displayed, perhaps on a thread around the neck, though exactly when and by whom we cannot know in the Shapwick context, except to note that the sites on which they found were domestic and certainly not high status. What message then was intended by the wearer? Perhaps the coins were used as a kind of secular badge and intended as a lucky charm, a kind of sympathetic magic to attract good fortune. There are examples of fourteenth or fifteenth century badges in the form of an open purse containing coins just as there are also more elaborate lattice work pendants which actually contained imitation tin-alloy coins, the latter were probably aristocratic objects which Brian Spencer (1998, 315–317) has suggested were dress accessories designed to attract money to their owners or just possibly to remind their wearers of the importance of giving and receiving of alms. Either way, the habit of showing and wearing coins was not unknown in the later medieval period. Spencer also cites examples of coins adapted as brooches and of coin-like badges cast in pewter found in London (Egan and Pritchard 1991, 260–262) and tells us that this 'coincided with a widespread increase in the fashion for wearing coins as decorative amulets'.

Definite secular brooches of this kind seem to be of late fourteenth and early fifteenth century date. By comparison, the Shapwick examples seem intriguingly early and, of course, they are Roman coins rather than real or imitation medieval ones. Can it really be that Roman coins lacked symbolism altogether, that these coins began life again in medieval Britain entirely free of association and meaning in a new phase of their biography? I wonder whether what we might be seeing is a rather crude reflection of the use of Norman military insignia, which were in some cases themselves Roman intaglios, or of aristocratic and knightly seals and which in turn expressed a simplistic contemporary perception of cultural continuity between Roman and Norman which is found more explicitly in con-temporary literature. It is not that later medieval wearers of pierced Roman coins at Shapwick wished to show, or even that they possessed, an appreciation of Roman materials or values, but that these

apparently very average inhabitants were emulating higher status emblems and insignia which themselves drew upon the classical world. They were, in the words of one historian, 'meant to conjure up an image of power greater than the man who bore them' (Crouch 1992, 179). Whichever is the case, a comprehensive re-examination of these more 'minor' re-cycled finds across the region would certainly be welcome.

The inhabitants of medieval Shapwick, it would seem, were strangers neither to earlier artefacts nor to earlier settlements and sites in their local landscape. 'Abbelchestre', for example, was the target of a medieval stone robber called John Sherp. We know this from a reference in a mid-fourteenth century court roll (Ecclestone 1998, 213). John, who was in charge of the harvest at Shapwick in 1348, abused his position by taking two hay carts and loading them with stone which he then 'took by night to his own house at Glastonbury', a distance of over 10km. 'Abbelchestre', later 'Abchester', is one of several Roman sites whose location on the western extreme of the parish is given away by the field name and for which there is now good evidence from excavation. The site, a modest domestic farmstead of first century to fourth century date, must have been known long before John got there. He was certainly unlucky to be caught, for others had had the same idea and got away with it. At Sladwick, another Roman site of the fourth century and later date which lies to the north of the modern village, excavation demonstrated clear evidence of repeated stone robbing. A robber trench had been cut down through the rubble remains of a collapsed stone building to reach the foundation courses. The archaeological evidence was clear enough to show that the trench had been returned to on at least one other occasion, and the fill of the robber trench contained seven sherds of medieval coarseware pottery of twelfth–thirteenth century date (Gerrard forthcoming).

We can be quite certain then that later medieval people knew where some earlier settlement sites were located and deliberately targeted them for their building materials. Locally, the costs of quarrying and winning building stone were dictated by Glastonbury Abbey and it was primarily a cheap supply of building stone which the looters were after. Even though tile and brick was certainly present on sites which are known to have been dug over, none of the 183 fragments of Roman ceramic building material at Shapwick were recovered from later contexts. It was stone they were after and that decision was a practical one, there is nothing here to suggest anything more elaborate, for instance that later medieval buildings were constructed in an attempt to emulate Roman architectural forms or construction methods. This argument, which seems persuasive enough for major building projects such as Caernarfon Castle (Taylor 1963), Colchester Castle or the Tower of London (Wheatley 2004) where mythical and material links may have been deliberately intertwined to project an impression of continuity with imperial traditions, finds no echo here. This is casual re-use of stone, driven by economy rather than any particular associations (e.g. Greenhalgh 1989; Eaton 2000; Stocker and Everson 1990). Locally, all the documented examples of 'iconic re-use' of stone seem to be much later in date. For example, the NE buttress of the re-built nineteenth century chancel of the church at Compton Dando incorporates a Roman statue of Jupiter[1] (Pevsner 1979, 174); an opportunity grasped by Victorians to Christianise the community's Roman past.

It would be quite wrong, however, to imply that all this medieval recycling was random and thoughtless. There were processes of selection at work in what was collected. On the one hand, robbers left behind any Roman brooches they happened upon; all fourteen Roman brooches from Shapwick were recovered from known Roman sites. No attempt was made to recontextualise them, they had no value. On the other hand, they pocketed coins and the antler rake. On the face of it, the only re-cycled objects were those for which an easy practical use could be found or with which the finders were already familiar. Even though other objects were more abundant, these were left behind. They were cautious, uncertain even, in their actions and perhaps the clearest expression of this uncertainty are the two broken halves of the Roman antler rake, the manner of whose deposition hints at a rejection or suspicion of material links with the past.

An Object Out of the Ordinary: A Bronze Socket and Holder

Shapwick also provides another excellent if somewhat bizarre example of the later salvage and re-cycling of artefacts. Excavations south of Shapwick House (6767/A) uncovered a later medieval bronze socket and holder dated to the early twelfth century (Figure 10.3). There are good parallels both for the type of artefact and its decorative motifs in Ireland at this date and it is probably an ecclesiastical piece intended to hold a cross vertical (Gerrard and Youngs 1997). The Glastonbury connection, with its links to Irish saints St Patrick, Bridget and Indracht seems to provide a plausible local context, especially since Shapwick was one of the Abbey's holdings, but there is one more remarkable thing we have yet to note. The medieval socket and holder has fitted into its tip a re-worked Bronze Age blade. This simple statement takes a

moment or two to absorb though the juxtaposition of prehistoric and medieval should not be entirely unfamiliar; prehistoric artefacts have been found before in later contexts. To take just one recently published example, an Early Bronze Age bronze axe was recovered from the medieval garderobe of the Great Hall at the Templar preceptory at South Witham (Lincs.; Davey 2002), but what we have in this case is a single composite artefact whose two components were originally intended for a quite different purpose and setting and were manufactured thousands of years apart.

We must first establish something of the object's archaeological context. It was found in a roughly dug straight-sided hollow which had been backfilled with a loose fill of Lias blocks, charcoal spreads and domestic debris and then capped with clay. Among the datable material was a lead shot pellet, a medieval knife guard hilt-plate and the blade of a peat spade. This eclectic mix of later medieval and post-medieval artefacts was also reflected in the pottery assemblage from this feature, which included twelfth and thirteenth century coarsewares as well as seventeenth and eighteenth century dishes and porringers. The latest closely dated pottery was a fragment of mid-eighteenth century stoneware bowl. The interpretation placed on the stratigraphy is that this and other holes had been roughly (and probably quickly) filled by shovelling in soil from the immediate area, an explanation which seems confirmed by the fact that sherds from this feature join with others from an adjacent ditch a few metres away. The conclusion drawn is that the pits were dug out and occupation material scooped together to be deposited into the hollows, the topsoil and natural clays then being spread about on top to smooth the contours. The fact that so many later medieval artefacts were found in the topsoil suggests that earlier features and layers were disturbed.

It seems certain that this process of landscaping occurred during the emparkment of the northern part of Shapwick sometime between 1765 and 1785 (Figure 10.4). The plot where the bronze holder was found lay on the corner of three streets where the 1765 map and survey of Shapwick records the home of William Chapman (DD/SG13). Put crudely, William's house was erased. Excavation here by Charles and Nancy Hollinrake found that none of the walls were left standing to a height of more than one or two courses and very little cultural material remained in the way of possessions, only a handful of broken clay pipes and occasional sherds of glass and pottery. The bronze socket and holder seems rather exceptional in this modest domestic context.

Surprisingly perhaps, there is almost no published

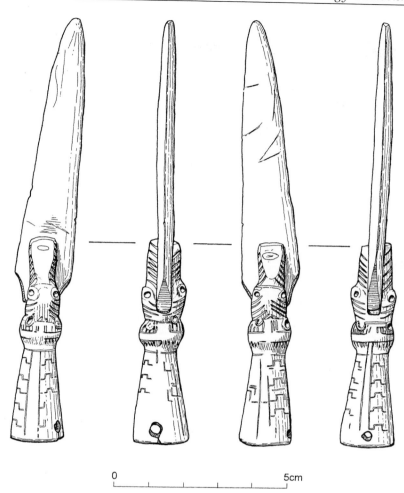

0   5cm

Fig. 10.3 Bronze socket and holder excavated south of Shapwick House, Shapwick. Drawn by Rob Read.

archaeological work which documents the processes of creation of an eighteenth-century landscape. As David Crossley (1990, 72) has noted, 'the archaeological potential of the villages displaced by eighteenth-century emparking has not been tested'. At Shapwick we are at least able to make a start on understanding some of the processes involved. Changes began in the second half of the eighteenth century, though they were not completed for many years. Buildings were demolished, ponds filled in and grassed over, contours smoothed. Wherever possible demolition rubble was disposed of by burying it; a rectangular rock-cut ornamental pond dug in the first half of the eighteenth century was filled in again before 1810 with rubble generated by the re-facing of the south front of Shapwick House. The best local parallel for events is West Quantoxhead where Mick Aston used the map sequence to show roads being re-routed after 1770 and the number of dwellings declining steadily from ten in 1761 to four by the middle of the next century when the church itself was re-sited (Aston

1985, 56). At Shapwick the process was faster and involved more houses; the fact that the church was not involved probably eased the process. Archaeology shows that fences were torn down, ditches filled, buildings dismantled and anything not re-usable was burnt. In order to smooth out the contours, holes were dug and filled with domestic rubble, and the soil from the fill spread about. Only some of the existing trees were left untouched, creating what was, in effect, an instant park. The bronze socket and holder seems somehow to have survived all this and may have been shovelled about several times before finding its way into the pit in which it was discovered. As we have seen, the best archaeological evidence for this landscaping process comes from joining sherds between contexts from the same trench though there are also joining sherds from different trenches some distance apart from one another. Several pottery sherds from a trench cut across West Street to the south of the mansion (6152/E) actually join with sherds found in the excavation of the moat around Shapwick House

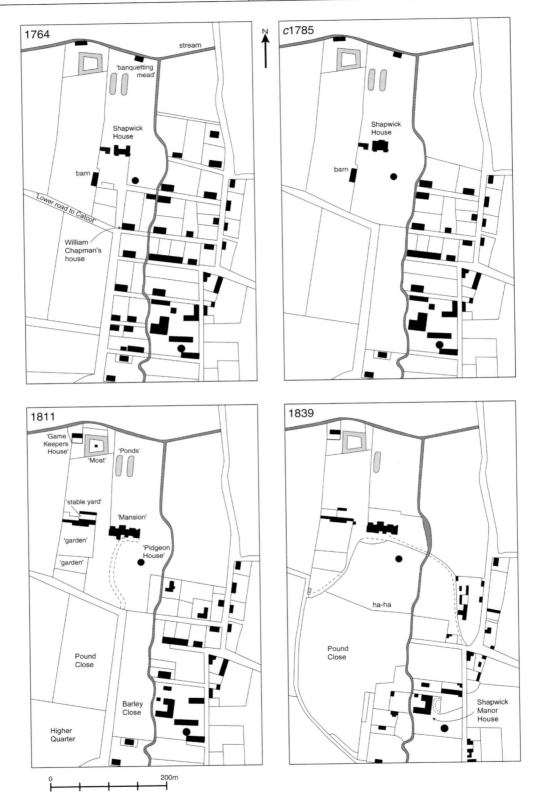

Fig. 10.4 *The process of emparkment to the south of Shapwick Park 1765–1839. Map created by Alejandra Gutiérrez from originals of 1764 (DD/SG 41 c206), c.1785 (DD/SG/50), 1811 (A/BED 1/3) and the 1839 tithe map of Shapwick. All these can be found in the Somerset Record Office.*

(6477/F) while two fragments of thirteenth-fourteenth century floor tile, undoubtedly from the chapel at the medieval curia (later Shapwick House) were recovered some way to the south during excavations on the line of the pipeline through Shapwick Park (Figure 10.5). It would seem then that material from the medieval manor was spread across the Park, especially at the time of emparkment in the second half of the eighteenth century, but also before that date.

To summarise, though the archaeological evidence is not conclusive, the bronze socketed mount and holder may derive from Shapwick House in the second half of the eighteenth century. But what exactly was it? The most plausible explanation at present is that this is not a fake, in that fakes or forgeries were intended to deceive, but some sort of curio, probably with a secondary function as a knife holder. It is possible that the two parts of the curio were sourced locally. The Irish connection with Somerset and Glastonbury, however obscure, was being emphasised by the Abbey in the twelfth century. In 1184 the relics of Patrick, Indracht and Dunstan, among others, were exhumed for display and perhaps the object was carried there by a monk or given as a gift. The socket and holder might then have found its way to the Abbey's manor house at Shapwick, perhaps most likely to the chapel there or to the parish church. The chapel may well have survived until the Dissolution but quite when the prehistoric blade and the medieval cross holder were brought together is much more difficult to answer. From archaeological evidence the composite object was already lost and buried by about 1765. Otherwise, the most telling observation I can offer is that during the first half of the eighteenth-century most antiquarians displayed little interest in medieval artefacts and had scarcely more respect for medieval buildings (Gerrard 2003, 20). Overall, this object hardly seems the product of a rigorous

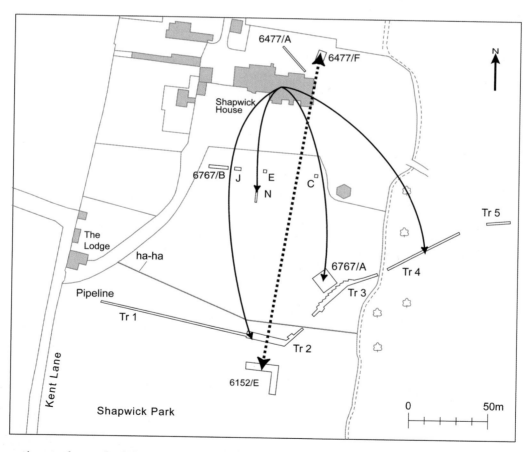

Fig. 10.5 Excavations to the south of Shapwick House in Shapwick Park. The trenches are coded by field and letter, thus 6477/ A is to the north of Shapwick House. The solid arrows indicate the likely movement of artefacts originating from Shapwick House to their place of discovery in the excavation trenches. The dotted arrow shows the findspots of two fragments of joining pottery. Taken together, this evidence suggests substantial landscaping and earth movement to create a new park to the south of Shapwick House in the late eighteenth century. Map created by Alejandra Gutiérrez.

antiquarian mind but rather more of a 'curiosity' which might belong in the cabinet of a catholic collector of 'rarities' as described by MacGregor (1985b) for the seventeenth century.

Who could have owned or commissioned such a piece? If the object is indeed later sixteenth or seventeenth century in manufacture then suspicion must fall upon the owners of Shapwick House in the immediate post-Dissolution period and particularly upon the Rolle family who purchased the manor in 1621. Sir Henry Rolle followed a successful career as a lawyer and was appointed a judge in 1645, advancing to Lord Chief Justice, a post he held between 1648 and 1655 (Henning 1983). He or his immediate family certainly had the necessary wealth and contacts to obtain these artefacts, but would he have had the inclination? Almost the only personal detail we have of Rolle is that he was a staunch Puritan, contemporaries saw him as 'just, but by nature penurious; and his wife made him worse' (Dick 1958). These characteristics he seems to have shared with other members of his immediate family who were also noted for their temperance and moderation (Cliffe 1984, 58). But what effect did religion have on daily life in the Rolle family? Common characteristics of Puritans were regular church attendance, instruction of the household through reading and prayer, a hatred of popery and despair at licentious behaviour (Morgan 1986, 13), but is it possible to detect a 'Puritan archaeology'? Probably not, for while there is some evidence of austerity and deliberate excess in dress codes was undoubtedly avoided, social distinctions would have been maintained. It would not necessarily have been outside the character of Puritan gentry to maintain an interest an antiquarian objects. More surprising perhaps is that a cross holder should have survived in this context. That it did so at all may be precisely because it is not an overt symbol of Catholic belief (such as a rood screen or a relic) but could instead be retained and mutilated. In effect, a sign of divine power (a cross) was transformed to a symbol of secular power in a new domestic context. The difficulty is knowing whether the holder was selected for symbolic reasons or simply because it was lying around. As Tarlow (2003, 115) has commented, 'much post-medieval re-use of pre-Reformation material should be interpreted as iconic rather than casual because of the potent cultural meanings of ecclesiastical material culture in the sixteenth and seventeenth centuries'. Sadly, we cannot know whether the prehistoric blade was already there or arrived later, but an antiquarian find does not seem an inappropriate suggestion. In any case, by the mid eighteenth century the two objects had been fused together to provide a secondary function probably as a knife holder and was about to be lost under the newly created park.

An Object Out of Place: A Cowrie Shell

My last find is an extremely unusual one, a large specimen of *Cypraea moneta* L. an exotic species of marine mollusc better known as the 'money cowrie' which was found during routine fieldwalking at Shapwick in October 1994 (Figure 10.6). It is certainly an experienced traveller. Its origins are Indo-Pacific; that is to say the small snail-like creature it once housed lived in the waters of the Red Sea or warm seas to the south and east which include the Persian Gulf, Arabian Sea and the Indian Ocean; the Maldive and Laccadive islands supplied most of the world's trade until the eighteenth century in shells of this kind (Light forthcoming). This particular example is not modified in any way, neither polished nor pierced. Almost the only fact we can be sure of is where it was found, in a field on the eastern edge of the modern village. Other finds from the same field include prehistoric flint, Roman and later medieval pottery and a particular abundance of seventeenth to nineteenth century pottery and associated structural materials such as brick, roofing slate and tile, and domestic debris including animal bone, clay pipes and metalwork. No field at Shapwick produced more pottery at a higher density than this field, over 1000 sherds were collected here alone, almost a sherd per metre walked along lines spaced 25m apart. Such quantities of material are too high to be explained by manuring, the most common mechan-

Fig. 10.6 The 'money cowrie' (Cypraea moneta L.) from Shapwick. Photograph by Jeff Veitch.

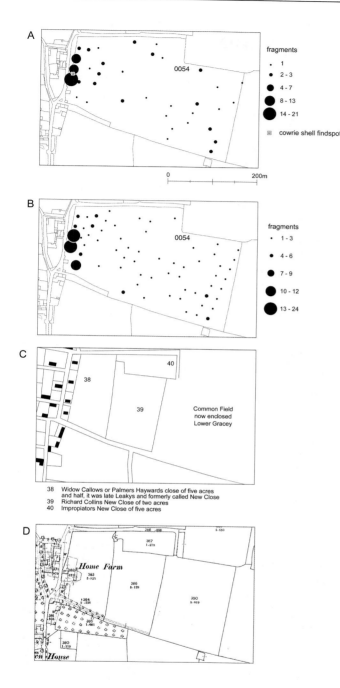

Fig. 10.7 Field 0054 in Shapwick parish. Fieldwalking distribution of 1720–1820 pottery (A) and nineteenth–twentieth century pottery (B). Map evidence for 1754 (DD/ SG c/206 36 1754) (C) and 2nd edition 25 inch OS map dated 1880 (D). Map created by Alejandra Gutiérrez.

ism by which finds make their way into arable fields; a more likely explanation is demolition. This is confirmed by the map sequence for the village which clearly shows an alignment of four buildings in this location on the 1754 map (DD/SG c/206 36 1754), succeeded by 1880 by farm buildings associated with Home Farm. These buildings were themselves ruined by 1971 and have since been demolished (Figure 10.7). The cowrie shell comes from the centre of this demolition spread and might be associated with either set of buildings, or indeed their predecessors in the same location. The shell itself cannot be dated, of course, but on the basis of provenance and the weight of finds from the same part of the field the object might be seventeenth, eighteenth or nineteenth century.

What do we know of cowrie shells circulating at this date? They were certainly being exported from South Asia to Europe in the early eighteenth century when they were used to pack crates of china. They were then re-exported by Dutch and English traders from Europe to Africa where they were exchanged with coastal West African groups for the slaves who were transported to the New World. Indeed, cowrie shells are sometimes referred to as 'the currency of Africa', though they also had special uses for divination, funerals, initiation and bride wealth. In particular they were used for decoration, not just as necklaces or in braided hair, but on drums, headdresses, masks, furniture, for game playing and counting. There is good archaeological evidence to confirm that enslaved Africans took cowries with them across the Atlantic, perhaps worn as jewellery or attached to clothing. A dump of cowries dating to about 1760 has been excavated on the property of a slave-trading merchant in Yorktown, Virginia, and a single example was also excavated from a street of slave houses and craft shops along Mulberry Row, adjacent to Thomas Jefferson's mansion (www.monticello.org). The latter cowrie had been pierced and showed evidence of abrasions from a thread which had been passed through it. Smaller, more personal finds such as these are one of very few material expressions of black identity found by North American archaeologists, because so many of the artefacts in play among slaves, such as pottery, were English. Similarly distinctive African artefacts include clay tobacco pipes and beads of glass, coral and ivory which Yentsch (1994, 191–192) also considers to be significant markers of cultural and social identity. In one example cited by Yentsch from Barbados an elderly man was buried with a necklace of carnelian stone, cowrie shells, fish vertebrae, canine teeth and beads. African-American women also continued to dress finely and made use of similar materials of varying colours and significance, combining objects of real value such as silver with those symbolic of natural wealth such as the cowrie.

Surprising as it may seem, there is an unlikely link between the European colonization of the New World and Shapwick. One of the owners of Shapwick House and the local squire, Denys Rolle (1725–1797) was a man of some influence in the West Country, he was High Sheriff of Devon, mayor (twice) and chief magistrate of Great Torrington and member of Parliament for Barnstaple. By the 1780s his estate comprised 45 manors in Devon and Cornwall, with principal residences at Stevenstone in north Devon and Bicton in the south-east of the county, as well as a town house in Exeter, and substantial estates in Hampshire, centred on East Tytherley. In Somerset, the manors of Bawdrip, Higham, Wookey, East Curry, North Curry and Well were all Rolle manors (Legg 1997).

In 1760 Denys first travelled by packet-boat to New York and then on to Philadelphia. Four years later he was granted 20,000 acres of unsettled land in Florida and set sail with a party of colonists who found their way to a promising site a little way upriver from Picolata, about 30 miles from St Augustine, which Rolle named Charlottia or Charlottenburgh, though it became known as Rollestown. Here, at Mount Pleasant on the east bank of the St John's river, not far from the present town of Palatka, he planned a town and advertised details of his settlement in West Country newspapers describing settlers' houses and gardens, a mansion house, a square and a churchyard. In his work he employed African slaves, indeed in a pamphlet of 1766 designed to encourage settlement in Florida, 'the most precious jewel of his majesty's American dominions', as Rolle called it, he promised the 'purchase of a Negro' as part of the settlement package (Rolle 1766; Mowat 1943, 51). Rollestown, however, was not without its share of misfortunes, the eccentric Rolle fell out with Governor Grant and his settlers, mostly London vagrants, deserted him for the enticements of St Augustine. Without doubt, he was something of an idealist and for over 20 years he doggedly pursued his dream of a Utopian colony so that by 1782 the total area of his new town, together with its rice plots, vineyard, fruit trees and plantation amounted to a substantial 80,000 acres. A year later, when Florida was returned to Spain, Rolle received only a third of the financial recompense he felt he deserved though he was at least granted 2000 acres on Great Exuma in the Bahamas (Legg 1997). Of the 106 slaves working in Florida, 42 died during the move there, but eventually Rolle was able to establish two settlements on the island: Rolleville in the north and Rolletown in the south.[2] His plan was a simple one, the English appetite for cotton offered him a chance to

recoup the losses he had suffered in Florida, so he set his slaves to clearing the island for cotton fields. Even so, his grand enterprise was doomed; over-intensive cropping, erosion and disease blighted his cotton plantations. Although Denys' son, John Rolle, seems at first to have supported his slaves, he directed in his will of 1842 that the family's land in the Bahamas should be sold. In truth, the Rolle plantations had long since failed to show any profit, many fields were abandoned and there were even instances of slave unrest on Rolle land in 1829 before all slaves were finally freed on August 1st 1838.

All in all, Denys perhaps spent four or five years of his life in East Florida. And though Denys was to be the last of the Rolle family line to make use of Shapwick mansion (now Shapwick Hotel), he made quite an impact on the village and its immediate landscape. His obituary explains that his favourite pastime was 'husbandry', and that he would dress as a peasant to work in his own fields. 'He has been often mistaken, in this dress, for a common husbandman, and, in this disguise, has directed many an enquirer to his own house' (Anon 1797c). We also know from his obituary that he was a keen botanist, great traveller, great walker and great talker (Anon 1797b) and it was almost certainly Denys' idea to empark the northern part of the village and plant up the newly created parkland nearest the house with Cedars of Lebanon. He did precisely the same at his principal residence at East Tytherley in Wiltshire. But the changes did not end here. It was probably Denys who was responsible for Shapwick's first 'ring-fence farm' at Northbrook in about 1780 and he was certainly actively involved with drainage in the Brue Valley. The enclosure of 1015 acres in 1784 seems initially to have brought profitable arable cultivation to replace pasture but, once exhausted, the fields returned to pasture again (Williams 1970, 131–140). The drainage of the whole of the Brue Valley was completed between 1780 and 1790 and catalogues of his libraries at Stevenstone and Bicton, his principal Devon residences, show that Rolle subscribed to *The Annals of Agriculture* and owned many books on botany and practical farming methods. Moreover, he had a taste for 'improvement', writing disapprovingly of the wastes of Dartmoor and Exmoor and undertaking marling experiments on his own estates, on at least one occasion 'freighting a vessel with mould from Hounslow' to improve his Devon heath land (Anon 1797b). Shapwick Heath was by no means his most ambitious enclosure project, at Sarsden (Oxon.) he enclosed 3030 acres of common fields and 1100 acres of waste in spite of local opposition (Legg 1997). Further interest in 'improvement' can be found in the quantities of amorphous slag collected during fieldwalking at Shapwick. In spite of apparent scepticism at the time, there is a close correlation between slag concentrations identified by field walkers and areas of pasture and meadow where the effect on productivity was reckoned to be most visible. The main problem on the peat, however, was the lack of surface drainage caused by defects in the outfall which was compounded by the effect of underground pipes draining water down off 'improved land' on the Poldens and flooding the lower lying peats.

So, returning to our find, Denys not only had an intimate knowledge of Shapwick and his lands there, but he also regularly crossed the Atlantic to the very place where cowrie shells were to be found in abundance. Florida was a key location for shell dealers (Claassen 1998, 233). There is one further connection and that is between Denys and the spot where the cowrie was picked up. In the middle of the eighteenth century there were four cottages on the eastern side of (now) Station Road, at the exact spot where the cowrie was found. One of them was referred to as a 'new cottage' in 1754 (Survey DD/SG16), and it seems likely they were all built at about this time. One of these cottages had disappeared by the time of the 1839 tithe map and another had gone by the date of the first edition Ordnance Survey 6 inch map in the 1880s. Today the sole survivor of the original row of four is No 50 Station Road. This was originally a 2-room cottage which was added to in the early nineteenth century and later subdivided into 2 dwellings (SVBRG 1996, 67). The debris collected by field walkers includes abundant pottery dating to the period 1780–1820, including creamwares, blue shell-edge and blue-printed pearlware, bone china, decorated porcelain, decorated red wares and refined blackwares which are very likely to be from these dwellings (Gutiérrez forthcoming). The Rolle connection is that he owned all four cottages. Could this cowrie have travelled the Atlantic twice? Once on board a slave ship, and later on a return voyage with Denys Rolle? Single un-stratified finds like this one rarely provide definitive answers but it would seem that Rolle took great interest in the personal affairs of his tenants, especially 'the rising generation' (Anon 1797a, 618). He was judged to be 'generous to his tenantry, indulgent to his servants and, above all, extensively benevolent to the poor' (Anon 1797c). Is it really possible that his generosity rose to the giving of souvenirs from his travels?

At this stage it is worthwhile considering other finds of cowrie shells in Europe and the Mediterranean to see if that provides any clues (Reese 1991). In fact, although money cowries (*Cypraea annulus* and *Cypraea moneta*) are the most common of the Indo-Pacific shells

in those regions, they are still quite rare finds and there is no real clustering in their dates or contexts which range from the Neolithic in Turkey to another dated AD 1375–1400 from Jerusalem. The cowries found occasionally in prehistoric contexts, such as the perforated Mesolithic example from Ulva cave in western Scotland are a different species (Bonsall *et al.* 1992). Sweden provides the most known examples, dating mostly between AD 600 and the tenth century, but of course the distribution map depends upon methods of recovery and standards of recording across many countries. In England, no finds are known to the writer of prehistoric or Roman date (Steve Willis pers. comm.) or indeed outside of the early medieval period, where with very few exceptions (e.g. Puddlehill, Bedfordshire; Matthews and Hawkes 1985, and Viking Jorvik) they are found in women's graves. We are fortunate in having a detailed study of imported grave goods of this date (Huggett 1988), though the different varieties of cowrie shells are considered together there and it is hard to be precise about numbers because many of the original reports from which Huggett took his data are vague as to the actual numbers found. With those caveats in mind, Huggett records 34 cowrie shells from 23 different Anglo-Saxon cemeteries including Camerton in Somerset (Wedlake 1958). They appear mostly in seventh-century burials like the sumptuous female graves at Lechlade (Miles 1986), though there are earlier examples (Sam Lucy pers. comm.), while marked concentrations in Cambridge-shire and Kent suggest a near-monopoly over their import which also seems to be true for amethyst beads, wheel-thrown pottery and glass vessels. Huggett's view is that access to these items outside these eastern counties may be 'limited to the 'wealthy' or those of higher social status', though clearly the picture may be complicated by other factors such as local fashion and the presence of foreigners.

In an early medieval context then, cowries were exotic and rare, particularly so outside Kent and Cambridgeshire. They represent one of a suite of imported goods which included Byzantine gold coins and copper-alloy 'Coptic' bowls which were acquired in the Eastern Mediterranean and, as Hinton (1990, 21) suggests, routed through Italy, across the Alps, along the Rhine and across the Channel. It has been suggested that these more fabulous goods were used to buy political favour and influence territorial control; certainly they suggest high level exchange among equals perhaps designed to reinforce marriage, trade or tenure. All this raises the question of what was supplied to Europe in return. Dogs, wool, cloth and slaves have all been suggested, but in Somerset the obvious product to be traded is lead from Mendip.

Cowries have no practical use and the 'ritual' context in which they are generally found suggests special meaning beyond that of simple personal adornment or as a status marker. They are certainly visually distinctive, combining a smooth polished surface with an unusual purity of natural colour, a coolness to the touch and an elaborate intricacy of form. When displayed about the person in a ritual context, they may have been 'read' in symbolic ways. The association between cowries, womanhood, fertility, procreation and wealth is well known (for example, they were worn in Roman Pompeii to prevent sterility); the shell is seen to resemble female genitalia among many modern cultures in Africa, India and the Pacific and the idea of rebirth may have been thought important in the afterlife. Claassen (1998, 211) cites their monetary uses, roles in fortune-telling and games and explains how they can be strung in different combinations to convey a range of emotions from friendship to enmity. Alternatively, the cowrie also resembles a half-open human eye and was used to guard against the Evil Eye and therefore against harm (Dubin 1995, 105). 'Eye beads' of one sort or another, are a feature common to many societies even today and can be simply stones incised with eye designs, or stones with banded colours or made of glass. Modern ethnographical study of amulets and their wearers suggests that the credibility and power of the talisman is enhanced by such factors as its age, ritual and ceremonial links and proofs of efficacy (Skeates 1995). These properties doubtless served well those who controlled their supply and we may imagine that their value was raised precisely by encouraging these associations. Either way, though their life histories came to an end once they were buried in a cemetery, this served to maintain their rarity and value.

If this cowrie shell is early medieval, then what is it doing in Shapwick? It is most likely to have come from a hitherto unknown cemetery, for which there is no supporting archaeological evidence from fieldwork in this location and which is likely to have been located some distance from settlement. The only certain contemporary settlement we know of lies in Church Field some 600m to the east, with another postulated at 'worthy' to the west (Figure 10.1). Our cemetery 'therefore' lies more or less equidistant between those two sites. All this is possible, if unproven and all the more intriguing when we add the fact that 450m further to the north of this find there are human remains which have been radiocarbon dated to AD 430–640 at 95.4% probability (AD 530–620 at 67% probability – SUERC-2938). This burial at 'Sladwick' is extraordinarily interesting for all kinds of reasons, not least because it was inserted into the structural

collapse of a fourth century Roman building. Like the cowrie shell, this event seems to pre-date the arrival of 'Anglo-Saxon culture' in the region. The 'coming of the English' to this area, the historical and place-name for which is reviewed by Costen (1992, 80–110), suggests that political and religious transformations began at more or less the same time, in the second half of the seventh century. Shapwick, as part of an Old British estate centre which came into the hands of West Saxon kings after AD 650, was then transferred to Glastonbury Abbey in the early eighth century. Our cowrie shell probably arrived in the area some time earlier, an artefact which had crossed political divides during the early seventh century or earlier. As such, it is a symbol of the penetration of Anglo-Saxon culture into an area under British influence, but might also be seen as a link between cultures on the margins of the spread of Christianity, a statement of pagan tradition against advancing cultural and religious change. This is an idea which strikes a chord with our interpretation of the burial in the Roman building at Sladwick. Could this burial have been intended to strengthen links with a 'British' or 'Roman' past before the arrival of Anglo-Saxon culture in this region? A statement of continuity of social relations perhaps, a linking of past time with present?

How might we choose between such wildly differing interpretations of this find? The weight of archaeological evidence, at least at a national level, may favour this being an early medieval object from a grave. The location of a cemetery in Field 0054 also seems to fit what we know of the contemporary landscape. And yet there is no evidence at all from this field of human skeletal remains among the considerable quantities of later bone which have survived the rigours of the plough soil. To use a favourite Aston adage 'is absence of evidence really evidence of absence?' On the other hand, the Rolle explanation also has its merits. The historical connections between people and places are real, however implausible they may seem, and the suite of artefacts from this particular field certainly fits better with an eighteenth century origin. Our inability to choose between these alternatives reflects our uncertainty in just how far we can push the evidence of an unstratified find. To take our interpretation further requires more fieldwork, geophysics perhaps in the first instance or trial trenching which might provide further stratigraphical or dating clues.

Conclusion

I have been interested in artefacts, specifically medieval ones, for most of my archaeological career.

At the same time I am always slightly horrified by the daunting catalogues of objects which accumulate in excavation monographs and museum catalogues. Other than the indulgence of feasting the eye on fine drawings, identifying artefacts, dating and naming them, the material still seems indigestible and there is often little appetite on the part of the author to say anything more. The impression given, all too often, is that these are lost and discarded items which have relatively little to tell us, except as a dating tool. Perhaps it has something to do with the way excavations are reported, artefact reports being penned by specialists who may lack a real understanding of the context of discovery and a main report drawn together by the excavator who, at worst, regards artefacts as an expensive inconvenience. But if that were true, then why do prehistorians seem to have a more enlightened view of their material?

The answer, as ever, comes down to the different academic trajectories of prehistory and historic archaeology. Prehistorians are in closer touch with anthropology and thus with the ways in which artefacts can be invested with meaning in order to create or maintain social relationships. Put another way, they understand that a simple functional explanation for the presence of an artefact on an archaeological site may be insufficient. A useful tool in this argument and one which appears in several recent texts is the idea of the biography of an object (Jones 2002, 83–102); the mapping of the entire life of an artefact, from production, through consumption and use, re-use, until the final point of deposition before its rediscovery by archaeologists. Such an simple and attractive idea should encourage us to think more expansively about our artefacts, about particular people with whom an artefact might have been associated (as I have tried to do here with Denys Rolle and the cowrie shell, for example), about how the meaning of an artefact is contingent on its context which may change as the artefact moves from place to place and through time (as it did for the bronze socket and mount) and, in particular, about the assertion that rubbish disposal, at the very end of an artefact's life, is not always structured according to practical considerations (as in the case of the antler rake). We should be alive to the possibility that attitudes to certain types of 'rubbish' in later medieval Britain reflect cultural practices as well as practical necessity. In the case of the three artefacts under consideration here, I find it hard to argue in any of these cases that those who possessed and handled these objects acted entirely in a rational manner or out of simple necessity. In each case more complex forces were at work and during their lifetime the objects became bound up in the construction and display of social and cultural identities. They were used as a means of communication, not merely used and then discarded, and at each phase in their life cycles they gained new meaning and status.

Notes

1 Other later re-furbishings sometimes featured medieval architectural features such as windows and doorways, among them the medieval pier bases for the columns of the aisles at Winford which were re-cycled from the same site when the church was re-built in 1796 (Pevsner 1979, 340) or the medieval window tracery re-used in the church of St Andrew at Wiveliscombe re-built in 1829 (Pevsner 1985, 350), while the church dedicated to St Dubricus at Porlock has two fragments of Saxon cross-shaft in one of its walls, probably placed on view there in the late nineteenth century (Pevsner 1985, 275), all effective ways to commemorate the long tradition of worship in their respective parishes. Elsewhere, medieval features were sometimes introduced to a wholly new structure, as in the case of the rood screen at the church of St Mary Magdalen in Exford which came from the medieval church of West Quantoxhead (Pevsner 1985, 169) or the fifteenth century doorway from Dunster in the early twentieth century church of St Michael at Alcombe (Pevsner 1985, 75). It would be useful to have a comprehensive analysis of re-used stone in medieval and later buildings in the South-West, to understand better which stone types were being re-used and when this re-use was taking place.

2 Both Rolletown and Rolleville are still there and Great Exuma has recently been described by the Washington Post as one of the '10 most desirable international locations' (www.peace and plenty.com). According to the same website 'many old walls and foundations... can still be found in Exuma's undergrowth', the remains of cotton planter's estate buildings. The name Rolle is today borne by one third of all Exumians.

Acknowledgements

I am grateful to Dr Sam Lucy for additional data on cowrie shells from early medieval cemeteries and to Dr Steve Willis for his views on the apparent absence of Roman cowries, and to my colleagues, past and present, in the Department of Archaeology at the University of Durham for discussions on theory and material culture. Were it not for the work of Robert Legg, the Rolle connections made above would never have been made, and all the original work in this regard is his alone.

References

Anon. (1797a) Obituary of remarkable persons; with biographical anecdotes. *Gentleman's Magazine* LXVII, 617–618.
Anon. (1797b) Additions to, and corrections in, former obituaries. *Gentleman's Magazine* LXVII, 885.
Anon. (1797c) Additions to, and corrections in, former obituaries.

Gentleman's Magazine LXVII, 1125.

Aston, M. A. (1985) *Interpreting the Landscape: Landscape Archaeology and Local Studies*. London, Batsford.

Aston M. A. and Gerrard, C. M. (1999) 'Unique, traditional and charming', The Shapwick Project, Somerset. *Antiquaries Journal* 79, 1–58.

Bonsall, C., Sutherland, D., Lawson, T. and Russell, N. (1992) Excavations at Ulva cave, western Scotland 1989: a preliminary report. *Mesolithic Miscellany* 13(1).

Chapman, J. (2000) *Fragmentation in Archaeology. People, places and broken objects in the prehistory of South Eastern Europe*. London, Routledge.

Claassen, C. (1998) *Shells*. Cambridge, Cambridge University Press.

Cliffe, J. T. 1984. *The Puritan Gentry. The Great Puritan Families of Early Stuart England*. London, Routledge.

Costen, M. D. (1992) *The Origins of Somerset. Manchester*, Manchester University Press.

Costen, M. D. (forthcoming) The field-names of Shapwick, in C. Gerrard with M. Aston *The Shapwick Project, Somerset. A rural landscape explored.*

Crouch, D. (1992) *The image of aristocracy in Britain 1000–1300*. London, Routledge.

Crossley, D. (1990) *Post-medieval archaeology in Britain*. London, Leicester University Press.

Davey, P. (2002) *The prehistoric flat axe, in P Mayes Excavations at a Templar preceptory. South Witham, Lincolnshire 1965–67. Society for Medieval Archaeology Monograph 19*. Maney, Leeds.

Dick, O. L. (1958) *Aubrey's Brief Lives*. London, Secker and Warburg.

Dubin, L. S. (1995) *The History of Beads*. London, Thames and Hudson.

Eaton, T. (2000) *Plundering the Past: Roman stonework in Medieval Britain*. Stroud, Tempus.

Ecclestone, M. (1998) Field names in the Shapwick Court Rolls, in M Aston, T. A. Hall and C. M. Gerrard (eds) *The Shapwick Project. A topographical and historical study. The Eighth Report*, 211–216. Bristol, Department for Continuing Education, University of Bristol.

Egan, G. and Pritchard, F. (1991) *Dress accessories c.1150–c.1450. Medieval finds from excavations in London: 3*. London, HMSO.

Gerrard, C. M. (2003) *Medieval Archaeology. Understanding traditions and contemporary approaches*. London, Routledge.

Gerrard, C. M. (forthcoming) Excavations at Shapwick, in C. Gerrard with M. Aston, *The Shapwick Project, Somerset. A rural landscape explored.*

Gerrard, C. M. and Youngs, S. M. (1997) A Bronze socketed Mount and Blade from Shapwick House, *Somerset. Medieval Archaeology XLI*, 210–214.

Greenhalgh, M. (1989) *The Survival of Roman Antiquities in the Middle Ages*. London, Duckworth.

Grinsell, L. V. (1960) The breaking of objects as a funeral rite. *Folklore* 71, 475–91.

Gutiérrez, A. (forthcoming) Medieval and later pottery, in C. M. Gerrard with M Aston (eds) *The Shapwick Project, Somerset. A rural landscape explored.*

Henning, B. D. (1983) *The House of Commons 1660–1690*. London, Secker and Warburg.

Hinton, D. (1990) *Archaeology, Economy and Society. England from the fifth to the fifteenth century*. London, Seaby.

Huggett, J. W. (1988) Imported grave goods and the early Anglo-Saxon economy. *Medieval Archaeology* 32, 63–96.

Jones, A. (2002) *Archaeological theory and scientific practice*. Cambridge, Cambridge University Press.

Legg, R. (1997) *A Pioneer in Xanadu. Denys Rolle: 1725–97*. Hants. Furrow Press.

Light, J. (forthcoming) Marine mollusks, in C. Gerrard with M. Aston, (eds.). *The Shapwick Project, Somerset. A rural landscape explored.*

MacGregor, A. (1985a) *Bone, antler, ivory and horn. The technology of skeletal materials since the Roman period*. London, Croom Helm.

MacGregor, A. (1985b) The Cabinet of Curiosities in Seventeenth-Century Britain, in O. Impey and A. MacGregor (eds), *The Origins of Museums. The Cabinet of Curiosities in Sixteenth- and Seventeenth-century Europe*, 147–158. Oxford, Clarendon Press.

Matthews, C. L. and Hawkes, S. C. (1985) *Early Saxon settlements and burials at Puddlehill, near Dunstable, Bedfordshire. Anglo-Saxon Studies in Archaeology and History 4*, 59–115.

Miles, D. (1986) Lechlade Saxon cemetery. *Rescue News* 38, 3.

Morgan, J. (1986) *Godly learning. Puritan Attitudes towards Reason, Learning and Education, 1560–1640*. Cambridge, Cambridge University Press.

Mowat, C. L. (1943) *East Florida as British Province 1763–1784*. Berkeley and Los Angeles, University of California Press.

Pevsner, N. (1979) *The Buildings of England. North Somerset and Bristol*. Harmondsworth, Penguin.

Pevsner, N. (1985) *The Buildings of England.South and West Somerset*. Harmondsworth, Penguin.

Reese, D. (1991) The trade of Indo-Pacific shells into the Mediterranean basin and Europe. *Oxford Journal of Archaeology* 10(2), 159–196.

Rolle, D. (1766) *An Extract from the Account of East Florida, Published by Dr Stork... With the Observations of Denys Rolle, who formed a Settlement on St John's river...* London, privately printed.

Skeates, R. (1995) Animate objects: a biography of prehistoric 'axe amulets' in the central Mediterranean region. *Proceedings of the Prehistoric Society 61*, 279–301.

Spencer, B. (1998) *Pilgrim souvenirs and secular badges. Medieval finds from excavations in London: 7*. London, The Stationary Office.

Stocker, D. and Everson, P. (1990) Rubbish recycled: A Study of the Re-Use of Stone in Lincolnshire, in D. Parsons (ed.) *Stone. Quarrying and Building in England AD 43–1525*, 83–101. Chichester, Phillimore.

Stoodley, N. (1999) *The Spindle and the Spear. A critical enquiry into the construction and meaning of gender in the early Anglo-Saxon Burial rite. BAR British Series 288*. Oxford, Archaeopress.

Tarlow, S. (2003) Reformation and transformation: what happened to Catholic things in a Protestant world? in D. Gaimster and R. Gilchrist (eds). *The Archaeology of Reformation 1480–1580*. Leeds: Maney and The Society for Post-Medieval Archaeology, 108–121.

Taylor, A. J. (1963) 'Caernarvon' in H. M. Colvin, A. J. Taylor and R. A. Brown. *A History of the King's Works*, volume 1, 369–95. London, HMSO.

Webster, C. J. (1992) Excavations within the village of Shapwick, *Proceedings of the Somerset Archaeology and Natural History Society* 136, 117–126.

Wedlake, W. J. (1958) *Excavations at Camerton, Somerset*. Camerton, Camerton Excavation Club.

Wheatley, A. (2004) *The Idea of the Castle in Medieval England*. Woodbridge, York Medieval Press.

Williams, M. (1970) *The draining of the Somerset Levels*. Cambridge, Cambridge University Press.

Yentsch, A. E. (1994) *A Chesapeake family and their slaves. A study in historical archaeology*. Cambridge, Cambridge University Press.

Chapter 11

'Of Naked Venuses and Drunken Bacchanals': Tong Castle, Shropshire, and its Landscapes

Paul Stamper

Tong stands close to Shropshire's eastern boundary (Figure 11.1). It is a small and picturesque place, blighted only by the M54 motorway which thunders its disinterested way past, joining Shropshire and its Blue Remembered Hills to Birmingham and the Black Country. In the village, and scattered among the surrounding countryside, hamlets and farms, are echoes of past glories: a fine church with an astonishing richness of medieval tombs, a curving lake hinting at a lost landscape park, and a plethora of follies and follified buildings. But of any great house whose owners might have commissioned such things there is no sign. This brief paper sets out to explain how that became about: to tell the story of Tong Castle's end, and more importantly to explore what kind of place it was, and what kind of landscape – or landscapes – it stood within.

From the Middle Ages Tong was one of those places that, later on, would be characterised as belonging to the gentry class. It already had a castle, and by 1273 a deer park (Wrottesley 1885, 54). The park probably had an unbroken existence through to the early eighteenth century (below), occupying the south-east corner of the parish; certainly Saxton's county map of 1577 places a park hereabouts. A moated site shown on a map of 1759 on the edge of Old Lodge Close presumably enclosed the medieval park lodge (SA 3581/1). As for the castle little is known of it, and uncertainty about its early history is introduced by the presence just south of Tong Norton, a hamlet a kilometre north of Tong village, of a sandstone mound called Castle Hill, which in the 1930s was believed to be the site of the first castle. This remains to be investigated. But whatever its origins, by the fourteenth century Tong castle apparently occupied the site of its later namesakes, on a slight bluff on a dogleg bend taken by the Tong Brook 600m south-west of Tong church; amateur excavations in 1976 appeared to find traces of it, but they remain unpublished

(Robinson 1980, 59). In 1381 the castle's owner, Sir Fulk Pembridge, acquired a licence to crenellate, although what if any work was undertaken as a consequence is unknown (Mercer 2003, 116). Almost certainly what that licence signified was less a concern about security but rather a wish by him to be seen in midland society as a coming man, one who by the very purchase of this permission was at least nominally in the king's favour (Coulson 1994, 93; 2003; Liddiard 2005, 43–4). His new castle may have expressed that self-perception in architectural form; indeed, given the quality of another of the family's commissions 20 years later, it would seem highly likely the licence accompanied a house of some pretension.

That commission, which forms the most splendid reminder of the family, and its apparent wealth, aspirations, and piety (or more cynically its concern to speed its souls through purgatory) stands in the form of Tong church and its tombs (Gaydon 1973, 131–2). The existing church at Tong (Figure 11.2) was endowed as a college of priests in 1410 by Fulk's widow Isabel. The principal function of the warden and four chaplains was to intercede for the souls of Isabel and her three husbands (Fulk, d.1409, had been the last). They were to live together, each with a chamber to himself, and were to be careful to talk in a low voice, to eat and drink modestly, and to refrain from hunting and hawking. Their collegiate buildings have disappeared, but lay to the south of the church; they survived until 1757 but were ruinous soon thereafter. Also living at Tong College were thirteen almspeople and two clerks, the other element of Isabel's foundation. Their almshouses, like the ruins of the college, survived until the earlier nineteenth century when they were relocated into the village.

The church itself was almost wholly rebuilt soon after the college's foundation (Eric Mercer (2003, 75) suggests perhaps completion within the next 20 years). Its form reflected its function, the choir lengthier than

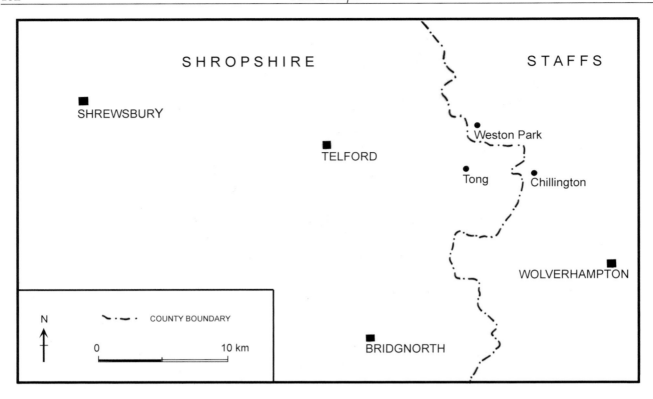

Fig. 11.1 Tong, Shropshire: location plan.

Fig. 11.2 Tong church from the south, showing the Vernon chantry chapel projecting from the crossing (Paul Stamper).

the nave and with a long chancel for the college's clergy. Pevsner (1958, 302) characterised it as 'a very spiky, battlemented and pinnacled building of red sandstone with a tower over the crossing. The tower starts square and turns octagonal. It ends with battlements and pinnacles and a stone spirelet.' On the death of Sir Fulk Pembridge in 1409 Tong had passed to his great-nephew Sir Richard Vernon of Haddon Hall (Derbyshire), and that he and his wife were buried there suggests that a decision had been taken to accord this newly acquired property, 75 km south-west of the Vernons' main seat, a special function: that of family mausoleum. One can only assume that the main attraction – putting to one side there was no burial place at Haddon – was the presence of the college of priests, who might now be expected to intercede on behalf of the Vernons' souls as well as those of their Pembridge kinsmen. Richard's son Sir William (d.1467) was also buried there, and then before his death in 1515 his son Sir Henry reinforced Tong's role as mausoleum by founding a chantry. To accommodate this an architecturally sophisticated chapel was built south of the south aisle, which has Shropshire's only fan vault. For Eric Mercer (2003, 88) the chapel's inspiration was metropolitan. The Vernons (for whom see Nigota 2004) of Haddon were of north midland gentry stock, and both Sir Henry's grandfather and father had been ambitious gatherers of offices and properties, his father gaining a reputation for violence and disputation. Somehow Henry managed to rise above his inherited station and make an aristocratic marriage to Anne, sister of the third earl of Shrewsbury. Clearly a wily and shrewd operator, one whom Christopher Hussey characterised as a man 'who had contrived throughout the Wars of the Roses to be on the winning side' (1946, 578), by 1474 he had become a member of the king's household as an esquire of the body. In 1485 he switched his support to Henry Tudor, fought for him at Stoke in 1487 and against the Cornish rising of 1489, and was knighted (somewhat tardily, in part because of his changing allegiances) in November 1489. This was also the occasion when the king's son was made Prince of Wales, and in 1492, when in his later forties, Sir Henry was made the prince's governor and controller.

For Pevsner (1958, 302) Tong was 'a museum of effigies, to the detriment of the architecture and the individual monuments'. But as a middling county family's mausoleum it has few equals. Perhaps the point actually is, that at the turn of the sixteenth century the Vernons were aspiring to more than this. The earliest of the monuments is that of Fulk and Elizabeth Pembridge, a plain alabaster affair whose mundane quality is at odds with the building which

houses it. Next in the sequence, of Sir Richard Vernon of Haddon Hall (d.1451; Figure 11.3), is judged by Brian Kemp (1980, 23) to be among the finest alabaster tombs in England. Originally the tomb would have been painted and gilded, enhancing its magnificence; in fact, overall the Vernon chantry must have resembled a jewel box, and little wonder that it became known as the Golden Chapel (Mercer 2003, 88). Other tombs are of a similar quality including the last of the freestanding monuments, the two-tiered affair of Sir Thomas Stanley (d.1576) and his wife Margaret Vernon.

Meanwhile, before his death in 1515 Sir Henry Vernon had rebuilt Tong Castle in brick, a fact noted by John Leland (who describes the event as recent) in the course of his 1539 tour of the northern counties (Chandler 1993, 397). This was a precociously employment of brick in a county where its use in gentry

Fig. 11.3 Tong church: the tomb of Sir Richard Vernon (d.1451) and his wife (English Heritage/National Monuments Record).

buildings only began more generally *c.*1570 (Mercer 2003, 159), and its style may have been equally up-to-date. The sole record of the house, an engraving of the early 1730s by the Buck brothers (Figure 11.4), is difficult to interpret, but shows a place with a central, well-fenestrated yet relatively low and small hall (with louvre) set between ranges which incorporated square and octagonal towers (including what was probably a lodgings tower at the south end) and tall, decorative, brick chimneys. As at Great Chalfield (Wilts.), a house built *c.*1480 for a wealthy clothier, within the superficial general symmetry of the façade external ornamentation as well as architectural vocabulary differentiated between the functions of the parts and expressed clearly their importance (Cooper 1999, 60). As a brick house it has the feel of contemporary places like Beaulieu (Essex) a royal house of 1516 and later (Thurley 1993, 44–5), East Barsham Manor (Norfolk) of *c.*1520–5 (Cooper 1999, 61–5), and Compton Wynyates (Warws.) of the early sixteenth century (*ibid.* 66), all, without doubt, gentry houses of the first order. Overall, Tong was quite a place in the early sixteenth century, and with his chantry and castle Sir Henry Vernon deliberately proclaimed to society in architectural terms his political, financial, and especially social achievements, and also his increasing attachment to Shropshire, his wife's home, rather than to the more northern counties where the family's traditional

power-base lay. If proof were needed of this we have it in the form of Sir Henry's own words, his will instructing his executors to build a sumptuous tomb at Tong for his wife and himself, 'the better and the more honourable for the blood that my wyff is comyn of' (P. R. O. PROB 11/18, fol. 66*r*, quoted by Nigota 2004).

Tantalisingly, at that point the story goes cold for 250 years, and during that period Tong is only occasionally glimpsed in the historical record (but see below, Acknowledgments). If there are documents revealing how life was lived at Tong during perhaps the greatest period of its history, in the time of Sir Henry's heir Richard (d.1517) and his son George (d.1565), they have yet to come to light. A few references relate to the fact that, while almost certainly indefensible against any determined attack, Tong Castle was garrisoned in the Civil Wars (Captain Richard Symonds called it 'a fayre old castle': Symonds 1879, 273), gaining the dubious distinction of being the first Shropshire stronghold to be taken by the Parliament, on December 28 1643. The outgoing Royalist garrison is said to have burned the place, but it would seem unlikely the damage was severe as the house was occupied during the Commonwealth (Hussey 1946, 578).

In 1764 Tong (which, as an aside, tradition says had seen the birth eight years earlier when tenanted by the

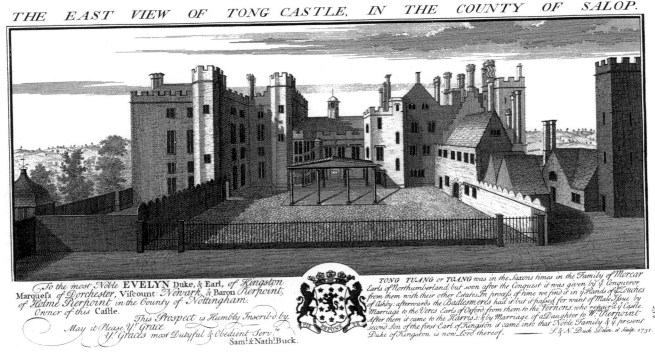

Fig. 11.4 Tong Castle: the Buck brothers' view of 1731 (author's collection).

Smythes of Acton Burnell of the later Mrs. Fitzherbert, the unlawful wife of George IV: Levy 2004) was sold for £40,000 to George Durant, who although only in his early thirties had already acquired a large amount of capital (Jeffery n.d.; Jeffery in preparation). His career began in 1757 when, newly down from Oxford, he was appointed clerk to the Pay Office. A year later he was made paymaster for the British troops involved in an expedition to Guadeloupe, a key episode in the Seven Years War of 1756–63. Family papers suggest a rakish – positively Flashmanesque – relish for dubious adventure and self-advancement while in foreign parts. By the time of his return in 1759 he may well have acquired modest wealth, and in 1761 had his portrait painted by Joshua Reynolds, by then well-established as the leading British portrait painter. Durant then set off as paymaster to the forces in the Cuban expedition of 1762, a further instalment in the Seven Years War, which appears to have provided the opportunity – in the form of the sack of Havannah in August of that year – for Durant to accrue a substantial personal fortune. This enabled him to fulfil his ambition of buying an estate in the neighbourhood of Worcester, where the family had lived in the seventeenth century (Hussey 1946, 580). Later Durant was to name one of his newly-created inclosed farms in the northern part of Tong 'Havannah', presumably as an ever-present reminder of the source of his wealth. Or at least a part of it. The Very Reverend Jeffery, who has made a study of the Durants, has had sight of family papers which indicate an involvement in the slave trade, and notes the frequency of the name Durant in the modern Windward Isles.

Within a year or so of purchasing Tong George Durant had brought in Lancelot 'Capability' Brown to put in hand improvements both to the house and to its surrounds (Figure 11.5). Brown at this time was well established as England's leading place-maker, and in the previous year had been appointed as royal gardener at Richmond, St. James's, and Hampton Court where he moved into Wilderness House (Phibbs 2004). His practise was active at several places on the Shropshire-Staffordshire border in the early 1760s, and it would seem that, one way or another, one contract flowed from another as good reports circulated of the amiable and able landscape gardener. About 1760 he had begun work at Chillington (Staffs.) 7km to the east of Tong, while 1765 was also the year he began work for Sir Henry Bridgeman at Weston Park (Staffs.), the estate immediately to the north of Tong (for Chillington and Weston see English Heritage 2005). At Tong, house building probably preceded park-making. Probably incorporating parts of the early sixteenth century Vernon residence (Hussey 1946, 578),

Tong Castle was reconstructed on a grand scale in the new gothick style (Figure 11.6), its first appearance in the county (Mercer 2003, 192, 199). The east (front) and west (garden) facades were symmetrical and different, although both were heavily dressed with loopholed towers, ogee-headed openings, and bay windows, and topped with battlements, a baroque dome, and Jacobean cupolas; locally it was said to have a Moorish flavour, and if academically incorrect this does capture something of its exotic character (*ibid.* 199–200; Hussey 1946, 580). Internally, the arrangement of space was equally up-to-date: the hall was no bigger than either of the drawing rooms, was smaller than the dining room, and was less than half the size of the saloon. While it is not impossible that a local architect was employed to work on the project – and Thomas Farnolls Pritchard, the conceiver of the iron bridge is a strong candidate (Mercer 2003, 352 n.37) – the concept was probably Brown's and his account book for 1765 (at the Royal Horticultural Society's Lindley Library) includes [fol.95] 'Various Plans for the alterations of Tong Castle. My journeys there several times' and [fol.119] 'George Durant Esqr of Tong Castle in Shropshire. Various plans & elevations made for Tong Castle & for journeys there £52 10s. 00'. He certainly employed this type of Strawberry Hill gothick elsewhere, probably in the same year, for instance, for the unexecuted lodge at Rothley in Northumberland. Johnny Phibbs tells me that this charge, 50 guineas, was a middling one by Brown's standards, and would have provided for outline plans and proposals both for house and grounds, but not the execution thereof.

Within the landscape at Tong, modifications matched those at the castle. An estate map of 1759 (SA 3581/1; Stamper 1996, pl. 15), perhaps drawn up in anticipation of the sale of the estate, shows the house standing on a slight peninsula, above a stream already dammed to make a pool. Eastward of the house was a wilderness, and a simplified *patte d'oie* arrangement of avenues of trees which ran across inclosed fields, the northerly arm leading to the church and the most southerly to the edge of the former medieval deer park. This was disparked by 1725 (Vaughan 1879, 257–8), although probably not long before that date, as while the 1759 map shows the park to be inclosed and under arable cultivation it also shows the pale as still standing. Tong Park Farmhouse, a five-bay brick building which stands within the former park and which has a 1736 datestone, was clearly built to cultivate what would have been a reasonably large farm by contemporary standards. By 1759, although clear traces of former open field land can be seen on the map, all of the parish's arable lands were in several

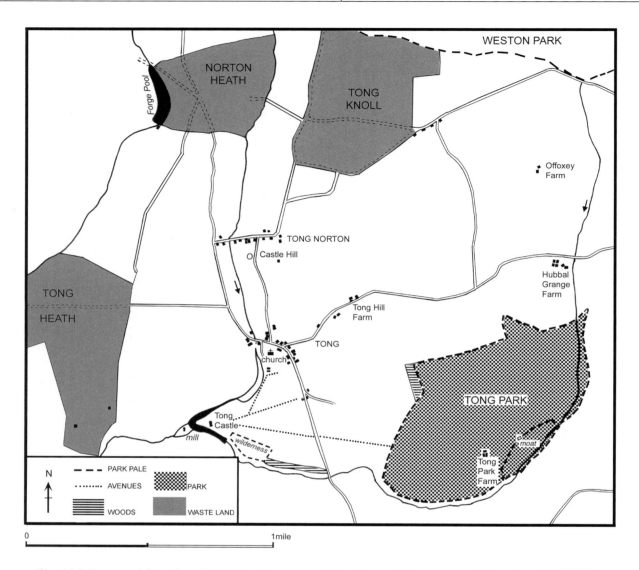

Fig. 11.5 Tong parish in the mid eighteenth century, before Brown's improvements (based on SA 3581/1).

cultivation. While some areas of straight-edged fields (as in the former park) hint at recent improvements, Norton Heath and Tongue Knoll (or Knowle) survived as large open commons in the north part of the parish along with a third, Tong Heath, half a mile west of the castle.

Brown – or whoever was executing his vision – began by constructing a large dam near the castle and thereby extending the pool around it to some 1,400m in length, the part nearer the castle being called Church Pool or North Pool, and that beyond the Newport Road Castle Hill Pool. George Durant petitioned to do the work in 1770, and was presented at Quarter Sessions in 1775 for 'digging a pool across the highway' (Robinson 1980, 54, 63), so lake making may have

followed on from the work on the house. Another dam was used to extend the pool south of the house eastward to the Wolverhampton road. Tong Castle now appeared to stand on a great river, a typical Brownian conceit (Figure 11.7).

Other engineering projects followed before the death of George Durant in 1780, notably the creation of an interlinked pair of lakes, Norton Mere to the north of Tong Norton, and Lodge Lake to the west of the castle (Figure 11.8). Again, the scale, ambition and indeed the very concept itself suggests the design was Brown's (he lived on until 1783), although as we have heard he probably played no part in over-seeing the works. Norton Mere was probably created at much the time that Norton Heath was inclosed, and partly

Fig. 11.6 Tong Castle: the garden front in the late nineteenth century (SA, Francis Frith postcard).

Fig. 11.7 Tong Castle c.1900: the North Pool arcs past the entrance front like a great river – the view from the village carriage drive (English Heritage/National Monuments Record BB89/S942).

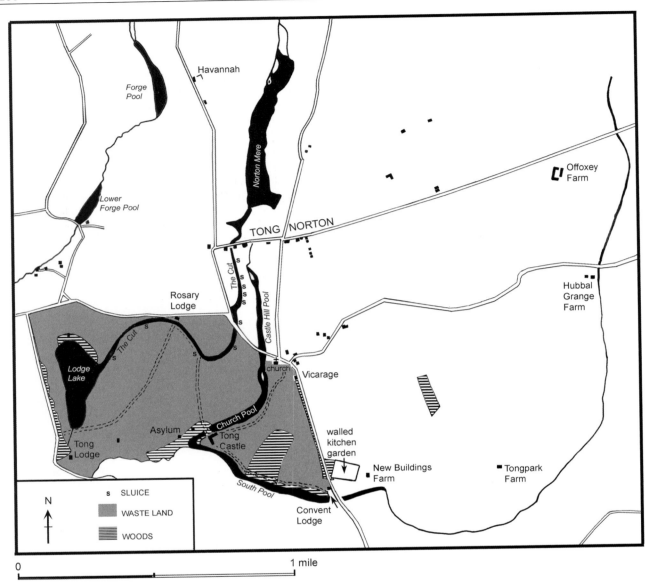

Fig. 11.8 Tong parish in the later eighteenth century, after park-making and improvement.

encroached upon it. The former heath was divided into straight-sided fields and an improving farmhouse built, named Havannah in memory of the place which brought George Durant good fortune thirty-odd years before (above). Similarly Lodge Lake occupied the area of the former Tong Heath which was inclosed by 1796 as was the third large common, Tong Knoll (SA 5233/1). While probably ornamental in its own right, and later planted around with trees, the principal purpose of Norton Mere was apparently to act as a supply for Lodge Lake by means of 'The Cut', a 1,800 m long channel 'several yards wide and three or four feet deep' (Robinson 1980, 52). A subsidiary purpose of

The Cut (a device used by Brown elsewhere, for instance at Chillington (Staffs.), where the river-like Canal is 1,000 m long) was to water meadow land – the 1891 Ordnance Survey six-inch map shows a sequence of nine sluice gates (the last removed in the early 1970s: Robinson 1980, 53) for this purpose (Shropshire sheet XLIV.NE) – and again this chimes with what is known of other designs by Brown. Johnny Phibbs has made the point (Phibbs 2004) that his parklands – and this was what the area north of the castle was being made into at this time as old field boundaries and the avenues of trees were removed – far from being 'bare and bald' were in fact hay meadows 'which brought the central, socially levelling episode of the agricultural year right into the heart of the estate.' Elsewhere he has suggested that mowing 'was a spectator sport, to be enjoyed from the windows of the big house' (Phibbs 2003, 129). At Tong Castle a climb to the battlements and a telescope would probably have been needed to enjoy a distance glimpse of the mowers, although they could have been seen from several of the public roads around the village as well as by anyone walking or riding in the park. Interestingly, something of the making of lakes and meadows was remembered by Tong's rector in the 1870s who recalled that Durant 'expended immense sums upon improving and beautifying the property. He formed Tong Lakes, and the canal which feeds it, upwards of two miles in length, and made arrangement for the irrigation of the park' (SA 3848/Misc/19). A somewhat crude estate map of 1796 (SA 5233/1) records the Brownian landscape, and shows the house, park (divided into compartments), new waters, and kitchen gardens sited just outside the park. The map is too badly drawn to allow certainty, but it is highly likely that other improvements visible on later maps had also been made during the same period beyond the new park, notably to the parish roads which had been straightened and rationalized, and to fields which had had their boundaries and sizes regularized notably north and east of Tong Norton. Sadly, today only fragments of the Brownian park landscape survives; a view which can still be enjoyed from Tong churchyard of the North Pool curving out of sight, and a few nineteenth-century photographs, are tantalising remembrances of what has been lost.

As for buildings in the park very little, if perhaps anything, had been done by the time George Durant the elder died in 1780. Durant's heir was his four-year-old son George, and over the following years the castle was let. We get an excellent (and opinionated) account of the place in 1792 when it was visited by the Hon. John Byng, which not only describes the (intentional) pastoral setting of the house but also makes clear that just as no expense had been spared on the house and the park, (and probably the wider estate too, for, as has been observed above, large-scale inclosure and associated improvements also took place during the time of George Durant I) so too there had been heavy spending on the contents because, to borrow the late Alan Clark's put-down, as 'new money' the Durants had had 'to buy their own furniture':

> This place, purchased by Mr. Durant has been rebuilt in a most overgrown taste; and would require a very large fortune to keep up. How people can build these pompous edifices without a sufficiency of surrounding estate is wonderful ! And yet how commonly it is done ...

> It is a grand and beautiful place; attended by the housekeeper I surveyed the house; – the staircase is very fine, the rooms well-sized, and well furnished; the vast bedchambers excellent; there is on the first floor a vast music room; but no library !Your hasty wealth thinks not of that. Every part of this house is covered by pictures – from Christie's – and other auctions, of dying Saints, naked Venuses, and drunken Bacchanals.

> Now why all this offensive show, disgusting to every English eye that has not been hardened in Italy ? Surely the intention of paintings was to clear the mind, and restore your pleasures; to survey your ancestry with conscious esteem; to view the beauties of Nature; to restore the memory of famous horses, and of faithful dogs. But why produce savage, and indecent exhibitions, before your children's eyes ? Why is Ovid's Metamorphoses to be produced in full display ?

> Why are the glorious feats of Jupiter to be held before our eyes; and why are we to be encouraged by Satyrs to peep at naked, sleeping beauty ? ...This would be a grand place; as it is some West-Indians [that is planters] may hire it for a few years; but, if once deserted, these great houses soon tumble to pieces. The pleasure ground behind the house is pretty, and the trees, and shrubs grow well. The water that twines through the park is beautiful, but might be much improved: neither its banks or the park are half planted but this is the case everywhere – views – and wind form the present taste.

(Andrews 1934–8, vol. 3, 139–40 [with spelling and punctuation modernised]).

Sadly, this is virtually all we know of the interior appearance of the house whose layout was mentioned above, although some areas of rococo plasterwork survived to be photographed before the castle was demolished. This was of a sufficient quality to suggest to John Harris the hand of Thomas Farnolls Pritchard, the Shrewsbury architect who has already been mentioned in connexion with Tong and who was the leading regional exponent of rococo carving and plasterwork (Ionides 1999, 277–9). While there is no proof of this attribution it is an indication, taken with Byng's purse-lipped description, of the quality of the interiors, whose exuberance clearly matched the castle's exterior.

George (II) came into the property in 1797, aged 21. To call him eccentric is to underplay matters, and even by contemporary standards his conduct as a husband and landowner drew adverse comment. On his death in 1844 the *Shrewsbury Chronicle* characterised him as 'Highly educated, of great natural abilities, and possessed of those intrinsic qualities which caused his society to be courted in public; yet his domestic circle was far from being that happy home it ought to have been. Although blessed with an amiable wife and family of children any gentleman might be proud of he, like the fallen Majesty of Denmark, left the Royal Feast to prey on Garbage.' (Jeffery n.d.)

Chief of his perceived faults was his sexual incontinence (for what follows Jeffery n.d.). He had several children by long-term mistresses (one of whom was found installed with her brood in the servants' wing at Tong by Mrs. Durant; her husband moved his paramour, but only into the laundry), although it must be said that he does appear to have made provision for them, one being made vicar of Tong many years later against the wishes of the bishop. More widely he is alleged to have fathered children in every cottage on the estate, taking on the role of godfather to these offspring and bestowing upon them names such as Napoleon Wedge, Columbine Cherrington, Louis Quatorze James, and (because she lived at the forge) Cinderalla Greatback. Needless to say such concern for his illegitimate children played poorly with his wife (who left and divorced him) and his fourteen illegitimate children (or at least those that survived, several dying young including poor Mark who in 1815, aged seven, was thrown fully clothed into Castle Pool by his father to learn to swim but drowned). In 1829, the year after his first wife's death, Durant married again, to his children's governess, Celeste Lefevre. They had a further six children, four of whom died in infancy.

Whether the cause of any death was fright we are not told, but it would not be surprising as Durant chastised his children by locking them in a wooden hut in the castle grounds with a black interior painted with luminous demons (Jeffery n.d.). The commissioning of eccentric buildings (and for once follies is a reasonable catch-all description) was a recurrent theme through the younger George's time at Tong, and while not all survive today illustrations and descriptions catch the flavour of those which have been lost. In fact what does still survive is far from clear, and a thorough study of the estate will be needed before all his architectural whimsies are brought to light. Griffiths, a nineteenth-century historian of Tong, wrote 'His eccentric character is indicated by the quaint buildings, monuments with hieroglyphics and inscriptions alike to deceased friends, eternity, and favourite animals which were then to be found on every path in the demesne'.

The most sympathetic description of the Tong follies was written in 1946 by Christopher Hussey, whose visit in 1946 found the place in rapid decline. He began with Convent Lodge, which still stands at the main east entrance to the site, at the end of the principal drive and close to the site of the kitchen garden (Figure 11.9). This is a striking two-storey stone building, crenellated, decorated with recessed crosses,

Fig. 11.9 A view of c.1850 of the main entrance to Tong Castle's grounds, with the stepped profile of Convent Lodge rising within the shrubbery (SA).

and with a broken wall to one side to suggest its ruination (although not sufficient to prevent occupation by a female gate-keeper in the guise of a nun (Auden 1937–8, 9)). This still stands, sadly ill-used by paintballers. To its side gateposts were heavy with 'hindoo-gothic' ornamentation which in the mid twentieth century charmed Barbara Jones along with the baronial Coalbrookdale gates which hung from them (1974, 125–7). The gateway was removed to Wolverhampton in 1978, but still surviving are sections of sandstone flanking walls decorated with carved relief and inset depictions of the castle, a butterfly, a bell, a harp, and various other devices including, like the lodge, Latin and Maltese crosses. Most extraordinary was a very good copy of Shrewsbury Abbey's fourteenth-century refectory pulpit which was perched on top of the wall, wherein Mr. Durant liked to perch and converse with passersby. Authorship of lodge and pulpit (and, it must follow, the flanking walls) is generally attributed to Lancelot Brown, although Johnny Phibbs knows of nothing like it elsewhere by Brown. Nor does the gate complex appear on the 1796 map (SA 5233/1) and although the cartographer (or his copyist) was crude he *was* fond of marking buildings with big square inky blobs. Indeed, it appears that the drive from this point east to the castle had yet to be built, the map showing the main approach at that time to have been across the park from Tong village. Two pieces of evidence in fact firmly suggest a construction date twenty-odd years later. The pulpit (which survived until 1975: Robinson 1980, 56–7), like so many of the other follies on the Tong estate, carried a lengthy verse inscription (Auden 1931, 81–2), which Christopher Hussey identified as coming from the *Irish Melodies* of Thomas Moore (1777–1852), who became the national lyrist of Ireland after his *Irish Melodies* – new lyrics for traditional Irish airs arranged by Sir John Stevenson – began to be published in 1808 and who found fame with verse lampoons (at the prince regent's expense) collected in *The Twopenny Post-Bag*, published in 1813. As an aside, it may be purely coincidental, but Moore, like the Durants (above), had West Indian links through his appointment as registrar of the naval prize court in Bermuda in 1803 (Carnall 2004). The second and probably conclusive point is an '1821' datestone which is recorded to have been incorporated in the wall (Auden 1931, 82). As has already been pointed out, the shared motifs on lodge and wall (above) suggest their likely contemporaneity, and unless evidence to the contrary is forthcoming in the future this can be fairly confidently taken as the date of the whole gate complex, including the pulpit.

There was supposedly another pulpit set on a wall

at Tong Norton Farm a kilometre or so to the north which fell down or was removed *c.*1870 (SA 3848/Misc/19, p. 128). Improbable though this would seem, weight is added to this contention by a 50m-long wall there which bears the self-same recessed Maltese and Latin crosses which adorn Convent Lodge and its flanking walls. The same motifs appear on a third location, the low flanking walls at the end of the drive from the house to Tong village (the recurring motif was noted by Auden 1931, 82). All three constructions are likely to broadly contemporary, that is *c.*1820, along with a Hermitage which stood in the stream valley below Convent Lodge and which shared with it its 'broken ruin' concept. This is shown in a watercolour of 1822 (SA 6009/338). As at other sites, such as Hawkstone in north Shropshire (Stamper 1996, 52), a hermit – Charles Evans, or to give him his stage name Carolus – was employed to recite verse and corncockle philosophy for the dubious pleasure of visitors. His death was announced in the *Gentleman's Magazine* in October 1822, which recorded that the 'Hermit of Tong' had lived for seven years 'in a lonely and romantic cell on the domains of G. Durant Esq.' – which, had he been the first holder of the post, would place the construction of the Hermitage around 1815, which fits neatly with the broad chronology developed above for this group of structures. Three years later the vacant Hermit's position was taken up by an army pensioner from Birmingham named James Guidney, or 'Jimmy the Rockman', but he quit after a month. In 1855 the building was let to a wheelwright, but later fell into ruins (Auden 1937–8, 9). Soon after the construction of Convent Lodge other diversions were provided for visitors (for the fullest general account see Boden 1931, 80–4): an arch of whale jaw bones over the Grand Drive from lodge to castle (Figure 11.10) and nearby, on the gate leading to the Dingle from the park, iron Aeolian harps (one of which survived in a dilapidated condition as late as 1844) which moaned in the wind (Griffiths 1844, 160). On the south lawn amusement was provided by a metal weeping willow which (as at Chatsworth, where one was installed at much the same time by Joseph Paxton: Elliot 1986, 79–80) drenched those innocent enough to sit beneath it.

Moving into the wider estate, one of the few securely dated structures was raised by George Durant about 1821, to celebrate the reduction in alimony payable to his first wife from £600 to £200 a year – achieved, allegedly, by using a corrupt solicitor. This was on Knoll Hill and took the form of a square, two-storey building, surmounted by octagonal piers some 80 feet high. A stone over the door proclaimed 'Optimo Adico TW'. This was blown sky-high by his children

Fig. 11.10 The collapsed arch of whale jaw bones, 1958 (Lady Higgs).

and tenants on the night of his death in 1844 – a measure of the affection in which he was not held – and is one structure of which no record apparently exists (Griffiths 1844, 161; Boden 1931, 84; Jeffery n.d.). It does not appear, for instance, in an album of distinctly amateur watercolours and annotated pen sketches of Tong's buildings (in private hands) which is the most comprehensive record of Durant's folly-mania. Presumably the work of one of the family, this records East and West lodges, both with towers; an 'Arabesque Pyramid' some 55 feet high; a monumental brick pigeon house; and a selection of the follified pigsties, privies, hen-houses, blacksmith's, and carpenter's shops (the last, in Tong Norton, with a representation of a coffin on the side) which the estate's tenants were forced to endure. Few structures escaped inscribed mottoes, poetry or sayings: a cottager who lived on Belle Isle in Norton Mere was provided with the latest in mod-cons, a pyramidal privy: over the door was PARVA SED APTA – small but necessary (Robinson 1980, 51–2). 'Mottomania' is the very apt description coined by Gwyn Headley and Wim Meulenkamp (1990, 192–5). For the last of his eccentric buildings Durant turned to polychrome brickwork, for Rosary Lodge (demolished; photo Hussey 1946, 581) and for what is undoubtedly the most spectacular of Tong's surviving buildings, the

Egyptian Aviary, a pyramidal hen house of 1842 at Vauxhall Farm (Jones 1974, 127–8) – the name another of Durant's rather weak puns, being a reference to London's notorious Vauxhall Pleasure Grounds.

Meanwhile the chantry in Tong church – the Golden Chapel – was turned into the family pew: the walls were panelled, a fireplace constructed, and settees introduced. On Sundays George Durant had his lunch there, delivered on a tray half-way through the service (Jeffery n.d.).

The Durants were a large, and largely undistinguished, family. Several died young (one of eating cherries) and few rose above the lower ranks of the church, army, or East India Company. The only event of note recorded at Tong in the nineteenth century was the great Aquatic Tournament, which took place on Lodge Lake in September 1839, the year after Queen Victoria's accession to the throne (Boden 1931, 77). This was attended by some 3,000 spectators, and took the form of a jousting match on boats between five-man teams – each comprising a bugleman and four others – in medieval costumes led by Cecilia, Lotus, and the Water Witch. On a signal from the Queen of Love and Beauty (the four-year-old Cecilia Durant) the teams first made a ceremonial circuit of the lake, and then began to joust. 'When the boats meet, the Bugle sounds the charge, and the Champion standing on the stern, with his lance advanced, will endeavour his antagonist.' The day ended with a coracle race round the lake between six contestants.

Odd though this event sounds – and probably was – we can provide a context for it. A modest revival of interest in gothic architecture began in the 1740s with Sanderson Miller and Horace Walpole, and soon spread to a general fancy for furniture and decoration in the medieval style, including suits of armour, and a readership for gothick tales. Soon after, in the early nineteenth century, came the string of influential works from the 'Great Enchanter' Sir Walter Scott – Ivanhoe came out in 1819 – which inspired hundreds of paintings on a medieval theme from leading artists of the day. Then, around 1840, came something of a vogue for families to trace their lineage in the hope of reviving long-lost titles and baronies, and a mania for heraldry among some members of the aristocracy (and would-be aristocracy). Thus we should not be surprised to find 'medieval games' being held, and probably the direct inspiration for Tong's Acquatic Tournament was the most celebrated piece of costumed tomfoolery, the Eglinton Tournament of late August 1839 (Anstruther 1963).

George Durant II died in 1844, and by the mid nineteenth century the castle was in poor repair and was sold. It was last occupied just before the First World War (during which an offer for it to be used for German POWs was declined because of the lack of bathrooms), stripped of fixtures soon after, and its shell finally blown up in 1954 (Hussey 1946, 581–2; Robinson 1980, 58; SA, photos in Tong file). Then, in 1983, the M54 motorway was built over its site.

Acknowledgements

I make no claims to great substance for this piece, which verges on antiquariansm. But it shows how a place can rise and fall, and rise again; how landscapes can be rapidly changed as well as evolving gradually; and how human choices and actions can play a dramatic part in shaping a place. It is very much a report on a work in progress, where most time so far has been spent in record office and library. The field archaeology of the place – the search for hump, bumps, and buildings and the whole wonderful grab-bag of 'techniques' that Mick's subject embraces – is still largely to come. For how that work ought to be done, with inquisitiveness tempered by humanity, with bustle balanced by gentle rumination, and with a liberal supply of red wine to assist musings with friends, Mick's work provides a model I wholeheartedly approve of.

I am grateful to Lady Higgs for sight of family papers and for permission to reproduce Figure 11.10. Also to Johnny Phibbs for supplying me with references from Brown's account book, for sight of his work in progress and for his thoughts on Brown's work at Tong, and to the Very Revd. R. M. C. Jeffery for permission to use his unpublished lecture on the Durants and for sight of chapters from his forthcoming book on the family which will tell its full extraordinary story. Tom Williamson, Gareth Williams and George Baugh also kindly looked at sections of the text and made useful suggestions. Typically, when too late to do anything about it, a chance conversation with my colleague Pete Smith drew to my attention the fact that Tong's 'missing' seventeenth and eighteenth century documents may be at Nottingham University Library (see Smith 1999, 97, for reference to a 1725 inventory which includes Tong Castle).

Abbreviations

P. R. O. Public Record Office, now National Archives, Kew
SA Shropshire Archives, Castle Foregate, Shrewsbury

References

Andrews, C. B. (ed.) (1934–8) *The Torrington Diaries. Tours made between the years 1781 and 1794.* 4 vols. London, Eyre and Spottiswoode.

Anstruther, I. (1963) *The Knight and the Umbrella.* London, Geoffrey Bles.

Auden, J. E. 1937–8 Some Erroneous Traditions. *Transactions of the Shropshire Archaeological Society 49*, 1–18.

Boden, G. H. (1931) *The History of Tong Church, College and Castle* (3rd edn).

Carnall, G. (2004) Thomas Moore (1779–1852). *Oxford Dictionary of National Biography.* Oxford, Oxford University Press.

Chandler, J. (1993) *John Leland's Itinerary: Travels in Tudor England.* Stroud, Alan Sutton.

Cooper, N. (1999) *Houses of the Gentry 1480–1680.* New Haven and London, Yale University Press.

Coulson, C. (1994) Freedom to Crenellate by Licence – An Historiographical Revision. *Nottingham Medieval Studies 38*, 86–137.

Coulson, C. (2003) *Castles in Medieval Society.* Oxford, Oxford University Press.

English Heritage (2005) *Register of Historic Parks and Gardens* (available via English Heritage website).

Elliot, B. (1986) *Victorian Gardens.* London, Batsford.

Gaydon, A. T. (ed.) (1973) *The Victoria History of the County of Shropshire*, 2. London, Oxford University Press.

Griffiths, G. (1844) *A History of Tong* (2nd edition).

Griffiths, G. (1894) *History of Tong and Boscobel.*

Headley, G. and Meulenkamp, W. (1990) *Follies* (revised edition).

Hussey, C. (1946) Tong Shropshire, II. *Country Life* 27 Sept. 1946, 578–81.

Jeffery, R. M. J. (in preparation) *Discovering Tong: its History, Myths and Curiosities.*

Jeffery, R. M. C. (n.d.) The Durants of Tong Castle. Unpublished lecture; copy in SA 4717.

Jones, B. (1974) *Follies and Grottoes.* London, Constable.

Ionodes, J. (1999) *Thomas Farnolls Pritchard of Shrewsbury Architect and 'Inventor of Cast Iron Bridges'*. Ludlow, Dog Rose Press.

Kemp, B. (1980) *English Church Monuments*. London, Batsford.

Levy, M. J. (2004) Fitzherbert, Maria Anne. *Oxford Dictionary of National Biography*. Oxford, OxfordUniversity Press.

Liddiard, R. (2005) *Castles in Context: Power, Symbolism and Landscape, 1066–1500*. Bollington, Windgather Press.

Mercer, E. (2003) *English Architecture to 1900: The Shropshire Experience*. Little Logaston, Logaston Press.

Nigota, J. A. (2004) Vernon family. *Oxford Dictionary of National Biography*. Oxford, Oxford University Press.

Pevsner, N. (1958) *The Buildings of England: Shropshire*. Harmondsworth, Penguin.

Phibbs, J. (2003) The Englishness of Lancelot 'Capability' Brown. *Garden History* 31.2, 122–40.

Phibbs, J. (2004) Lancelot Brown. *Oxford Dictionary of National Biography*. Oxford, Oxford University Press.

Robinson, D. H. (1980) *The Wandering Worfe*. Waine Research Publications.

Smith, P. (1999) West Dean House, Wiltshire. *Georgian Group Journal* 9, 86–106.

Stamper, P. (1996) *Historic Parks and Gardens of Shropshire*. Shrewsbury, Shropshire Books.

Symonds, R. (1879) Diary of the Marches of the Royal Army During the Great Civil War. *Transactions of the Shropshire Archaeological Society* 2, 273–82.

Thurley, S. (1993) *The Royal Palaces of Tudor England*. New Haven and London, Yale University Press.

Vaughan, H. F. J. (1879) Some Account of the Ruckley Grange Estate. *Transactions of the Shropshire Archaeological Society* 2, 213–72.

Wrottesley, G. (1885) The Stone Chartulary. *Collections for a History of Staffordshire* VI part i. Stafford, William Salt Archaeological Society.

Chapter 12

Clear Fountains and Turbid:
Archaeology's 'Crisis' of Communication?

Nick Corcos

The Bristol conference held early in December 2004 was intended to celebrate the contribution to our profession of someone who has dedicated almost his entire working life to communicating his infectious passion for the subject to people not directly involved in it. This is, indeed, probably Mick's greatest contribution, and it is impossible to overstate its importance; because it is a stark fact, lost on far too many members of the profession today, and especially those from the academic side, that without public support, we are nothing. My theme is therefore intended to link in with that aspect of Mick's work, and to develop an argument that focuses mainly, although not exclusively, on one particular element of our communication strategy with the wider, non-specialist public; that is, in the way that we *write*. I make no apologies for the fact that this is a highly personal, and therefore by definition, subjective, survey, by someone who is himself an outsider. I came into dirt archaeology as a landscape historian, and have had to come to terms with the use of archaeological evidence in the course of my own research work, a sometimes painful experience which at least in part underpins this paper. There are few specifics here; little that could actually be characterised as empirical. It is all pretty anecdotal and circumstantial. But the evidence *is* there: open any number of peer-reviewed journals or academic books, and it stares you in the face.

My main thesis is straightforward enough: it is simply that far too much of our modern archaeological literature, at all levels but especially in the more academic realms of books, journals and site reports, is tedious, sterile, badly written, unengaging, abstruse, and at times just downright unreadable. I would argue very strongly that as a profession, our relationship with those outside the subject is *defined* by the way we communicate with them. And I am convinced that we are failing, spectacularly, to convey effectively our enthusiasm, our passion, for our discipline, to that

wider audience upon whose support we so crucially rely. The case for effective communication is well expressed by Paul Bahn: "archaeology's ultimate goal – if it is to have any meaning or justification – must be to convey its findings not only to students and colleagues, but above all to the public which generally footed the bill for the work and paid the salaries.......if public funding were to dry up, so would most archaeology" (Bahn 1996, at 88 and 93). But certainly as far as archaeological publications are concerned, if they were forced to conform to the standards encapsulated in the logo shown as Figure 12.1, far too many would simply fail.

There is of course little new or original in what I am saying here, and calls for clarity in what we write surface intermittently from within the profession. I am certainly not alone in holding the view that a major cultural shift is needed, and my simple justification for this paper, if any were needed, is that these things just cannot be repeated often enough.[1] The fundamental nature of these concerns is cogently articulated by Simon Denison (1997a, 11):

Fig. 12.1 Crystal Mark logo reproduced by kind permission of the Campaign for Plain English.

All too often, even in books intended for the 'general reader', there is an excruciatingly detailed examination of the minutiae of sites and objects...presented in an overblown, pseudo-technical language, and with too little interpretation of what life may have been like for the people who used these sites and objects in the past. Publishers who tolerate such bad writing deserve their share of the blame.

Earlier on Denison had himself quoted a clearly exasperated Francis Pryor:

Why are we so scared of our peers' opinion? Why can't archaeologists write in vivid English?

Likewise, in a recent review of a volume of conference proceedings on medieval landscapes, Andrew Fleming remarks that:

many of the essays are highly readable, an outcome perhaps not entirely unconnected with the absence of archaeologists. (Fleming 2003, 100)

Although one suspects that Fleming's tongue may be at least partly in his cheek here, nonetheless the observation is a highly revealing one.

So here we have two major figures in British archaeology, both of them scholars and academics of the highest professional standing, one implicitly and one explicitly expressing their concern in this respect. But there are others who have said the same thing. Neil Faulkner, reviewing the journal *Antiquity*, recently revamped under its new editor Martin Carver, remarks how:

Academic journals can be dry as dust -with articles full of impenetrable jargon and obscure detail of no interest to anyone outside a tiny handful of fellow specialists. Is it really true that archaeology has become so abstruse and complicated that, like computer science, it is incomprehensible to the uninitiated? Should we simply enjoy the results the academics feed us, without enquiring as to how they are achieved? Is archaeology irrevocably divided between professionals on the one hand and *Time Team* viewers on the other? Of course, it is not so. It all depends on how things are written. Anyone can appear clever by writing in a way that is obscure and exclusive. But the job of any good archaeologist is partly to communicate what they are doing to a wide audience. (Faulkner 2004, 548)

Critics will of course say that the colour of Dr Faulkner's archaeological politics is well known, and that he would say that wouldn't he? True enough, perhaps. But in my opinion, we dismiss this perspective at our peril.

Francis Pryor himself has put his money firmly where his mouth is by producing *Britain BC* (Pryor 2003). By his own admission a highly personal view, Pryor has nonetheless succeeded in brilliantly high-

lighting what is arguably the greatest of the lies promulgated by some high-powered academics. There is a certain mindset, an insidious culture, that requires the erection of an intellectual Berlin Wall, which we transgress at our peril, even, I suspect, to the cost of our academic careers. One can be *either* academic and scholarly, *or* engaging and accessible; but *not* both at the same time, and even to make the attempt is to incur from some quarters a level of venom that one might not have thought possible in a milieu of supposed intellectual liberalism. On the broadcast media side, Mick himself knows all about this only too well: it is quite clearly attested in the deeply negative tone of some of the initial published reaction to *Time Team* from alleged colleagues within the profession. This culture of mutual exclusivity pervades our archaeological literature; however, the whole idea is of course not only completely absurd, but actually dangerous and corrosive. There are numerous examples of senior, respected, academic scholars writing at the highest level of rigorous analysis but who are yet capable of producing narratives that at once engage the reader, and convey with elegant, economic simplicity and precision, their often highly complex themes. To pluck just one name from mid-air: give an intelligent non-specialist virtually any book by Richard Bradley, and in terms of understanding themes both broad and detailed, they'd probably have absolutely no problem with the overwhelming majority of it. And the crucial point here is that generally, Bradley is *not* consciously aiming at this wider audience, but at his peers, a point to which I will return later. If someone like Bradley can achieve this, why can't others?

In far too many minds within our discipline, accessibility is a dirty word. To write accessibly is to be immediately branded as in some abstract way 'second-rate', not to be taken too seriously, to be at best tolerated, at worst, made the subject of often vitriolic condemnation. The equation 'accessible = simplistic' seems to have slipped into our collective subconscious, but it is false. A recent short book review in *British Archaeology* praised an author for producing "a still convincing and entertaining search for complexity in the history and meaning of archaeology, as antidote to accessibility's drive for simplicity" (Pitts 2005, 37). The word seems clearly to be used here in a pejorative sense, but surely accessibility means, above all, *clarity*: it is simply disingenuous to suggest that highly complex concepts cannot, almost by definition, be presented in an accessible way. And what higher goal can an academic scholar set him or herself, than to open the minds of those to whom our discipline is almost literally a closed book?

A major part of the problem lies in the perception that academic credibility requires, indeed absolutely demands, the use of a certain kind of *language*. This again is a cultural issue. Like those unfortunate children years ago who, being naturally left-handed, at school were actually beaten into using their right hands; so are we forced to conform in our use of language. Dissent, academically, is fatal. So for example we use passive verbs, rather than active; and use of the first person is strictly forbidden. No-one has yet been able to tell me exactly why it is inherently any more scholarly to say "the liquid was poured into the test tube", rather than "I poured the liquid into the test tube". And yet this simple change to the use of the active verb and the first person, renders language once dull, lifeless and sterile, now immediate, personal, and engaging. I, the writer, am talking directly to you, the reader. The entrenched closed-mindedness that vehemently eschews such directness is something I have never understood, and indeed, when writing my own doctoral thesis, I tried as far as I could to put my own views into practice by littering the narrative with active verbs and first persons. I well remember the battle I had with both my joint supervisors over this, which frankly I had not expected. But the interesting point is that in fact *neither* had any inherent, intellectual objection to my consciously *personal* usage. Rather, both were concerned, on my behalf, at the impression it might convey to my examiners about my academic rigour, or lack of it. Neither is this concern confined to an older generation of scholars. I was surprised to have exactly the same disagreement with one of my PhD colleagues, many years my junior, and for exactly the same reasons: a perception that the first person is unscholarly and inappropriate in an academic narrative. The specific reason or reasons for this belief always turn on *tradition* as the final arbiter: it is, quite simply, the way we have always done it. It is of course a completely ridiculous argument. It was 'traditional' for many years to send small children up chimneys to clean them; that did not necessarily make it a good thing. As it turned out, my viva examiners gave me a hard time over other matters, but *not once* did they either explicitly or implicitly criticise my writing style.

The irony about all this is that the same people who set themselves up as arbiters of correct, appropriate academic usage, are quite happy to produce impenetrable, jargon-ridden narratives loaded with meaningless but fashionable buzz words and phrases that obscure understanding, add nothing in terms of the clear exposition of themes, and actually say very little. This kind of material is designed not to *communicate*; but to impress at the meretricious funding fiasco that is the RAE. Surely it really cannot

be true that, to misquote Shakespeare, these are tales told by idiots, full of sound and fury, signifying nothing? (Macbeth, Act 5, Scene 5). The answer to this, of course, is no, at least, not invariably. And therein, for me, lies the most tragic aspect of this whole issue. There are surely few professional archaeologists, whether academics or field practitioners, who would now dispute at least the principle that an effective body of theory is absolutely central to the continued relevance and vigorous development of the discipline. And in some cases it is absolutely clear that caught in the all-entangling net of obscure, technical prose, there are outstandingly important ideas struggling to get out – ideas which will change our view of the world, and which represent defining moments in our attempts to construct the robust and meaningful theoretical frameworks which should inform and underpin our narratives across *every* period of study, not just the prehistoric (for the Roman period see the various volumes of TRAC, the *Proceedings of the Theoretical Roman Archaeology Conference*; and for the medieval period see the recent ground-breaking survey by Chris Gerrard, 2003). These deserve to be widely disseminated, discussed, debated and assimilated. But when, for the overwhelming majority of readers, *including* professional archaeologists, they are presented in a form in which large chunks are effectively unreadable, what chance do they have, beyond a tiny peer group? This is just sad beyond measure, precisely because it is so unnecessary. Paul Bahn, who I quoted earlier, hit the nail squarely on the head: at all levels of the discipline, we ought constantly to be reminding ourselves just who it is, ultimately, that funds our work and pays our wages (Bahn 1996, 88).

One small example of the kind of thing I mean will suffice, although it is one of my favourites. We're no longer allowed simply to take evidence into consideration. We now have to "factor it in". This is pretentious, pseudo-intellectual clap-trap of the most invidious kind. I have no idea about its origins except to say that it looks suspiciously like yet another attack on our mother tongue by transatlantic corporate-speak. But it is precisely this sort of unnecessary usage (and this is by no means the worst example) that seems calculated to alienate rather than engage the 'average', intelligent but non-specialist reader. And I use the word 'calculate' quite deliberately. For there is absolutely no doubt in my mind that in stark contrast to the man whose contribution in this field is celebrated in this volume, there is a worrying minority of professional, academic archaeologists, the abstruseness of whose written prose is actually *intended* to do exactly that – to *exclude*, through language and usage, the vast majority of that enthusiastic lay audience outside the heady atmosphere of the elite gentleman's club to which academic archaeology seems far too often to aspire. The noxious whiff of intellectual snobbery should act as a wake-up call to every one of us who cares about the way we are perceived by those outside the academic branch of our profession – and that *includes* other archaeologists. The attitude of this school towards the general public is brought home forcefully in the well-known cartoon reproduced here as Figure 12.2.

There is a strand of English topographical writing, of which, let us remind ourselves, archaeology was *itself* once part, which, when we look back on it, shows us as archaeologists what we have lost. Look at anything by H. J. Massingham, Joan Thirsk, Maurice Beresford, H. P. R. Finberg and of course, W. G. Hoskins himself, and my meaning will, I hope, become clear. There are probably far too many archaeologists who will need reminding, or indeed telling, that 2005 marked the fiftieth anniversary of the publication of one of the greatest and most influential works of English history ever written: Hoskins's seminal *Making of the English Landscape* represents a defining moment in the development of our understanding of, and approach to the historic environment, with as much significance for archaeologists as for historians; a fact now at long last recognised, in some quarters of the profession at least, and Hoskins's contribution to this field is currently the subject of a major critical reassessment by one of our leading theoretical archaeologists, Matthew Johnson (2007).

Of these, only Beresford had an explicitly archaeological background, and was also a highly-regarded medieval economic historian in his own right; but Hoskins and Finberg *were* landscape scholars of the highest professional standing, and indeed, I think it is fair to say that Mick himself stands firmly in this tradition. There were at the conference two figures, Chris Taylor and Chris Dyer, an archaeologist and medieval economic historian respectively, who regularly produce narratives that are at once both intensely scholarly, but also fluid and immediately engaging. Purely archaeological writers could learn a great deal through close study of published work by members of the Leicester School of English Local History, which has a long and splendid tradition in this context. One of my own personal icons in this respect, is the former head of that Department, Alan Everitt. His book *Continuity and Colonisation* (1986) is not only a pioneering study of the evolution of a regional English landscape, at times as highly technical as any excavation report, especially when discussing place-names, but is also one of the most profoundly engaging, beautifully written books you will ever read. It is quite simply a sublime pleasure from first page to last. A non-specialist could pick it up and immediately feel completely at home. How many scholarly books by *archaeologists* could you say that about?

And what is the common thread that connects these authors and their writing? It is, quite simply, a quality of *lyricism*. By their very particular use of language and imagery, these writers, and others like them, are able to convey to their readers a highly personal,

Fig. 12.2 The public as 'irritating distraction'. Reproduced from Bahn 1996, 73.

almost celebratory perspective on their subject, in which analytical, scholarly rigour is tempered by a degree of simple humanity, emotional involvement, and empathy with both reader and subject, that is all too rare in archaeological writing today. One thinks particularly, for example, of Jacquetta Hawkes´s affectionate celebration of the British landscape, *A Land* (1951). The best of this writing, indeed, makes a claim to be considered literature in its own right. F. W. Maitland´s classic work *Domesday Book and Beyond* (1897) is a case in point. I am of course not suggesting for one moment that modern archaeological narratives should strive for this goal. That would clearly be absurd. But there is no doubt that the readability and engagement of so much of it would be vastly improved if writers were to expend just a little more effort on speaking directly to the reader on a personal level, and with a little more emotional involvement and commitment.

There are probably many and complex reasons why as a profession we write as we do (i.e. generally, badly), but we can perhaps define two major ones. Firstly, and ironically, a major part of the problem lies in the very eclectic nature of the discipline itself, something which usually, and quite rightly, is seen as one of its fundamental strengths. In drawing on ideas from a whole range of other disciplines, archaeology has gained crucial insights into the way that past societies develop, thrive, and collapse. Cross fertilisation from sociology and anthropology has been especially important in this respect; but in importing some of these ideas wholesale, regrettably, the often highly technical language of these disciplines has come as part of the baggage, undigested, misunderstood and misused, like a great Trojan horse carrying within it the forces that will eventually be our undoing. In archaeology, this second-hand language has become academically 'fashionable', and this is indeed a dangerous development. I am not the first person to say this, and I hope I am not the last. But I think we need to look very closely at how much of this stuff we actually need for our own purposes, and discard that element of it superfluous to requirements: which will I suspect be a lot. Language is not immutable: it can and should be bent to our will.

Secondly, but closely related to the first, is that there is a generation of scholars still active who in the 1960s were trained in the then-fashionable processual school of archaeology, one of the main tenets of which was total emotional detachment in an attempt to interpret the evidence, derived from empirical observation using specific methodologies, from as objective and 'scientific' a perspective as possible. This is directly related to the way that scholars of that generation

write, and indeed, so tenacious have the processual tenets been that they continue to influence the writing styles of younger scholars trained in later traditions. That the goal of absolute objectivity was rapidly recognised as both impossible and not necessarily desirable is implicit in the rise of post-processual archaeology. This is an approach which seeks explanations of human behaviour in ways which, far from attempting artificially to distance the observer emotionally from past societies, seeks instead to involve him or her far more directly in their emotive "and often idiosyncratic responses to particular conditions", as attested through material culture (Bahn 2001, 365).

Of course, it is absolutely true that all intellectual and technical disciplines have their own language, which we would call jargon; specialist words and phrases that pass for a kind of shorthand between trained practitioners. This is both totally understandable, and probably unavoidable. How far we can consider it *desirable* is altogether another question. Nowhere is this kind of language more to the fore than in excavation reports, and there are doubtless many professionals who would say that this is probably the one context where technical language really *has* to be used, or clarity and understanding may suffer. This is an argument I would reject. The practical result is that many excavation narratives, although by no means all, are among the most turgid, dry, tedious and just plain boring texts that one could possibly read. But as with academic work, there are examples to show that it really doesn't have to be like this; such as almost anything with Philip Rahtz's hand in it, whether as editor or author. Others have advanced the argument that non-specialists have no place looking at excavation reports anyway – the implicit reasoning clearly being that they should not be meddling in matters of which they have no understanding. The proper place for these enthusiasts, we are told, are the 'popular', non-academic syntheses – the kind of thing that Tempus, for example, does so well. Overviews and general surveys such as these are indeed incredibly useful sources for readers at *all* levels, from non-specialists with merely a casual passing interest, to professional academics.

But this raises yet another question which to my mind has never received a satisfactory answer. If, after reading one of these more 'accessible' works, a non-specialist is actually inspired to seek out the primary data on which it is based, in the form of more technical reports, does he or she not have the absolute right to expect that that information should at the least be readable and broadly comprehensible? We ought to be encouraging non-specialists to get stuck in to the nuts and bolts of our discipline – vicariously to dirty their hands and muddy their boots through our excavation reports – we should be opening up to them our bizarre and fascinating but all too introspective world of cuts, fills, stratigraphy, and all the rest. The writers of popular synthetic works perform an admirable and crucial task. But we also need to convey the message to our supporters among the general public that such works, by and large, represent merely opinions based on overviews of *some* of the primary data. They are not, and never can be, accurate portrayals of what actually happened in the past, and obviously no professional scholar would ever, one hopes, claim that that was the case. Again, there's nothing new in this, others have said it. But what I think we should also be doing is the greatest service that any discipline can do for its non-specialist enthusiasts: giving them the raw evidence directly and engagingly, and letting them make up their own minds.

There is now more than enough evidence, from Community Archaeology Projects and other schemes, that, certainly as far as the *practical* side of the work is concerned, with the correct guidance, non-specialists can become first-rate fieldworkers; better, in fact, in terms of sheer commitment, competence and enthusiasm, than many so-called professionals (see, for example, Pearce and Cale 2005). Surely we should be doing all we can to draw this constituency in to the more abstract elements of the archaeological discipline, and showing them that their fieldwork may have implications in a far wider context.

Greater understanding at the technical and theoretical level of the subject must inevitably have positive, direct implications for our relationship with the wider public. I have seen few excavation reports which could not be improved out of all recognition for *everyone* just in terms of straightforward readability by a little more care over language and expression, and probably more robust editing. After all, as Mike Pitts has crucially reminded us recently, "you can write intelligently about archaeology for people who are not archaeologists, and if you do it well, it becomes important for archaeologists too" (Pitts 2004, 43).

There are perhaps hints that at last, things in this respect may be beginning to change. David Price, Chairman of the Editorial and Publication Board for the Mary Rose Trust, recently went out of his way to make the point that as far as the project's full archaeological reports were concerned, "it is the firm objective of the ………..Trust to provide a text that will satisfy the demands of specialist researchers – but also to be accessible to the general reader. We believe that this policy objective has generally been

successful". It is surely both highly significant, and encouraging, that general accessibility should at the least, and from the outset, be a key stated aim of those in charge of producing "one of the largest studies of a British archaeological excavation to come out in recent times" (Price 2004, 573, speaking about the publication of Marsden 2003). Another example of the way the tide may be turning in this respect is Andrews (ed.) 2003, published by Wessex Archaeology. It is, to all intents and purposes, a full, technical excavation report. But it costs only five pounds, and is written specifically to be accessible to a non-specialist readership. Its use of clear, full colour diagrams, plans and sections is an object lesson in clarity. Its approach to the whole question of how to deal with specialist reports that would normally take up valuable space and which, let's face it, may only be of direct interest to other specialists, may point the way for the future, because they can be found on the excavation's web site. This has meant that the authors have been able to use the space released to produce something far more akin to a *story* – a coherent, structured historical narrative. A solution which archaeological publishers will increasingly adopt is to put the specialist reports on a CD-ROM. An example is Foreman *et al.* (eds), 2002, one of a series from another of our big contracting units, Oxford Archaeology. It has a splendid range of illustrations, including many maps and photographs again in full colour, in a hard cover, for only £10. This is a really remarkable bargain and an indication of the disproportionate amount of space taken up by specialist reports.

The essential point, though, is this: if the Mary Rose reports, and other publications like them, *are* successful in this respect, and that success translates directly into numbers of copies sold, then maybe other authors, editors and publishers of excavation reports had better sit up and take notice.

All this begs a fundamental question: why do we write? For many academic archaeologists the answer to that is straightforward: we write to be read by, and to impress with our learning and scholarship, our *peers*, our fellow club members, and the devil take the hindmost. As I have already intimated, some professional academics use words like 'engaging' or 'accessible' as negatives, in a highly pejorative sense; indeed it is a fact that at least one has explicitly accused those who espouse these goals of being 'anti-intellectual'. This is totally absurd, and in fact quite the opposite is true. Far from 'dumbing down', the presentation of often complex themes to an intelligent lay audience in a style that is at once rigorous, clear and engaging, without at the same time being patronising, is one of the most intellectually demanding tasks that any specialist scholar can undertake. It forces the researcher to crystallise his or her ideas in their own mind; to strip them down to the fundamentals and ask themselves an often very difficult question: what *exactly* am I trying to say here? And when seen in these terms, the sad fact is that there are simply far too many professional archaeologists who are either simply not up to the job, or even worse, consciously choose to write in a certain style.

Paul Bahn has something to say about this very subject in his incomparable little book, *Bluff Your Way in Archaeology*. Bahn provides a number of useful ruses in the field of archaeological publication. Under the heading Obfuscating, he says this:

> Another way to sidestep criticism is to make your prose so obscure and tortuous that nobody, including yourself, is quite sure at the end of it what you have been saying. This smokescreen effect, particularly common in theoretical work, is very useful when it turns out that you were wrong, or new finds alter the situation: you can simply claim that you were misunderstood and that you said nothing of the kind. (Bahn 1989, 37)

As an example of the kind of thing he means, Bahn quotes this sentence from a piece of published work:

> The notion of structural contradictions resulting in societal change relates to the operation of causative variables at a different epistemological level from that assumed in analysis of interlinked variables and entities resulting in morphogenic feedback processes. (Bahn 1989, 15).

I have tried to make sense of this statement on numerous occasions. I am of average intelligence, with a reasonable vocabulary, and consider myself reasonably well informed. But I have simply failed to understand what the writer is trying to say here. Did he *himself* know (and it *is* a 'he'!)? As I read and re-read this, my overwhelming feeling is that I am being patronized and talked down to by someone who has absolutely no interest in trying to help me understand his ideas; but is extremely interested in letting me know how clever *he* is, and how stupid and far outside the close-knit circle of cognoscenti *I* am. I actually corresponded with Bahn about this quote as I was curious about its source. He told me I was the first person in 16 years to ask for that information! It transpired that the author of this particular piece of obfuscation is one of our leading theorists, and it is surely a matter for concern that some of the profession's most eminent academics think it acceptable, indeed necessary, to write in this way. Bahn's point, of course, was satirical. But it strikes firmly home precisely because it has a disturbing ring of truth about it that reminds us of a fundamental, guiding principle:

that if something cannot be expressed concisely and with clarity, then it is probably just not worth saying. It speaks volumes that when confronted outright with these concerns the tendency of some theoretical specialists is to resort to what might strike us as frankly rather desperate special pleading; evidence, perhaps, that consciences have been pricked and raw nerves struck (see, for example, the highly revealing interview with Michael Shanks conducted by Simon Denison for *British Archaeology*: Denison 1997, 14).

Lewis Binford, that colossus of archaeological theory, was once famously quoted as saying that he would be worried if someone claimed actually to have understood, at first reading, a sentence he had written, because it would suggest to him that the person had not read it properly, or had missed his point. In such cases he would then

> take that sentence and make a whole paragraph out of it to make sure that [the reader] understands what is different about what I am saying. I write so that people have got to read and reread it so that maybe they have got the meaning.

He further added that

> the clearer the writing is, the more ambiguous the terms are…..In other words the clearest sentence would be the sentence that everybody would give meaning to immediately…..if I'm trying to manipulate a reader I can't do it by making him think he knows what I'm saying. Because if I think I'm saying something that he doesn't know; or I think I'm saying something new, then why should he think it's all so clear and he's thought it all along? (quoted in Sabloff, 1998. I am very grateful to Jim Dixon for this reference).

This is little short of disingenuous, and its logic convoluted and tail-chasing. It represents nothing less than a licence for deliberate, cynical and systematic obfuscation – Binford's somewhat paradoxical argument is that he writes in a certain way to *force* the reader into understanding through repeated rereading. However, it seems to me that there is a disturbing subtext here, and the inference which I draw from these remarks is that he is not, in fact, actually concerned with the reader's understanding of his writing; he does not regard clear communication as his job. As long as Binford and his ilk can justify their ideas as somehow 'different', then he, and they, are content. But there must be an absolute here – a point where, no matter how many times one rereads a piece of prose, it simply does not click; and surely if a narrative is *disconcertingly* difficult to understand, to the extent of being effectively unintelligible, how is the reader then to make an informed judgment about whether or not it *is* actually different from anything he has come across before, as Binford himself is apparently so anxious that he should? We return to my fundamental point: complex concepts that are both meaningful and radical most emphatically *can* be conveyed through the written word, with clarity, elegance and economy, *if* it is the writer's conscious purpose to do so.

Elsewhere, Bahn has remarked that "theoretical archaeology should not be taken too seriously – it's easy to laugh at those who do become obsessed with it: in fact, it's essential" (Bahn 1996, 74). There can be little doubt that, although perhaps expressed in rather extreme terms, there are many in the profession who have at least some sympathy with that sentiment; and who would privately agree that if this is indeed the way in which the theoreticians are sometimes perceived, they have no-one to blame for it but themselves. For example, take Oxley and Morton's well-known Archaeological Buzz-Word Generator (www.york.ac.uk/depts/arch/yccweb/aids/buzz.htm). Three columns in a table of 20 numbered rows contain random selections of fashionable, and generally abstruse words, and by choosing a word from each column, it is possible to construct scholarly-sounding but in fact completely meaningless phrases with which one can litter one's own work. A boon for first year undergraduates wanting to make an impression but baffled by modern archaeological theory ("for additional fun and excitement, why not get a friend or Cambridge colleague to pick the numbers for you!"). Although of course intended only as a bit of fun, the crucial point is that the Generator works on a humorous level exactly because it so effectively satirizes theoretical pretentiousness, and everyone, probably even the theorists themselves, knows it.

I am in complete agreement with Simon Denison, who I quoted earlier, in suggesting that editors and publishers who happily pass material like this into print, actually bear as much, if not more blame than the people who write it. It should simply not be published, but rather, should be subject to almost automatic, and robust refusal, and accepted back *only* if the author is prepared to rewrite into plain English. If this happened on a regular basis, the message would get through soon enough, but at present, the self-proclaimed guardians and arbiters of what constitutes archaeological scholarship continue to promulgate abstruseness over clarity, apparently blinded by false learning masquerading as academic rigour. They have a lot to answer for. The phrase 'emperor's new clothes' may be somewhat hackneyed, but is also frankly difficult to avoid in the context of this kind of writing.

But is this whole issue of clear communication with the general public *really* so important? Am I, and others, just making mountains out of molehills, creating 'crises' where in fact, there are none? This question turns to a large extent on one's view about the social 'usefulness' of archaeology itself. There is a widespread school of thought that sees the discipline as non-essential. We don't actually *need* it, as a society, to survive. Indeed, this is a common enough view held by those both inside and outside the profession. An example of the former, yet again, is Paul Bahn, who remarks that "archaeology is undeniably a 'luxury' subject which constantly needs to justify its existence" (Bahn 1996, 6). A contrary view, however, highlights the crucial political and social implications of the archaeological record, and holds that this knowledge alone, and the lessons it holds for society as a whole, more than justifies the continued existence and development of the discipline:

> we do need accounts of the past; how many stable and viable societies survive without them? Politically.....we need archaeology (particularly a self-critical archaeology) to stand against, for example, fascistic and racist myths about the past – to not have the archaeology we have at present would mean having something else in its place and.....the alternatives are truly frightening… (*pers. comm.* Chris Cumberbatch).

Whether or not we perceive archaeology as socially expendable, we could ask the same question of art, or literature or music, or any number of other liberal disciplines. The fact that all these things profoundly and deeply enrich us culturally and intellectually is irrelevant in this context. The central point here is that *whatever* position one takes on this question, both ultimately conjoin at a tacit consensus: that archaeology as a discipline should be vigorously defended. The only difference between the two schools of thought is that one considers some kind of 'external' justification for archaeology is necessary, the other that it is manifestly *self*-justifying.

However much it may be denied in certain quarters, the inescapable fact is that our survival depends on the continuing goodwill, interest and often vociferous support of an army of non-specialist enthusiasts. The material culture which we dig up, and the human stories we weave around it, which at best probably enjoy only a nodding acquaintance with the truth, belong as much to them as it does to us. It is their right to know, and to learn about their collective pasts. So the message is: we communicate or die. Properly mobilised and informed, we know how powerful public opinion can be when important archaeology is under threat. One has only to look at the campaigns over the Rose Theatre in London, or the Newport medieval ship. In both cases it was not the purely *archaeological* argument that won the day, but the overwhelming public outcries that followed in the wake of these discoveries. And there are numerous other examples, briefly but tellingly reviewed by George Lambrick (2002, 28).

A recent straw poll of leading specialists and professionals asked what, in their opinion, was the most important archaeological development in this country in the twentieth century (Denison 1999, 180). Hedley Swain, a Departmental Head at the Museum of London, was in no doubt: it was *Time Team*. Why?

> Because TT is the thing that's done best what archaeology is supposed to do – engage with ordinary people.

The visual broadcast medium is well taken care of. It is really about time we learned the same lessons as far as the *written* word is concerned.

In 1946, George Orwell published an essay entitled "Politics and the English Language". His thesis was that the politicians of the day were directly responsible for a marked decline in clarity of expression, particularly in the written word, that was beginning to pervade society as a whole. Among other problems, he draws our attention to

> lack of precision. The writer either has a meaning and cannot express it, or he inadvertently says something else, or else he is almost indifferent as to whether his words mean anything or not…[pretentious] words…are used to dress up simple statements and give an air of scientific impartiality to biased judgements…it is often easier to make up words of this kind…than to think up the English words that will cover one's meaning. The result, in general, is an increase in slovenliness and vagueness…in certain kinds of writing…it is normal to come across long passages which are almost completely lacking in meaning…modern writing at its worst…consists in gumming together long strips of words which have already been set in order by someone else, and making the results presentable by sheer humbug. The attraction of this way of writing is that it is easy. (Orwell 1946, 129–134, passim)

Sound familiar? It is surely a disturbing thought, and to the shame of our discipline, that 60 years on, Orwell's words strike home like a heat-seeking missile upon so much of modern archaeological writing. Indeed, he might well have written them with archaeologists, and not politicians, in mind. It is impossible to improve on the straightforward, commonsense solutions to these problems with which Orwell presents us, and they provide a perceptive summary of everything that I have been arguing here:

> A scrupulous writer, in every sentence that he writes, will ask himself at least four questions, thus: What am I trying to say? What words will express it? What image or idiom will make it clearer? Is this image fresh enough to have an effect? And he will probably ask himself two more: Could I put it more shortly? Have I said anything that is avoidably ugly? (Orwell 1946, 135)

Despite his concerns, however, Orwell was also optimistic that the damage could be halted, and that, with commitment and application on the part of the individual, the process of linguistic degradation was reversible:

> Modern English, especially written English, is full of bad habits which spread by imitation and which can be avoided if one is willing to take the necessary trouble. If one gets rid of these habits one can think more clearly, and to think clearly is a necessary first step towards political regeneration: so that the fight against bad English is not frivolous and not the exclusive concern of professional writers. (Orwell 1946, 128)

Orwell's essay is a goldmine of insightful perspectives on the state of the written language in his own day; it holds crucial lessons for many in our own profession, especially its more academic practitioners, whose tortuous and abstruse usage may be choking at birth ideas of seminal importance. Forget Renfrew and Bahn (2004). If I had my way, every first-year archaeology undergraduate would be given a copy of Orwell's paper, and be told to read it, burn its message on their hearts, and strongly encouraged *throughout* their university career to put its lessons into practical, day to day use in their essay and dissertation writing. It does not matter how brilliant the student; if they cannot express themselves, if they cannot convey their brilliant ideas to others in clear, elegantly simple, economic prose, then no matter how intense the scholarship, it counts for nothing. And the same, needless to say, applies even more so to professional academics.

Early in the nineteenth century, the English poet Walter Savage Landor penned some words that for me strike at the very heart of what I have attempted to argue here, and from which I have taken my title:

> Clear writers, like clear fountains, do not seem so deep as they are; the turbid look the most profound. (Landor 1824)

I would argue very strongly that as a profession, our best writers, our "clearest fountains", are among our most valuable assets. Profound scholarship, lightly worn, and communicated with instinctive clarity in engaging, humane narratives that have, as it were, a twinkle in the eye. Unlike the turbid works of lesser scholars, writing like this will always stand the test of time, and will always retain its power to draw in especially those who are not *themselves* practitioners in our profession.

I have painted a perhaps depressing picture of how at present we stand in our relationship with the wider public in terms of the way we communicate with it through the written word. I will doubtless be told that, frankly, it is tough luck. That is how it is, that is how we do things, nothing is going to change, and the world is thus. Another ivory-tower lie. The world is *not* thus. But rather, as someone once said, thus have we *made* the world. And if we really want to, if we are really serious about getting our message across to the people who pay our wages, and support us at every turn with seemingly inexhaustible interest, we can, and should, *un*make it.

Note

1   This paper was completed by November 2004, but by coincidence an article published very recently in *Antiquity* presents similar arguments, and has a major source, Orwell 1946, in common with this discussion. See Bentley 2006.

Acknowledgement

I am very grateful to Chris Cumberbatch for reading and commenting on a draft of this paper. All views expressed here, and responsibility for any errors of fact or judgment, are solely my own.

References

Andrews, P. (ed.) (2003) *The Spirit of Change: The Archaeology of Kingston Riverside*. Salisbury, Wessex Archaeology.

Bahn, P. (1989) *Bluff Your Way in Archaeology*. London, Ravette.

Bahn, P. (1996) *Archaeology: A Very Short Introduction*. Oxford, Oxford University Press.

Bahn, P. (ed.) (2001) *The Penguin Archaeology Guide*. London.

Bentley, A. R. (2006) Academic copying, archaeology and the English language, *Antiquity* 80.307 (March 2006).

Denison, S. (1997) Getting Behind Theory's Bad Reputation, *British Archaeology*, March 1997, No 22.

Denison, S. (1997a) Archaeology and the Art of a Good Story, *British Archaeology*, September 1997, No 27.

Denison, S. (1999) *Time Team* vs Sutton Hoo vs C14 Dates, *British Archaeology*, December 1999, No 50.

Everitt, A. (1986) *Continuity and Colonisation: The Evolution of the Kentish Landscape*. Leicester, Leicester University Press.

Faulkner, N. (2004) Review of *Antiquity* in *Current Archaeology* 192, June 2004.

Fleming, A. (2003) Review of *Inventing Medieval Landscapes. Senses of Place in Western Europe*, in *Landscape History* 25.

Foreman, S., Hiller, J. and Petts, D. (eds) (2002) *Gathering the People, Settling the Land: The Archaeology of a Middle Thames Landscape, Anglo-Saxon to Post-Medieval*, Oxford, Oxford Archaeology.

Gerrard, C. (2003) *Medieval Archaeology: Understanding Traditions and Contemporary Approaches*. London, Routledge.

Hawkes, J. (1951) *A Land*. London, Cresset Press.

Johnson, M. (2007) *Ideas of Landscape*. Oxford, Blackwell.

Lambrick, G. (2002) Why Newport Breathes New Life Into Public Participation, *British Archaeology*, October 2002, Issue 67.

Landor, W. S. (1824) Imaginary Conversation Between Southey and Porson, collected in C. G. Crump (ed.), *Imaginary Conversations by W S Landor*. London, Dent, 1891.

Maitland, F. W. (1897) *Domesday Book and Beyond*. Cambridge, Cambridge University Press.

Marsden, P. (ed.) (2003) *Sealed by Time: The Loss and Recovery of the Mary Rose*. Portsmouth, Mary Rose Trust.

Orwell, G. (1946) Politics and the English Language, reprinted in S. Orwell and I. Angus (eds), *The Collected Essays, Journalism and Letters of George Orwell, Vol 4, In Front of Your Nose, 1945–1950*. London, Secker and Warburg, 1968.

Pearce, I. and Cale, K. (2005) Not Just Batter Puddings, *British Archaeology* March/April, Issue 81.

Pitts, M. (2004) *The Archaeologist*, Spring 2004, No 52.

Pitts, M. (2005) Review of *Digging the Dirt*, in *British Archaeology* March/April 2005, Issue 81.

Price, D. (2004) *Current Archaeology* 192, June 2004.

Pryor, F. (2003) *Britain BC*. London, Harper Collins.

Renfrew, C. and Bahn, P. (2004) *Archaeology: Theories, Methods and Practice* (4th edn), London, Thames & Hudson.

Sabloff, P. (1998) *Conversations With Lew Binford: Drafting the New Archaeology*. Norman, University of Oklahoma Press.

Chapter 13

Reconstructing Past Landscapes: What Do We See?

Christopher Taylor

I went to Scotland and found nothing that looked like Scotland. (Arthur Freed, Producer of *Brigadoon*)

I want to start this paper by recounting three true stories. The first occurred many years ago at a meeting in my village at which planning officers explained the new Structure Plan. At question time after the talk an elderly lady asked "Why are the maps you use wrong?". The stunned silence was broken by the senior planning officer explaining that the maps used were all official Ordnance Survey ones and were of course correct. The old lady swept this aside. She knew they were wrong. "How are they wrong?" asked the baffled planner. "Well" said the lady, "I have lived here for eighty years and I know that my daughter's house on one side of the village is much further away from the centre than mine on the other side. Yet your maps show it to be exactly the same distance".

The events in my second story took place in 1961 soon after I joined the Royal Commission on Historical Monuments. While working in West Cambridgeshire the Investigators were treated to a visit by the great W. G. Hoskins. Amongst a number of sites we visited was Caxton Moats, where we showed Hoskins an area of curious earthworks. We explained to him that, although we did not know their function, the earth-works were probably very late in date because, as he could see, they overlay slight ridge-and-furrow. Hoskins reply was "What ridge-and-furrow?". It was clear that, like the old lady and the planner we and Hoskins were seeing completely different landscapes.

My third story also goes back some years to when I was the historical advisor to the makers of a television programme on the English landscape. When the final script arrived I rang up the producer and said "This won't do". "What's the matter?" he asked. "Well" I said, "amongst other things you have missed out the whole period between 410 and 1066". "Yes, I know" said the producer, "but nothing important happened then, did it?". When I remonstrated he agreed that one or two things did take place but, and I quote, "Your version doesn't make a very good story, does it?". My plea for even a half-truthful landscape history was rejected with contempt. The television men knew what sort of landscape history the viewers wanted and it was not mine.

These stories illustrate, in their different ways, some of the problems of researching, writing, teaching and popularising landscape history, something that Mick Aston and I have spent most of our working lives doing. You will notice that I call the subject that both Mick and I study landscape history, not landscape archaeology. This is because history is a discipline and archaeology merely a technique. We are all trying, or should be trying, to write history or prehistory.

I start with the last story. This seems to me a good example of the way that landscape history is manipulated, altered and sanitised by non-historians, and some historians, for political, social and economic gain as well as for entertainment. Of course it was ever thus. History has always been used and misused. But when, as with landscape history the past is visual, it is much more obvious. And when it is seen by someone who has spent his life trying to re-construct that past it becomes personal. One can only smile when politicians talk of "our precious land" or "our glorious past", or similar fatuous expressions. But when these same politicians can, for example, order the massive alteration or destruction of areas of land, claiming that among other things they are not very old and therefore of little historical interest, hackles rise. It is not necessarily that I object to the countryside being destroyed, although sometimes I do. There may be very good reasons for it to happen. I just dislike specious history being invoked as an additional reason for allowing the process to take place. Or even in the reverse situation using bad history to protect the landscape.

This separation of historic landscapes from other, non-historic ones, is an affront to a landscape historian who, following the teaching of Crawford, Hoskins and Beresford, believes that there is only one landscape that has changed and developed, for better or worse, over the last 12,000 years or so. Or put the other way, all landscapes are historic.

The idea that there are indeed separate landscapes stems, I think, from the early antiquarians who were interested in the, usually relict, features of the remote past. For them, barrows, hill forts, moats etc. and later churches and castles were the past, all the rest of the landscape was the present. As interest in the past developed, more and more features in the landscape were recognised as worthy of study. Now, at the academic level at least, the logical development of landscape history as a proper subject means that everything in the landscape is of historic interest whether it be railways, pillboxes, cottages, or pre-historic fields, together all forming a dynamic whole. But, outside academia the process seems to have stopped in the late nineteenth century. Curiously, perhaps, this was almost certainly because of the growing interest in the remains of the past and the increasing threat to them. The need for protection to past features that led, for example, to the first Ancient Monuments Acts and to the establishment of the National Trust, led to the defining, both legally and pragmatically, of individual pieces of the landscape as historic. Although this was probably inevitable it formed the public and official perception of the visible past for the succeeding century. The past became ring-fenced and could thus be scheduled and later listed and registered. As appreciation for past landscapes continued to grow, the process was expanded to include Conservation Areas, National Parks, Country Parks, AONBs and eventually provided protection, by law, by agreement or by ownership, to thousands of individual sites and areas from destruction or mutilation.

All this was, of course, a good thing. But it also had downsides. By removing the past from the present and separating them by a firm physical or legal boundary, the past could not only be protected, it could be exploited. Again not a bad thing, especially if the exploitation provided money for its upkeep, facilities for education and, particularly, pleasure for those who visited it. But it also meant deceiving people about their history. People have begun to believe that the only place the past can be seen is within the fence and thus they must drive to it on holiday or at weekends. And, of course, be charged for it. This is perhaps one reason for the institutional and political support for a ring-fenced landscape history. With suitable management it can be very profitable.

But the primary reason for separating the visual past from the present is that it provides a clear line both on a map and on the ground beyond which politicians, developers, planners, and landowners have much more freedom to do what they want, or what is necessary. That is, by enclosing the past, the present becomes easier to manage and the future less difficult to plan for. Again, I am not saying that this is wrong. Much of it has to be like this to cope with what we all, landscapes historians included, want in the 21st century. But it does affect the public's perception of what is the past.

And this perception is further refined by the initial choice and subsequent treatment of what is deemed to be an historic landscape. Because of the background and education of those who make the decisions, most historic landscapes tend to be aesthetically pleasing to the eye, either to start with, or are later deliberately made so. At individual sites grass is well-mown, loos are carefully hidden, gift shops and cafes placed in otherwise redundant buildings or designed in glass and stainless steel by up-and-coming architects. Signage is discreet and paths are all-weather. And in most cases it is all "steeped" in history, although I have never learnt how you distinguish a steeped landscape from an unsteeped one. In wider historic landscapes, grassland and grazing animals are pre-ferred to arable and combine harvesters, deciduous trees to coniferous plantations, split oak paling to barbed wire. Anything that is either offensive or dangerous to the increasingly fastidious, litigious and urban-based visitor has to be removed, cleaned up, or fenced off. Real farm animals are replaced by cuddly lambs, real people are replaced by bad actors in smocks, doublets and wenching dresses. Yet again all this is fine. Much of it can be interesting, most of it is usually enormous fun, if not taken too seriously, sometimes it is even educational. And, if well organ-ised, it can make very large sums of money. But please, do not call it history, and especially not landscape history.

It is certainly not the landscape history, that wonder-ful kaleidoscope of the interaction of past peoples with their worlds, that I have studied and taught for nearly fifty years. I have to sit and grind my teeth as the history of the landscape is distorted and spoiled for the sake of a "good story" or a ten per cent increase in visitors. Of course landscape historians are not alone in being upset by the constant manipulation of their chosen subject. Friends and colleagues in other branches of history, in the social sciences, in medicine and in the applied and theoretical sciences I know feel the same way about the public perception of what they do.

One reaction to this, for some historians at least, is

to abandon any attempt to pass on the results of their work to the wider world and to retreat further into their own. But, are their closeted perceptions any more acceptable than those of the general public. Here we come to the second of my stories, where professional academics, in this case Royal Commission Investigators and the great W. G. Hoskins, saw completely different landscapes. For the fact that we, collectively, see such different landscapes, and as a result interpret them in different ways, means that it is difficult if not impossible for the public, including politicians, planners and the television men, to understand and value historic landscapes. And this, when the landscapes themselves are under the greatest pressure to be changed. Here, of course, is another dichotomy. It is only by the research that produces these different perceptions that our subject, or indeed any subject, advances. But by the very nature of modern research, not only are there almost as many views of past landscapes as there are landscape historians, but the speed at which research advances, means that those views are changing all the time. It is thus difficult for those not directly involved in research to make use of it for non-academic purposes. Some of the older members of our profession, including myself, who have seen the rapid and confusing changes in *our* perceptions of historic landscapes have more than a little sympathy with those who want to use our results, even television programme makers. Just a few examples will suffice. Stonehenge and similar monuments have changed from being temples, to astrological clocks, and then to computers, all in my lifetime, reflecting modern rather than ancient perceptions. The originators of the English village have changed from 5th century democratic Saxons with a good training in physical geography, to late Saxon and post-Conquest landscape reorganisers and planners. Medieval castles have developed from mighty military machines to status symbols, the arrival of agriculture in Britain has retreated from around 2000 BC to before 5000 BC.

In more philosophical terms, the determinism of the 1950s and 1960s, derided by landscape historians of the 1970s and 1980s is now back in fashion. The old form of narrative landscape history, which after all is the one most of the general public understand by history, has been replaced by landscapes of perception, of ritual, and of social organisation. All these changes have been tremendous and have increased our understanding of the landscape and its people enormously. As landscape historians we must be pleased to see how our chosen and relatively new subject has developed in the last 20 or 30 years. But do we see the history of the landscape as a whole any more clearly than we did? I suspect not. In fact we probably see it

less clearly and thus understand it less well than we used to. Again this is as it should be. But it does not help those who try to both use and enjoy the results of our labours. So, if their versions of landscape history appear crude to us, it is precisely as a result of our successes.

My first story, of the elderly lady and the trouble with maps, illustrates the problem of understanding what people actually see, or saw, in the landscape. In the case of the old lady it was not just a matter of maps but again of different ways of looking at the world. Just what did, indeed do, people see of the landscape that we study? And more importantly can we ever, as historians, understand what they see or saw? Back in the 1950s and 1960s our early attempts were certainly simplistic. We looked then, and inevitably still look, at past landscape through the blinkered and blurred eyes of the present. Thus our view of the past was based on the materialistic and functional appearance of our own world of the 1950s. Since then we have developed more sophisticated, some would say merely different, ideas as to how past peoples saw their world. We now have landscapes of folklore, beliefs and symbolism, perhaps reflecting the increasing uncertainties of the world in which landscape historians lived in the 1980s and 1990s. Recently, with the advent of the latest technologies, and especially with GIS and associated modelling techniques, there has been a return to deterministic interpretations of past people's perceptions of landscape.

Once again this is all inevitable. We can never write about the past outside the confines of the present. And it really does not matter. Provided that we do not believe, as some historians used to and a few still do, that we are somehow writing the final and unchangeable story of a past that was logical and coherent. As G. R. Elton put it, 'History is the mess we call life reduced to some order, pattern, and possible purpose'.

All this might be regarded as the inevitable ravings of a grumpy old man who has given up on his subject. But I have not. I remain enormously optimistic about landscape history, the direction in which it is going and the way that it is developing. Of course our views will be misrepresented, our arguments with colleagues more heated and our understanding of the minutiae less clear. But that should not stop us. We need to continue our research, modifying and changing ideas and to pass them on to both students and to the wider world. How else can we hope to extend knowledge, expand minds and educate the public? Many of us have always believed this and have spent a lifetime working towards these aims. And the one person who has certainly encouraged me, and I know many others, in our beliefs and aims, is Mick Aston. No one exemplifies my optimism for landscape history more than Mick. Through his work on the subject at all levels, in his books and academic papers, in his work in specific areas such as Shapwick and at small individual sites he has taught us all to look more carefully at the world. Through his interest in monastic sites he has show us how detailed research can push the boundaries of a subject into areas hitherto not reached. Through his teaching, from evening classes, through university lectures to his research students, he has passed on his enthusiasm and skills to two and more generations of both the public and future professionals. And through his work in the media he has also educated lay people and influenced policy making. But, and perhaps most important of all, at least to me, through his work everywhere, his great knowledge and his ever-present humour he has shown us all what we desperately need to take on board. Landscape history is great fun.

Index

Abbotsbury Abbey, *Benedictine*, 68, 70
Abbotsbury, Dorset, 66, 70, 71
Abingdon Abbey, *Benedictine*, 163
Abingdon, 46
Adare Castle, Co. Limerick, 120–122
Adomnan, 54
aerial photography, 2
Agen, dép. Lot-et-Garonne, 99
agriculture, adoption of, 23
Aïnhoa, bastide, dép. Pyrénées-Atlantique, 107
Albigensian Crusade, 107
Aldwick, Somerset, 64
Alexander III, pope, 99
Alfonso VII, King of Castile, 99
Algeria, 53
alloidal land & owners, 63, 64, 70
alluviation, 24
Alphonse of Poitiers, count of Toulouse, 107
Alward, 64
ancient demesne, 63
Anglo-Saxon Chronicle, 86
Anglo-Saxon estates, 67, 68
Angoulême
    cathedral, 137
    canons, 137
Aquatic Tournament, Tong Castle, 192, 193
Aquitaine, 91
archaeological literature, 196
Arianism, 53, 54, 56
Arthous, Premonstratensian abbey, dép. Landes, 96, 102, 107, 110, 114
Ascot-under-Wychwood, Oxfordshire, 80
Athanasius, bishop of Alexandria, 55, 56
Athelney Abbey, *Benedictine*, 83, 84
Augustinian canons, 137, 141
aurochs, 31
availability model, 51
Avebury, Wiltshire, 15, 16
Aveline's Hole, 8, 24
Axe, river, 10

Bampton, Oxfordshire, 59
Bangor, 54
Banwell, Somerset, 131

baptism, 53, 55, 57
    of infants, 57
Barnard Castle, 76
Batch, early Norman castle, 78
barrows, 9
    bank, 7
    Bronze Age, 1
bastides, 106–107
Bath Abbey, *Benedictine*, 56
Bayonne, 96
Beacon Hill, Somerset, 18
Beaker pottery, 12
Beaulieu, Essex, 184
Beaumarchés, bastide, dép. Gers, 110
Beckery, Somerset, 57
Bede, The Venerable, 54–56, 58
Béhaune-en-Lantabat, Premonstratensian priory, dép. Pyrénées-Atlantiques, 91, 100, 103
bell-founders' pit, 139
Bellpuig de los Avellanas, Premonstratensian abbey, 98
Benedict Biscop, 56
Benedict XIII, antipope, 113
Benedictinism, 56
beorg, 83
Bernard Jourdain de l'Isle, 95
Béziers, Hérault, 98
Birdcombe, Wraxall, Somerset, 24, 26, 29, 32, 46, 51
Bishop of Winchester, 64
bishop's retinue, 131
bishops' residences, repairs, 135
bishops's register, 131
Bishopstone, Somerset, 82
Black Death, 111
Black Down, Somerset, 16, 18
Black Prince, 111
Blackford, bishop's residence, Somerset, 131
Blackshouse Burn, Lanarkshire, 14
Blackstone Rocks, N. Somerset, 32
Blashenwell, Dorset, 72
Bobbio monastery, *Benedictine*, 56
Bonnegarde-en-Chalosse, bastide, dép. Landes, 110
bookland, 62, 64
Bordeaux, 107

Bordesley Abbey, *Benedictine*, ix
Brean Down, 4
Bronze Age,
   early monuments, 15
   flint, 29
   hut circles, 37
   monument builders, 39
   pottery, 29
   scrapers, 26
   settlement, 44
bronze socket and holder, 170–4
Broome Heath, Norfolk, 26, 46, 49
Brown, 'Capability', 185
Bryanston, Dorset, 64
Buck brothers, engravers, 184
Buckland Ripers, Dorset, 68, 69, 70
Bug-Dniester groups, 41
burial
   evidence, 24
   rites, 160
   site, 24
burials, 141, 147, 150, 154, 157, 158
Burrington Combe, 7

Caernarfon Castle, 170
Caistél Dúin Leódha, 119
Calvinism, 113
Campagne-sur-Arize, bastide, dép. Haute Garonne, 109
Canterbury, 58
Caput Montis, borough, 85
Carn Brea, Cornwall, 46, 49
Carrickfergus, 125
Carthusian Order, 90
Cashel, 119, 120
castellologists, 76
castellology, 117
Castle Batch, 80
Castle Cary castle, Somerset, 77
   demolition, 82
   excavations, 78
   great tower, 81
   ringwork, 80
Castle Cary, Lodge Hill, 81
Castle Cary, roman religious tradition, 80
Castle, Ballyderown Castle, Co. Cork, 120, 122
castles,
   Angevin, 118
   earthwork castles, 76
   earth-and-timber, 117, 119, 124
   iconographic symbolism, 76
   military role, 76
   motte-and-bailey, 121
   phenomenology, 118

ringwork, 120
Romanesque, 117
royal and baronial, 118
siege castle, 81
stone, 118
Cathar heresy, 94
cave burial, 8, 9, 10
caves and swallets, 7
caves, 8
caves, liminal places, 9
Cazères-sur-l'Adour, bastide, dép. Landes, 111
Celestine II, pope, 106
Celtic fields, 4
ceorls, 62
Cerne Abbey, *Benedictine* 68, 69, 70
Chaffcombe, Somerset, 65
chantry, Tong, 183, 192
Chardstock, Dorset, bishop's residence, 130
Charles VII, king of France, 110
Charlottia, als. Rollestown, Florida, 176
charter, Portesham, 68, 70, 71
Charterhouse Warren Farm Swallet, 12, 29, 31
Charterhouse, Somerset, 4, 14, 32
Cheddar Gorge, 4, 7, 29
Cheddar Man, 24
Chelmscombe Cave, 9
Chew Magna, Somerset, bishop's residence, 131
Chew Valley, Somerset, 16
Chillington, Staffordshire, 185
church dues, 68
Church Fathers, 53
Church Knowle, Dorset, 72
church of St Nicholas, Carrickfergus, 120
churches, impropriated, 106
Cistercians, 90, 94, 97, 107, 137, 163
Civil War, English, 184
Clava cairns, 15
Claverton, Somerset, bishop's residence, 131
clay floor, Mesolithic, 37
Clement of Alexandria, 10
Clevedon, Somerset, 32
Cluny Abbey, 117
Cnut, 61, 68
Coastline, 6
Cockroad Wood Castle, Somerset, 78, 80
coins as amulets, 169
Colchester Castle, 170
colluviation, 24
Columban monks, 58
Columbanus, 56
Combelongue, Premonstratensian abbey, dép. Ariége, 93, 95, 102, 107, 113, 114
Compton Wynyates, Warwickshire, 184
Congresbury, 58

Constantine, Emperor, 53
Corfe, Dorset, 71
Corton, Dorset, 68
cottars, 65
Councils of the Church,
     Alexandria, 55
     Carthage, 54
     Ephesus, 53
     Milevis, 54
     Nicaea, 53
     Orange, 53, 56
cowrie shell, 174, 175
     as currency, 175, 177, 178
     ritual use, 177, 178
Cranborne Abbey, Dorset, 73
Cranmore, Somerset, 64
Crawford, O. G. S., 2
Croyde, Devon, 63
Cucuteni-Tripolye farming culture, 41
Curry Rivel, rector of, 135
customary dues, 68

Dagan, bishop, 55
Damerham, Wiltshire, 65
Dartmoor, 2
Dax, 97
De Colombers family, 85
deliberate breakage, 168
demic diffusion, 23
Deverill, Wiltshire, 65
Devon, 63, 64, 65, 66
diffusionist theory, 41
diffusionists, 23, 24
Dinnington, Somerset, 64
Divielle, Premonstratensian abbey, dép. Landes, 94,
     97,103, 113, 114
Dogmersfield, Hampshire, bishop's residence, 131
Dolebury Warren hillfort, 4
Domesday Book, 62, 63, 64, 68, 73, 74, 78, 82
Domesday Book, Exeter, 64
domesticated species, 51
Donatists, 53
donjon, of Carrickfergus, 120
donjons, 118, 121 122, 123, 124, 125, 126, 127
Donkin, Robin, 90
Dorchester, Dorset, 66, 70
Dorset, 63, 64, 65, 66
double houses, 91
Dover castle, 124, 127
Downend castle, 84, 85
Downend, motte and bailey, 80
Downend, Somerset, 77
Dublin, Holy Trinity Cathedral, 120
Duhort-Bachen, bastides, dép. Landes,111

Duiske Abbey, Cistercian, Co. Kilkenny, 120
Dún Mór, Co. Galway, 119
Dundry, Somerset, 16
Durance, bastide, dép. Lot-et-Garonne,111
Durance, Premonstratensian priory, dép. Lot-et-
     Garonne, 93, 99, 103
Durant, George, 185
Durant, George, junior, 189, 190
Dyfed, 55

Eadred, king of the English, 71
Eadwig, king of the English, 72
Ealhstan, bishop, 86
Eanwulf, ealdorman, 86
East Barsham, Norfolk, 184
East Chinnock, Somerset, 64
East Harptree, Somerset, 18
Easter controversy, 54
Easter, 55, 58
Eaton Heath, 46
Ebbor Gorge, Somerset, 7, 32
Ecgberht, 58
Ecumenical Church Councils, 53
Edith, queen, 63
Edithmead, early Norman castle, 78
Edmer Ator, 64
Edmer, 64
Edward I, king of England, 110, 118, 163
Edward II, king of England, 110
Edward III, king of England, 110, 111
Edward the Confessor, king of the English, 63, 163
Eglinton Tournament, 193
Egypt, 56
Eleanor of Aquitaine, 91, 163, 164
Elvod, Archbishop, 54
Embrun, 94
emparkment, 170
Environmental determinism, 2
eremitical life, 56
escort duties, 65
Eskmeals, Cumbria, 46, 49
estates, bishop of Worcester, 62
Eustace of Beaumarchés, 109
Evercreech, Somerset, bishop's residence, 133
exchange of artefacts, 41
Exeter, 78
Exmoor, Somerset, 23

Failand Ridge, Somerset, 24, 29
farmers, Neolithic, 42, 49
farming frontier, 40, 44, 49
field systems, 67
field-walking, 166
filiation, 91

Fitzgerald family, 127
five-hide units, 73
flint knapping, 23, 26, 37
    scatters, 24
    tools, Mesolithic, 38
Florida, 176
Fondarella, Premonstratensian abbey, 98
Fontcaude, Premonstratensian priory, dép. Herault,
    93, 94, 98, 102, 113, 114
Fontevrault Abbey, 163, 164
fonts, 57
Fontvive Abbey, Cistercian, 137
foragers, 42
Forts of the Saxon Shore, 58
Fosseway, 83
Fox, Sir Cyril, 2
Friar Waddon, Dorset, 68
Frome, 4
Fuentesclaras, Premonstratensian abbey, 98
Fulk Pembridge, 181

Gascony, 90, 107
Gaul, church in, 55
geld, 63
Geoffrey de Marisco, 121
Geraint, King of Dumnonia, 55
Gerald II of Blaye, bishop of Angoulême, 137
Geþyncðo, 61, 64
Gildas, 54
Gimont Abbey, Cistercian, 101
Glastonbury Abbey, *Benedictine* 64, 65, 83, 84
Glastonbury, 57, 58
Godwin, Earl, 64
Gorsey Bigbury henge, 19, 32
Gothic architecture, 120
gothick style, 185
Gough's Cave, Cheddar, 8
Gough's New Cave, Cheddar, 24
Goujon, Premonstratensian nunnery, 100
granges, 100, 105
grange,
    Bordères, 106
    Gergovie, 106
    St Sauveur d'Orthecole, 106
grave goods, 9
Great Chalfield, Wiltshire, 184
greenstone axehead, 12
Grooved Ware, 12
Grosbot Abbey, Cistercian, 137, 161
    estates, 139
Gussage, Dorset, 64
Guyenne, 90
Gytha, 63

Hadrian, Archbishop of Canterbury, 57, 58
Hales castle, 78
Ham Hill, hillfort, Somerset, 83
hammerstone, 26
Hampshire, 63
Harold, earl & king of the English, 63, 64, 78
Hartland, Devon, 63
Hastingues, bastide, dép. Landes, 110
Hauverne, Marseilles, Premonstratensian priory, 99,
    105, 106, 113
Hawkcombe Head, Somerset, 24, 35, 38, 51
    Mesolithic flint, 37
    spring, 37
Hay Wood Cave, Hutton, Somerset, 9, 32
Hazleton north long barrow, 46, 49
Hedingham Castle, 120
Hembury causewayed enclosure, 26, 46, 49
henges, 7
Henri of Lausanne, 94
Henry de Tracy, 81
Henry II, king of England, 91, 120, 163, 164
Henry III, king of England, 163
Henry Vernon, 183
heresy, 53, 54, 94
heretics, 55
hermitages, 58
hermits, 56
Herston, Dorset, 73
Hexham, Northumbria, 58
hidation, 63
hides, 62, 68
historic landscapes, 205
History, 205
Holy Cross of Waltham Abbey, 84
Honoratus, 56
Honorius, Emperor, 54
Hooke, Dorset, 73
Hoskins, W. G., 2
hospital, 96, 99, 100
Hugh de Fosses, 91
Hugh de Lacy, 124
human remains, Totty Pot, 29
Hundred Years' War, 113
hundreds, 62
hunter-gatherers, 23, 26, 46, 49
    rituals, 10
hunting, 38
Husserl, Edward, 3

Ilchester, Somerset, 67
'indigenism', 42
indigenists, 23
Ine, King of Wessex, laws, 57
Iona, 58

Ireland and Rome, contacts, 54
Irish bishops, 55
Irish monasteries, 58
Irish, northern, 54
Iron Age hillforts, 4
    pottery, 9
    sites, 72

Jarrow, 58
John Byng, 189
John, king of England, 123

Kilmalkedar, Galway, 57
Kimmeridge, Dorset, 72
Kingcombe, Dorset, 73
Kingdom of Castile, 91
Kingdom of Navarre, 91
Kingston Russell, Dorset, 66
Kingston, Dorset, 71, 72
knights, 61

l'Oraison-Dieu Abbey, dép. Haute Garonne,
    Cistercian, 100
La Bastide-de-Serou, bastides, dép. Arièges, 108,
    113
La Capelle, Premonstratensian abbey dép. Haute
    Garonne, 95, 113
La Casedieu, Premonstratensian abbey, nr Tarbes, 91,
    94, 95, 96, 98, 105, 106, 110, 111, 113, 114
La Rochefoucauld family, 161, 163
labour services, 65
Lahonce, Premonstratensian abbey, dep. Pyrénées-
    Atlantiques, 96, 114
Landkey, Devon, 58
landscape
    archaeology, 1, 2
    Dorchester/Weymouth, 68
    experiential, 3
    Mendip, 4
    phenomenological, 3
    places, 3
    ritual, 14
    of South Cadbury, 67
    subjective, 3,
Langton Matravers, 71, 72
Languedoc, 107
Lannes, Premonstratensian priory, dép. Lot-et-
    Garonne, 99, 102, 106
Lanprobus, Celtic monastery, Sherborne, 58
lar, 80
Lateran baptistery, 53
Laurence, Archbishop of Canterbury, 54, 55, 57
lay benefactors, 137
Leland, John, 183

Lérins monastery, *Benedictine*, 56, 57
Lieu-Dieu-en-Jard, Premonstratensian abbey, Poitou,
    95, 101
lithic scatters, 7
Llandegai 'A' henge, 12
London, 58
long barrows, 16
Long Bredy, Dorset, 66
Louis IX, king of France, 163
Louis, VIII, king of France, 107
Lower Woodford, Wiltshire, bishop's residence,
    130
Lusignan family, 164
Luxeuil monastery, *Benedictine,* 56
Lynton, Devon, 38

magnetometer survey, 15
Malmesbury Abbey, *Benedictine,* 58, 59
manors, 62, 64
March Hill, 49
Marciac, bastide, dép. Gers, 111
Marseilles, 56, 106, 113
Marten, Wiltshire, 65
Mathilda, 81
mausoleum, Grosbot, 137, 139–164
mausoleum, Tong, 183
Maynooth Castle, Co. Kildare, 121, 127, 128
medieval bishops, 130
Mendip
    animal bone, 4
    caves, 1
    cereal cultivation, 4
    Hills, 4, 32
    Lords Royal, 4
    Neolithic sites, 4
    prehistoric environment, 4
    Royal Forest, 4
    Woodlands, 4
        clearance, 6
Mesolithic
    chipping floor, 24
    flint, 24, 35
    flint, Hawkcombe Head, 37
    microburins, 26
    microliths, 24, 29
    open-air sites, 1
    period, 51
    tools, 29
    use of caves, 31
Mesolithic, late, 24, 49
Mesolithic to Neolithic overlap, 44
Mesolithic-Neolithic transition, 23
miles, 62
military determinism, 118

mining liberties, 4
minster,
    churches, 57, 58
    Dorchester, Dorset, 72
    Wareham, Dorset, 72
Mirambeau, Saintonge, Premonstratensian nunnery, 101
Monasteranenagh Abbey, Cistercian, Co. Limerick, 121
monasticism, 55–57, 90
Monkwearmouth monastery, *Benedictine*, 58
Monophysitism, 53
Montacute, Somerset, 77, 78
Montacute Castle, 82, 83
Montacute, St Michael's Hill, 83
Montesquieu-Volvestre, bastide, dép. Haute-Garonne, 107
monument builders, 49
mos teutonicus, 161
motte castle, 120
motte, 119
motte-and-bailey, 83, 84
mottes in Normandy, 76
Mudford, Somerset, 64

naked Venuses, 189
Nechtan, king of the Picts, 58
Nenagh Castle, Co. Tipperary, 120, 122, 123
Neolithic,
    burial traditions, 9
    early, 6, 8, 23, 49
    farmers, 4
    Mendip, 7
    monuments, 1, 15, 18
    period, 26, 40
    Revolution, 23
    tomb builders, 49
Neroche Castle, Somerset, 80, 85
Nestorians, 53
new geography, 2
New York, 176
Newcastle-upon-Tyne castle, 124
Newgrange, 15
Norman Conquest, 61, 65
Normandy, 63
North Cadbury, Somerset, 73
North Hill, Somerset, 18, 19
North Molton, Devon, 63
Northumbria, 58
Northumbrians, 54
Norton Priory, 163
Notre Dame de Sarrance, Premonstratensian priory, dép. Pyrenees-Atlantiques, 100, 105, 113, 114
nuns, 95

Obazine Abbey, Cistercian 137, 139
Odcombe, Somerset, 64
Old Red Sandstone, 18, 19
Orc, *huscarle*, 68, 70
Orford castle, 124, 127
Origen, 55
Osric, ealdorman, 86

Palestine, 56
park, Tong, 181
parochia, 68
    of Corfe, 72
pastoralism, shifting, 4
peat formation, 6
Pecthelm, 58
Pelagians, Pelagianism, 53–55, 58
Pelagius, 53, 56–57
Pen Hill, Somerset, 18
Penitential of Theodore, 54, 55
Peter de Bruis, 94
Peter the Venerable, Abbot of Cluny, 94
Petrobrusians, Petrobrusian heresy, 94–95
Philadelphia, 176
Philip IV, king of France, 110, 111
Pictish stone monuments, 58
Picts, 54
Pierre, count of Bigorre, 96
pilgrimage to Notre dame de Sarrance, 100
Plaisance d'Armagnac, bastide, dép. Gers,111
Pleinselve, Premonstratensian abbey, dép. Gironde, 91, 94, 101, 102, 113
ploughlands, 63
Polden Hills, 85, 177
Poldowrian, 49
Porchester Castle, 126
Porlock Beach, submerged forest, 37
Portesham, Dorset, 68
Portland, Dorset, 68, 70, 71
Post Track, 49
Potterne, Wiltshire, bishop's residence, 130, 134, 135
Premonstratensian abbeys, architecture, 101–103
Premonstratensians,
    canons, 90, 91
    circaries, 91
    general chapter, 91
    nuns, 100
Prémontré, 91, 101
Priddy Circles, Somerset, 12, 14, 19, 21
Priddy long barrow, 19
Purbeck, Dorset, 66, 71, 72
Purse Caundle, Dorset, 83

Quantocks, 10
Queen, Edith, 64

quern stones, 18

radiocarbon date, 24, 26, 29, 38
Rahan church, Co. Offaly, 123
Ralph Lovell, 80, 81
Ralph of Shrewsbury, bishop of Bath and Wells, 133, 134
Ramsbury, Wiltshire, bishop's residence, 130, 134
Raymond VII, count of Toulouse, 108
Retuerta, Premonstratensian abbey, 98
Richard I, Duke of Aquitaine, King of England, 91
Richard Mitford, bishop of Salisbury, 133,134
Richard Vernon, 183
Rimont, bastide, dép. Ariéges, 109
Rimont, Premonstratensian abbey, dép. Arièges, 114
ringwork castles, 83, 120
Ripon, Durham, 58
River Adour, 96
River, Axe, 10
River Brue, 84
River Garonne, 91
River Parrett, 84, 86
Robert, count of Mortain, 64, 78, 82
Robert, earl of Gloucester, 81
Roger IV, count of Foix, 108
Rolle, Denys, 176
Rolletown, Great Exuma, Bahamas, 176
Rolleville, Great Exuma, Bahamas, 176
Rollington, Dorset, 73
Roman,
    mining, 4
    pottery, 9
    road, 14, 66
    sites, 72
    stone re-used, 58
Romanesque architecture, 118, 119, 120, 121
Rome, 53–54, 57–58
Rowberrow Cavern, Somerset, 32
Royal Commission on Historical Monuments, 205
Ruaidhri Ua Conchobhair, 119

Saintonge pottery, 91
Salisbury, 130
San Salvador, Urdax, Premonstratensian abbey, 98, 107
Santiago de Compostela, 93, 94, 95, 96, 100
Sauer, Carl, 2
schism, 53
sedentism, 23
sergeants, 62
Shapwick, Somerset, 73, 166, 177
    Home Farm, 175
    House, 171, 174, 176
    Park, 173
Sherborne, Dorset, 58

Sherborne castle, bishop's residence, 130
Shilvinghampton, East and West, Dorset, 68, 70
shire courts, 62
Shropshire, 181
siege, Bristol castle, 81
    Castle Cary, 81
Simon of Ghent, bishop of Salisbury, 131
Sixtus III, pope, 53
Skellig Michael, 57
skin-working, 39
slaves, 65
slave trade, West Indian, 185
slaves, West African, 175, 176
Sock Dennis, 65
Somerset, 63, 65, 66
Somerset Levels, 6
Somerton, Somerset, 135
Sonning, Berkshire, bishop's residence, 130, 134
South Cadbury, Castle, 73
    landscape, 67
Spain, 98
St Aldhelm, bishop of Sherborne, 55, 58
St Anne, Arros? Premonstratensian priory, 98
St Anthony, 55
St Augustine of Canterbury, 54, 57, 58
St Augustine of Hippo, 53–56, 58, 91
St Augustine's Abbey, 163
St Benedict, Rule, 56
St Bernard of Clairvaux, 94
St Columba, 56
St Columban, abbot, 55
St Cuthbert, 54
St David's, Pembrokeshire, 57
St Denis Abbey, *Benedictine* 163
St Dominic, 94
St Germanus of Auxerre, visits Britain, 54
St Jean-de-la-Castelle, Premonstratensian abbey, dép. Landes, 83, 96, 99, 107,111, 113, 114
St Jerome, 56
St John Cassian, 56, 58
St Martin of Tours, 55
St Norbert of Xanten, 91, 94
St. Jerome, 54
Stanton Drew, geology, 15–17
Stanton Drew, N Somerset, megalithic complex, 15
Ste Marguerite, La Rochelle, Premonstratensian nunnery 101, 105
Ste Marie-à-la-Porte-de-France, Marseilles, Premonstratensian priory, 105
Stephen, king of England, 78, 81
St-Gilles, dép. Gard, 94
Stock Hill, 4
stone circles, 7
Stonehenge, 12

Stowey castle, 78, 80
Strand, London, bishop's residence, 131
struck flints, 7
swallets, 10, 12, 14, 31
    Bronze Age, 12
    Neolithic deposits,12
Swanage, Dorset, 71, 72
Sweet Track, Shapwick, Somerset, 26, 46, 49
Symbolism of materials, 15
Synod of Macon, 56
Synod of Mag Lene, 54
Synod of Whitby, 59

Tanchelm, 94
Tarbes, 95
Tatton, Dorset, 68, 69, 70
Taunton, County Museum, Somerset, 35
thegns, 61, 62, 64, 65, 68, 69, 70, 73
Theodore, Archbishop of Canterbury, 54, 57, 58
Thirty Years War, 114
Thomas Langton, bishop of Salisbury, 131
Thomas Moore, 191
Thorpe Common, 49
Tole, widow, 68, 70
Toller Porcorum, Dorset, 73
Tom Tivey's Hole, 8
tombs, 183, 184
Tong
    Castle, 181, 183, 185, 186
    church, 181, 192
    College, 181
Totty Pot swallet, Somerset, 24, 29, 31, 32
    burial, 29
Toulouse, 91, 95, 96
Tovi, sheriff, 83
Tower of London, 170
transition sites, 49
transition to farming, 42
Trim Castle, Co. Meath, 121, 124, 125, 126, 127, 128
Tuam, Co. Galway, 119
tufa mound, 20

ua Conchobhair kings, 128
urban property, 106
Urban V, pope, 101

Ven Combe springs, 35
Ven Combe, 37
    springs, 35

Vic-Fezensac, Premonstratensian priory, dép. Gers, 93, 96, 103, 113
Viking armies, 85
    fortifications, 86
Viking's Pill, 86
villeins, 65

Waddon, Dorset, 68, 70
Waldensians, 94
Walter de Lacy, 125
Walter of Douai, 78, 80
Waltham Abbey, *Benedictine*, 84
wave of advance, 23, 40
Wedlake Collection, 35
Wellow Brook, Somerset, 20
Wells, Somerset, bishop's residence, 131
Wells, Somerset, 134
Wessex, 57–59, 63
    Caving Club, 29
    landscape, 62
Weston Park, Staffordshire, 185
Westward Ho!, Devon, 49
Weymouth, Dorset, 66
whetstones, 18
Whit Stones, 37
Whithorn, Galloway, 58
Whitwell Long Cairn, Derbys, 26, 46, 49
Wilfred, 56, 58
William I, the Conqueror, king of the English, 61, 83
William IX, Duke of Aquitaine, 164
William of Malmesbury, 83
Wiltshire, 63, 65, 66
Wimble Toot, motte, 80
Windmill Hill, Wiltshire, 19
    bowls, 9
    vessel, 8
Wiveliscombe, Somerset, bishop's residence, 131, 134
Woodford, Wiltshire, bishop's residence, 133
Wookey Hole, Somerset, 10
Wookey, Somerset, bishop's residence, 131, 134
Woolston, Somerset, 73
Worth Matravers, Dorset, 71, 72
Wulfstan, Archbishop of York, 61
Wyke, Dorset, 68, 70

Yatton Keynell, Wiltshire, 73
York, 58

Zubernoa, Premonstratensian abbey, 93